*"We, representatives of Palestinian civil society, call upon
organizations and people of conscience all over the world t
implement divestment initiatives against Israel, similar to t
the apartheid era. We appeal to you to pressure your respec...
and sanctions against Israel. We also invite conscientious Israelis to support this Call, for the sake of justice and genuine peace."*
        Palestinian Civil Society Call for Boycott Divestment and Sanctions, 2005

"There are concrete steps that people can take, learning from the lessons of the first Intifada and the Boycott, Divestment and Sanctions campaign to dismantle the South African Apartheid regime; strategies of popular resistance, strikes, occupations, direct actions. From the streets into the offices, factories and headquarters is where we need to take this fight, to the heart of decision-makers that are supposedly making decisions on our behalf and the companies making a killing out of the occupation. The third intifada needs to be a global intifada."
        Ewa Jasiewicz, from the besieged Gaza Strip, January 2009

"Israel is committing a grave crime in Gaza. 350 children have been reported dead. It's absolutely disgusting that weapons are being made in our cities in our country that are being used to kill innocent women and children and are being used indiscriminately; it's about time that something was done about it. If the law and the police can't do anything about it, it's about time somebody else did."
  Tom Woodhead, one of the 'EDO Decomissioners', January 2009. Hours after giving this interview Tom broke into EDO MBM, an arms manufacturer supplying weapons to Israel, and destroyed the production line.

"Clearly, the BDS movement is coming of age and is raising the cost of corporate complicity with Israeli war crimes. Strategic BDS campaigns are proving, through every day successes, that BDS is the most effective form of solidarity needed to challenge Israel's system of colonialism, occupation and apartheid"
  Jamal Juma, commenting on the court order to liquidate key BDS target, Carmel Agrexco. Jamal is coordinator of the Stop the Wall Campaign and member of the Palestinian Boycott Divestment and Sanctions National Committee (BNC) secretariat.

A BDS Handbook

Foreword

by Ewa Jasiewicz

'Targeting Israeli Apartheid: a BDS handbook' is the guide many of us in the movement have been waiting for: a map to demystify and expose the daily reproduction of the occupation of Palestine. This forensic, clear, and systematic account details the where, who, how and why of the flows of capital and contracts, which enable the colonisation of Palestine to continue.

'Targeting Israeli Apartheid' tells us the names, addresses, profit margins and zones of activity of the corporate web that sustains this injustice. With this information, and an understanding of these processes, our ability to intervene is enhanced. With this handbook, activists will be better equipped to target the companies that are violating human rights and international law and to undermine the ability of companies to ignore and repress Palestinian human rights. When campaigning, many of us encounter anti-Semitic claims that the reason the occupation and colonisation of Palestine has gone on for so long is because Jews control the world, that there is a Jewish conspiracy. This book busts that racist myth. There is no conspiracy; capitalism has no ethnicity. The primary reason the occupation and colonisation of Palestine has gone on for so long, with little intervention by states to stop it, is because it is an international phenomenon rooted in material power interests and benefits for capital and state authority. This oppression is lucrative.

'You make history when you do business'. Contracts can sign away the sovereignty of a people with a pen's stroke. History is made everyday, the everyday is consigned to history. To intervene in history, to co-make it, is to realise one's own agency.

This book re-frames the occupation as an international economic and cultural dynamic that we can identify in our own countries, on our streets and in our own homes. We can change the world, build a culture of resistance which can open new space, bring down borders to understanding, and create participatory democracy and power from below. This book is a book of the movement and for the movement. Read it, organise and take action!

Ewa Jasiewicz is a journalist, union organiser and a coordinator of the Free Gaza Movement

Introduction

Our rationale for writing this book is pure and simple: information for action. We believe that the direct action of ordinary people is vital for the success of the Palestinian struggle for justice. The end of Israeli apartheid, militarism and occupation will not be achieved by representatives, governments and politicians but through grassroots solidarity.

The book takes its cue from the unified Palestinian call for Boycott, Divestment and Sanctions (BDS) against Israel.[1] The background to that call was Israel's brutal crushing of the Palestinian Authority (PA) during 'Operation Defensive Shield' in 2001, when the Israeli army reoccupied the main cities of the West Bank and Gaza, launched air strikes and demolished houses. 6,500 Palestinians were killed and tens of thousands imprisoned. Government infrastructure was destroyed as the Israeli state prepared to remake the PA as client caretaker rulers of the subjugated Palestinian population. The intention was to provide the occupiers with an occupation from within.

At the same time, Israel embarked upon a new project, profitable for Israeli corporations but extremely costly to Palestinian communities: the 700km long apartheid wall. The wall is intended to steal more Palestinian land, ghettoize Palestinians and annex many Israeli settlements to the Western side of the wall.

Palestinian communities across the West Bank rose up against the wall, organising demonstrations in affected villages. The movement was met with bullets and tear gas by the occupying army.

In 2004, a case against Israel's wall was brought to the International Court of Justice (ICJ) in the Hague. Amid solidarity demonstrations, the ICJ gave an advisory ruling that the wall was illegal and that rendering assistance to it was prohibited.[2]

A year later Israel was still building the wall in defiance of this ruling. In response, a coalition of civil society groups issued a call for international solidarity. Palestinians appealed to people around the world to implement boycotts, divestment campaigns and press for sanctions against Israel until "it withdraws from all the lands occupied in 1967, including East Jerusalem, and removes all its colonies and walls in those lands; implements United Nations resolutions relevant to the restitution of Palestinian refugees rights; and recognizes the right of its Palestinian citizens to full equality."[3]

The Palestinian Boycott Divestment and Sanctions National Committee later explained: "The key lesson learned from South Africa is that, in order for world governments to end

---

[1] The full call can be found at www.bdsmovement.net/call, [accessed September 2011].
[2] The full International Court of Justice ruling can be read at www.icj-cij.org/docket/index.php?pr=71&code=mwp&p1=3&p2=4&p3=6&case=131&k=5a, [accessed September 2011].
[3] www.bdsmovement.net/call, *Idem.*

their complicity with Israel's grave and persistent violations of human rights and international law, they must be *compelled* to do so through mass, well organized grassroots pressure by social movements and other components of civil society. In this context, BDS has proven to be the most potent and promising strategy of international solidarity with the Palestinian people in our struggle for self determination, freedom, justice and equality."[4]

BDS is thus not just about the wall, or the occupation of the West Bank and Gaza. It is a holistic approach to Israel's militarism and its racist and apartheid policies against Palestinians, both inside 1948 Israel and in the Palestinian territories occupied in 1967: from the ethnic cleansing of 1947-9 to the state-orchestrated marginalisation of majority Palestinian municipalities, such as Nazareth; from the current state-orchestrated Judaization of Jerusalem to the harassment and house demolitions intended to push communities out of areas coveted by the state for Jews, both in the villages of the West Bank and the unrecognised Palestinian villages within Israel. BDS presents countless possibilities for effective grassroots campaigning, ranging from consumer action to workplace organising and direct action. The BDS movement has the potential to bring the Palestinian struggle to the doorsteps of those who profit from Israeli apartheid.

---

[4] http://www.bdsmovement.net/2011/before-and-after-september-7154, [accessed September 2011].

Credits

Written and researched by Tom Anderson, Therezia Cooper, Jack Curry, Georgia Clough, and Pete Jones.

Additional research by Karen Hallel.

Comic strip sequences written by Sean Michael Wilson and illustrated by Rejena Smiley.

Cover illustration by Jamie Martin.

Foreword by Ewa Jasiewicz.

Edited and produced by Tom Anderson, Therezia Cooper, Jack Curry and the Corporate Watch cooperative.

Published by Corporate Watch.

Layout and design by Tartan Pixie.

Printed by Russell Press.

ISBN: 978-1-907738-04-3

About this book

The BDS movement has enjoyed significant success since 2005. Many international companies, such as Deutsche Bahn,[1] have pulled out of projects in occupied Palestine following pressure from boycott campaigns. Companies with stakes in the occupation economy, such as the Dutch Dexia banking group, have been forced to divest their shares,[2] while Israeli conglomerate Africa Israel has been forced to announce to campaigners that it will not work in the settlements.[3] Since Israel's massacre in Gaza in 2009, Israeli companies have faced significant drops in exports, particularly to Europe.[4]

This book is intended as a point of reference for BDS campaigners. By providing information on the Israeli and international companies complicit in Israeli apartheid, occupation and militarism, we intend to provide information on who to target and what to prioritise.

Our focus here is on companies, but of course, BDS is not only about corporations. The academic boycott, the boycott of Israeli institutions and the call to artists not to perform in Israel, as well as the boycott of sports-people and artists who accept Israeli state funding, are integral parts of the BDS campaign.

The book is in three parts. The first looks at each sector of the Israeli economy, its relative importance and the corporate protagonists within it. Part two provides detailed geographical case studies, examining the effect of corporate activities in specific geographical areas. The final section focuses on the UK, looking at British arms companies, retailers, investors and charities complicit in Israeli occupation, militarism and apartheid.

The book was conceived in 2008, weeks before Israel commenced its three-week massacre in the Gaza Strip. In 2010, Corporate Watch researchers spent time in Israel, the occupied West Bank and Syrian Golan. In February 2010, the Corporate Occupation blog (corporateoccupation.wordpress.com) was set up as a resource for BDS campaigners. The blog has received over 30,000 visitors. During 2010-11 Corporate Watch gave dozens of workshops and presentations to groups of BDS campaigners and at festivals and gatherings highlighting the need for increased action in the BDS movement. This book is the culmination of this work.

---

[1] http://www.palestinemonitor.org/spip/spip.php?article1802, [accessed September 2011].
[2] http://archive.globes.co.il/searchgl/NIS per cent20600m per cent20asking per cent20price per cent20for per cent20Dexia per cent20Israel_h_hd_2L34oDZOtELmnC30mDZCtDZ0nBcXqRMm0.html, [accessed September 2011].
[3] http://www.coalitionofwomen.org/?tag=africa-israel-investments&lang=en, [accessed September 2011].
[4] http://www.guardian.co.uk/world/2009/apr/03/israel-gaza-attacks-boycotts-food-industry, [accessed September 2011].

Therezia Cooper and Tom Anderson are long-term BDS activists. They have volunteered in Palestine with the Jordan Valley Solidarity project, the Tel Rumeida Project and the International Solidarity Movement (ISM), and have taken part in numerous campaigns and actions against the sale of Israeli goods in British supermarkets, the manufacturing of arms for Israel in the UK and the sale of settlement goods. Tom is a member of the Corporate Watch cooperative.

Jack Curry is a researcher and freelance journalist who has been writing about the occupation of Palestine for a number of years. In early 2011 Jack travelled to the West Bank to engage in solidarity work and write on the situation of Bedouin living in the Jordan Valley.

Georgia Clough is a writer for Red Pepper magazine and radical newsheet, SchNEWS. She has a special interest in the Israel-Palestine issue.

Pete Jones and Karen Hallel have both volunteered with the ISM in Palestine and have been active in the UK BDS movement.

Sean Michael Wilson is a comic book writer from Scotland, who now lives and works in Japan. He has had more than a dozen books published by a variety of US, UK and Japanese publishers.[5]

Rejena Smiley is from Detroit, Michigan. She studied Comic Art at Minneapolis College of Art and Design.[6]

---

[5]To see more of Sean's work visit http://sean-michael-wilson.blogspot.com.
[6]To see more of Rejena's work visit http://www.rejenasmiley.com/blog.

Acknowledgements

This book could not have been written without the firm foundations laid by BDS campaigners over the last ten years. Particular credit must go to the Coalition of Women for Peace (www.coalitionofwomen.org) who created the Who Profits website (www.whoprofits.org). Special mention must also go to the Palestinian Grassroots Anti-Apartheid Wall Campaign (www.stopthewall.org) and the Boycott National Committee (www.bdsmovement.net).

We also thank Jordan Valley Solidarity (www.jordanvalleysolidarity.org www.brighton palestine.org), the International Solidarity Movement (www.palsolidarity.org), the Free Gaza Movement (www.freegaza.org), the popular committees of Bil In and Nabi Saleh, *Adalah* in Haifa (www.adalah.org), *Al Maarsad* in the Israeli occupied Syrian Golan (www.golan-marsad.org), *Kav LaOved* (www.Kav LaOved.co.il), the Palestinian General Federation of Trade Unions in Tulkarem, the Regional Council of Unrecognised Villages in the Naqab, the Alternative Information Centre (www.alternativenews.org) and Anarchists Against the Wall (www.awalls.org).

In the UK, we would like to thank War on Want (www.waronwant.org), the Boycott Israel Network (www.boycottisraelnetwork.org), Campaign Against the Arms Trade (www.caat.org.uk), the British Committee for the Universities of Palestine (www.bricup.org.uk) and Jews for Boycotting Israeli Goods (jews4big.wordpress.com).

Thanks to the Amiel Melburn Trust, Donal O'Driscoll, Don Atherton, Jamie Martin, Phunkee, Sophia Miller, Uri Gordon and the Corporate Watch cooperative for proof reading and help in producing this book.

Finally, we dedicate this book to the memory of our friend Simon Levin. A committed BDS campaigner, Simon bore witness to Israeli incursions in Balata refugee camp during the Second *intifada*, took part in blockades of Agrexco's UK depot and, in 2009 during the Gaza massacre, helped sabotage the production of weapons bound for Israel. Simon died during the writing of this book.[1]

---

[1] To read more about Simon see http://www.indymedia.org.uk/en/2011/07/481974.html, [accessed September 2011].

About Corporate Watch

Corporate Watch is a research group exposing the environmentally destructive and socially divisive projects of corporations and dragging the corrupt links between business and power, economics and politics into the spotlight.

From Corporate Watch's beginnings looking at PFI road-building we have broadened out to examine the oil industry, globalisation, genetic engineering, the food industry, toxic chemicals, migration, privatisation and many other areas, to catalogue corporate crimes and build a picture of the nature and mechanisms of corporate power, both economic and political. We have worked with and provided information to people and groups including peace campaigners, environmentalists, and trade unionists, large NGOs and small autonomous groups, journalists, MPs and other members of the public.

Over nine years we have become a respected professional research and campaigning organisation, run effectively as a workers' co-operative. We are currently supported mainly by donations from individuals and those few independent trusts and foundations willing to support an organisation such as ours. We do not take money from corporations or governments.

Corporate Watch
c/o Freedom Press
Angel Alley
84b Whitechapel High Street
London, E1 7QX
t: +44 (0)207 426 0005
e: contact[at]corporatewatch.org

Contents

Part one: Overview of the Israeli Economy

Page 1	Israel's export trade
Page 3	The effect of the BDS movement on exports
Page 5	Holding companies
Page 7	Banking and financial services
Page 16	Agriculture
Page 36	Extractive industries
Page 47	Energy
Page 55	Telecommunications
Page 61	Tourism
Page 68	Freight transport
Page 73	Public transport
Page 77	Academia
Page 88	Manufacturing overview
Page 91	Israel's settlement industrial zones
Page 124	Military industry
Page 149	High-tech
Page 161	Diamonds
Page 168	Pharmaceuticals
Page 178	Construction and real estate
Page 215	Franchises

Part two: Geographical Case Studies

Page 221	The Syrian Golan
Page 230	The Jordan Valley
Page 240	East Jerusalem
Page 255	The Dead Sea
Page 259	The Naqab

Part Three: The UK - Bringing the Fight Home

Page 277	Arms companies in the UK
Page 288	Israeli companies with British shareholders
Page 291	Banks
Page 294	Retail
Page 307	Universities
Page 317	Pension funds
Page 329	Charities

Maps

Page 52   Gaza Marine Zone
Page 195 The West Bank apartheid wall
Page 221 Syrian Golan
Page 230 The Jordan Valley
Page 232 The Allon Plan
Page 240 East Jerusalem
Page 259 The Naqab

Comic Strips

Page 32   The fruits of apartheid
Page 120 The wall against the Bedouin
Page 145 Bil'in
Page 271 The Jewish National Fund
Page 344 Boycott, Divestment and Sanctions

Appendices

Page 347 Select Bibliography
Page 350 Glossary
Page 356 Index

We have provided thorough footnotes to enable the reader to delve deeper into the source material used. Books and reports have been referenced by author, date and page number. Where possible we have provided a hyperlink. Articles and company websites have sometimes been referenced simply by a web link to conserve space. We have provided an access date for hyperlinks to facilitate the recovery of information, which is no longer on the web from internet archives.

Ibid: signifies that the information is from the same source as the previous footnote

Idem: signifies that the source has been referenced in full earlier in the book.

Part One

An Overview of the Israeli Economy

1
Israel's Export Trade

Foreign exports, worth an estimated $55 billion in 2010, are vital to the Israeli economy. Israel's exports include high-tech goods such as aviation products and arms, communications equipment, computer software and hardware, medical electronics and equipment and fibre optics. Israel's low-tech exports include wood and paper products, potash and phosphates, food, beverages, tobacco, caustic soda, cement, metals, chemical products, plastics, diamonds, textiles and footwear. Israel's most important exports are cut diamonds, high-tech goods, chemicals and arms.

The US remains Israel's main export market, with exports to the US amounting to some $24.5 billion in 2010. In 2007 these exports included cut diamonds (45.6 per cent), medical/pharmaceutical products (12.9 per cent), telecommunications equipment (3.6 per cent), aircraft and aircraft parts (5.1 per cent), medical equipment (3.1 per cent), electronic and computer equipment (3.7 per cent), and other military equipment (1.3 per cent).[1]

In 2009, EU imports from Israel amounted to €8.8 billion ($12.45 billion), consisting of machinery and transport equipment (25.2 per cent), chemicals (24.5 per cent) and agricultural products (11.1 per cent), particularly vegetable products (8.4 per cent).[2] In addition, Israel sold €3.7 billion ($5.23 billion) worth of services to EU countries. Roughly half of these were business services, while half were related to transport and tourism.[3]

---

[1]http://www.suite101.com/content/top-israeli-imports-exports-a59994, [accessed September 2011]. A breakdown of Israel's exports to the US from 2002 to 2010 can be found at www.census.gov/foreign-trade/statistics/product/enduse/imports/c5081.html#questions.
[2]http://ec.europa.eu/trade/creating-opportunities/bilateral-relations/countries/israel/, [accessed September 2011].
[3]*Ibid.*

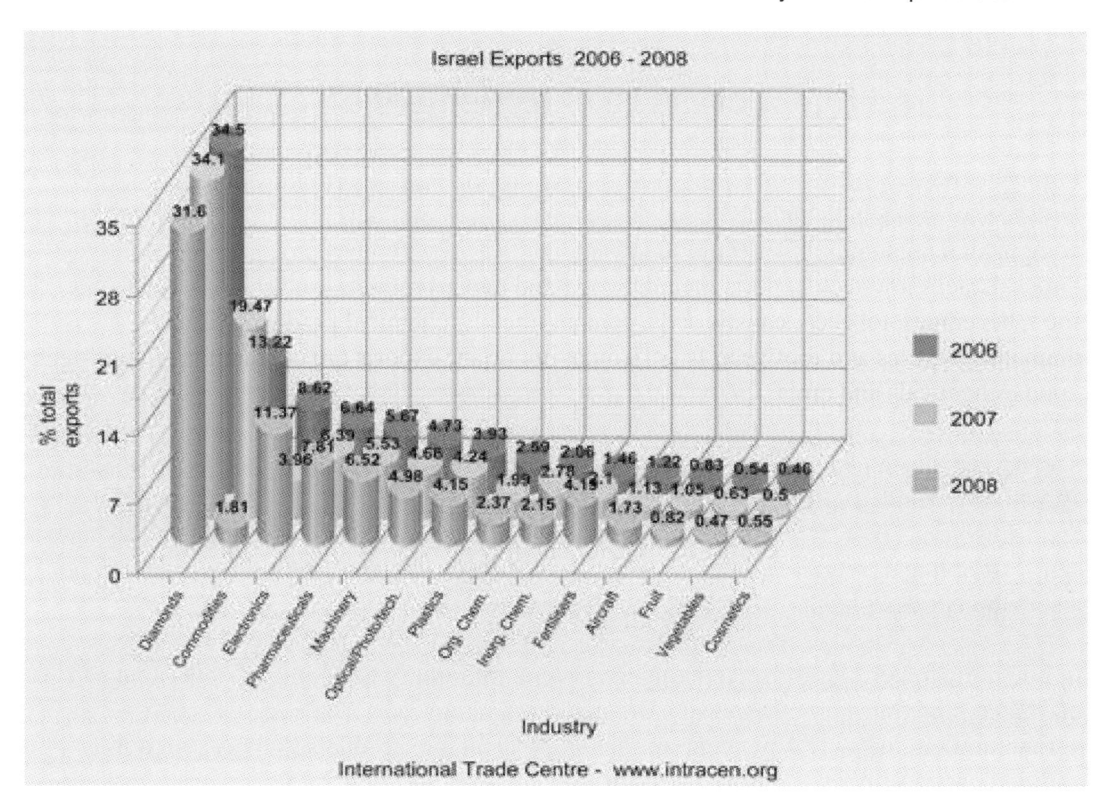

Overview of the Israeli Economy: Israel's Export Trade

Israel Exports 2006 - 2008 (% total exports)

Industry	2006	2007	2008
Diamonds	31.6	34.1	34.5
Commodities	1.81	—	—
Electronics	19.47	13.22	11.37
Pharmaceuticals	3.96	7.81	8.62
Machinery	6.39	6.52	6.64
Optical/Phototech	5.53	4.98	5.67
Plastics	4.66	4.15	4.73
Org. Chem	4.24	2.37	3.93
Inorg. Chem	2.59	2.15	2.79
Fertilisers	2.06	4.19	4.1
Aircraft	1.46	1.73	1.13
Fruit	1.22	0.82	1.05
Vegetables	0.83	0.47	0.63
Cosmetics	0.54	0.55	0.46 / 0.5

Israel Exports 2006 - 2008 ($ Billion/Yr.)

Industry	2006	2007	2008
Diamonds	19.1	18.4	16.13
Commodities	1.11	—	—
Electronics	10.53	6.97	6.19
Pharmaceuticals	2.14	4.78	4.03
Machinery	3.46	2.99	3.11
Optical/Phototech	2.99	3.06	2.65
Plastics	2.52	2.55	2.29 / 2.21
Org. Chem	1.84	1.45	1.32
Aircraft	1.21	1.08	—
Fertilisers	1.52	2.14	—
Inorg. Chem	0.98	0.61	0.68
Vegetables	0.57	0.57	0.34
Fruit	0.39	0.5	0.29
Cosmetics	0.25	0.21	0.27 / 0.34

International Trade Centre - www.intracen.org

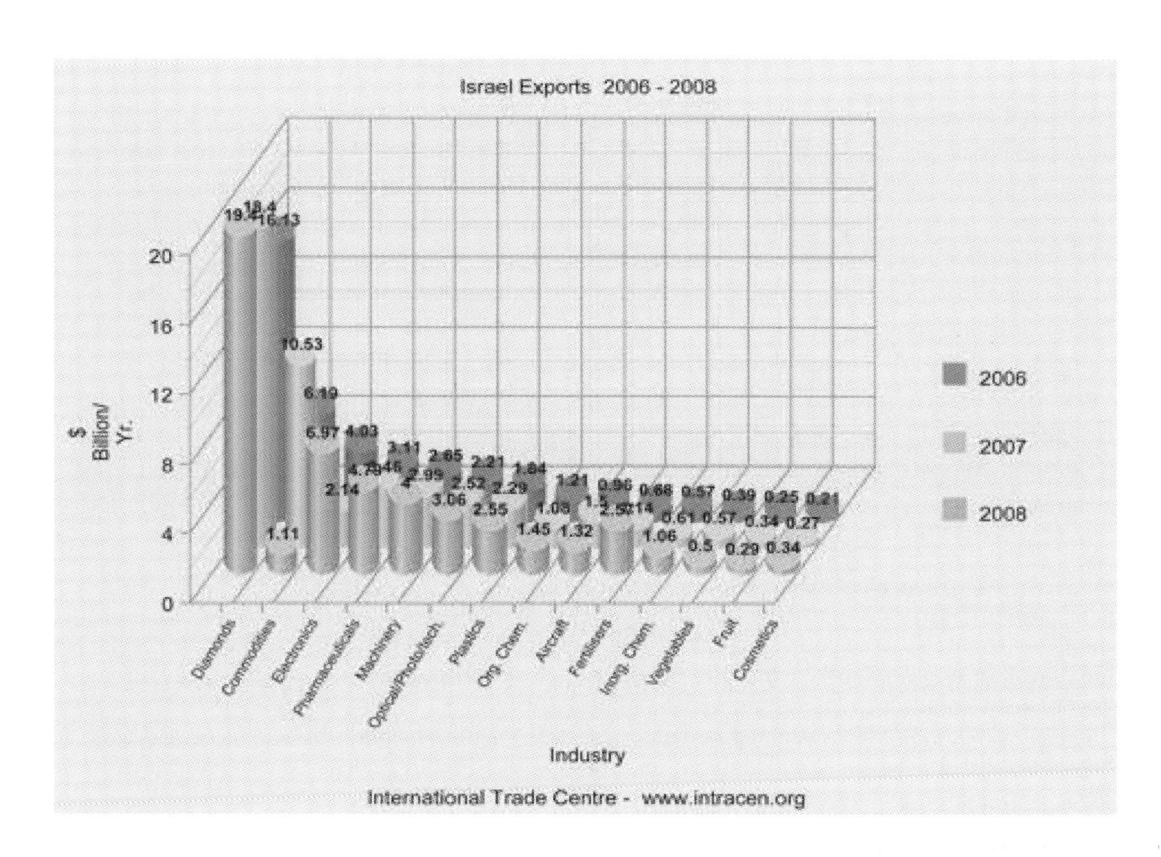

2
The Effect of the BDS Movement on Exports

"The horrific images on TV and the statements of politicians in Europe and Turkey are changing the behaviour of consumers, businessmen and potential investors. Many European consumers boycott Israeli products in practice."

Nehemia Stressler, Israeli economics journalist[1]

It is difficult to measure the effects of the BDS movement on Israeli exports. However, in April 2009 a report by the Israel Manufacturers Association reported that 21 per cent of 90 Israeli exporters questioned had experienced a drop in demand due to boycotts, mostly from the UK and Scandinavian countries. In March 2009, a report from the Israel Export Institute claimed that 100 out of 400 polled exporters received order cancellations because of Israel's 2009 assault on Gaza. The same year, Gil Erez, Israel's commercial attaché in London, complained that "organisations are bombarding [British] retailers with letters, asking that they remove Israeli merchandise from the shelves."[2]

In July 2011 the Knesset, rattled by the threat posed by the BDS movement, passed the 'Bill for prevention of damage to the state of Israel through boycott'. The new law penalizes any person or organization that calls for an "economic, cultural or academic" boycott of "a person or other party" because of its "relation" to Israel, Israeli institutions, or "any area under [Israel's] control."[3] This repressive move by the Israeli state shows that the boycott is now seen as a serious challenge.

In 2011, Carmel-Agrexco, Israel's largest agricultural exporter, revealed a €33 million loss and massive debts,[4] which it attributed partly to losses in Europe. Agrexco had lost business from several European supermarkets, including the Italian Coop chain, due to boycott pressures.[5] Similar campaigns are being waged in the UK, France, Spain and Sweden. On 11th September 2011 Agrexco was ordered into liquidation by a court in Tel Aviv (*see our later chapter on agriculture*). As respected Israeli economist Shir Hever has stated, the European-wide campaign against the company was among the factors that led to the company's downfall. Hever explains that "the company has been found to produce misleading reports, and did not warn its investors of the possible impact of the BDS campaign to boycott the company products. Many farmers have left the company, opting to work with competing ones which have not yet been at the focus of the BDS campaign, and as a result Agrexco entered a liquidity crisis. Several companies have considered bidding to

---

[1] http://www.guardian.co.uk/world/2009/apr/03/israel-gaza-attacks-boycotts-food-industry, [accessed September 2011].
[2] *Ibid*.
[3] http://www.hrw.org/news/2011/07/13/israel-anti-boycott-bill-stifles-expression, [accessed September 2011].
[4] http://www.jpost.com/Business/Globes/Article.aspx?id=226399&R=R9, [accessed September 2011].
[5] http://www.bdsmovement.net/2010/two-of-italys-biggest-supermarket-chains-suspend-sales-of-settlement-produce-694, [accessed September 2011].

buy Agrexco, but have withdrawn their bids after a brief research, which has no doubt uncovered the company's prominence in the BDS campaign, among other things."[6] Agrexco's brand, at the time of writing, was being sold as a going concern.

Such damage to Israel's national exporter seemed an impossible dream when campaigns against Agrexco began in 2004 and is a testament to the continuing success of the BDS campaign.

---

[6] http://www.bdsmovement.net/2011/palestinian-civil-society-welcomes-agrexco-liquidation-calls-for-celebration-of-this-bds-victory-8010, [accessed September 2011].

3
Holding Companies

The Israeli economy is dominated by groups of companies, often controlled by families, which control a huge amount of the economy's capital. The relationships between these companies are complex and often deliberately obfuscated. Writing about the situation in 2002, political economists Jonathan Nitzan and Shimshon Bichler argued "many of [the] firms were linked through complex and often circular cross-ownership ties, and even when these ties were conceptually straightforward, their origins were often concealed by long ownership chains leading to offshore shell companies."[1]

Nitzan and Bichler go on to identify five groups of companies that, in 1999, owned 82 out of 652 companies on the Tel Aviv Stock Exchange.[2] The groups have since changed and the table below shows some of the current concentrations of capital in the Israeli economy:[3]

Israel's Chamber of Commerce in Tel Aviv (Corporate Watch 2010)

---

[1]Nitzan, J and Bichler, S (2002), *The global political economy of Israel*. Pluto Press, p.97.
[2]*Ibid*, p.99.
[3]Figures taken from http://www.bdicode..co.il/Rank_ENG/34_0_0/Holding Companies According to Assets, [accessed September 2011].

Overview of the Israeli Economy: Holding Companies

Holding Company	Finances	Companies Controlled
IDB Group Controlled by the Nochi Danker, Livnat and Manor Families	$74 million assets $20 million revenues	Clal Koor Cellcom
FIBI Holdings Controlled by the Lieberman family and Zadik Bino through the Bino Group	$28 million assets $1.5 million revenues	**First International Bank of Israel** **Paz**
Delek Group Main shareholder is Yitzhak Tshuva	$22 million assets $12 million revenues	**Delek Real Estate** **Delek Petroleum** **Delek Investments and Properties**
Arison Group Controlled by the Arison family	$22 million assets	**Bank Hapoalim** **Israel Salt Company** **Shikun&Binui**
Israel Corporation Controlled by the Ofer family	$12 million assets $13 million revenues	Zim **Israel Chemicals Ltd** **Oil Refineries Limited** (37%)
Africa Israel Controlled by Lev Leviev	$7 million assets $2 million revenues	AFI Properties Danya Cebus AFI Hotels AFI Industries Alon USA

The Israeli state owns a significant number of companies including, amongst others, the **Israeli Electric Company**, three major arms companies; **Israeli Military Industries, Israeli Aerospace Industries** and **Rafael** and the **Mekorot** water company.

The details of this network of holding companies are significant as their complexity can mask the complicity of companies in Israeli apartheid, militarism and occupation. For instance, BDS campaigners may choose to target the investors and CEOs at the helm of these corporate groupings, many of whom are resident outside Israel.

4
Banking and Financial Services

In 2009 the financial sector contributed 26.1 per cent to Israel's GDP,[1] with banking activity alone accounting for over a quarter of this total.[2] The Israeli banking sector is highly consolidated with five main holding banks: **Bank Hapoalim, Bank Leumi, United Mizrahi-Tefahot Bank, First International Bank of Israel** and **Israel Discount Bank**.

Whilst controlled by FIBI Holdings, First International Bank of Israel (FIBI) is linked to Israel Discount Bank, with the latter holding 26.53 per cent of FIBI shares.[3] Together these banks and their subsidiaries control 95 per cent of the market, contributing around 4.1 per cent of GDP from banking activities alone.[4] It is, however, difficult to obtain exact figures on the banking sector's contribution to GDP because the numbers are buried in overall GDP from services and trade.

Even within this highly concentrated system, most of the deposits, credit card mutual funds, and underwriting activities are monopolised by the two largest banks, Hapoalim and Leumi.[5] According to the **Bank of Israel**, the total value of assets held by Israeli banks at the end of 2009 was NIS 1.088 trillion ($274.424 billion).[6] Of this, 56 per cent was equally shared between Bank Hapoalim and Bank Leumi.

---

[1] Israeli Bureau of National Statistics, cited by Shir Hever in private correspondence with the authors, April 2011.
[2] Bank of Israel (2009), *Israel's banking system – annual survey 2009*. Available: http://www.bankisrael.gov.il/publeng/publeslf.php?misg_id=15, [accessed 23/02/2011].
[3] Who Profits (October 2010), *Financing the Israeli occupation*, Available: http://www.whoprofits.org/articlefiles/WhoProfits-IsraeliBanks2010.pdf.
[4] Bank of Israel (2009), *Israel's banking system – annual survey 2009, Idem*. Note: This figure excludes the contribution of mortgage lending, commercial banking, consumer lending via credit card companies, and banking activities abroad.
[5] Sokoler, M (2006), *Changes in the Israeli banking system,* Bank of International Settlements, BIS Papers No. 28., Available: www.bis.org/publ/bppdf/bispap28p.pdf, *[accessed 01/03/2011]*.
[6] Bank of Israel (2009), *Israel's banking system – annual survey 2009 Idem*.

Bank Leumi: a Zionist history

The history of Bank Leumi extends beyond that of the state of Israel; the bank is a creation of the Zionist movement. Established in London in 1902, Leumi is Israel's oldest bank, beginning life as the **Anglo Palestine Company (APC)**, which was an offshoot of the **Jewish Colonial Trust** established at the Second Zionist Congress. The Trust was an answer to a call by Dr. Binyamin Ze'ev Herzl, in an article published in 1897, for a financial institution to help realise the goals of the Zionist movement.[7] In August 1903, APC subsidiary the **Anglo Palestine Bank (APB)** opened its first branch in Jaffa. The core aim of the APC was to develop and nurture business initiatives in industry and agriculture.[8] One of APB's major projects in its formative years was the extension of loans to the **Ahuzat Bayit Association** for its Jewish housing development on the outskirts of Jaffa.[9] As the Zionist presence in Palestine grew, a debate raged about how economic expansion could accommodate the need to absorb increasing Jewish immigration. During the 1930s, APB, in collaboration with the Jewish Agency, established a fund to support industrialists and help increase the economy's "absorptive" capacity.[10] After the State of Israel was established in 1948, APB was responsible for designing the new state's monetary system and ordering and distributing currency notes. Within three months, official bank notes were distributed bearing the name of Anglo-Palestine Bank and the signatures of APB chairman Ziegfried Hoofien and general manager Aaron Barth.[11] To overcome the problem of the official bank of the State of Israel being a British firm, a company called **Leumi Le'Israel** was created in Tel Aviv during 1950, assuming the obligations and assets of APB[12] and, thus, Bank Leumi was created.

In its latest financial statement, Bank Leumi announced a net profit of NIS 1.859 billion ($507.2 million) for the first nine months of 2010.[13] Bank Hapoalim recorded NIS 1.515 billion ($420 million) net profit in the same period.[14] Net profits for the five banking groups in 2009 were NIS 5.4 billion ($1.484 billion).[15] Figures for 2010 had not been published at the time of writing.

---

[7]http://www.bdicode.co.il//CompanyTextProfile_ENG/55_752_0/Bank per cent20Leumi per cent20le-Israel per cent20BM, [accessed 04/03/2011].
[8]*Ibid*.
[9]http://english.leumi.co.il/LEStruc/Leumis_Heritage/5491/, [accessed 04/03/2011].
[10]Kampf, A (2010), *Reception of the development approach in the Jewish economic discourse of mandatory Palestine, 1934-1938*. Israel Studies. Vol 15, No.2. p.80-103.
[11]http://english.leumi.co.il/LEStruc/Leumis_Heritage/5491/, [accessed 04/03/2011].
[12]*Ibid*.
[13]http://english.leumi.co.il/LEFinancialStatements/Financial_Statements/3334/, [accessed 23/02/2011].
[14]http://www.bankhapoalim.com/wps/portal/!ut/p/_.cmd/cs/ce/7_0_A/s./7_0_CR/_s.7_0_A/7_0_CR, [accessed 23/02/2011].
[15]Bank of Israel (2009), *Israel's banking system – annual survey 2009 Idem*.

The mortgage market is similarly consolidated. In 2005, Mizrahi merged with rival bank, Tefahot, to create the largest mortgage lender in Israel,[16] controlling some 35 per cent of the market.[17] **Leumi Mortgage Bank** controls a further twenty-five per cent,[18] meaning that just two institutions dominate 60 per cent of the market. A large proportion of the remaining home loans are provided by Bank Hapoalim and **Discount Mortgage Bank**.

Independent and foreign banks

In addition to these banking behemoths, there are three independent banks in Israel: **Union, Bank of Jerusalem** and **Dexia Israel**. The latter, however, is a subsidiary of Belgian-French financial group Dexia. The BDS movement has successfully induced Dexia to pull out of Israel and the company is reportedly planning to sell its shares to Bank of Jerusalem.[19] Dexia is so keen to divest that it is planning to sell its Israeli assets even if it incurs a loss.[20]

Four foreign banks also operate branches in Israel: **HSBC, BNP Paribas, Citibank** and **State Bank of India**. These four foreign banks control only 1.6 per cent of Israeli assets,[21] yet their importance to the economy should not be underestimated. Foreign branches operate within a niche customer base - targeting wealthy private individuals, government bond markets, and Israeli companies wanting to raise money in international capital markets.

Barclays Bank operates an office in Israel and, in August 2011, was granted a license to operate branches in Israel.[22] Barclays is also the only British bank to own significant investments in Israeli companies.[23] Both Barclays and HSBC have their headquarters in London.

Beyond banking

Hapoalim and Leumi are more than just banks. They are huge conglomerates, influencing every facet of the Israeli economy. Leumi has the widest reach, owning a 15.72 per cent stake in **Paz Oil**, and 18.14 per cent in **Israel Corporation Ltd**.[24] The latter is one of Israel's largest holding companies, whose portfolio includes shipping and container provider **Zim** and chemical company **ICL**.[25] Hapoalim has a 10 per cent share in **Clal Insurance**

---

[16] http://www.animaweb.org/en/pays_israel_financesbanques_en.php, [accessed 23/02/2011].
[17] Who Profits (October 2010), *Financing the Israeli occupation*, Idem.
[18] http://seekingalpha.com/instablog/533793-israel-s-financial-expert/42532-israel-s-housing-bubble-set-to-pop
[19] http://www.globes.co.il/serveen/globes/docview.asp?did=1000650344&fid=1725, [accessed 04/03/2011].
[20] *Ibid*.
[21] Bank of Israel (2009), *Israel's banking system – annual survey 2009*, Idem.
[22] http://www.ynetnews.com/articles/0,7340,L-4109211,00.html, [accessed 04/03/2011].
[23] Orbis database, Bureau Van Dijk, [accessed 19/08/2011].
[24] http://www.bdicode.co.il//CompanyTextProfile_ENG/55_752_0/Bank per cent20Leumi per cent20le-Israel per cent20BM, [accessed 04/03/2011].
[25] http://www.israelcorp.com/Holdings/HoldingsChart.aspx, [accessed 04/03/2011].

Enterprise Holdings, which is majority owned by the **IBD Group**. Clal owns 85 per cent of the shares in **Nesher Israel Cement Enterprises**, which provides cement for the construction of the wall and settlements.[26]

Banking on occupation

A 2010 report by Who Profits highlights six areas in which the Israeli banking sector provides direct financial support that services, enables and profits from, settlements in the occupied West Bank and occupied Syrian Golan:[27]

1. Providing mortgage loans to settlers
2. Providing special loans for building projects
3. Providing financial services to Israeli local authorities in the West Bank
4. Operating branches in settlements
5. Providing financial services to businesses in settlements
6. Benefiting from access to the Palestinian monetary market as a captured market

Bank Hapoalim's branch in Bnei Yehuda settlement, occupied Syrian Golan (Corporate Watch 2010)

Mortgage provision

All major Israeli banks, as well as the Bank of Jerusalem, have mortgage subsidiaries offering housing loans to Israelis wishing to live on settlements. Not only does this allow them to collect profits in the form of interest, it also gives them a direct stake in the

---

[26]http://www.whoprofits.org/Company per cent20Info.php?id=682, [accessed 04/03/2011].
[27]Who Profits (October 2010), *Financing the Israeli occupations*, Idem.

settlements. This is because, as with all mortgage agreements, the property acts as collateral against the loan. Therefore, until the loan is paid off, the bank part-owns the property and, should settlers default, the bank would own the property.

Who Profits argues: "By providing these mortgage loans for the construction or the purchasing of homes in settlements, the banks turn themselves into active participants in the development and sustainment of the Israeli settlements in the occupied territory."[28]

An advertisement for a construction project in the settlement of Zufin. At the bottom it says "mortgages in preferential conditions by Leumi mortgage bank." (Coalition of Women for Peace 2009)

Construction loans

Housing construction in Israel is dependent on loans provided under favourable terms known as "accompaniment agreements" (*Heskem Livui*).[29] Research by Who Profits shows that all of the major Israeli banks provide these loans to construction companies building in settlements. As with mortgage loans, these agreements mean that the banks hold the property as collateral against the loan, until all housing units have been sold to occupiers.

An example of this is the Nof Zion housing project in occupied East Jerusalem, which is being constructed by **Digal Investments and Holdings**. Credit for the project was provided by Leumi. When Digal was unable to repay either Leumi or its bondholders, **Nof Zion**, Digal's main asset, became a bargaining tool.[30] Palestinian-American businessman Basher al-Masri offered to buy Digal's stake in Nof Zion, much to the disapproval of Israel's national-

---

[28]*Ibid*, p.11.
[29]*Ibid*.
[30]http://english.themarker.com/leumi-rescinds-threat-to-dissolve-digal-after-agreement-is-reached-1.346586?localLinksEnabled=false, [accessed 04/03/2011].

Overview of the Israeli Economy: Banking and Financial Services

religious parties.[31] After settler groups threatened to boycott the bank, Leumi accepted a lower bid from Jewish-American supermarket mogul Rami Levi, who had had a previous financing offer turned down.[32]

In 2007, Bank Hapoalim loaned money to **Heftsiba** for a settlement construction project. Heftsiba had been building housing units in the East Jerusalem settlement Har Homa and the Nofei Sela project in Ma'ale Adumim settlement on the outskirts of Jerusalem.[33] Leumi, Discount and Mizrahi-Tefahot also loaned money to Heftsiba,[34] although it is unclear whether this was related to the construction of settlements.

Israeli banks finance the settlement construction business knowing full well what it entails. In fact, under an accompaniment agreement, the banks appoint officers to monitor and supervise the development of the project.[35]

Services to settlement authorities

Local and regional councils and municipalities in settlements across the West Bank and occupied Syrian Golan rely on the financial services provided by the major banks and their subsidiaries.[36] These services include loans, the opening and running of bank accounts, and the transfer of funds from central government.

For example, Who Profits uncovered seventeen loans made by Dexia Israel to illegal settlements between the end of 2008 and 2009. This included two loans to the local council of Kedumim settlement, totalling NIS 1.5 million (approximately $409,000) and three loans to the regional council of Mateh Benyamin settlement totalling NIS 5 million ($1.37 million).[37] Overall, Dexia Israel provided more than NIS 23 million (approx $6.5 million) of loans to settlements between June 2008 and the end of 2009.[38]

Business loans

As well as providing credit for the construction of settlements and the purchase of settlement homes, the banks also provide capital for settlement industry. Some of these businesses operate solely within the occupied Palestinian territories (OPT) and settlement property is often used as collateral against the loan.[39]

---

[31]*Ibid*.
[32]http://www.jpost.com/NationalNews/Article.aspx?id=210406, [accessed September 2011].
[33]http://www.haaretz.com/print-edition/business/hapoalim-heftsiba-is-lying-in-its-motion-to-halt-legal-steps-1.227160, [accessed September 2011].
[34]http://www.haaretz.com/print-edition/news/police-plan-to-grill-bank-execs-in-heftsiba-collapse-1.227873, [accessed September 2011].
[35]Who Profits (October 2010), *Financing the Israeli occupations*, Idem.
[36]*Ibid*.
[37]Who Profits (October 2010), *Financing the Israeli occupations*, Ibid.
[38]*Ibid*.
[39]*Ibid*.

Examples include financing from Leumi and Hapoalim to the **City Pass** consortium, which is constructing the Jerusalem light rail line.[40] This transport network will connect settlements and settlement neighbourhoods in East Jerusalem with West Jerusalem and the rest of Israel.

Capturing the Palestinian market

Because of the economic agreements signed in the Paris Protocols (the predecessor to the Oslo Accords), the OPT have been denied the right to develop an independent monetary system. This includes a lack of national currency, leading to the inability to set interest rates and control inflation. Instead, the Palestinian market operates using four different currencies: the Israeli shekel, the US dollar, euros and the Jordanian dinar.[41]

As most of the goods bought in the OPT come from Israel, most transactions are carried out in shekels. Out of NIS 20 billion in annual transfers, 80 per cent goes from the OPT to Israel.[42] Despite the dominance of the shekel, Palestinian banks do not have access to shekel clearing houses. This means they have to buy clearing-house services from Israeli banks.

Hapoalim and Discount Bank provide the clearing services for Palestinian banks but place severe restrictions on agreements in order to increase profits. There are limitations on the amount that can be transferred in each transaction, increasing the amount of transactions needed and the amount of charges.[43] This, coupled with the extortionate commission charged by the Israeli banks for each transaction, cripples the already fragile Palestinian banking system.

Blood money

There are a number of small banks in Israel with a niche client base tied in with the occupation. **Bank Otsar Ha-Hayal** (Bank of the Soldier Treasury) was set up under the British Mandate to serve Jewish veterans of the British armed forces.[44] Today it serves the Israeli army, employees of defence institutions and the Israeli aerospace industry, as well as the general public. Ostar Ha-Hayal is a subsidiary of First International Bank of Israel, which holds 68 per cent of its shares.[45]

Yahav Bank for Government Employees is 50 per cent-owned by Mizrahi and 25 per cent by the Histradrut (the Israeli umbrella trade union confederation).[46] Banking services include loans to state employees on favourable terms. Considering that almost every facet of the state

---

[40] http://english.themarker.com/economy-finance/jerusalem-train-on-disaster-track-1.224870, [accessed September 2011].
[41] Who Profits (October 2010), *Financing the Israeli occupations*, Idem.
[42] *Ibid.*
[43] *Ibid.*
[44] http://www.bankotsar.co.il/bankOtsar/site/en/bankOtsar.asp?pi=1689&doc_id=4564, [accessed September 2011].
[45] Who Profits (October 2010), *Financing the Israeli occupations*, Idem.
[46] http://www.whoprofits.org/Company per cent20Info.php?id=889, [accessed September 2011].

apparatus contributes to the occupation of Palestine and the oppression of Palestinians, Yahav, and the customers it serves, are complicit in Palestinian suffering.

International links

Israeli banks operate 158 offices and branches abroad either directly, through representatives, or indirectly through subsidiaries. At the end of 2009, these overseas operations held NIS 145 billion ($39.7 billion) in assets, totalling 14 per cent of the banking groups' total assets.[47] This includes a Bank Leumi operation in London, which provides high street banking and mortgage provision to UK customers. Hapoalim also has an office in London.

However, according to the Bank of Israel activity abroad, especially in developed markets, has failed to provide a steady profit stream for Israeli banks due to competition from more established local banks. As a result, Israeli banks have been targeting emerging markets by buying local banks with a well established domestic base.

The banks also act as a conduit for international finance to operate within Israel. Hapoalim is the exclusive Israeli issuer of **American Express** (Amex) cards for payments in shekels, although Bank Leumi has signed a deal with Amex for foreign currency payments.[48] Hapoalim is, however, the sole franchise holder for American Express cards in Israel through its **Isracard Group** subsidiary.[49] Isracard is the largest credit card company in Israel, with a growing customer base encompassing almost half of the Israeli population.[50]

As highlighted above, major international banks such as HSBC and Citibank with operations in Israel are complicit in underwriting the activities of the Israeli state by helping it issue bonds on the world market.[51] At least nine British financial companies are known to own Israeli government bonds: **Artemis Investment Management, Ashmore Investment Management, Barclays Global Investors, Capital International Ltd, Fortis Investments, Investec Asset Management, Morley Fund Management, Pictet Asset Management UK Ltd** and **State Street Global Advisors UK Ltd.**[52]

Because it is difficult to pinpoint exactly how the money from each bond issuance is used, we cannot track how this helps the occupation per se. However, considering the huge amount of Israeli government expenditure on subsidising settlement expansion and industry, not to mention the over-inflated military budget, it is not difficult to see how bond issuance aids the occupation.

---

[47] Bank of Israel (2009), *Israel's banking system – annual survey 2009, Idem.*
[48] http://www.globes.co.il/serveen/globes/docview.asp?did=769384, [accessed September 2011].
[49] *Ibid.*
[50] http://www.reuters.com/article/2010/11/15/isracard-results-idUKLDE6AE0AK20101115, [accessed September 2011].
[51] http://electronicintifada.net/v2/article10402.shtml, [accessed September 2011].
[52] *Ibid.*

Resistance

The successful campaign against Dexia, prompting the bank to divest from Dexia Israel, is an example of what is possible in terms of BDS action around banking. Since 2008, the 'Israel Colonises – Dexia Finances' campaign has pressured the Franco-Belgian bank to divest from Dexia Israel. The campaign, which has been active in France, Luxembourg, Belgium and Turkey, persuaded 42 municipalities that hold shares in Dexia to pass motions calling for divestment, with demonstrations held outside Dexia offices, parliamentary questions raised about the company and shareholder actions at AGMs.[53]

Since 2009, a campaign has been underway in the US to persuade the labour movement to divest its Israeli state bonds.[54]

Where next?

Because Israeli banks derive most of their business from the domestic economy, the BDS movement should target the pool of companies that provide services or franchises to Israeli banks. The obvious example is American Express. Equally, Leumi's small presence in the UK market could be easily targeted with concerted campaigns, as could Barclays and the four other international banks operating in Israel. In addition, it is of paramount importance to ensure that the Israeli government cannot access global bond markets and raise the funds needed to continue its settlement expansion and oppressive military occupation. Therefore bondholders such as Barclays should be targeted, whilst HSBC should be targeted for helping Israeli companies raise money in capital markets.

BDS activists demonstrate at Dexia's AGM, May 2011, Brussels (Globalise Solidarity 2011)

---

[53]http://www.bdsmovement.net/2011/dexia-looking-6361, [accessed September 2011].
[54]http://dumpisraelbonds.com/?page_id=2, [accessed September 2011].

5
Agriculture

> Agriculture is important for the BDS movement as it is the sector, which has, perhaps, the biggest overall impact on Palestinian communities. The industry is closely controlled by the Israeli state, which allocates land and water resources and gives subsidies for farming activities and visas for foreign workers. For Palestinians living in rural areas the impact of settlement farms has been catastrophic: not only are their lands confiscated for agricultural settlement expansion at an alarming rate, their natural water resources are also stolen by the Israeli state. But it is not just rural Palestinians who are affected by Israeli farming. Palestinians are also used by Israel as a 'captive workforce' for the settlements. Urban workers commute through checkpoints at dawn in order to get to their jobs in the fields and packinghouses. Once there, they receive around half of the minimum wage and receive no contracts, sick pay or health insurance. For Palestinians at least, Israel's fruits taste bitter.

Israel's revenues from the agriculture industry account for 2.6 per cent of the country's GDP, with about 2 per cent of the population working in agricultural production.[1] Israel is also quickly expanding its agricultural technologies industry. In 2007, revenue from the export of agriculture equipment and related products amounted to $2.2 billion dollars.[2] Around 240,000 people work within the area of services for agriculture, bringing the total of agricultural and secondary agricultural workers to between 8 and 9 per cent of the workforce.[3]

On the face of it it might seem like the BDS movement spends a disproportionate amount of energy on agricultural produce considering the relatively small contribution it makes to Israeli GDP. However, agriculture has always been closely connected to the Israeli occupation and has one of the biggest and most direct impacts on the lives of Palestinians. At the creation of Israel, agriculture was seen as a top priority for the new state, which saw quick agricultural expansion as necessary in order to "settle the underdeveloped areas of the country for geopolitical security."[4] After the occupation of the West Bank in 1967, Israel immediately started to build settlements, with a special focus on the Jordan Valley, where the objective was to reset the borders of Israel to include the Valley.[5] Since then, the Jordan Valley has grown to be one of the largest agricultural centres in the country, providing a livelihood for settlers living in over 30 illegal settlements located there.

---

[1] http://www.indexmundi.com/israel/economy_profile.html, [accessed 3/3/2011].
[2] OECD (2010), *OECD Review of agricultural policies: Israel, 2010*. Available: http://www.oecd.org/dataoecd/53/0/45189389.pdf, p.61. Please note that the OECD report states that the review is "not intended to cover the territories known as the Golan Heights, the Gaza Strip or West Bank. However, for technical reasons, this review sometimes uses Israel's official statistics, which include data relating to the Golan Heights, East Jerusalem and Israeli settlements in the West Bank."
[3] *Ibid*, p.54.
[4] *Ibid*, p.80.
[5] http://www.btselem.org/english/Settlements/Jordan_Valley.asp. [accessed 3/3/2011].

60 per cent of Israeli agricultural production consists of vegetables, fruit and flowers, with the remaining 40 per cent being livestock and related products such as meat, milk and eggs.[6] The growth in fruit and vegetable sales is mainly driven by the export market[7] so it continues to be an important focus for the boycott movement. The livestock market is almost exclusively domestic, so it provides limited scope for the BDS movement and will, therefore, not be discussed at length here.

Greenhouses belonging to the illegal settlement of Argarman in the Jordan Valley (Corporate Watch 2010)

The EU, followed by the USA, is the most important market for the export of Israeli fruit, vegetables, herbs and flowers, with vegetables currently being the fastest growing product.[8] Within the EU, the main importer of Israeli agricultural products is the Netherlands (17 per cent), although produce that arrives in the Netherlands often gets reshipped to other countries,[9] hence complicating the process of tracking it through labeling. This is particularly pronounced when it comes to flowers which tend to go from Israel straight to the big Dutch flower auction houses such as **Flora Holland**,[10] and then on from there in mixed-country consignments that do not require the country of origin to be stated. The UK is the second largest importer of Israeli fresh produce (12 per cent).[11]

---

[6]OECD (2010), *OECD Review of agricultural policies: Israel, 2010, Idem*, p.50.
[7]*Ibid*, p.19.
[8]*Ibid*, p.50.
[9]*Ibid*, p.66.
[10]For information about Flora Holland, see http://www.floraholland.com/en/Pages/default.aspx, [accessed 9/3/2011].
[11]OECD (2010), *OECD Review of agricultural policies: Israel, 2010, Idem*, p.67.

Overview of the Israeli Economy: Agriculture   **18**

Israel is Europe's biggest supplier of flowers, and Israeli exports totalled $1.5 billion in 2004, representing a greater return than weapons sales for that year.[12] However, growing flowers for export is an important business in Israel, representing around 20 per cent of agricultural exports.[13] Markets are captured by providing flowers out of season, such as the provision of peonies to Europe when the Dutch growing season finishes at the end of spring.[14] In comparison, due to Israel's relentless siege on Gaza, only a third of the estimated 30 million flowers grown in the strip were allowed to reach international markets in 2010 because of border closures.[15]

Flowers grown for export by settlers in the Jordan Valley (Corporate Watch 2010)

Two areas of Israeli agriculture currently growing rapidly are organic farming and rural, or 'agro', tourism.[16] So far agricultural tourism, which accounts for around 20 per cent of Israel's total tourism market and is state-supported jointly through the ministries of tourism and agriculture, is expanding, mainly through domestic tourism.[17] However, the BDS movement should keep this in mind for the future as the internet has opened up new ways for alternative destinations to advertise themselves.

---

[12]Morgenstern, J (2004), Economic development: flowers beat missiles, *Globes*. Available: http://www.israelforum.com/board/showthread.php?5451-Economic-development-Flowers-beat-missiles, [accessed 13th July 2010].
[13]http://en.wikipedia.org/wiki/Agriculture_in_Israel#cite_note-CBS-3, [accessed 13th July 2010].
[14]KKL-JNF (2011), New Agricultural Innovations at Western Negev R&D Station, *Jerusalem Post*, Available: http://www.jpost.com/GreenIsrael/PEOPLEANDTHEENVIRONMENT/Article.aspx?id=210041, [accessed September 2011].
[15]http://teleflora.com/flower-news/post/gaza-crossing-closure-has-hurt-israels-flower-industry-800487276.aspx, [accessed 13th July 2010].
[16]OECD (2010), *OECD Review of agricultural policies: Israel, 2010, Idem*, p.73 and p.180.
[17]*Ibid*, p.73.

Organic produce seems to be the next big growth area, with increasing demand for organic goods in Europe and with areas used for organic farming having doubled in Israel during the last decade. 75 per cent of organics are grown for export, with a massive 90 per cent destined for the EU market.[18] Corporate Watch's own research in the occupied territories has shown that a lot of organic produce destined for Europe originates from illegal Israeli settlements but is still packaged in boxes showing accreditation from international standard setting bodies for organic goods, such as the **International Federation of Organic Agriculture Movements (IFOAM)**.[19] IFOAM's own guidelines state that its accredited operators should "respect the rights of indigenous peoples, and should not use or exploit land whose inhabitants or farmers have been or are being impoverished, dispossessed, colonized, expelled, exiled or killed, or which is currently in dispute regarding legal or customary local rights to its use or ownership."[20]

A captive workforce

There are 18,000 Palestinian workers with Israeli work permits employed in illegal settlements throughout the West Bank.[21] A further 20,000 permit holders work inside Israel.[22] Most Palestinians employed by Israeli businesses work in agriculture, construction or in one of the industrial zones.[23] The Israeli high court ruled in 2007 that Israeli labour laws had to be extended to Palestinians employed by Israelis in the occupied territories and, since then, Palestinians have been legally entitled to the Israeli minimum wage and other benefits such as holiday pay, payslips and health cover.[24] However, Palestinian settlement workers in general, and agricultural workers in particular, have seen few changes in their working conditions as a result, as there is almost no enforcement of the high court ruling inside the occupied territories.[25] In the few instances where the pay of settlement workers has increased, it has only done so after court cases on behalf of individuals. Most of those cases have been brought by employees in industrial zones rather than agricultural workers.[26]

On top of the figures for security-cleared workers with permits, there are an estimated 10,000 'illegal' Palestinian settlement workers. Almost all of them work in the agricultural

---

[18] *Ibid*, p.180.
[19] See for instance http://corporateoccupation.wordpress.com/2010/08/12/hadiklaim-in-the-jordan-valley/ and http://corporateoccupation.wordpress.com/2010/04/08/further-information-about-edom-uk-signs-of-more-mislabelling/, [accessed 10/3/2011].
[20] *The IFOAM basic standards for organic production and processing.* Available: http://www.ifoam.org/about_ifoam/standards/norms/norm_documents_library/IBS_V3_20070817.pdf, [accessed 10/3/2011].
[21] Alenat, Salwa (2010), *Working for survival: labor conditions of Palestinians working in settlements*, Kav LaOved, Available: http://www.kavlaoved.org.il/media-view_eng.asp?id=3048, [accessed 10/3/2011].
[22] Roy Wagner from *Kav LaOved*, interview with authors, March 2010.
[23] Alenat, S (2010), *Working for survival, Idem.*
[24] *Kav LaOved* (2007), *Precedent setting ruling*, Available: http://www.kavlaoved.org.il/media-view_eng.asp?id=1123, [accessed 10/3/2011].
[25] Alenat, S (2010), *Working for survival, Idem.*
[26] *Ibid.*

industries, a majority in the Jordan Valley.[27] There are also Palestinians working within agriculture illegally inside Israel, especially in the Arava region.[28] The conditions for these illegal workers are especially dire. Not even superficially protected by any law, they are, as a captive workforce with few options, especially vulnerable to exploitation. Their working conditions show it: they work long hours, have no right to unionise, receive no health insurance, sick pay or holiday pay and get paid, on average, 60-80 NIS per day - around half of the minimum wage that they are entitled to. They do not have contracts, meaning that they can be fired, or simply asked not to come back without any notice, even after years of service.[29] As these workers are not regulated, child labour is common in the settlements, especially in the fruit picking fields, where Corporate Watch found children as young as 11 years old working adult shifts. The legal minimum age for such work is 16.[30] Produce exported from settlements where these kind of working conditions exist can regularly be found on British supermarket shelves.

Working for agricultural illegal settlements is a complicated issue for Palestinians. To get a permit to be a 'legal' settlement worker, they have to go through security checks administered by the Israeli security authorities every three to six months.[31] Sometimes the security services demand collaboration from the Palestinians in exchange for them passing the clearance process, resulting in a certain amount of suspicion of settlement workers within their own communities.[32]

In a bitter twist of fortunes, Palestinian workers often work for a pittance on illegal settlements on land stolen from Palestinian families, while workers who commute to the agricultural areas from further afield have to deal with checkpoints and intimidation on a daily basis to reach their jobs. With settlement workers starting around six o'clock in the morning, many have to start travelling in the middle of the night to be sure of arriving in time as they have to go via Israeli checkpoints, where they may be held, questioned and searched for hours before being let through.[33]

Since the mid-1990s, the number of Palestinians working inside Israel has decreased because of what Israel generally terms 'security issues'. Since less Palestinians are issued with work permits, the number of migrant workers has increased, with an estimated 24,000 being

---

[27] *Ibid.*

[28] Roy Wagner, interview, *Idem*.

[29] These facts are based on around 50 field studies carried out with settlement workers on the ground by Corporate Watch between March and May 2010. Some of articles on this issue can be found at http://corporateoccupation.wordpress.com/. There are also many other reports on this subject from various sources, one of the best being the *Kav LaOved* website, (www.kavlaoved.org.il).

[30] Interview with Roy Wagner from *Kav LaOved*, *Idem*. The youngest settlement worker Corporate Watch interviewed during our research was 11 years old. There were a large amount of workers under 16 years of age.

[31] Alenat, S (2010), *Working for survival, Idem*.

[32] Interview with Roy Wagner, *Idem*.

[33] See http://corporateoccupation.wordpress.com/2010/05/25/the-start-of-the-working-day-for-settlement-workers-in-the-jordan-valley/. There are good, constantly updated reports published by *Machsom Watch* (Checkpoint Watch). Available: http://www.machsomwatch.org.

employed in the agriculture sector at the time of writing. The majority of these workers are from Thailand but there are also some from Nepal, Vietnam and China.[34]

Many Palestinian settlement workers have told Corporate Watch that most foreign workers earn more than they do, yet they still do not earn the minimum wage that they are entitled to. Recent publications by *Kav LaOved*, an independent Israeli workers rights hotline, show that there are many disturbing practices in the Israeli migrant labour market. The most common issues are similar to the ones experienced by Palestinian workers: lack of payslips and delayed or unpaid wages,[35] while migrant workers often live in substandard accommodation provided by their employer on-site. *Kav LaOved* has found that a majority of human trafficking offences being investigated in Israel concern Thai agricultural workers. Despite a recent Israeli law stating that it is illegal for private agencies to take a mediator fee from workers who are migrating to work in the country the average amount that these workers paid out in 2010 for the benefit of being exploited by the Israeli agriculture business amounted to over $10,000 per person.[36] The fact that most migrant workers would have had to borrow money to pay this sum[37] makes them very vulnerable and easy to manipulate as they cannot afford to lose their jobs and be sent back to their home countries while still in debt.

Palestinian settlement workers, on their way to work, being searched at Al Hamra military checkpoint (Machsom Watch 2010)

---

[34]Rosenthal, N (2010), *2010 Activity summary report - migrant workers in agricultural settlements, Kav LaOved,* Available: http://www.kavlaoved.org.il/UserFiles/File/Thaieng.pdf, [accessed 15/3/2011].
[35]*Ibid.*
[36]*Ibid.*
[37]Interview with Roy Wagner, *Idem.*

With the Palestinian Authority now supporting a settlement boycott and urging Palestinians not to take jobs in the settlements, it seems likely that the number of foreign workers will overtake Palestinian workers inside the West Bank. It is imperative, therefore, that the issue of migrant worker exploitation is not ignored by the BDS movement.

Bleeding Palestine dry

Much is made these days of the growing water crisis in Israel, and one of the country's priorities is to develop its 'advanced technologies' sector that could improve irrigation techniques.[38] An astonishing 1,127 million cubic metres of water out of 2,147 per year (or 57 per cent of Israel's total water consumption) is used for agricultural production. Only around 60 million cubic metres is allocated to the Palestinian Authority,[39] making the water issue - and hence agriculture - one of the best examples of how Israel's apartheid policies are implemented on the ground.

All water, and 94 per cent of the land in Israel, is 'public', with only 6 per cent in private ownership. Israeli farmers, including settlers, receive water subsidies and do not pay the full price for water,[40] while Palestinians living under occupation find it hard to get access to water. Even when they do have access they pay double the Israeli rates. In settler agricultural areas, such as the Jordan Valley, the Israeli national water company **Mekorot** controls 98 per cent of the water supply. Almost all of this is used by the settlers, with many Palestinian communities having to drive for miles, sometimes through Israeli checkpoints, to collect water by tractor. Israel claims state ownership of all water, including natural wells,[41] and does not generally allow Palestinians to use them. In the rare instances when a community is not prohibited from using their natural water sources, it is often of little consolation: Palestinians in area C, for example, are not allowed to drill their wells deep enough to compete with Mekorot, which has led to most natural wells drying up.[42]

94 per cent of the land within Israel is managed by the **Israel Land Administration (ILA)**, with land controlled either by the state, the **Jewish National Fund** (JNF) or the Israel Development Authority.[43] Agricultural land is divided into three priority zones: A, B and C. Zone A is the highest priority area for settlement and development. Israelis moving to zone A and B areas get substantial support from the state in the form of subsidies and tax breaks.[44] Although official reports tend to focus on the priority areas inside Israel, most illegal settlements in the West Bank fall into the A and B categories, with Israeli government funds channelled through third parties, often parastatal organisations, such as the **World Zionist**

---

[38] OECD (2010), *OECD Review of agricultural policies: Israel, 2010, Idem.*
[39] *Ibid*, p.152-155.
[40] *Ibid*, p.94.
[41] *Ibid*, p.161.
[42] Information based on numerous personal interviews by Tom Anderson and Therezia Cooper with Palestinians in the Jordan Valley, 2006-2010.
[43] *Ibid*, p.84-85.
[44] *Ibid*, p.84. Please note that these A, B and C areas are Israeli development zones and do not refer to the A, B and C zones implemented by the Oslo accords.

Organisation.[45] The two places with zone A and B status inside Israel are the Naqab and the Galilee.[46] The JNF is currently running a programme called Blueprint Negev to encourage Jewish settlement in the Naqab,[47] while Al Araqib, one of the unrecognised Bedouin villages in the Naqab, has been demolished completely by the ILA (which is controlled by the JNF) a dozen times during the last year alone.[48]

Company profiles

There are many Israeli agricultural companies that can be targeted. Some have already received much attention, while some are new. Here are profiles of some of the companies that we consider priorities for the boycott movement.

Carmel-Agrexco, the Israeli national exporter, was ordered into liquidation on September 11th 2011. It trades in fruit, vegetables and flowers. 30 per cent of the company was owned by the Israeli government, with a further 25 per cent owned by growers, including settlers, represented by Israel's production and marketing boards. The board of directors was dominated by government employees. The final 25 per cent was owned by the **Tnuva** cooperative. In September 2011 Agrexco was ordered into liquidation by a Tel Aviv court. It is unclear, at the time of writing, what will become of the company's various assets.

Carmel-Agrexco was deeply involved in the trade of settlement goods. It had a regional office in the occupied Jordan Valley and worked with growers in most of the settlements there. During the trial of seven UK activists who had blockaded Agrexco's UK depot in 2004, Amos Orr, Agrexco's general manager, gave evidence that Carmel Agrexco marketed between 60 and 70 per cent of all agricultural produce grown in Israeli settlements.[49] From personal interviews with settlement workers who deal with Agrexco's produce in the Jordan Valley, it became evident that the company was complicit not only in land grabs and water exploitation, but also in profiting from illegal labour conditions.[50] Agrexco traded under the brand names **Carmel**, **Carmel Bio Top** (organic produce), **Alesia**, **Coral**, **Jaffa** and **Jordan Plains**. It had subsidiaries in France, Italy, Germany and the US.

In 2011, Agrexco revealed a €33 million loss and massive debts,[51] which it attributed partly to losses in Europe. Agrexco had lost business from several European supermarkets

---

[45] B'Tselem, *Land expropriation and settlements*. Available: http://www.btselem.org/english/settlements/migration.asp. [accessed 16/3/2011].
[46] OECD (2010), *OECD Review of agricultural policies: Israel, 2010, Idem*, p.84.
[47] Jewish National Fund, *Blueprint Negev*. Available: http://www.jnf.org/work-we-do/blueprint-negev/, [accessed 16/3/2011].
[48] See for instance http://www.middleeastmonitor.org.uk/articles/arab-media/1385-al-arakib-and-villages-in-the-negev-as-part-of-israels-judaisation-scheme, [accessed 16/3/2011].
[49] Chris Osmond, defendant in the 2006 case at Uxbridge Magistrates Court, personal notes.
[50] Corporate Watch and the Jordan Valley Solidarity Group have conducted interviews with workers in the area frequently from 2006-2011. There are various examples of personal evidence of Agrexco's practices on www.brightonpalestine.org and corporateoccupation.wordpress.com.
[51] http://www.jpost.com/Business/Globes/Article.aspx?id=226399&R=R9, [accessed September 2011].

including the **Italian Coop** chain due to boycott pressures.[52] The Israeli state, who owned 30 per cent of Agrexco, refused to bail it out, presumably due to the nascent neoliberal consensus in Israel and the company was forced to search for bidders. Agrexco issued tenders for the sale of the company, valued at between €120 and 160 million. **Total Produce**, an Irish agricultural exporter, was one company that purchased a tender. In response the Palestinian BDS national committee wrote to the company warning: "Purchasing Agrexco would deem your company complicit in Israel's violations of international law, and make it, therefore, a legitimate target for legal action and popular boycotts." Total Produce ultimately opted not to make a bid for Agrexco. At the last moment an Israeli company, **Kislev Forwarding and Customs Clearing Ltd**, owned by Zvi Grinberg, offered 190 million NIS for Agrexco but this was not enough to save the company. Tel Aviv District Court, on September 11th 2011, ordered Agrexco's liquidation.[53] The BNC has called on the movement to target companies which "purchase Agrexco assets and brand names or seek to replace the company as the primary Israeli agricultural exporter."[54]

On October 11th 2011 Tel Aviv District court ruled that Agreco could be sold to Gideon Bickel, of **Bickel Flowers** and Chen Lamdan, of **Orian SM Ltd**.[55] *(See our later chapter on freight transport for more on Agrecco).*

Beresheet's depot in the settlement of Merom Golan, Occupied Syrian Golan (Corporate Watch 2010)

---

[52]http://www.bdsmovement.net/2010/two-of-italys-biggest-supermarket-chains-suspend-sales-of-settlement-produce-694, [accessed September 2011].
[53]http://www.globes.co.il/serveen/globes/docview.asp?did=1000672903&fid=1725, [accessed September 2011].
[54]http://www.bdsmovement.net/2011/palestinian-civil-society-welcomes-agrexco-liquidation-calls-for-celebration-of-this-bds-victory-8010, [accessed September 2011].
[55]http://www.globes.co.il/serveen/globes/docview.asp?did=1000689920, [accessed October 2011].

Beresheet is an Israeli fruit export and marketing company based in the Galilee and occupied Syrian Golan. It has a depot and packing house in the illegal settlement of Merom Golan. The company has dozens of plantations on illegal settlements in the occupied Syrian Golan[56] and advertises that it exports to Europe. Produce advertised on its website includes apples, peaches, nectarines, pears, cherries, kiwi fruit, lychees, pears and persimmons. An address in Merom Golan is given on the site as the company's main contact address.[57]

According to its website, Beresheet markets and produces 50,000 tonnes of produce annually. The company lists the following illegal settlement *kibbutzim* as partners: El Rom, Avnei Eitan, Merom Golan, Yonatan, Ein Zivan and Ortal. Beresheet also operates a visitors centre in the illegal Israeli settlement of Ein Zivan.

Truck bearing Edom's logo picking up agricultural produce from Tomer settlement, Jordan Valley (Corporate Watch 2010)

Beresheet claims it has a 30 per cent share of the Israeli fruit export market and exports produce to England, Russia, Cyprus, South Africa and more. Its goods are marketed under the **Duet** and **Genesis** brand names.[58]

Edom UK is an Israeli company founded in 2003 dealing with major supermarkets including **Waitrose**. British companies **Valley Grown Salads (VGS)** and **Glinwell PLC** each own 20 per cent of the shares in **Edom UK**. Another 30 per cent is owned by **Chosen Agricultural**

---

[56] A map of Beresheet's plantations can be found on http://www.pri-beresheet.co.il/map/, [accessed 28/3/2011].
[57] http://www.pri-beresheet.co.il/contactus/, [accessed 28/3/2011].
[58] This company profile was first published by Corporate Watch here: http://corporateoccupation.wordpress.com/2010/04/22/beresheet-exporting-the-fruits-of-occupation/, [accessed 28/3/2011].

Products, which consists of farmers from *moshavs* in the Arava region, and a further 30 per cent by **Magnolia UK Holdings**.[59] Jimmy Russo, the director of Valley Grown Salads, is also the chairman of Edom UK.[60]

Edom UK specialises in the export of peppers and tomatoes and produces organic goods - a growing market in Israel and worldwide. **Edom Fruits** is a subsidiary of Edom UK.[61] Valley Grown Salads imports tomatoes and peppers from **Edom Israel**, especially during the winter months.

Palestinian workers picking dates on the land of Kalia settlement
(Corporate Watch 2010)

VGS claims that its produce does not come from settlements but exclusively from the Arava region in Israel. However, Corporate Watch has established that Edom has exported wrongly labelled produce grown in the illegal settlement of Tomer during 2009.[62]

As a company with strong British links, Edom UK, through Valley Grown Salads, could be an important target for BDS campaigners.

Hadiklaim is an Israeli date growers cooperative that deals with several major supermarkets

---

[59] http://www.whoprofits.org/Company per cent20Info.php?id=864, [accessed 28/3/2011].
[60] http://www.v-g-s.co.uk/about/edom/, [accessed 28/3/2011].
[61] http://www.edom.co.il, [accessed 28/3/2011].
[62] For the full story of Corporate Watch's research on Edom UK see http://www.corporatewatch.org.uk/?lid=3660, [accessed 28/3/2011].

in the UK, including **Sainsburys**, **Marks & Spencer**, **The Cooperative**, **Tesco** and **Waitrose**. It exports to 30 countries. Tesco and Marks & Spencers' own-branded dates are Hadiklaim produce.

Hadiklaim exports under the **King Solomon Dates** and **Jordan River** brand names and its products are marketed by **Almog Tradex**.[63] The company boasts that its growers and packing houses "have approvals from international standard setting bodies – **ISO, BRC, EUREPGAP, Bio USDA** and **IFOAM** – as well as the Israeli Ministry of Agriculture and the **Israeli Bio-Organic Agriculture Association**." Indeed, its produce is often certified as organic in the UK market. But, though the company highlights its growers inside Israel, it also works from the illegal settlements of Beit Ha'Arava and Tomer in the Jordan Valley.

Hadiklaim specialises in Medjoul dates, the kind most frequently used by Muslims for breaking their fast in Ramadan. Boycott campaigns against Israeli dates have run for the last few years around the Islamic holy month.[64]

After consumers started to question the origins of Hadiklaim date boxes labelled 'Produce of South Africa', it has come to light that **Karsten Farms**, a South African company, is exporting dates through Hadiklaim. Karsten Farms has an office in the UK and is an approved supplier of grapes to Tesco.[65] By buying South African dates and repackaging them in Hadiklaim boxes, the company might think it can get round the boycott by confusing consumers, while at the same time extending its trading period by exporting dates all year round (as South African dates are harvested at a different time of year than Israeli ones). Consumers and activists should make it clear to Karsten and any other company working with exporters from illegal settlements that this trade makes them complicit in the occupation of Palestine and equally a target for the BDS movement.[66]

Mehadrin Tnuport Export (MTEX) is one of Israel's largest growers of fruit and vegetables with yearly sales of around $200 million, 70 per cent of which being for export. The company is set to gain from Agrexco's ill fortunes and may replace Agrexco as Israel's largest exporter.[67] Mehadrin focuses on citrus fruits and is one of the biggest suppliers of the Jaffa brand worldwide. The company also markets dates, grapes, avocados, potatoes and pomegranates.[68] MTEX is 100 per cent-owned by **Mehadrin Group.** Other subsidiaries of the parent company include **Mehadrin Tnuport Marketing UK** (100 per cent owned), **MTEX Holland B.V** (100 per cent owned), **MTEX UK Food Service** (100 per cent

---

[63] http://www.whoprofits.org/Company per cent20Info.php?id=688, [accessed 28/3/2011].
[64] See for instance http://www.guardian.co.uk/uk/2010/aug/04/israeli-dates-boycott-ramadan, [accessed 28/3/2011].
[65] http://www.fruitnet.com/content.aspx?cid=2102&ttid=6&sid=355, [accessed 28/3/2011].
[66] For our full investigation into the Karsten Farms issue, see http://corporateoccupation.wordpress.com/2010/09/07/partnership-between-south-african-and-israeli-agribusiness-fuels-apartheid/, [accessed 28/3/2011].
[67] http://www.jnews.org.uk/commentary/why-did-agrexco-go-bankrupt, [accessed October 2011].
[68] http://www.mtex.co.il/, [accessed 28/3/2011].

owned), **Topgro UK** (50 per cent owned), **Pri-Or** (99.86 per cent owned) and **Miriam Shoham** (50 per cent owned).[69]

Mehadrin sources its produce from growers in at least one illegal settlement, Beqa'ot in the Jordan Valley. When Corporate Watch researchers visited Beqa'ot, we found that the grapes and dates packaged there were all labelled 'Produce of Israel'. During several interviews with Beqa'ot workers, we also found that they earned even less than the average Palestinian in the Valley, with workers mentioning wages as low as 56 NIS a day.[70]

Mehadrin works with **Tesco** in the UK and has 'certificates of conformity' from the supermarket chain viewable on its website.[71] Although it is unclear whether Tesco deals with any Mehadrin settlement growers, there is no doubt that, by importing Mehadrin produce, the retailer is helping this occupation industry flourish.

Lately, through conversations with Norwegian Palestine solidarity groups, it has been revealed that Mehadrin also acts as an exporter for some Palestinian produce through a relationship with **Sinokrot/Palestine Gardens** and, hence, helps in strengthening the normalisation of the occupation through establishing Palestinian exporters as junior partners in a relationship dependent on the maintenance and consolidation of the occupation.[72] Corporate Watch is not aware if any Sinokrot/Palestine Gardens produce exported to the UK goes via an Israeli company.

BDS resistance to Israel's agricultural apartheid so far

Of all the different areas that the boycott movement has focused on, resistance to agricultural imports from Israel, especially from the illegal settlements, has so far been the most active. There are several reasons for this. Firstly, the effects of agricultural practices on Palestinian communities are obvious to anyone visiting the area. Secondly, fruit, vegetables and herbs are the kind of products that people are most likely to come across on a trip to the shops within the EU. Thirdly, the way that agricultural trade is conducted means that there are diverse ways in which people can involve themselves in boycott campaigning. The following are some selected examples of BDS activities surrounding agriculture.

Lobbying

There has been sustained lobbying going on in BDS circles during the last five years, especially around the issues of settlement produce and labelling and against the continuation

---

[69] Figures from http://www.whoprofits.org/Company per cent20Info.php?id=967, [accessed 28/3/2011].
[70] Corporate Watch's full article on Mehadrin: http://corporateoccupation.wordpress.com/2010/05/18/mehadrins-business-in-beqaot-settlement-and-tescos-complicity/#more-724, [accessed 28/3/2011].
[71] http://www.mtex.co.il/certifications.aspx, [accessed 28/3/2011].
[72] Private correspondence between the authors and *Boycott Israel* about the import practices of Bama, Norway.

of the EU-Israel Association Agreement, which gives Israel preferential trade terms with all EU countries.[73]

In 2009, the UK's Department for Environment, Food and Rural Affairs (DEFRA) issued new guidelines regarding the labelling of products being imported to Britain from the West Bank. The guidelines state that "the Government considers that traders would be misleading consumers, and would therefore almost certainly be committing an offence, if they were to declare produce from the OPT (including from the West Bank) as 'Produce of Israel'".[74]

The publication of these guidelines constituted a big victory for the BDS movement, which had been working on labelling issues for years. In 2007 a group of activists from the Brighton Jordan Valley Solidarity Group entered the Tomer settlement in the Jordan Valley and found produce intended for Tesco. The goods were labelled 'Produce of Israel' despite being grown and packaged in the West Bank.[75] Evidence gathered on the ground was then used by activists to pressure supermarkets and DEFRA representatives to consider the labelling issue more seriously. This led supermarkets to change their labels to 'produce of the West Bank', with the DEFRA guidelines going one step further and urging retailers to include information about whether produce originates from a settlement.[76] Although part of the reason for the change in the government's attitude might be the realisation that tolerating wrongly labelled produce makes it possible for Israel to avoid paying tax on products not covered by the preferential trade agreement (i.e. exports from the Palestinian Territories), it is nonetheless one step on the way to victory for the agriculture-related activities of BDS campaigners.

Direct action

The BDS movement has never relied solely on isolated lobbying but values creativity and diversity of tactics. Awareness-raising and direct action have always been part of its arsenal. Throughout the UK and Europe, supermarket leafleting, 'occupations' and 'trolley actions' - where Israeli produce is removed from the shelves or bought, then returned with a complaint at the customer service desk - have been carried out on a weekly basis in many locations for years.[77]

---

[73]The agreement can be found at http://eur-lex.europa.eu/LexUriServ/LexUriServ.do?uri=O J:L:2000:147:0003:0156:EN:PDF, [accessed 18/3/2011]. For information about the campaign to oppose the trade agreement see http://www.bdsmovement.net/?q=node/179, [accessed 18/3/2011].
[74]DEFRA (December 2009), *Labelling of produce grown in the occupied Palestinian territories*, Available: www.defra.gov.uk/foodfarm/food/pdf/labelling-palestine.pdf, [accessed 18/3/2011].
[75]Brighton Jordan Valley Solidarity http://brightonpalestine.org/node/100, [accessed 18/3/2011].
[76]DEFRA (December 2009), *Labelling of produce grown in the occupied Palestinian territories, Idem*.
[77]Some examples of supermarket actions http://brightonpalestine.org/node/642, [accessed 18/3/2011], http://www.indymedia.org.uk/en/2009/03/425650.html, [accessed 18/3/2011] and http://infowars.org/2009/03/19/pro-palestinian-supporters-enter-french-supermarket-remove-israeli-products/, [accessed 18/3/2011].

Much activism has focused on Israel's national agricultural exporter Carmel-Agrexco, which has had to endure persistent direct actions, such as blockades of its warehouse in Hayes, in the UK, since 2004.[78] There have also been blockades and actions against Agrexco in Belgium, Italy and France. In 2009, activists from France, Switzerland and Italy set up a Coalition Against Agrexco (CAA) to fight the new docking location in the port of Sete in France, as well as working on building resistance to Agrexco in these countries. Legal action was taken by CAA against Agrexco in relation to the new French port, in which Agrexco was accused of fraud because of its export practices regarding labelling of settlement produce. In February 2011, the court found that Agrexco had avoided customs duty in France by importing settlement goods as 'Israeli'.[79]

A supermarket 'trolley action' (London Indymedia 2010)

One of the many blockades of Agrexco's London depot (UK Indymedia 2009)

Interestingly, it has been almost impossible for activists to provoke Agrexco to take any legal action against them as a result of these direct actions. In the UK, there has not been a single successful legal action initiated by the company against activists obstructing the flow of

---

[78]For a summary of all direct action against Carmel Agrexco see http://www.indymedia.org.uk/en/actions/2008/carmelagrexco/, [accessed 18/3/2011].
[79]http://coalitioncontreagrexco.net/node/57, [accessed 18/3/2011].

goods from its depot since 2006, when seven activists were acquitted of aggravated trespass at the Agrexco distribution centre in Hayes following a judge's ruling, after half-time submissions, that the protesters had no case to answer.[80] It seemed that Agrexco was willing to put up with blockades, protests, office invasions and even damage to its premises,[81] rather than have the legality of its practices exposed and challenged in court.

At the time of Agrexco's liquidation new campaigns against it were developing in Norway and the Netherlands, with increased interest in Sweden and Denmark.[82] It is essential that this energy is channelled into targeting the companies which take Agrexco's place.

Where next?

The BDS movement has worked very hard on agriculture issues and has achieved some impressive successes along the way. So far, most efforts have focused on settlement produce. It is important that this is seen as a strategic approach, with the main goal being a total boycott of Israeli goods and the end of Israeli exports to Europe. As Corporate Watch's research has shown, there is no way of distinguishing between Israeli and settlement produce, with products constantly being wrongly labelled and exported under false pretences. Shir Hever, a researcher at the Alternative Information Centre in Jerusalem and author of *The Political Economy of Israel's Occupation*, agrees that a settlement-only boycott would fall short of the movement's objectives. When asked if there was any data on how much of Israel's agricultural exports originated from settlements, he answered: "I'm afraid that your question is one of the mysteries that are yet to be cracked. The Israeli government obviously does its best to conceal this information, and even Professor Arie Arnon (probably the most prominent Israeli economist that studies the occupation) had to admit that the data is just not available. This lack of separation is one of the main arguments why a boycott of all Israeli goods is justified."[83]

So the current challenge for the BDS movement is to broaden mainstream BDS activity by:
- Highlighting why produce from inside Israel should be boycotted too.
- Targeting secondary companies, the importers of Israeli produce, the supply depots and freight companies transporting produce to supermarkets and the supermarkets themselves. A good focus could be the British investors in Edom UK, as there is a direct connection between its business and the Israeli exporter.
- Working against any attempts by Israel and anti-boycott groups to undermine the effectiveness of the boycott by confusing issues. The BDS movement should resist the temptation to see limited trade of Palestinian produce through Israeli exporters, such as Mehadrin and Hadiklaim, as a step forward. The boycott needs to facilitate real independent Palestinian alternatives, such as Zaytoun products (www.zaytoun.org) in the UK, or it is likely to fail.

---

[80] See for instance electronicintifada.net/v2/article4438.shtml, [accessed 18/3/2011].
[81] www.indymedia.org.uk/en/2007/08/378741.html, [accessed 18/3/2011].
[82] http://www.bdsmovement.net/?q=node/797, [accessed 18/3/2011].
[83] Private e-mail correspondence between the authors and Shir Hever, March 18, 2011.

FRUITS OF APARTHEID
JUST TELL ME IN YOUR OWN WORDS PLEASE, YUSIF.
YOU DON'T MIND ME TAPING THIS?
NO, IT'S OK.
I WANT PEOPLE TO KNOW WHAT'S GOING ON HERE IN THE JORDAN VALLEY.
AFTER THE WAR IN 1967, THE MEHOLA SETTLEMENT WAS ESTABLISHED.
IT QUICKLY GREW TO TAKE OVER MOST OF THE LAND THAT USED TO BE PART OF EIN EL-BEIDA VILLAGE.
MY FAMILY HAD A LARGE FARM BACK THEN, BUT IT WAS ALSO SWALLOWED UP BY THE SETTLEMENT.
I DIDN'T WANT TO DO IT, BUT... WELL, THERE WASN'T MANY OTHER OPTIONS - EVENTUALLY I HAD TO START WORKING IN THE SETTLEMENT.
IN A CARMEL AGREXCO PACKING HOUSE.

IT WAS VERY DEPRESSING WORKING THERE.
I COULD SEE OUR OLD LAND FROM THE PACKING HOUSE WINDOW, NOW CLOSED OFF BEHIND SETTLEMENT FENCES.
THEY WERE GROWING BANANA TREES THERE.
YOUNG, GREEN, BEAUTIFUL BANANAS.
WHILE I WAS PACKING PRODUCTS, GROWN ON OUR LAND, FOR EXPORT TO EUROPE.

Fruits of Apartheid by Sean Michael Wilson and Rejena Smiley — **34**

BUT INSTEAD, THEY DISMISSED ME THE NEXT DAY.
NOW I WORK WITH MY FATHER.
WE CAN HARDLY GET BY!
ALL WORKERS OF CARMEL AGREXCO IN THE MEHOLA SETTLEMENT LACK CONTRACTS, PENSIONS, SICK-PAY, THE RIGHT TO JOIN A UNION OR ACCIDENT INSURANCE. THIS IS PROFIT OVER PEOPLE.
ISRAELI GOODS PAY NO TAX WHEN ENTERING EUROPE UNDER THE EU ISRAEL ASSOCIATION AGREEMENT.
EUROPE IS THE BIGGEST RECIPIENT OF AGREXCO PRODUCE. AS LONG AS THAT TRADE CONTINUES, EUROPEAN GOVERNMENTS ARE EFFECTIVELY AIDING THE ISRAELI OCCUPATION OF PALESTINE AND THE EXPANSION OF ILLEGAL SETTLEMENTS.
AGREXCO BOAST THAT THEIR GOODS CAN REACH EUROPE IN 48 HOURS WHILE MOST PALESTINIAN GOODS CANNOT EVEN REACH THE LOCAL MARKET AS THEY ARE HELD UP AT CHECKPOINTS.
THE PALESTINIAN HARVEST OFTEN ROTS IN THE VALLEY.

6
Extractive Industries

> **International law and natural resources in the occupied territories**
>
> UN General Assembly Resolution 1803 states that permanent sovereignty over natural wealth and resources is a "basic constituent of the right to self-determination".[1]
>
> Israel's status as occupying power in the West Bank and Gaza was reaffirmed in 2004 by the International Court of Justice, which also reaffirmed the right of self-determination of the Palestinian people.[2]
>
> The Hague Conventions state that "the occupying State shall be regarded only as administrator and usufructuary of public buildings, real estate, forests, and agricultural estates... situated in the occupied country. It must safeguard the capital of these properties, and administer them in accordance with the rules of usufruct."[3]
>
> The Rome Statute of the International Criminal Court states: "Destroying or seizing the property of an adversary unless such destruction or seizure be imperatively demanded by the necessities of the conflict" is "a war crime."[4]

Israel is relatively poor in natural resources. Its extractive industries consist of the lucrative mineral extraction from the Dead Sea, extraction of salt, quarrying for construction materials and extracting natural gas. The majority of Palestinians have been denied access to the Dead Sea, and the economic gains that can be made from it, since the land in the West Bank on the northern coast of the Dead Sea was illegally occupied by Israel in 1967. Israeli settlers are also involved in quarrying in the West Bank and occupied Syrian Golan. This has continued despite legal challenges asserting its illegality under international law.

Mineral extraction

The mineral extraction industry has expanded rapidly since the 1980s, as Israel has increased its ability to extract and process minerals into high-value products such as fertilizers, pesticides, petrochemicals, cosmetics and plastics.[5] In the decade leading up to 2002, the sales of chemicals tripled to $8 billion, 14 per cent of the country's total industrial production at the time.[6]

---

[1] http://www2.ohchr.org/english/law/resources.htm, [accessed 18/3/2011].
[2] http://www.icj-cij.org/docket/index.php?pr=71&code=mwp&p1=3&p2=4&p3=6&ca, [accessed 18/3/2011].
[3] http://www.icrc.org/ihl.nsf/full/195, [accessed 18/3/2011].
[4] http://untreaty.un.org/cod/icc/statute/romefra.htm, [accessed 18/3/2011].
[5] http://www.mfa.gov.il/mfa/mfaarchive/2000_2009/2002/1/facets per cent20of per cent20the per cent20israeli per cent20economy- per cent20resource-based per cent20indu, [accessed 18/3/2011].
[6] *Ibid.*

Mineral extraction from the Dead Sea is estimated to have a profitability of $143 million per year.[7] **Dead Sea Works** is the world's fourth largest producer of potash products, and the second largest producer of bromine after the US.[8] **Dead Sea Magnesium Ltd** is the world's largest magnesium chloride production plant.[9] Not surprisingly, salt is another major product. The **Israel Salt Company** extracts salt from the Red Sea, the Dead Sea and the Mediterranean.[10]

Dead Sea Works, owned by Israel Chemicals Ltd, South-West Dead Sea coast (Corporate Watch 2010)

The corporate exploitation of the Dead Sea is rooted in the history of Zionism. In 1929, the British Mandate, after successful Zionist lobbying of the British parliament, granted mining rights to Polish Zionist Moshe Novomeysky.[11] Novomeysky set up the Palestine Potash Company, based in London, and established a mining site in the north of the Dead Sea. He also set up settlements for his workers on land controlled by the British mandate at Kalya and Beit Ha'Arava.

The shoreline in the occupied Palestinian territories (OPT) was occupied by Israel in 1967 and Israeli-run tourism now dominates the beaches, while settlements dominate the coast.[12] Further south, inside 1948 Israel, the picturesque shores of the north are replaced with enormous and domineering extraction plants. In fact, the entire southern part of the sea has

---

[7]http://foeme.org/uploads/publications_publ22_1.pdf, [accessed 18/3/2011].
[8]http://b7prt05.iclfertilizers.com/irj/servlet/prt/portal/prtroot/com.sap.portal.navigation.portallauncher. anonymous?NavigationTarget=ROLES://portal_content/com.sapro.iclportal/roles/com.sapro.portal_us er/Production_Marketing/com.sapro.Cleveland_Potash/com.sapro.Cleveland_About_Us, [accessed 18/3/2011]. See also http://www.scienceviews.com/geology/bromine.html, [accessed 18/3/2011].
[9]http://www.matimop.org.il/company.aspx?code=2603, [accessed July 2011].
[10]http://www.salt.co.il/intro_en.php, [accessed July 2011].
[11]Weizmann Institute, *Moshe A. Novomeysky; founder of dead sea industries*. Available: http://www.weizmann.ac.il/ICS/booklet/16/pdf/novomersky.pdf, [accessed June 2011].
[12]Donald Macintyre (14/6/2008), Palestinians barred from Dead Sea beaches to 'appease' Israeli settlers, *The Independent*.

been turned into an industrial site.[13] Palestinians who lived near the southern shore were expelled in the 1950s.[14]

After 1948, what was left of the Potash company in the Israeli-controlled area was nationalised and eventually became Dead Sea Works. It holds the only concession, valid until 2030, for the extraction of minerals from the Dead Sea.[15] The company was state-owned until it was sold off in the mid-1990s to the Ofer brothers' holding company, **Israel Corporation**, a deal that meant the entire natural resources of the Israeli state would be controlled by private interests.[16] Dead Sea Works is now a division of multinational company **Israel Chemicals Limited (ICL)**.

The southern Dead Sea extraction plant of Dead Sea Works is the largest factory in Israel.[17] The company's corporate propaganda boasts: "at the Dead Sea Works the spirit of Zionism and the initiative of industry have been successfully joined together."[18] Minerals extracted at Dead Sea Works are used in a whole range of household products, beauty products and industry. All Israeli Dead Sea minerals, including the minerals found in cosmetic products, come from Dead Sea Works.[19] Dead Sea Works is a major client of **Krashin Metal Industries**, a manufacturer of machinery and equipment based in the Barkan industrial zone in the occupied West Bank.[20]

The Dead Sea is shrinking at an alarming rate. It is estimated that 25-30 per cent of this shrinkage is due to extraction by Dead Sea Works.[21]

Copper ore is a more recently discovered Israeli resource, found in the ancient caves of the Timna Valley, near the Arava.[22] The windfall discovery is heralded as a new lucrative endeavour for Israel in terms of encouraging foreign investment. The mine was leased and developed by Mexican company **Altos Hornos de Mexico SA (AHMSA)**.[23]

---

[13] http://foeme.org/www/?module=projects&project_id=21, [accessed July 2011].
[14] Hunaiti, H (2008), *The Arab Jahalin; from the Nakba to the wall,* Stop the Wall, Available: http://stopthewall.org/activistresources/1720.shtml, p.50-51, [accessed September 2010].
[15] http://www.iclfertilizers.com/Fertilizers/DSW/Pages/OurHistory.aspx , [accessed July 2011].
[16] Adam Hanieh (2003), *From State-led growth to globalization: The evolution of Israeli capitalism*, Journal of Palestine Studies, Vol. 32:4 p.12-13.
[17] http://foeme.org/uploads/publications_pub168_1.pdf, p. 21.
[18] Dead Sea Works electronic presentation recorded by the authors at Dead Sea Works in 2010.
[19] http://corporateoccupation.wordpress.com/2010/08/23/israel-opportunity-2010-a-chance-to-invest-in-apartheid/, [accessed July 2011].
[20] http://www.whoprofits.org/Company per cent20Info.php?id=870, [accessed July 2011].
[21] Ward Anderson, J (2005), For Dead Sea; A slow and inexorable death, *Washington Post.* Available: http://www.washingtonpost.com/wp-dyn/content/article/2005/05/18/AR2005051802400_pf.html, [accessed July 2011].
[22] Hopkins, S (4/9/07), Israel's new, old copper mine, *Wealth Daily*.
[23] *Ibid.*

Another major export product is salt, produced by the **Israel Salt Company** and exported as table, cooking and industrial salts.[24]

Company profiles

Israel Chemicals Industries (ICL) is one of the most lucrative transnational corporations on the Tel Aviv Stock Exchange.[25] Following privatisation, the company made the most of the Israeli state's new neoliberal stance put into force by the 'Economic Stabilisation Plan' of the 1980s. This encouraged globalization, a process that ICL has grasped with gusto.[26]

ICL is a fertilisers and chemicals company that consists of **ICL Fertilizers, ICL Industrial Products** and **ICL Performance Products**.[27] The principal shareholder in the company is **Israel Corporation**.[28] ICL is a producer of potash and bromine, a chemical used in automobile engines, and is the only company with rights to extract minerals from the Dead Sea and phosphates from the Naqab.[29] It has production facilities in Israel, Europe, North and South America and China.[30] The company also mines potash and salt in Spain, through subsidiary **Iberpotash**, and in the UK, through its subsidiary **Cleveland Potash UK**.[31] In 2010, ICL had a net income of $1.02 billion.

The **Universities Superannuation Scheme**, the pension scheme for most UK higher education workers and the UK's second largest pension fund, is an investor in ICL.[32]

Ahava is the largest Dead Sea cosmetics company. Almost all of Ahava's products, barring tweezers and hair-clips, which are sourced from the Far East, come from its factory situated in the illegal West Bank settlement of Mitzpe Shalem, just north of the Green Line on the Dead Sea coast. Ahava also has a visitors centre in kibbutz Ein Gedi, a few miles south, and sells its goods in the illegally occupied West Bank tourist attractions of Qumran and the Kalya beach resort.[33]

Ahava sources the minerals used in its products from Dead Sea Works,[34] while excavating

---

[24] http://salt.co.il/index.php?sitelang=en, [accessed July 2011].
[25] http://www.tase.co.il/TASEEng/General/Company/companyDetails.htm?ShareID=00281014&CompanyID=000281&subDataType=0, [accessed July 2011].
[26] Hanieh (2003), *From state-led growth to globalization*, Idem.
[27] http://www.icl-group.com/ICLSegments/Pages/ICLSegments.aspx, [accessed July 2011].
[28] http://www.tase.co.il/TASEEng/General/Company/companyDetails.htm?ShareID=00281014&CompanyID=000281&subDataType=0, [accessed July 2011].
[29] http://corporateoccupation.wordpress.com/2010/08/23/israel-opportunity-2010-a-chance-to-invest-in-apartheid/, [accessed July 2011].
[30] http://corporateoccupation.wordpress.com/2010/08/23/israel-opportunity-2010-a-chance-to-invest-in-apartheid/, [accessed July 2011].
[31] http://www.iclfertilizers.com/Fertilizers/DSW/Pages/BUHomepage.aspx, [accessed July 2011].
[32] http://corporateoccupation.wordpress.com/2011/06/19/1230/, [accessed July 2011].
[33] Observed by Corporate Watch researchers, March 2010.
[34] Bags of Dead Sea Works minerals were photographed inside the Mitzpe Shalem factory. Private Correspondence, February 2011.

Dead Sea mud from the northern coast (within the West Bank). As such, Ahava is guilty of exploiting occupied Palestinian resources.[35]

Ahava's shareholders include the West Bank settlements of Kalya (7.5 per cent), Mitzpe Shalem (37 per cent) as well as **Hamashbir Holdings** (37 per cent) and **Shamrock Holdings** (18.5 per cent), both of which are major investors in the occupation industries.[36]

Israel Salt Company was another company established under the British Mandate, with a concession granted by the mandatory government to the **Jewish Colonisation Association** to extract salt from the Mediterranean coast in 1922.[37] The company has a facility near Kibbutz Kalya on the North Coast of the Dead Sea inside the West Bank. According to its website, this facility is on the site of an old Palestine Potash Company facility.[38] The facility is on illegally occupied territory confiscated by Israel in 1967. The company also has facilities in Eilat on the Red Sea and Atlit on the Mediterranean coast. It claims to export 25 per cent of its products to the Far East, Africa, Europe and the USA.[39] Israel Salt Company is fully owned by **Arison Investments**, a powerful holding company controlled by the Arison family.[40] Israel Salt Company owns the '**Salt of the Earth**' ('**Melach Ha'aretz**') and 'Salit' brands.[41]

Israel Salt Company manufactures salt products for dishwasher maintenance, which are marketed under **Reckitt Benckiser**'s **Finish** brand name.[42] The UK is listed as one of Reckitt Banckiser's key markets for the Finish brand. Israel Salt Company claims that all of its products marketed under the Finish brand name are manufactured in Eilat, however it remains unclear from where the salt is extracted.[43]

Quarrying

There are currently 10 quarries in the West Bank,[44] producing 12 million tons of construction material a year, according to a report by the Israeli Ministry of Interior.[45] These illegal

---

[35] http://www.whoprofits.org/Company per cent20Info.php?id=575, [accessed July 2011].
[36] *Ibid.*
[37] http://salt.co.il/index.php?pid=55, [accessed July 2011].
[38] *Ibid.*
[39] http://salt.co.il/index.php?pid=55, [accessed July 2011].
[40] *Ibid.*
[41] http://www.whoprofits.org/Company per cent20Info.php?id=893, [accessed July 2011].
[42] Reckitt Benckiser is an international company with offices in the UK. The company can be contacted at Finish Consumer Services, PO Box 4044, Slough, SL1 0NS, UK and Reckitt Benckiser Ireland Ltd, 7 River Walk, City West Business Campus, Dublin 24, Ireland
[43] http://www.whoprofits.org/Company per cent20Info.php?id=893, [accessed July 2011].
[44] Bronner, E (2009), Desert's sand and rocks become precious resources in West Bank dispute, *New York Times*. Available: http://www.nytimes.com/2009/03/07/world/middleeast/07westbank.html, [accessed September 2011].
[45] Nieuwhof, A (2011), Multinational companies mining occupied Palestinian land, *Electronic Intifada*, [accessed July 2011].

quarries provide nearly a quarter of the sand and gravel that Israel uses annually.[46] One quarter of this is used in the OPT, the vast majority for the construction of the apartheid wall and the settlements and the rest in 1948 Israel.[47] Several Palestinian quarries are also in operation, but most of their products are also sold in Israel.[48]

Israeli quarry near the settlement of El Rom, occupied Syrian Golan (Corporate Watch 2010)

As Ethan Bronner wrote in the *New York Times*, "Sand and rocks might seem like trivial resources in a country that is half desert. But with strict environmental restrictions on quarrying...they turn out to be surprisingly valuable. Building contractors are often caught in the Negev desert stealing them by the truckload in the dead of night. A 2008 government study predicted a serious shortage of raw building materials within a decade."[49]

Israeli quarrying in the occupied territories began when the land was seized in 1967.[50] Palestinians are forced into the position of buying the stolen produce back from the Israeli companies on the open market. All taxes and revenues are fed back into the Israeli treasury rather then that of the PA. It is claimed that the operations also damage the Palestinian economy through unequal competition.[51]

---

[46] Bronner, E (2009), *Desert's sand and rocks, Idem.*
[47] Nieuwhof, A (2011) *Multinational companies mining occupied Palestinian land, Idem.*
[48] *B'Tselem, Israeli quarries in the West Bank.* Available: http://www.btselem.org/english/settlements/20100922_israeli_quarries_in_the_west_bank.asp, [accessed July 2011].
[49] Bronner, E (2009), *Desert's sand and rocks, Idem.*
[50] *B'Tselem, Israeli quarries in the West Bank. Idem.*
[51] Nieuwhof, A (2011) *Multinational companies mining occupied Palestinian land, Idem.*

According to Michael Sfard, a lawyer for Israeli rights group *Yesh Din*, Israeli quarrying for construction materials in occupied Palestinian land constitutes "illegal transfer of land in the most literal of senses."[52]

Alongside its illegality, Israeli quarrying in the West Bank has a damaging impact on the environment. It affects the area's biodiversity as well as destroying agricultural land. Pollution caused by the quarries also has negative health implications, causing increased levels of asthma amongst children living nearby.[53] In fact, it is the more relaxed environmental laws in the occupied Palestinian territories that make them such an attractive business prospect for Israeli companies. In Israel, there are stricter laws about noise and dust pollution and more resistance to quarries amongst civilians living nearby. Authorities in Palestine are unable to enforce environmental laws on Israel, which controls the territory.[54] Israel has never sought to regulate its quarrying activities in the West Bank.[55]

This exploitation of resources has been the subject of various legal challenges. Notably, in March 2009, *Yesh Din* took the Israeli state and 11 Israeli corporations operating quarries in the West Bank to the Israeli High Court of Justice, producing a petition demanding that all quarrying and mining activities in the territory be suspended, that no current licences to quarry be extended and that no concessions for new operations be issued.[56]

The demand for a halt to quarrying activities was not granted. Instead, the Israeli high court simply requested responses from the parties involved, meaning they could carry on as usual. Two months later, in May 2009, the state announced it would freeze expansion of quarrying activities in the West Bank but the existing quarries were left to carry on undisturbed.[57] There has been no further court action since then.

Company profiles

Cemex is a Mexican company that owns, through its subsidiary **ReadyMix Industries**, 50 per cent of the Yatir quarry.[58] The Yatir quarry lies near the settlement of Teneh Omarim in the occupied West Bank. ReadyMix also owns plants in various Israeli settlements, including Mevo Horon, the Atarot and Mishor Edomim settlement industrial zones, which are in the West bank, and Katzrin settlement industrial zone in the Golan Heights.[59] Cemex has annual revenues of over $1 billion.[60]

---

[52]Quoted in *Ibid*.
[53]Frykberg, M (2009), Israel stripping West Bank quarries, *Electronic Intifada*, Available: http://electronicintifada.net/content/israel-stripping-west-bank-quarries/8210, [accessed July 2011].
[54]*Ibid*.
[55]B'Tselem, *Israeli quarries in the West Bank. Idem.*
[56]*Yesh Din* (2009), *Legality of quarrying activity in the West Bank*, Available: http://www.yesh-din.org/infoitem.asp?infocatid=15, [accessed July 2011].
[57]B'Tselem, *Israeli quarries in the West Bank. Idem.*
[58]Nieuwhof, A (2011), *Multinational companies mining occupied Palestinian land, Idem.*
[59]*Ibid*.
[60]http://www.whoprofits.org/Company per cent20Info.php?id=704, [accessed July 2011].

Cemex is a registered participant in the UN Global Compact, an initiative for transnational corporations to commit to 'sustainable' and 'responsible' business practices. The Global Compact states that "businesses should support and respect the protection of international human rights within their spheres of influence, and make sure they are not complicit in human rights abuses."[61]

The company operates in the UK, with a head office in Surrey.[62] The company's UK revenues make up approximately 8 per cent of the company's net sales.[63] Cemex UK has shares in **Cemex Israel**.[64]

ReadyMix plant in Katzrin settlement industrial zone, occupied Syrian Golan. ReadyMix is owned by Cemex (Corporate Watch 2010)

Heidelberg Cement is a German corporation that operates the Nahal Raba quarry in the West Bank through its subsidiary **Hanson Israel**.[65] Hanson Israel also has two concrete plants in the settlements of Modi'in Illit and Atarot and an asphalt plant near the Elqana settlement.[66]

A truly multinational company, Hanson operates in the UK under the name **Hanson UK**, and is the leading supplier of heavy building materials to the construction industry.[67] Its UK

---

[61] Nieuwhof, A (2011), *Multinational companies mining occupied Palestinian land, Idem.*
[62] Cemex UK head office address is: Cemex UK Operations, Coldharbour Lane, Thorpe, Egham. Surrey TW20 8TD.
[63] http://uk.reuters.com/business/quotes/companyProfile?symbol=CX.N, [accessed June 2011].
[64] OSBIS Database, bureau Van Dijk, [acessed August 2011].
[65] Nieuwhof, A (2011), *Multinational companies mining occupied Palestinian land, Idem.*
[66] *Ibid.*
[67] http://www.heidelbergcement.com/uk/en/hanson/about_us/index.htm, [accessed June 2011].

headquarters are in Maidenhead.[68] Two British pension funds, the **Lothian Pension Fund** and the **Universities Superannuation Scheme (USS)**, hold shares in Heidelberg Cement.[69]

Although it has not yet removed itself from the OPT, Heidelberg Cement at least had the decency to remove itself from the UN Global Compact. Yet the company claims on its website that its corporate social responsibility and sustainability strategy includes a commitment to "the fair distribution of natural resources to current and future generations."[70]

Other companies involved in quarrying in the occupied territories include **Ben Hasharon**, a subsidiary of **Hofrey Hasharon** that is involved in large-scale quarrying in the Barkan stone quarry.[71] **Shapir Civil and Marine Engineering** owns and operates a cement plant in the industrial zone of the settlement of Atarot, and a stone quarry, called Natuf, in the occupied West Bank, thus, in the words of Who Profits, "exploiting Palestinian natural resources for the needs of the Israeli construction industry."[72]

Ashtrom Group, a construction and engineering firm that supplies materials for checkpoints and the Israeli Ministry of Defence, operates a quarry near the settlement of Beithar Illit.[73] A main shareholder in the group is international investment fund **Allied Holdings**.[74] Allied Holdings is owned by the **Gutwirt Inheritance Fund** through **RIH LTD**, which is controlled by **Trust A.G** (Jersey).[75]

Privately owned by the Kalev family, the **Salit (Mishor Edomim) Quarry and Plant** has a plant and a stone quarry in Mishor Edomim industrial zone, which is a settlement in the occupied West Bank.[76]

Resistance

One of the most visible and successful BDS campaigns has been against Ahava. The company's flagship UK store in Covent Garden, London, has closed after a two-year campaign.[77]

The store's opening in 2007 was followed, a year later, by the start of a concerted campaign by pro-Palestinian activists, which has been going on ever since. The tactics employed have

---

[68] Hanson UK head office: Hanson House, 14 Castle Hill, Maidenhead, Berkshire SL6 4JJ.
[69] Information obtained through an FOI request to the Lothian Pension Fund and on the USS website, [accessed September 2011].
[70] Nieuwhof, A (2011) *Multinational companies mining occupied Palestinian land, Idem.*
[71] http://www.whoprofits.org/Company per cent20Info.php?id=700, [accessed June 2011].
[72] http://www.whoprofits.org/Company per cent20Info.php?id=699, [accessed June 2011].
[73] http://www.whoprofits.org/Company per cent20Info.php?id=480, [accessed June 2011].
[74] http://www.whoprofits.org/Company per cent20Info.php?id=733, [accessed June 2011].
[75] *Ibid.*
[76] http://www.whoprofits.org/Company per cent20Info.php?id=698, [accessed June 2011].
[77] http://www.thejc.com/news/uk-news/47284/protests-drive-ahava-out-covent-garden, [accessed June 2011].

been diverse. The most visible have been the fortnightly demonstrations outside the shop, which drew Zionist and fascist counter-protests and a policing nightmare.

Activists lock on inside an Ahava store. The company's store in London was repeatedly forced to close for the day by occupations of the store. (ISM London 2010)

Ahava after being targeted by BDS saboteurs, the store has closed as a result of protests (London BDS 2009)

Behind the scenes, complaints were made to Camden Trading Standards and the police, regarding the misleading labels, which do not accurately reflect the geographical origin of the products. An investigation into this is ongoing at the time of writing with the shop also accused of offences under the Proceeds of Crime Act. Campaigners argue that trading from settlements encourages more settlers into the OPT, in breach of the Geneva Convention and the Rome Statute of the International Criminal Court. Complaints were also made to the police about Ahava's fraudulent claiming of the benefits of the EU-Israeli Association Agreement, as the produce is manufactured on settlement land and not in Israel, as claimed.

The shop has been forced to close on dozens of occasions by activists locking-on inside the shop and blockading its entrance. Other actions saw damage to the shopfront and the front door super-glued shut. The combination of direct action, engaging the public through demonstrations and mounting legal challenges has proved successful in forcing Ahava UK to close its doors, while publicising the BDS movement as an active and effective form of opposition to Israeli apartheid.[78]

---

[78] See, for example, http://www.indymedia.org.uk/en/2009/12/443271.html, [accessed June 2011].

Resistance to Ahava has also been strong in the US, where campaign group Stolen Beauty[79] has successfully targeted Ahava's celebrity endorsers[80] and persuaded US stores not to stock Ahava products.[81] Ahava protests have also taken place in Holland,[82] France,[83] South Africa,[84] Australia and New Zealand.[85]

Where next?

The international nature of the companies involved in the Israeli extractive sector, including Hanson, Cemex and Heidelberg Cement, makes them viable as targets for BDS campaigns around the world.

Although Ahava has closed its store in London, it still operates in the UK via its sister brand, **Ahava UK**'s mail order and supply depot, in Cheltenham. The company also claims to be looking for new premises to replace its London store.[86] The strength of argument regarding the illegality of Ahava's operations that made targeting it so successful should now be channelled into challenging these alternative UK operations.

Ahava is also involved in research into nanotechnology conducted by the EU and the Natural History Museum.[87] Other partners in the programme include King's College London and Imperial College.[88] Whilst universities can be pressured by their students, the EU can, and should, be forced to answer for its willingness to work with corporations complicit in the illegal occupation of Palestinian territories.

Israel Chemicals Ltd, a company owned by one of the largest conglomerates in Israel, and which is responsible for a large proportion of the shrinkage of the Dead Sea, should be a major BDS target. As indicated above, the company has premises around the world, including in the UK, and has many international investors.

---

[79] http://www.codepink4peace.org/section.php?id=415, [accessed June 2011].
[80] http://electronicintifada.net/content/ahava-campaign-comes-court/8881, [accessed June 2011].
[81] http://www.jta.org/news/article/2011/01/14/2742561/the-bay-drops-ahava-but-not-because-of-boycott, [accessed June 2011].
[82] http://londonbds.org/tag/protest/page/2/, [accessed June 2011].
[83] http://www.youtube.com/watch?v=-J3-d2pRXdA&feature=player_embedded, [accessed June 2011].
[84] http://www.bdsmovement.net/2011/uproar-against-ahava-false-labelling-7265, [accessed June 2011].
[85] http://www.bdsmovement.net/2011/seacret-flashmob-7216, [accessed June 2011].
[86] http://www.corporatewatch.org.uk/?lid=3942, [accessed June 2011].
[87] http://cordis.europa.eu/fetch?CALLER=FP7_PROJ_EN&ACTION=D&DOC=1&CAT=PROJ&RCN=89919, [accessed June 2011].
[88] *Ibid*.

7
Energy

The Israeli energy sector has traditionally been dominated by state-owned companies.[1] Israel has reserves of fossil fuels[2] but also imports crude oil, gas and petroleum from other countries.

Palestinians are almost entirely dependent on Israel for fuel, which is transported to fuel terminals in the West Bank and Gaza and then distributed by the Palestinian Authority. Israeli companies benefit from this dependency.

Gaza Power Plant after Israel bombed it with F-16s (International Solidarity Movement 2006)

The Gaza Power Plant produces around two thirds of the electricity needs of the Gazan population. However, the power plant is dependent on Israeli private company **Dor Alon** for its fuel supply. Fuel is used as a political weapon by Israel, with supplies of fuel to the Gazan authorities regularly shut off by Dor Alon as an act of collective punishment at the behest of the Israeli state. The Gaza Power Plant was bombed in 2006, after the abduction of Gilad

---

[1]OECD (2009), *Economic survey of Israel 2009*. Available:
http://www.oecd.org/document/53/0,3746,en_2649_33733_44384757_1_1_1_1,00.html, p.24.
[2]CIA, *World factbook*. Available:
https://www.cia.ghttp://www.oecd.org/document/53/0,3746,en_2649_33733_44384757_1_1_1_1,00.ht mlov/library/publications/the-world-factbook/geos/is.html, [accessed June 2011].

Shalit.[3] The remainder of the electricity needs of the West Bank and Gaza are met by the **Israeli Electric Company**. Israeli and international companies also benefit from the generation of wind energy from farms in the occupied Syrian Golan.

Gas: Israel had 30.44 billion cubic metres of natural gas reserves in 2010.[4] The piping of gas is administered by a state-owned firm, **Israel Natural Gas Lines Ltd**, but private companies, such as **Dor Alon** and **Paz**, are responsible for commercial gas supply. In 2008, a new gas pipeline was completed from Al-Arish in Egypt to Ashkelon in Israel.[5] This pipeline has been attacked several times in 2011 by Egyptian saboteurs.[6] **Delek,** along with US firm **Noble Energy**, plan to exploit several Mediterranean gas fields over the next five years. The Gaza Marine Field, owned by the British **BG Group**, remains unexploited.

Oil: Israel had reserves of 1.94 million barrels (bbl) of oil in 2010.[7] The Israeli oil sector is now completely privatised.[8] Israel's largest oil refinery is located at Haifa Bay. The Haifa refinery was established during the British mandatory period by **Shell** and the **Anglo-American Oil Company** (now **Esso**) to receive oil piped from Iraq (then also under British control). The refinery was sold to the Israeli state in 1958 due to fears that the Arab oil producers would boycott Shell. The Israeli state set up **Oil Refineries Ltd (ORL)**, which had a monopoly on oil production and ran the Haifa refinery and the Ashdod Oil Refinery. In 2006 **Paz Oil** took control of the Ashdod refinery, while ORL became publicly traded.

Wind: Israel has been developing wind energy in the occupied Syrian Golan since the 1990s.[9] In 1992, **Mei Golan Wind Energy** established a wind farm there, providing energy for companies in the Katzrin industrial zone and to the Israeli national grid. In 2008, **Mei Golan** acquired a license to build further wind turbines from an area close to the occupied Syrian village of Majdal Shams to the settlement of Alonei Habashan. Mei Golan is negotiating with the US energy firm **AES** to build the turbines.[10]

Another planned wind project in the occupied Golan, led by **Green Wind Energy Ltd,** was approved in August 2010. Green Wind Energy is negotiating a partnership with **DE Wind,** a subsidiary of **Daewoo**, to carry out the construction work.[11]

---

[3] *B'Tselem*, *Act of vengeance*. Available: http://www.btselem.org/english/publications/summaries/200609_act_of_vengeance.asp, [accessed June 2011].
[4] CIA, *World factbook, Idem*.
[5] OECD (2009), *Economic survey of Israel 2009, Idem*, p.148.
[6] See, for instance, http://www.france24.com/en/20110730-militants-attack-gas-pipeline-egypts-sinai, [accessed September 2011].
[7] CIA, *World factbook, Idem*.
[8] OECD (2009), *Economic survey of Israel 2009, Idem*, p.148.
[9] http://www.haaretz.com/print-edition/business/aes-mei-golan-to-build-wind-turbines-farm-1.243996, [accessed June 2011].
[10] *Ibid*.
[11] http://www.globes.co.il/serveen/globes/docview.asp?did=1000580394&fid=1725, [accessed June 2011].

Company profiles

The Israeli Electric Company (IEC) remains a state-owned company and has a monopoly on electricity provision. However, moves toward privatisation may result in the involvement of private companies in the sector.[12]

After 1967 IEC became the main electricity supplier to the newly occupied Palestinian territories. IEC supplies the West Bank directly and through **Jerusalem District Electric Company (JDEC)** (*see our later chapter on East Jerusalem for more information on JDEC*). The company supplies around 33 per cent of Gaza's electricity, the remainder coming from the Palestinian Gaza Power Plant.[13] IEC derives 5-6 per cent of its income from its supply to the West Bank and Gaza.[14]

IEC's bills to its Palestinian customers are collected by JDEC and the Palestinian Authority. Unpaid bills are retrieved by IEC from the taxes collected by the Israeli government on behalf of the PA.[15]

Dor Alon has a monopoly over the supply of fuel to the Gaza Strip. The company, which is, at least partly, dependent for its profits on sales to this captive Palestinian market,[16] has helped to implement Israel's siege of Gaza by cutting off the supply of fuel when the Israeli state wishes to instigate punitive measures against Gaza's population.[17]

Dor Alon is the Israeli representative of **Chevron** and **Aral lubricants**.[18] The company operates in the US as **Alon USA Energy Inc**, which is listed on the New York Stock Exchange (NYSE) and operates petrol stations under the **FINA** brand name. **Blue Square**, another Dor Alon subsidiary, is also listed on the NYSE.

The **Alon Group** is the franchisee of **KFC** and **Pizza Hut** in Israel and holds 49 per cent of the shares in **Diners Club Israel**.[19]

Paz Oil is the largest Israeli energy company,[20] with profits of 1,834 million NIS ($534 million) in 2010.[21]

---

[12] OECD (2009), *Economic survey of Israel 2009, Idem,* p.148.
[13] Swirski, S (2008), *The burden of occupation*, Adva Center. Available: http://www.adva.org/.../aa-Full per cent20Report per cent20- per cent20Latest per cent20November per cent202008(1).pdf, p.23.
[14] *Ibid*, p.23.
[15] *Ibid*, p.23.
[16] *Ibid*, p.23.
[17] http://www.whoprofits.org/Company per cent20Info.php?id=469, [accessed June 2011].
[18] http://www.whoprofits.org/Company per cent20Info.php?id=469, [accessed June 2011].
[19] http://www.whoprofits.org/Company per cent20Info.php?id=452, [accessed June 2011].
[20] Swirski, S (2008) *The burden of occupation, Idem,* p.24.
[21] http://investing.businessweek.com/research/stocks/financials/financials.asp?ticker=PZOL:IT, [accessed June 2011].

Overview of the Israeli Economy: Energy **50**

Paz was founded in 1922 as **Anglo Asiatic Petroleum**. From 1927, it traded as **Shell Palestine** until 1958, when its assets were transferred to the company's French and English shareholders after Shell bowed to the Arab states' boycott of Israel. In 1998, Jack Lieberman, an Australian billionaire, bought a stake in the company.[22]

Today, **Paz Oil Company Ltd** engages in refining, producing, storing, importing, and marketing of oil, while **Paz Gas** is a supplier of domestic gas.[23]

Pazgas supplies domestic gas to Israeli settlements. Photo taken in the settlement of Merom Golan, occupied Syrian Golan (Corporate Watch 2010)

Paz has a monopoly on the sale of fuel to the PA in the West Bank and as such is taking advantage of the captive Palestinian market created by Israel's occupation. It also operates petrol stations in dozens of settlements in the West Bank and supplies cooking gas to the West Bank settlements.[24] Corporate Watch has also found that Paz is the gas provider in the settlement of Merom Golan in the occupied Syrian Golan.[25]

The principal shareholders in Paz are currently **Bino Holdings** (Israel), the **Clal Group** (Israel), **Dolphin Energy** (UAE) and **Instanz Holdings** (US).[26] Bino Holdings, a

---

[22] http://www.paz.co.il/en/about.asp, [accessed June 2011].
[23] http://investing.businessweek.com/research/stocks/financials/financials.asp?ticker=PZOL:IT, [accessed June 2011].
[24] http://www.whoprofits.org/Company per cent20Info.php?id=470, [accessed June 2011].
[25] http://corporateoccupation.wordpress.com/2010/04/21/corporate-watch-in-the-golan-heights-merom-golan/#more-555, [accessed June 2011].
[26] http://www.tase.co.il/TASEEng/General/Company/companyDetails.htm?ShareId=01100007&CompanyID=001363&subDataType=0, [accessed June 2011].

conglomerate controlling a group of companies that also includes **Israel Discount Bank**, is controlled by the Lieberman family and Zadik Bino. **Instanz** is owned by the Lieberman family, while Dolphin Energy's principal shareholders are **Occidental Energy** (US) and **Total** (France).[27]

Delek, established as a state-owned company in 1951, is one of the largest Israeli energy companies and Paz's main competitor. It was purchased by Yitzhak Tshuva in 1998 and is now part of the **Delek Group**, a conglomerate of real estate, retail and energy companies. Tshuva is one of the richest billionaires in the world.

Delek petrol station in the settlement of Katzrin, occupied Syrian Golan (Corporate Watch 2010)

Delek operates a chain of petrol stations in Israel, on settlements in the West Bank and occupied Syrian Golan.[28]

Delek Europe, a subsidiary of Delek, is attempting to expand into Europe.[29] US company **Noble energy** is Delek's partner in several Mediterranean marine gas projects.

Oil Refineries Limited (ORL) controls Israel's largest petrochemical/refinery facility at Haifa bay. The company advertises the capacity to produce 9 million tonnes of crude oil per year.[30] **Israel Corporation** owns a 37 per cent stake in ORL. **Israel Petrochemical Enterprises**, a subsidiary of **Avgol**, owns a further 36 per cent stake.[31]

---

[27]http://www.dolphinenergy.com/Public/our-company/aboutus-shareholders.htm, [accessed June 2011].
[28]http://www.whoprofits.org/Company per cent20Info.php?id=740, [accessed June 2011].
[29]http://www.delek.co.il/?CategoryID=298&ArticleID=195&sng=1, [accessed June 2011].
[30]http://www.israelcorp.com/Holdings/Energy/OilRefineriesLtd.aspx, [accessed June 2011].
[31]http://www.tase.co.il/TASE/Templates/Company/CompanyDetails.aspx?NRMODE=Published&NR

British Gas and the Gaza Marine Field

"On its coastal littoral, Gaza's limitations are marked by a different fence where the bars are Israeli gunboats with their huge wakes, scurrying beyond the Palestinian fishing boats and preventing them from going outside a zone imposed by the warships."

Peter Beaumont, *The Guardian*, 2009[32]

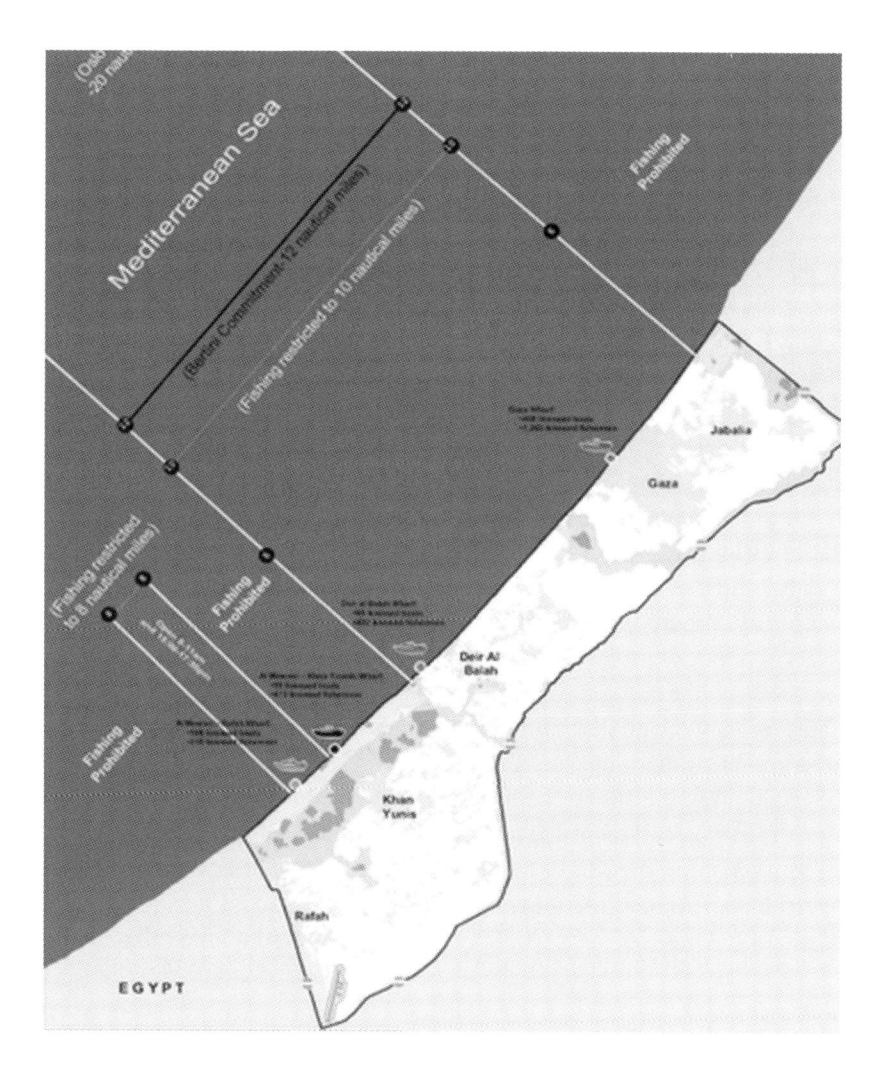

ORIGINALURL= per cent2fTASEEng per cent2fGeneral per cent2fCompany per cent2fcompanyDetails.htm per cent3fsubDataType per cent3d0 per cent26companyId per cent3d001408 per cent26ShareId per cent3d01118470&NRNODEGUID={64943F3E-1454-428C-BA65-88201752A602}&NRCACHEHINT=Guest&CompanyID=000259&subDataType=0&ShareId=02590 248 and http://www.google.com/finance?q=TLV:PTCH, [accessed July 2011].
[32]http://www.guardian.co.uk/world/2009/may/27/return-to-gaza, [accessed July 2011].

About 20km off the coast of Gaza lie natural gas fields in Palestinian coastal waters. The gas is estimated to be worth some $4 billion, making it Palestine's most valuable natural resource. The marine field is next door to Israel's waning deposits of natural gas.

The Gaza Marine Field is out of bounds to Palestinians. There is no way for the PA to make use of the gas and Gaza's coastal waters are patrolled by Israeli gunboats. The Israeli military has announced that it will enforce an exclusion zone of three nautical miles off Gaza's coast and, in reality, it even attacks boats on the Gazan shore. Since 2009, one Gaza fisherman has been killed and scores injured by Israeli naval vessels 'enforcing' this zone.[33]

BG Group owns the exploration rights to the Gaza gas fields. BG estimate that the gas fields contain one trillion cubic feet of gas.[34]

BG's original plans were to sell Gaza's natural gas to Egypt.[35] However, pressure from former British prime minister Tony Blair led the company to reopen earlier failed negotiations with Israel for a pipeline development that would land the gas at Ashkelon, a southern Israeli city with a petroleum refinery. In May 2007, the Israeli Cabinet approved a proposal by prime minister Ehud Olmert "to buy gas from the Palestinian Authority."

The proposed contract was for $4 billion, with profits in the order of $2 billion, of which one billion was to go to the Palestinians. Tel Aviv, however, had no intention of sharing the revenues with Palestine. An Israeli team of negotiators was set up by the Israeli Cabinet to thrash out a deal with BG Group, bypassing both the Hamas government and Abu Mazen's Palestinian Authority. Where the revenues from the marine field would go remained murky, with discussions of a 'pot of money' to go toward West Bank infrastructure projects.

BG Group states on its website that, in December 2007, it "withdrew from negotiations" with the Israeli government concerning the sale of gas from the Gaza Marine Field to Israel, and that it is now "evaluating options for commercialising the gas."[36] The company further reassured us that it had closed its office in Israel in January 2008 and that it is currently "in the process of relinquishing the Med Yavne licence" for its main gas field in Israel.[37] Media reports, however, have revealed that negotiations between BG and Israeli officials were, in fact, renewed in 2008. One observer, Michel Chossudovsky, concluded that "it would appear that Israel was anxious to reach an agreement with the BG Group prior to the *[2009]*

---

[33] http://fishingunderfire.blogspot.com/2010/01/fishing-under-fire-report-2009.html, [accessed July 2011].
[34] http://www.bg-group.com/InvestorRelations/Reports/db2010/country_profiles/africa_middle_east_asia/Pages/areas_of_palestinian_authority.aspx, [accessed July 2011].
[35] http://business.timesonline.co.uk/tol/business/industry_sectors/natural_resources/article1826739.ece. [accessed July 2011].
[36] http://www.bg-group.com/InvestorRelations/Reports/DB2009/global/amea/Pages/israel_palestinian_authority.aspx, [accessed July 2011].
[37] www.bggroup.com/OurBusiness/WhereWeOperate/Pages/pgIsraelandAreasofPalestinianAuthority.asp., [accessed July 2011].

invasion *[of Gaza]*, which was already in an advanced planning stage."[38]

As of 2011, the Gaza Marine Field remains an untapped resource, while Palestinians remain dependent on Israeli fuel.

Where next?

The Israeli energy sector has, thus far, been largely ignored by the BDS movement. However, Palestinians' enforced dependency on Israeli fuel is a key factor in the perpetuation of Israeli occupation. It therefore makes sense for BDS campaigners to concentrate energies on **Dor Alon** and **Paz**, the companies benefiting directly from the Palestinian captive market.

Dor Alon's US subsidiaries listings on the NYSE should be targeted by US BDS campaigners, while French company **Total**'s stake in Paz investor, **Dolphin Energy** should be a target for the French movement. British campaigners should remain vigilant over the future of **BG Group**'s gas concession in the Gaza Marine Field.

Gazans near Beit Lahiya protest against Israeli naval attacks on fishermen (Sharyn Locke 2009)

---

[38] www.globalresearch.ca/index.php?context=va&aid=11680. See also this timeline by David K. Schermerhorn: www.globalresearch.ca/index.php?context=va&aid=11787, [accessed July 2011]. For more background, see this Electronic Intifada article:
http://electronicintifada.net/v2/article4909.shtml, [accessed July 2011].

8
Telecommunications

The Israeli telecommunications market provides services to the Israeli military and settlers and operates infrastructure on stolen Palestinian land. Services are often provided selectively, for example excluding residents of Palestinian unrecognised villages in Israel, thereby strengthening Israeli apartheid.

Up until the Oslo accords in the 1990s, Israeli companies had a monopoly on the West Bank and Gaza telecommunications market. In 2000, a Palestinian private company, **Paltel**, was given a license to operate in these two regions.[1]

Revenue from landline, cellular and electronic communications accounts for around 4 per cent of Israeli GDP.[2]

Company profiles

For over three decades after 1948, Israel's telephone networks were run by a government agency.[3] In the 1980s, **Bezeq**, a state-owned company, was formed with a monopoly on the telecommunications market. Since the 1990s, the state has been selling off its stake in Bezeq.[4] The company is now owned by private consortia, including the London and New York based **Apax Partners**. Competition has been permitted in the landline market since 1997.[5]

Bezeq was privatised in 2005. It is the largest telecommunications provider in Israel and owns **Pelephone**, one of Israel's four leading cellular providers. The company offers cellular and landline services to the army, checkpoints and Israeli settlers, owns telecommunications infrastructure in the Occupied Territories[6] and provides discriminatory services within Israel.

Although Palestinian residents of the unrecognised Palestinian villages in the Naqab are Israeli citizens they are excluded from connection to landline services as building in these villages is prohibited by the Israeli state. Often telephone lines run above the houses of Palestinian residents of the Naqab but the inhabitants of those houses have no hope of ever being connected.[7] Furthermore, it has been reported by the Arab Human Rights Association

---

[1] Swirski, S (2008), *The burden of occupation*, p.24.
[2] http://www.tradingeconomics.com/israel/telecommunications-revenue-percent-GDP-wb-data.html, [accessed July 2011].
[3] http://www.jewishvirtuallibrary.org/jsource/Economy/eco2.html, [accessed July 2011].
[4] http://ir.bezeq.co.il/phoenix.zhtml?c=159870&p=irol-homeprofile, [accessed July 2011].
[5] http://www.jewishvirtuallibrary.org/jsource/Economy/eco2.html, [accessed July 2011].
[6] http://whoprofits.org/Company per cent20Info.php?id=738, [accessed July 2011].
[7] Interviews and correspondence between the authors and the Regional Council of Unrecognised Villages (RCUV), 2010-11.

that Bezeq has only ever recruited a handful of Palestinian Israeli citizens.[8]

There are currently four Israeli cellular phone providers: **Partner (Orange)**, **Cellcom, Pelephone** and **MIRS**.[9] These companies also provide SMS messaging, video conferencing and broadband internet access. 20 to 45 per cent of the West Bank and Gaza cellular market in 2008 was in the hands of Israeli companies. Israeli companies are at an advantage in the Palestinian market as Palestinian competitors, such as **Jawwal**, Paltel's mobile network, and **Wataniya**, are not permitted to build masts in Area C, comprising 59 per cent of the West Bank but Israeli companies are free to erect masts in settlements and military bases. Schlomo Swirski called this an 'unlicensed competition' to Palestinian mobile networks.[10]

Electricity and phone lines run above the heads of the residents of the unrecognised villages of the Naqab with no possibility of ever being connected (Corporate Watch 2010)

Partner Communications, a franchise of Orange, operates a network in Israel which covers occupied Palestine and the occupied Syrian Golan. An agreement by the mobile phone multinational, which is owned by **France Télécom**, licensed the Israeli company to use its name and logo.

Partner now run Orange shops or kiosks in many of the larger settlements in both the West Bank and the occupied Golan and advertises itself very heavily in them. For example Partner Communications, known as **Orange Israel**, has kiosks in the settlements of Pisgat Ze'ev[11]

---

[8]http://www.arabhra.org/hra/Pages/PopupTemplatePage.aspx?PopupTemplate=85, [accessed July 2011].
[9]http://whoprofits.org/Newsletter.php?nlid=46, [accessed July 2011].
[10]Swirski, S (2008), *The burden of occupation*, *Idem.* p.25.
[11]http://corporateoccupation.wordpress.com/2010/04/11/businesses-in-the-east-jerusalem-settlement-

and Modi'in Illit. It has erected over 160 antennas in the West Bank and has telecommunication infrastructure facilities on occupied territory.[12] Orange mobile phone masts, operated by Partner, are located both inside the settlements themselves and on land specifically confiscated for the masts. The masts are situated to benefit the settlements and the Israeli army. The Palestinian Authority, in its crackdown on settlements and enforcement of its settlement boycott, called in 2010 for all Israeli mobile phone networks, including Orange, to be banned in Palestinian cities. Although Orange is a separate company from Partner Communications, this does not mean that it is not complicit in profiting from the occupation.

Orange advertisement in the West Bank at the side of Route 90, a road used by Israelis and Palestinians. Tellingly the sign is written only in Hebrew (Corporate Watch 2011)

When Partner launched Orange Israel, the brand name was registered by **Hutchison Whampoa**, which was a major shareholder in Partner. The success of the new network, after its launch in 1999, is generally considered one of the most successful advertising efforts undertaken in Israel, largely due to the brand name. Hutchison Whampoa divested its shares from Partner in 2009. Since France Télécom took over **Orange PLC** in 2000, it has allowed the agreement to continue. The success of Partner relies heavily on Orange's brand recognition. By withdrawing the license for its brand name and logo, Orange could take a very visible stance against occupation and apartheid, rather than silently aiding it.

---

pisgat-zeev/, [accessed July 2011].
[12]http://corporateoccupation.wordpress.com/2010/05/20/orange-making-the-future-bright-for-israels-illegal-settlements/, [accessed July 2011].

Partner Communications is now controlled by Ilan Ben-Dov's company **Scailex Corporation**, which owns 51 per cent of its shares.[13] France Telecom is based in Paris with offices and franchises worldwide. The agreement between Orange and Partner is an ongoing one but stipulates: "the license agreement may be terminated by mutual agreement, or at our discretion, or by Orange International if a court determines that we have materially misused the brand and we continue to materially misuse the brand after such determination of material misuse."[14] It seems fair to say that the placing of antenna on illegally occupied territory is a misuse of the Orange brand and would be a basis for France Telecom to terminate the agreement.

Cellcom, part of a conglomerate of Israeli and international companies, the **IDB Group**,[15] began operating in Israel in 1994. It owns antennas in the occupied West Bank and Golan, as well as providing cellular services to Israeli soldiers and settlers.[16] Like Partner, the company also owns shops and stalls in illegal settlements in the West Bank.

In 2009, Cellcom launched a controversial TV advertising campaign showing Israeli soldiers playing football by the apartheid wall. The campaign prompted criticism of the company.[17] Seth Freedman, for instance, observed: "In Cellcom's eyes even the most tragic and traumatic experiences of an entire people can be harnessed to the selling of mobile phone services. That the wall is detested by millions of Palestinians, has been ruled wholly illegal by an international court, and has been proved to be a tool for blatant and brazen theft of Palestinian land is neither here nor there; at least, not when there's a cheap laugh to be had and an in-joke to be shared with the company's target audience."[18] The commercial was produced for Cellcom by the **McCann-Erickson** agency.[19]

MIRS Communications (MIRS) is a provider of cellular telecommunications services to the Israeli army and provides services to Israeli settlers. It also operates communications infrastructure on Israeli military bases and settlements.[20]

Until recently, MIRS was owned by **Motorola Israel**. In 2010 the ownership was transferred to the French Company **Altice**.[21] Altice owns the French companies **Numericable, Completel** and **Valvision** and the Swiss company **Green**.[22]

---

[13] http://www.whoprofits.org/Company per cent20Info.php?id=713, [accessed July 2011].
[14] http://www.wikinvest.com/stock/Partner_Communications_Company_ per cent28PTNR per cent29/Intellectual_Property, [accessed July 2011].
[15] http://whoprofits.org/Newsletter.php?nlid=46, [accessed July 2011].
[16] http://whoprofits.org/Company per cent20Info.php?id=712, [accessed July 2011].
[17] http://www.haaretz.com/print-edition/news/ahmed-tibi-joins-opposition-to-cellcom-commercial-1.279942, [accessed July 2011].
[18] http://www.guardian.co.uk/commentisfree/2009/jul/20/cellcom-advert-israel-palestinians, [accessed July 2011].
[19] *Ibid.*
[20] http://www.whoprofits.org/Company per cent20Info.php?id=543, [accessed July 2011].
[21] http://www.mirs.co.il/, [accessed July 2011].
[22] *Ibid.*

Pelephone, owned by **Bezeq,** owns over 200 antennas in the West Bank and the occupied Syrian Golan.[23]

Resistance

A concerted campaign has been waged by the US Campaign to End the Israeli Occupation against Motorola, which owned MIRS up until 2010. **Motorola Solutions**, the mother company of Motorola Israel,[24] is wholly owned by the US Motorola company.[25] The 'Hang up on Motorola' campaign in the US has had some initial success: US service provider **Credo** has agreed not to offer Motorola handsets with their contracts after campaign pressure,[26] and Motorola sold its **Government Electronics Department**, which manufactured bomb fuses, to Israeli military contractor **Aeronautics Defense Systems**.[27] However, Motorola Israel still has a contract to provide surveillance systems on the perimeters of Israeli settlements and the apartheid wall.[28]

Apax Partners, an investor in Bezeq, has been the target of direct action in London during Israel's 2009 massacre in Gaza and in 2011.[29] In 2010, UK NGO War on Want and the Palestine Solidarity Campaign launched a campaign against Bezeq's inclusion in the **BT Alliance**.[30] BT's management has been lobbied and a protest has been held against BT's British Olympic Ball.[31] The Israeli group Boycott from Within has written an open letter in support of the campaign.[32]

In 2011, French BDS campaigners wrote a letter to trade unionists working for France Telecom asking them to pressure the company to break its franchise agreement with Partner Communications.[33] One union, SUD PTT, has promised to raise the issue at every company meeting.[34]

---

[23] http://whoprofits.org/Company per cent20Info.php?id=714, [accessed July 2011].
[24] http://www.whoprofits.org/Company per cent20Info.php?id=992, [accessed July 2011].
[25] http://whoprofits.org/Company per cent20Info.php?id=992, [accessed July 2011].
[26] http://www.endtheoccupation.org/article.php?id=2463, [accessed July 2011].
[27] http://www.endtheoccupation.org/article.php?id=1939, [accessed July 2011].
[28] http://whoprofits.org/Company per cent20Info.php?id=992, [accessed July 2011].
[29] http://www.indymedia.org.uk/en/2009/02/422708.html, [accessed July 2011].
[30] http://www.waronwant.org/campaigns/justice-for-palestine/hide/action/17124-act-now-tell-bt-to-hang-up-on-the-occupation, [accessed July 2011].
[31] http://www.ism-london.org.uk/2341, [accessed 10/02/2011].
[32] http://disconnectnow.org/?p=162, [accessed 10/02/2011].
[33] http://bdsfrance.org/index.php?option=com_content&view=article&id=448:appel-aux-syndicats-de-france-telecom&catid=9:evenements-bds-france, [accessed 10/02/2011].
[34] http://bdsfrance.org/index.php?option=com_content&view=article&id=453:le-syndicat-sud-ptt-de-france-telecom-nous-repond-et-propose-une-petition&catid=9:evenements-bds-france, [accessed 10/02/2011].

Where next?

The complicity of the four cellular providers, along with Motorola, in Israeli militarism and occupation presents a number of lines of attack to the BDS movement. Orange and Motorola are household names globally. The global BDS movement should follow the example of the US campaign against Motorola. Pickets of stores selling Motorola handsets should be organised globally and a global effort made to persuade mobile service providers not to offer Motorola handsets as part of their consumer contracts. There also needs to be a push to persuade local and national governments to exclude Motorola from their service procurement. In the case of Orange, BDS campaigners should continue to pressure France Telecom to terminate its franchise agreement with Partner.

Altice, and its associated companies, should be a major target for the French BDS movement. In the UK, Apax Partners, a major investor in Bezeq, has offices in London and should be a BDS focus.[35] The campaign against BT has broad potential to be rolled out as a grassroots consumer campaign aimed at persuading consumers to switch providers if BT fails to end its business relationship with Bezeq.

BDS activists disrupt BT's Olympic Ball in London over their alliance with Bezeq (ISM London 2010)

---

[35] http://www.apax.com/offices/london.aspx, [accessed 10/02/2011].

9
Tourism

Revenues from tourism currently account for an estimated 6.4 per cent of Israel's GDP and are forecast to rise to 7.2 per cent by 2020.[1] It provides 8.9 per cent of jobs within Israel.[2]

Tourism is an increasingly important part of Israel's economy, with 2.7 million tourists visiting Israel in 2009 and 3.75 million in 2010.[3] Israeli tourism hit a low during the Second Palestinian *Intifada* in 2000 but has been steadily increasing ever since.[4] The largest group of visitors are from the US.[5] The largest groups of European visitors are French, British and Polish.[6] The majority of tourists in Israel, 69 per cent, are Christian,[7] surpassing even Jewish tourists in number. In 2008, Israeli airlines earned $540 million from inbound tourism and $1 billion from outbound flights.[8]

Israel's tourism industry is managed and promoted by the Ministry of Tourism, with a budget of 632 million NIS ($172.5 million) in 2008.[9] The industry is regulated by the Israeli 1976 Tourism Services Law.[10]

Many of the tourist attractions promoted by Israel lie within the territories occupied in 1967, for example the Al Aqsa Mosque, the Wailing Wall and the Church of the Holy Sepulchre in occupied East Jerusalem, the Church of the Nativity and Rachel's Tomb in Bethlehem, the old city of Al Khalil (Hebron), the North coast of the Dead Sea and the ski resorts of the occupied Syrian Golan. Occupied East Jerusalem is listed by the Israeli Ministry of Tourism as the most popular place for foreign tourists to visit "in Israel".

Israel has been heavily promoting itself as a tourist destination. Advertising campaigns, like the Think Israel campaign, have been targeted at European capitals. In October 2010, Israel hosted the Organisation for Economic Cooperation and Development (OECD)[11] tourism

---

[1] World Travel and Tourism Council, *Israel: key facts at a glance*. Available: http://www.wttc.org/eng/Tourism_Research/Economic_Research/Country_Reports/Israel/, [accessed 10/02/2011]. The OECD estimates the contribution of tourism in 2008 to Israeli GDP as 2 per cent – see OECD (2010), *Country profiles: tourism trends and policies, Israel*, Available http://www.oecd.org/document/24/0,3746,en_2649_34389_44607576_1_1_1_1,00.html, [accessed 10/02/2011].
[2] World Travel and Tourism Council, *Israel: key facts at a glance.*, Idem.
[3] Ya'r, C (2010), 2010 Record Year for Tourism to Israel, *Arutz Sheva*. Available: http://www.israelnationalnews.com/News/news.aspx/141382, [accessed 10/02/2011].
[4] OECD (2010), *Country profiles: tourism trends and policies, Israel*, Idem.
[5] Ya'r, C (2010), 2010 Record Year for Tourism to Israel, *Idem*.
[6] OECD (2010), *Country profiles: tourism trends and policies, Israel*, Idem.
[7] Ya'r, C (2010), 2010 Record Year for Tourism to Israel, *Idem*.
[8] OECD (2010), *Country profiles: tourism trends and policies, Israel*, Idem.
[9] *Ibid*.
[10] *Ibid*.
[11] http://www.oecd.org/document/38/0,3343,en_2649_34487_45697574_1_1_1_1,00.html, [accessed

A unique experience?

A 2010 Israeli Ministry of Tourism advertising campaign described a holiday in Israel as a "unique experience." Damn right it's a unique experience: interrogation by surly airport security, sharing buses with hordes of armed-to-the-teeth Israeli adolescents and the chance to see the old city of Jerusalem policed by racist goons with a quota of Palestinian residents to harass. For the more adventurous tourist, there are the deserted and terrorised streets of the old city of Al Khalil, daubed with xenophobic graffiti, the apartheid wall, collective punishment, targeted assassinations, house demolitions, torture and repression. The possibilities are endless.

The Israeli Ministry of Tourism promotes itself heavily in the UK (Advert featured in the Guardian's G2 2010)

conference. Israeli Tourism Minister Stas Misezhnikov said in 2010 that Israel's recent membership of the OECD was "of great importance in terms of building a positive image for the country, the positive image gained will have an effect on the tourist's choice to visit Israel, and it will attract foreign investors to the country, including, among others, investors in tourism."[12]

In 2006, the then Israeli foreign minister Tzipi Livni announced the ministry of Tourism would play a big part in the $7m "Brand Israel project" to "bridge the gap between the real Israel and its international image."[13] In reality, tourism in Israel helps normalise a colonial

---

10/02/2011].
[12] http://www.alternativenews.org/english/index.php/topics/news/2676-oecd-selects-jerusalem-to-host-its- tourism-conference, [accessed 10/02/2011].
[13] Israel Today (2006), British expert: Israel needs new image, Available: http://www.israeltoday.co.il/default.aspx?tabid=178&nid=10075, [accessed 17/02/2011].

apartheid state. The Boycott National Committee (BNC) states: "Internationally, tourism is overtly deployed by Israel to 'rebrand' the state as an attractive holiday destination, and to cover up its occupation, colonisation and apartheid policies."[14]

Normalising the occupation

Israel uses joint tourism projects with the Palestinian Authority (PA) as a tool to normalise the occupation. Under a joint PA-Israeli scheme in Bethlehem, the **Bethlehem Quick Impact Project (QIP),** Israeli tour guides will receive licences to operate in PA-controlled areas and special 'tourist-friendly' checkpoints will be set up to shield tourists from the reality of the occupation.

The stated aims of this project are: "Improving Palestinian marketing strategies and developing publicity campaigns for Holy Land travel focusing on Bethlehem, facilitating tourist access to the city in particular and the West Bank in general, rehabilitating tourist sites, improving the financial situation of the private sector by providing soft loans, investment guarantees, or matching grants and building capacity for the PNA Ministry of Tourism."[15] However, Stop the Wall, in a recent report, criticised the project for:

- Ignoring sustainable Palestinian domestic tourism (which the travel restrictions imposed by the occupation render impossible)
- Attempting to work around the Israeli military occupation
- Separating occupied Palestinians from tourists
- Relegating Palestinians to a secondary role in the QIP, with Israel as the primary partner
- Cementing the occupation through basing economic development on the current status quo.[16]

The Bethlehem QIP is just one example of the many joint tourism initiatives between the Palestinian Authority and Israel. These initiatives make the PA complicit in the normalisation of the occupation through the tourism industry, an industry where Palestinians are a junior partner and whose development is planned around the consolidation of Israeli occupation and apartheid.

The Bethlehem initiative is not the only joint tourism initiative between the PA and Israel. In 2009, a press conference was held in France to announce the launch of the "Israel-Palestine" programme by **Voyageurs du Monde,** with support from the Israeli National Tourism Office and the Palestinian Delegation in France (the equivalent of the Palestinian embassy). This joint initiative advertised tours in the old city of Al Khalil, which included a visit to the

---

[14]Boycott National Committee (September 2010), *Open letter to OECD regarding decision to host tourism conference in Jerusalem.* Available: http://bdsmovement.net/?q=node/773, [accessed 17/02/2011].
[15]Stop the Wall Campaign, *Development or normalisation, a critique of West Bank development approaches and projects.* Available: http://www.stopthewall.org/downloads/PRDPcritique.pdf, [accessed 17/02/2011].
[16]*Ibid.*

settlement of Kiryat Arba, whose residents have been responsible for terrorising local Palestinians. Al Khalil is described as having an "unusual and quaint characteristic: a Palestinian city 'blended' with settlements."[17]

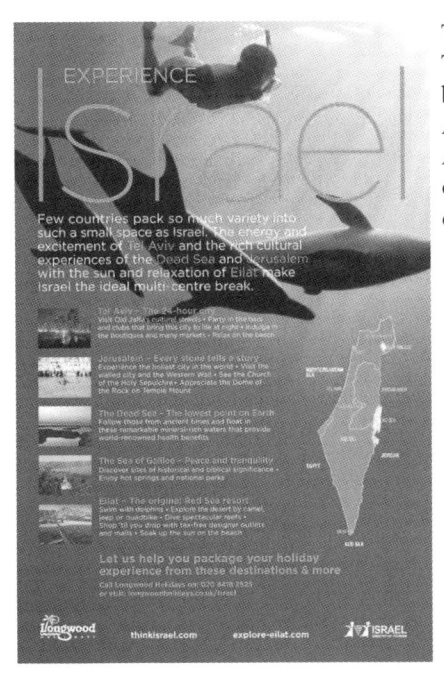

This Israeli Government Tourism Office advert was banned by the UK Advertising Standards Agency for depicting the occupied territories as part of Israel

Cementing the occupation

The tourist industry is also used to cement the occupation and dislocate Palestinians from their land. For example, in Silwan, in occupied East Jerusalem, 88 Palestinian homes have received demolition orders[18] to make way for an 'archaeological park' named King's Park. Zionist organisation **El Ad**, helped along the way by the **Israeli Antiquities Authority**, has spearheaded the excavation of the area, in an attempt to monopolise the land and make way for the project.[19]

The settlements as tourist attractions

The settlements themselves are promoted as tourist attractions. For instance, guestrooms in settlement kibbutzim are advertised in the Jordan Valley and the occupied Syrian Golan by international travel websites such as **Venere.com**[20] and **Booking.com.**[21] **The Lonely Planet**

---

[17]CAPJO EuroPalestine (26/11/2010), *Palestine: une tentative de normalisation de l'apartheid, par le torisme,* Available: http://www.europalestine.com/spip.php?article5645, [accessed February 2011].
[18]Architects and Planners for Justice in Palestine, *Silwan,* Available: http://apjp.org/silwan/, [accessed 17/02/2011].
[19]Hider, J (2009), Settlers dig tunnels around Jerusalem, *The Sunday Time*s. Available: http://www.timesonline.co.uk/tol/news/world/middle_east/article3463264.ece, [accessed 17/02/2011].
[20]http://www.vcnere.com/hotels/afik/hotel-kibbutz-afik/, [accessed 17/02/2011].

series of guidebooks lists settlements, such as Merom Golan in the occupied Syrian Golan,[22] as potential travel destinations. Settlements, such as Hebron's Beit Hadassah, encourage Zionist tourism to strengthen their hand in the battle to push Palestinians out of the old city of Al Khalil.[23] 12 new hotels are being built in the Har Gilo, Gilo and Har T'sion settlements in the Bethlehem region[24] and the Gush Etzion settlement block is expanding its tourist amenities.[25]

Tourists at Kalya beach on the North Coast of the Dead Sea, West Bank (Corporate Watch 2010)

Companies promoting tourism in Israel jointly with the Israeli Ministry of Tourism:
Explore Worldwide Ltd
Longwood Holidays
Voyageurs du Monde
Cox and Kings
Explore
Colette Worldwide Holidays
El Al Superstar Holidays
Page and Moy

---

[21] http://www.booking.com/hotel/il/kalia-kibbutz.en.html, [accessed 17/02/2011].
[22] http://shop.lonelyplanet.com/israel-and-the-palestinian-territories/israel-and-the-palestinian-territories-travel-guide-6/israel-and-palestine-territories-the-upper-galilee-and-the-golan-chapter-6?lpaffil=lpcomsearch-shoplinks, [accessed 17/02/2011].
[23] International Solidarity Movement (September 2010), *A ghost town beckons? Old City in Hebron under threat*, http://palsolidarity.org/2010/09/14368/, [accessed February 2011].
[24] Boycott National Committee, private correspondence with authors.
[25] *Ibid*.

Companies advertising holidays or guest rooms in Israeli settlements:
Venere.com
Travelbyclick.net
Voyageurs du Monde
Booking.com

Marketing companies working with the Israeli Ministry of Tourism:
Acanchi

Alternative tourism

Recognising the importance of visiting Palestine in building the global solidarity movement, many Palestinian and Palestine solidarity groups promote alternative solidarity tours to Palestine. Many of these groups tap into the constant supply of Christian groups wishing to visit the 'holy land'. These groups include the Alternative Tourism Group (www.atg.ps), The Olive Co-op (http://www.olivecoop.com) and the Holy Land Trust (www.holylandtrust.org). Groups like these allow tourism to strengthen resistance to Israeli apartheid, rather than benefit the occupiers. However, those thinking of visiting Palestine should consider whether their visit is placed firmly within the framework of solidarity.

Resistance

In 2008, activists in Valladolid, Spain, occupied the area close to the Israeli stall at the 14th Valladolid Tourism Fair. The following year, the Israeli delegation refused to participate in the fair.[26]

In April 2010, the UK Advertising Standards Authority (ASA) upheld a complaint by Palestine solidarity activists about Israeli Ministry of Tourism posters that implied that East Jerusalem was part of Israel. The posters were banned.[27] There has also been a concerted direct action campaign in London to subvertise and destroy Israeli Ministry of Tourism posters.[28]

Activists worldwide mobilised against the OECD's Tourism Conference in Jerusalem in 2010. As a result, five countries, the UK, Sweden, Ireland, Turkey and South Africa, withdrew from the conference.[29] The Alternative Tourism Group, the Arab Hotel Association, the Civic Coalition for Palestinian Rights in Jerusalem and several others lead a boycott

---

[26] See http://plataformapalestinavalladolid.blogspot.com/, [accessed February 2011].
[27] Sweeney, M (2010), Israeli tourism ad banned for using photo of East Jerusalem, *The Guardian*. Available: http://www.guardian.co.uk/media/2010/apr/14/israeli-tourism-ad-asa, [accessed February 2011].
[28] For example see Asad, A (2010), Activists 'decorate' Israel Ministry of Tourism billboards, *UK Indymedia*. Available: http://www.indymedia.org.uk/en/2010/07/455326.html, [accessed February 2011].
[29] See, for instance, Boycott National Committee Press Release (2010), *Five countries boycott tourism conference in Jerusalem*, Available: http://bdsmovement.net/?q=node/778, [accessed February 2011].

campaign against the International Tourism Conference in March 2011.[30]

Subvertised Israeli Government Tourism Office Poster (UK Indymedia 2010)

Where next?

Tourism is a major contributor to the Israeli economy and plays an important part in normalising Israeli apartheid and occupation. BDS campaigners should urge a boycott of tourism in Israel, challenge international tourism projects and joint PA-Israel initiatives and initiate action against companies organising tours to Israel.

The large number of Christian visitors to Israel presents a big opportunity for the BDS movement to raise awareness of the travel boycott among Christian communities and discourage pilgrimages to Israel unless they are positioned firmly within a framework of solidarity.

The promotion of tourism is an important part of the Israeli state's PR strategy, 'subvertising' Israeli Ministry of Tourism advertising campaigns and public events are important opportunities to counter this spin.

---

[30]Alternative Tourism Group (2011), *A conference in the Service of Israeli Colonization and Apartheid: The international tourism conference – Jerusalem*. Available: http://atg.ps/index.php?lang=en&page=news&news_item=129741502552, [accessed February 2011].

10
Freight Transport

The transport of Israeli goods to foreign markets is of particular importance to the BDS movement.

Shipping

Corporate Watch has examined bills of lading for ships leaving Israeli harbours[1] bound for the US (often via Europe and Asia) up to 2010. We found that the dominant shipping companies were **Zim** and **Maersk**. **Agrexco** also shipped goods to Europe via an in-house shipping line, although the future of Agrexco's transport network is unclear now that the company's liquidation has been ordered.

Company profiles

Zim is a shipping company owned by the Ofer brothers, who are part of one of the most powerful business families in Israel. Established in 1945, Zim boasts that it ships goods to Asia, Europe, Africa, North and South America and the Middle East.[2]

Zim is 99 per cent owned by the **Israel Corporation**, Israel's largest holding company, which also owns energy companies and **Israel Chemicals Ltd.**[3] Zim's European HQ is in Hamburg and the company has contact points across Europe, including in London.[4]

Zim has a 75 per cent stake in **UTI Logistics**, an international transport company established in 2007 that is involved in air freight and shipping. UTI has offices at all central shipping points in Israel, near Ben-Gurion International Airport (UTI's corporate headquarters); the Haifa Port; Ashdod and Eilat; Ben-Gurion International Airport's cargo center; and at land border crossings with Egypt and Jordan. The company employs 20,000 people and has logistics centres in 142 countries. The HQ of **UTI worldwide** is in the USA.[5]

---

[1] Corporate Watch looked at bills of lading up to and including 2010, primarily via the importgenius website.
[2] http://www.zim.com/content.aspx?id=158&l=4, [accessed June 2011].
[3] http://www.israelcorp.com/Default.aspx?tabid=64, [accessed June 2011].
[4] http://www.zim.com/Find_Agent.aspx?hidSubmit=false&id=153&l=4&cFullName=&isFromMap=false&searchType=9&ZimCode=A2&AgencyCode=GBLPL01&AgencyName=Represented+By+Zim+Uk+Ltd.&PageType=3&searchByNameTextBox=&selectArea=-1&selectCountry=-1&selectCity=-1, [accessed June 2011].
[5] http://www.bdicode.co.il/CompanyTextProfile_ENG/629_659_0/UTi per cent20Logistics per cent20Israel per cent20Ltd, [accessed June 2011].

Carmel-Agrexco, Israel's largest agricultural exporter, transported goods, prior to its liquidation order, from Ashdod on its own ships to Fos, near Marseille, and to Vado in Italy.[6] Agrexco brought 90 per cent of its produce to Europe by ship, with the remaining 10 per cent being road-freighted.[7]

Agrexco recently invested in a new terminal at the port of Sete. The terminal opened in May 2011 and handled predominantly Agrexco goods. It is run by Italian company **Reefer Terminal**, which is part of the **GF Group**.[8]

The company also air-freighted goods to its terminal at Liege, Belgium, from which goods were distributed across Europe, including to the UK.[9] In addition, it transported some goods by train from Italy to the Netherlands.[10] Agrexco's rail freighted goods were shipped to Trieste by Zim.[11]

Zim and Maersk shipping containers ready for loading at Haifa docks
(Corporate Watch 2010)

It is unclear what will become of this extensive transport network now that the Agrexco has gone into liquidation. Part of Agrexco's shipping network has already been taken over by **Cosiarma**, a company owned by the GF group. Cosiarma has chartered two vessels previously used by Agrexco and renamed them the Cala Pira and Cala Paradiso. They will

---

[6] http://www.agrexco.co.il/en/logistics.asp. and http://www.freshplaza.com/news_detail.asp?id=38681 and http://www.thegrocer.co.uk/articles.aspx?page=articles&ID=199967, [accessed March 2011].
[7] http://www.thegrocer.co.uk/articles.aspx?page=articles&ID=199967, [accessed March 2011].
[8] http://www.mail.fruitnet.com/content.aspx?cid=8872, [accessed March 2011].
[9] http://www.agrexco.co.il/en/logistics.asp, [accessed March 2011].
[10] http://www.thegrocer.co.uk/articles.aspx?page=articles&ID=199967, [accessed March 2011].
[11] http://www.brassicastoday.com/en/agrexco-on-an-agrotrain-to-europe-newsc-81.aspx, [accessed March 2011].

sail regularly from Haifa to Ashdod and from there to Sete and Genoa.[12]

Maersk is a Danish conglomerate and the largest container shipping company in the world. It makes numerous voyages from Israeli ports to Europe and the US. Companies shipping goods on Maersk's vessels in 2010 included **Carmel-Agrexco**, arms company **Elbit** and settlement company **Avgol**, which is based in the Barkan settlement industrial zone.[13] The company has offices worldwide.[14]

GBS offers Freight Forwarding Services from Israel to the UK. The company has offices in Kent and Suffolk.[15]

Thousands demonstrate against Agrexco's new port in Sete, The port and the transport network is now being run by GF group (UK Indymedia 2011)

Air Freight

Total air cargo movements through Israel's airports in 2010 totalled 302,903 tons. The main carriers were **El Al**, which carries cargo in the holds of their passenger planes, and **Cal**.[16]

---

[12] http://www.freshplaza.com/news_detail.asp?id=86056#Scene_1, [accessed september 2011].
[13] All info from importgenius, [accessed March 2010].
[14] Economist.com, Container shipping. 2005-05-11 [accessed 12/04/2007].
[15] http://www.gbsfreight.co.uk/freight/middle-east/israel, [accessed March 2011].
[16] http://www.reportsnreports.com/reports/70583-israel-freight-transport-report-q2-2011.html, [accessed March 2011].

List of freight companies operating in Israel[17]

Airgate Israel
Ashdod Bonded Ltd
Carmel International Shipping Services
Dynamic Shipping Services
GES Global Export Shipping
Goldline Shipping
Kamor Shipping Services
Maman Cargo Terminals
Sea Transport and Trading
Taavura Holdings
Unitag

Allalouf
Caspi Cargo Lines
CAL
El Al
Gadot Chemical Tankers and Terminals
Israir
Lucy Borchard Shipping
Mayan
Sharon
Unishipping Israel
Zim

Belgian activists blockade the air freighting of Israeli goods at Liege airport (BDS Movement 2011)

Resistance

BDS campaigners have put up strong resistance to Agrexco's transport network (*see the chapter on agriculture earlier in this book for a full run-down*) including blockades of Agrexco's UK logistics centre, two blockades of the Agrexco/Lachs terminal in Liege and mass demonstrations against the new Agrexco terminal in Sete.

After the Israeli attack on the Gaza Freedom Flotilla in 2010, dockworkers in Sweden, India, South Africa, Norway, Malaysia, Turkey and the US refused to unload Israeli goods.[18] Indian

---

[17] http://www.science.co.il/Transportation-Companies.asp, [accessed March 2011].
[18] See for example http://www.ynetnews.com/articles/1,7340,L-3909614,00.html, [accessed March 2011].

dockworkers also held a picket of Zim's offices in Cochin, while a 500-strong picket of Zim was held in Oakland, in the USA.[19]

Where next?

BDS campaigners should target Zim's logistics operations, both through workers' actions and through targeting its offices and depots. Pressure should also be placed on Maersk to cease transporting Israeli goods.

Railworkers' unions should monitor the fate of Agrexco's rail link from Trieste to the Netherlands and mobilise against any attempt by another company to transport Israeli goods by this route.

Dockworkers in Oakland picket a Zim container ship after the Israeli attack on the Gaza Freedom Flotilla (Libcom 2010)

BDS campaigners should closely monitor the fate of Agrexco's assets and target any company which attempts to purchase its transport network to transport Israeli goods. As such, Cosiarma and the GF Group should be key targets.

---

[19] http://palestinenote.com/blogs/news/archive/2010/07/06/dockworkers-at-indian-port-boycott-israeli-ships.aspx, [accessed March 2011].

11
Public Transport

The consumer transport sector in Israel is divided between a few key companies. International companies, **Veolia** in particular, have penetrated the Israeli transport market and should be top priorities for the BDS movement.

Buses

Dan, Egged and **Veolia** dominate the Israeli bus transport market. All three companies run services to Israel's West Bank settlements. Egged also operates in the Israeli occupied Syrian Golan.

Veolia run buses from West Jerusalem to the illegal West Bank settlement of Giv'at Ze'v (Corporate Watch 2010)

Egged is the largest public transportation company in Israel. It operates special bus lines and public transportation to almost all settlements, including remote outposts. Egged is also involved in the development of the light rail project in Jerusalem.[1] The company is in the process of listing itself on the Tel Aviv Stock Exchange.

Dan is the second-largest public transportation company in Israel. It provides public transportation services to West Bank settlements in the region of Shomron.[2] Dan is a

---

[1] http://www.whoprofits.org/Company per cent20Info.php?id=504, [accessed March 2011].
[2] http://www.whoprofits.org/Company per cent20Info.php?id=501, [accessed March 2011].

participant in the 'adopt a unit' programme, having adopted and organised joint events with an Israeli army combat unit.[3]

Veolia/Connex Israel runs bus services throughout Israel and to Israeli settlements in the West Bank, including Beit Horon and Givat Ze'ev along road 443,[4] a road upon which Palestinians are forbidden from driving (for 'security reasons').

Air travel

El Al, one of Israel's main air carriers, was set up by the Israeli state in 1948. The company has now been fully privatised[5] but still describes itself as the Israeli national airline.[6]

Activists in Athens delay an El Al flight after they blocked five check-in counters in protest against the blockade of Gaza and the Israeli attack on the Mavi Marmara, (Australians For Palestine 2010)

El Al has repeatedly been accused of racism. In 1999, Jabour Jabour, an Israeli-Palestinian, brought a discrimination case again the company after it refused to admit him to a flight attendant training course.[7] In 2010, the company was ordered to pay 30,000 NIS to two Israeli-Palestinians who faced discrimination when travelling with El Al from New York to

---
[3]http://www.dan.co.il/english/template/default.asp?maincat=&catId=25&PageId=706&parentid=&show=1, [accessed March 2011].
[4] http://www.whoprofits.org/Company per cent20Info.php?id=581, [accessed March 2011].
[5]OECD, *Economic survey of Israel 2009, Idem*, p.148.
[6]http://www.elal.co.il/ELAL/English/AboutElAl/History.htm, [accessed March 2011].
[7]http://radioislam.org/historia/Zionism/elal_dscrmn.html, [accessed March 2011].

Israel. Abd al-Wahab Shalabi, the claimant in the case, called on "everyone opposing discrimination" to boycott El Al.[8]

List of commercial airlines flying to Israel[9]

Adria	Aegean Airlines	Aeroflot
Aerosvit Airlines	Air Berlin	Air Canada
Air China	Air France	Air Sinai
AirBaltic	Alitalia	Arkia
AT Airways	Austrian Airlines	AZAL
Belavia	British Airways	Brussels Airlines
Bulgaria Air	Cimber Air	Croatia Airlines
Cyprus Airways	Czech Airlines	Delta
Donavia	EasyJet	EL AL Israel Airlines
Ethiopian Airlines	Georgian Airways	Germanwings
Iberia	Israir	Jet2
JetairFly	KLM	Korean Air
Kuban Airlines	LOT	Lufthansa
MALEV	Meridiana	Oren Air
Rossiya Airlines	Royal Jordanian	S7 Airlines
SAS	Smart Wings	Spanair
Swiss Continental Airlines	Tandem Aero	TAROM
Tatarstan Airlines	Thai Airways	TolAir Services
Transaero Airlines	TUIfly	Turkish Airlines
Ukraine International	United	Ural Airlines
US Airways	UTair	Uzbekistan Airways
VIM Airlines	Vueling Airlines	

Rail

Israel Railways, a state-owned company, runs all of Israel's railways. There are currently two major rail infrastructure projects, one in Jerusalem and one from Jerusalem to Tel Aviv, which are discussed below, in the construction chapter of this book.

In 2009, Israel Railways sacked all Israeli-Palestinian 'crossing guards' on the pretext that they had not served in the army and should not, therefore, carry a gun. Moves like this exclude non-Jewish citizens of Israel from jobs offering more responsibility and pay and consign them to low paid jobs such as cleaning. *Sawt al Amal*, a Palestinian trade union, took

---

[8]http://www.haaretz.com/print-edition/news/el-al-ordered-to-compensate-humiliated-israeli-arab-passengers-1.842, [accessed March 2011].
[9]http://www.skyscanner.net/flights-to/il/airlines-that-fly-to-israel.html?p1=1, [accessed March 2011].

up the case in Israel's labour courts and obtained an injunction against the dismissals.[10] The cases are still ongoing.

Resistance and ways forward

Veolia is, and should continue to be, the target of global campaigning for its involvement with projects in Israel and the occupied territories *(see our chapter on construction for more on Veolia)*. Egged has faced resistance since it won a public tender to operate buses in Holland.[11]

In July 2010, Greek activists delayed an El Al flight after they blocked five check-in counters in protest against the blockade of Gaza and the Israeli attack on the Mavi Marmara, part of a freedom flotilla attempting to break the siege of Gaza.[12] This kind of action could be replicated worldwide.

The crossing guards sacked by Israel Railways received international support from hundreds of international trade union branches and campaigning organisations. This level of support needs to be shown to all workers who are discriminated against by Israeli companies.

---

[10] http://www.ajras.org/en/?page=show_details&Id=32&table=news&CatId=-1 and Adalah (2009), *Targeted citizen: Israel Railway case (video)*. Available: http://www.adalah.org/eng/video_target.php, [accessed March 2011].
[11] http://www.haaretz.com/news/diplomacy-defense/pro-palestinian-group-in-the-netherlands-cals-for-boycott-of-israeli-bus-company-1.373546, [accessed March 2011].
[12] See, for instance Blumenkrantz, Z (2010), Anti-Israel protesters delay El Al flight in Athens, *Haaretz*. Available: http://www.haaretz.com/news/diplomacy-defense/anti-israel-protesters-delay-el-al-flight-in-athens-1.301921, [accessed March 2011].

12
Academia

"If in extreme situations of violations of human rights and moral principles... academia refuses to criticize and take a side, it collaborates with the oppressing system."

The late Israeli linguist Tanya Reinhardt[1]

While measuring the exact GDP contribution of Israeli academia is difficult, the importance of higher education institutions to Israel's economic growth goes without saying. It was through the innovation incubated and developed in universities across the country that both the military-industrial complex and high-tech sector developed. As with other states that adopted neoliberal policies during the 1990s, Israel has moved towards what is now seen as a 'knowledge economy'. Essentially, this means heavy investment in research and development with particular emphasis on industries such as computer software and electronics.[2]

Israeli higher education actually began during the British mandate period, when the **Technion** and **Hebrew University** opened their doors in 1924 and 1925 respectively. The creation of the State of Israel, and the population growth that followed brought a need to expand higher education on the back of social and economic requirements.[3] Not only were universities demanded in more rural areas of the country, but the construction of a modern state required an intelligentsia. In the 1950s and 1960s, five further universities were founded. Today there are seven Israeli universities: **The Hebrew University** in Jerusalem, **Tel-Aviv** and **Bar-Ilan** in Tel-Aviv, **Haifa** and the **Technion** in Haifa, **Ben-Gurion** in Be'er Sheva, and the **Weizmann Institute of Science** in Rehovot. Four of these - Hebrew University, Tel-Aviv, the Technion and the Weizmann Institute - are ranked among the top 150 universities in the world.[4] There are also numerous colleges and academic institutes, the biggest of which is the **Herzliya Interdisciplinary Center** (IDC).[5] Some of these have a prestige and status similar to the universities.

Licensing and accreditation for academia in Israel falls under the remit of the Council for Higher Education, an independent statutory body comprising between 19 and 25 members, appointed every five years. The head of the council is always the Minster of Education, whilst around two-thirds of its members are academics.[6] At least two student representatives, one for university students and one for college students, also sit on the Council. In addition

---

[1]Reinhardt, T (2003), *Why the world should boycott Israeli academic institutions*. Available: http://www.monabaker.com/pMachine/more.php?id=96_0_1_12_M5, [accessed 21st March 2011].
[2]Yacobi Keller, U (2009), *The economy of the occupation: academic boycott of Israel*, Alternative Information Center: A Socioeconomic Bulletin, No. 23-24 Available: http://electronicintifada.net/v2/article10945.shtml, [accessed 11th March 2011].
[3]Israeli Council of Higher Education. Available: http://www.che.org.il/template/default_e.aspx?PageId=279, [accessed 11th March 2011].
[4]http://www.voxeu.org/index.php?q=node/984, [accessed 23rd March 2011].
[5]Yacobi Keller, U (2009), *The economy of the occupation: academic boycott of Israel. Idem.*
[6]Israeli Council of Higher Education. *Idem.*

to being the only organisation with authority to give educational accreditation, the Council advises the government on developing and financing higher education and scientific research.[7] Under its guidance, Israel has become a world leader in scientific innovation, driven by heavy government investment in research and development which, at around 4.7 per cent of GDP, was the highest in the world in 2008.[8] As a result, universities are now seen as a source of immense national pride in Israel.[9]

The Ariel University Centre of Samaria, based in the West Bank settlement of Ariel (Michael Jacobson 2011)

These prestigious accolades have been put under threat since the turn of the millennium, as economic policy shifted to the right. Under the auspices of Ariel Sharon and his fiscally conservative finance minister Binyamin Netanyahu, government funding to universities was drastically cut in line with a wider contraction in public spending.[10] The Higher Education Budget stagnated, despite a growth in student numbers, and large budget cuts led to faculty dismissals and a reduction in scientific activity.[11] According to Shlomo Swirksi, the result has been a new reliance on overseas funding and deepening partnerships with private companies.[12]

---

[7]http://www.mfa.gov.il/MFA/Facts+About+Israel/Education/Higher+Education.htm, [accessed March 2011].
[8]Rose, H, and Rose, S (2008), *Israel, Europe and the academic boycott*, Available: http://rac.sagepub.com/content/50/1/1.abstract, [accessed 21st March 2011].
[9]Buck, T (2010), Israeli universities accused of anti-Zionism, *Financial Times*, Available: http://www.ft.com/cms/s/0/de5b3f7a-b11f-11df-bce8-00144feabdc0.html#axzz1Hcbpjdh1, [accessed 25th March 2011].
[10]Swirski, S (2008), *The burden of occupation*, Idem.
[11]*Ibid.*
[12]*Ibid.*

Window dressing the occupation

Dissident Israeli academic Ilan Pappe argues: "Israeli academia is the window dressing of the Jewish society's moral and cultural self-image."[13] Remaining largely uncritical, Israeli institutes of higher education and many faculty members who serve them are directly culpable in the occupation, providing the moral and scholarly grounding for the oppression of Palestinian people. Their complicity, in fact, runs much deeper. From discriminatory admission policies to research into next generation weapons used to crush dissent in the OPT Israeli universities are integral to the Zionist project.

Israeli bombing of Islamic University of Gaza, December 2008

Brothers in arms

While all Israeli universities have links with the Israeli arms industry in some way or another, perhaps the biggest culprit is the Technion. This extends from training arms industry managers and engineers to in-house research into building 'defence' and 'surveillance' tools designed to keep Palestinians living in giant open prisons.

One such project awarded research grants to Technion electrical engineering students, giving them access to **Elbit Systems'** 'Eye Tracking Laboratory'.[14] Another is the Ramtech rocket project, which was completed across five years with the help of 20 different students under the supervision of Professor Alon Gant, and **Rafael's** Yitzhak Greenburg.[15] The Technion also has the highest percentage of students serving in the reserve army, with many forming both the academic elite and the military elite.[16] Teaching is even tailored towards the

---

[13]Pappe, I (2004), *The meaning and objectives of the academic boycott, resisting Israeli apartheid: strategies and principles – an international conference on Palestine,* London, 5th December 2004. Available: http://www.bricup.org.uk/archive2.html, [accessed 24th March 2011].
[14]http://ir.elbitsystems.com/phoenix.zhtml?c=61849&p=irol-newsArticle_print&ID=1376090&highlight=, [accessed March 2011].
[15]*Structures of oppression: why McGill and Concordia universities must sever their links with the Technion University*. Obtained via personal correspondence.
[16]*Ibid.*

particular job at hand. In 2001, the Technion unveiled a three-year MBA program specifically for Rafael managers.[17]

As well as receiving funding from arms manufacturers, some universities have CEOs from the industry on their boards of governors. One example, at the Technion, is current CEO of **Boeing Israel**, General (Reservist) David Irvy. Irvy is also an advisory member of the Israel Missile Defence Association. He sits alongside other governors, such as Major General (Reservist) Yitzhak Hoffi, a former head of Mossad, and Schlomo Yanai, an ex-high ranking IDF officer and head of the security delegation at the Camp David negotiations.[18] Hebrew University, however, trumps all others. The chairman of the board of governors at the university is Michael Federmann, who also chairs the board at **Elbit Systems**.[19]

Manufacturing consent

At Haifa University, protests are banned on campus unless licensed by the Vice-Chancellor. Unofficial demonstrations, however peaceful, are disbanded and often filmed by security staff, with video evidence used as grounds for suspending or expelling students.[20] This came to a head in August 2007, when seven Palestinian and Jewish Israeli students staged a protest against racist remarks made by the Student Union spokesperson during a newspaper interview. Holding hands, with their mouths covered with tape, they stood silently and formed a human chain.[21] They were arrested and charged with "provoking a commotion" and "wild behaviour". When a disciplinary tribunal declared them innocent, the university appealed against the decision.[22]

Six months later, students faced a disciplinary for holding an unpermitted memorial service for the 13 Palestinian civilians killed in the October 2000 demonstrations across villages in the Galilee and Nazareth.[23] While all protests technically break Haifa University rules, the same barriers to freedom of speech have not been applied to unauthorised pro-Zionist demonstrations. When students held counter-protests in retaliation to rallies against the siege of Gaza and occupation of the West Bank, the university failed to hold them to account despite not having issued permits.[24]

---

[17] Ibid.
[18] http://people.forbes.com/profile/shlomo-yanai/78055, [accessed March 2011].
[19] http://ir.elbitsystems.com/phoenix.zhtml?c=61849&p=irol-govBoard_pf, [accessed March 2011].
[20] Cook, J (2008), Academic freedom? Not for Arabs in Israel, *Counterpunch*. Available: http://www.counterpunch.org/cook02292008.html, [accessed 22nd March 2011].
[21] Alternative Information Center (2007), *Haifa University harasses Jewish and Arab students who participated in peaceful anti-racist picket,* Available: http://www.pacbi.org/etemplate.php?id=576, [accessed 23rd March 2011].
[22] Rose, H and Rose, S (2008), *Israel, Europe and the academic boycott, Idem.*
[23] Traubmann, T (2008), Haifa U. to punish students for memorial of October 2000 riots, *Haaretz*, Available: http://www.haaretz.com/news/haifa-u-to-punish-students-for-memorial-of-october-2000-riots-1.239773, [accessed 23rd March 2011].
[24] Alternative Information Center (2007), *Haifa University harasses Jewish and Arab students who participated in peaceful anti-racist picket. Idem.*

This move is in line with the university's approach to Operation Cast Lead. A striking example came at the height of the military onslaught, when it released the following announcement:

> "As a show of solidarity with IDF soldiers fighting in Gaza and residents of the south, the University of Haifa has made its central tower into a national flag ... the university is not an ivory tower and is inseparably connected to the community. With this symbolic act, it expresses its great appreciation for the residents of the south and its support for the IDF's soldiers."[25]

Similarly, Haifa University was more than willing to allow an academic conference entitled 'The Demographic Problem and Israel's Demographic Policies'. The talk, from which Palestinian Israeli academics were excluded, focused on the differential birth-rate between Palestinian and Jewish Israelis, and how to achieve the political objective of a permanent Jewish majority in Israel.[26] Neither did they condemn geography professor Arnon Sofer when he argued in a press interview: "If we want to remain alive we will have to kill and kill and kill. All day, every day. If we don't kill we will cease to exist."[27] Sofer is a self-professed architect of the separation wall.

Yet when Israeli academics voice support for a boycott as a necessary tool to end the barbaric treatment of Palestinians, they are publicly denounced by fellow faculty members and management. For example, Ben-Gurion University president Rikva Carmi rebuked Professor Neve Gordon for advocating BDS in a 2009 Los Angeles Times op-ed, stating: "After [Gordon's]...extreme description of Israel as an 'apartheid' state, how can he, in good faith, create the collaborative atmosphere necessary for true academic research and teaching?"[28] Then, in April 2011, a major American donor threatened to cut funding unless Ben Gurion took greater action to denounce leftist professors. The unnamed benefactor was due to hand over millions of shekels for a new library and it is thought that Gordon was the target of his criticism.[29]

The Katz controversy: re-writing history

The dedication of Israeli academic institutions to Israel's dominant historical narrative became apparent in 2000, in what has been dubbed the 'Katz controversy'. Haifa

---

[25] http://azvsas.blogspot.com/2009/09/how-haifa-university-and-israels.html, [accessed 22nd March 2011].
[26] Rose, H and Rose, S (2008), *Israel, Europe and the academic boycott, Idem*, p. 1-20.
[27] *Ibid.*
[28] Horowitz, A, and Weiss, P (2010), The boycott divestment sanctions movement, *The Nation*. Available: http://www.thenation.com/article/boycott-divestment-sanctions-movement?page=0,3, [accessed 22nd March 2011].
[29] Alternative Information Center (2011), *Donor to Ben Gurion University wants condemnation of leftist statements*. Available: http://www.alternativenews.org/english/index.php/topics/economy-of-the-occupation/3540-donor-to-ben-gurion-university-wants-condemnation-of-leftist-statements, [accessed 10th June 2011].

postgraduate student Teddy Katz was sued for libel after claiming in his MA thesis that Israel had committed a massacre in the Palestinian village of Al-Tantura during 1948. The case was brought by veterans of the Alexandroni Brigade, which led the operation, some of whom had spoken to Katz as part of his research. While the paper was awarded an astonishing 97 per cent, the university appointed a committee to re-examine the thesis. The committee decided to overturn the original decision and fail it.[30]

In collecting data for his thesis, Katz relied heavily on the use of oral testimony as one of his basic methodological approaches. He interviewed over one hundred Israeli and Palestinian individuals who were in, or connected to, villages on the outskirts of Haifa during the 1948 war.[31] Katz concluded that during the conquest of Tantura by Jewish forces in late May 1948 a large number of individuals had been murdered, possibly as many as 225. To make matters worse, when Haifa historian Ilan Pappe publicly defended Katz, he was himself targeted for disciplinary action by the university. Following an international campaign the threat was revoked[32] but, due to Pappe's outspoken criticism of the occupation, his position became untenable. Pappe has left Israel and now teaches at Exeter University.

Two-tier education

Not only do Israeli universities stifle criticism of state policies towards Palestinians, they also actively participate in creating apartheid within the Israeli education system. This begins with the admission process before Palestinian Israeli students have even set foot in a lecture theatre. Every potential student has to undergo psychometric exams – a combined aptitude and personality test – which are criticised as culturally biased and discriminatory.[33] Because of this, psychometric tests were scrapped in 2003 in a bid to help 'weaker sections' of society gain university places, only for the Committee of University Heads to reinstate them upon learning the number of Palestinians entering university had risen sharply as a result.[34]

As a result of this process, coupled with a lack of higher education in the Palestinian areas of Israel, the disparity between Palestinian and Jewish students in university attendance is striking. While Palestinian citizens constitute more than 20 per cent of the Israeli population, they form less than ten per cent of the student body,[35] and one per cent of academic staff.[36] According to Uri Yacobi Keller: "Palestinian applicants are three times as likely to be rejected by Israeli academic institutions than Jewish applicants."[37]

---

[30] http://en.wikipedia.org/wiki/Ilan_Papp per centC3 per centA9#Katz_controversy, [accessed 10th June 2011].
[31] *Ibid.*
[32] BRICUP (2007), *Why boycott Israeli universities? British committee for the universities of Palestine*. Available from BRICUP, www.bricup.org.uk.
[33] Cook, J (2010), Racist Universities?, *Counterpunch*, Available: http://www.jkcook.net/Articles3/0517.htm#Top. [accessed 22nd March 2011].
[34] Cook, J. (2008), Academic freedom? Not for Arabs in Israel, *Counterpunch. Idem.*
[35] Cook, J (2010), Racist universities?, *Counterpunch. Idem.*
[36] Yacobi Keller, U (2009), *The economy of the occupation: academic boycott of Israel*, Idem, p.16.
[37] *Ibid.* p.16.

Even the success of gaining a university place does little to stem the tide of discrimination, and the life of a Palestinian student is made particularly difficult by barriers to campus accommodation. Allocation of dormitories is largely based on military service, from which Palestinian Israelis are automatically disqualified.[38] In August 2006, Haifa District Court issued a judgement stating that using military service as a criterion to determine allocation of student housing at the University of Haifa is illegal and that it discriminates against Arab students.[39] Yet the practice still persists across the board at Israeli academic institutions.

Palestinians are also deterred by the way in which student funding is structured. Unlike Britain, there is no government-backed loan scheme to cover tuition fees. The majority of students rely on scholarships to get them through a degree programme. Virtually all scholarships and grants are based on service in the IDF and vary according to station. Being a combat soldier is particularly lucrative: funds are often double the standard scholarship.[40] These benefits for IDF soldiers have been enshrined in law by the Absorption of Former Soldiers Law of 1994, which was passed by the *Knesset* in 2001.[41]

International links

Israel benefits from its status as an honorary member of the European Union, giving it access to funds provided by the European Commission for scientific research. While mostly civilian, some of these projects could be manipulated for military use. Others are direct collaborations with defence manufacturers. For example, the **University of Reading** has partnered with **BAE Systems** and Israeli firm **Athena GS-3** in the 'Security of Aircraft in the Future European Environment' (SAFEE) project. Led by **Sagem Défense Sécurité** of France, the aim of SAFEE is to construct an advanced aircraft security system designed to operate during terrorist scenarios on board aircraft.[42] While appearing to be research to protect people from a perceived future threat, it is another element of the increased securitisation of everyday life in Europe and Israel and fuels the Israeli military-industrial complex.

The British connection

Over the past 10 years, successive British governments have pursued an active policy of scientific collaboration between UK and Israeli universities. This culminated in the 2008 British-Israel Research and Academic Exchange Partnership (BIRAX), launched by Gordon

---

[38] Arshad, S (2011), *The impoverishment of Palestinian Arabs in Israel*, Middle East Monitor Briefing Paper, Available: http://www.scribd.com/doc/52038309/The-impoverishment-of-Palestinian-Arabs-in-Israel, [accessed 26th May 2011].
[39] Alternative Information Centre (2011), *Haifa-Ottawa exchange: evidence of discrimination against Palestinian students*. Available: http://www.alternativenews.org/english/index.php/topics/economy-of-the-occupation/3365-haifa-ottawa-exchange-evidence-of-discrimination-against-palestinian-students, [accessed 26th May 2011].
[40] Authors personal correspondence with an Israeli student and ex-IDF soldier.
[41] http://www.old-adalah.org/eng/pressreleases/pr.php?file=20_09_10_1, [accessed September 2011].
[42] http://cordis.europa.eu/fetch?CALLER=FP6_PROJ&ACTION=D&DOC=25&CAT=PROJ&QUERY=012ed96749d3:7815:19dcb036&RCN=72832, [accessed 21st March 2011].

Overview of the Israeli Economy: Academia **84**

Brown and Ehud Olmert, the UK and Israeli prime ministers at the time. The $1.6 billion scheme to award scientific research grants is mainly funded by the **Pears Foundation**, which presents itself as a philanthropic body.[43] During his November 2010 visit to Israel, UK foreign secretary William Hague announced 10 joint research projects which had been selected to receive the next round of BIRAX funding. The projects, which aim to tackle energy and environmental problems, involve nine British universities, including **Oxford**, **Bath**, and **Imperial College London.**[44]

Edinburgh was one of 23 universities occupied by students in solidarity with Palestine in February 2009 (UK Indymedia 2009)

The collaboration extends beyond scientific ventures. The Department of the Study of Religions at London's **School of Oriental and African Studies** (SOAS) is currently preparing a joint conference with the Hebrew University. The event, entitled 'Jewish Art in its Roman-Byzantine Context', is scheduled to take place in Jerusalem in May 2012.[45] The presence of SOAS in an occupied city normalises the situation and lends support to an Israeli academic institution with part of its campus on land stolen from Palestinians in East Jerusalem.[46] A similar situation arose in 2009 when a lecture series was held in conjunction with Tel Aviv University to celebrate the centennial of the city of Tel Aviv in the midst of Israel's bombardment of Gaza.[47] The Student Union at SOAS voted overwhelmingly for a motion to pressure their university to cancel the series but protests fell on deaf ears. This

---

[43] Cronin, D (2011), Who Benefits from EU-Israel academic cooperation?, *Electronic intifada*. Available: http://electronicintifada.net/v2/article11851.shtml, [accessed 21st March 2011].
[44] http://ukinisrael.fco.gov.uk/en/news/ministerial-visits/fs-visit/scientific-research, [accessed 21st March 2011].
[45] http://corporateoccupation.wordpress.com/2011/05/06/british-universities-links-to-israel-part-one-soas/, [accessed 21st March 2011].
[46] http://boycottZionism.wordpress.com/category/normalization/, [accessed 21st March 2011].
[47] http://www.bdsmovement.net/2009/soas-palestine-society-report-tel-aviv-university-part-and-parcel-of-the-israeli-occupation-502, [accessed September 2011].

may be explained by the fact that SOAS stands to gain from a continued state of militarisation and apartheid, as it holds investments in companies profiting from the occupation.[48] (*For more details of British university investments in Israeli apartheid and militarism see part three of this book*).

Resistance

Moves towards an academic boycott intensified with a 2002 letter published in the Guardian, led by Stephen Rose. This was seconded by a group of several hundred European academics, all of whom called for a moratorium on EU funding grants to Israeli cultural and research institutions.[49] This policy, it was argued, should remain in force until Israel complies with UN resolutions and makes serious concessions in peace talks with the Palestinians. That same year, the UK Association of University Teachers (AUT) decided to embrace the moratorium and, three years later, passed a motion to boycott Haifa and Bar-Ilan Universities. However, in 2006, the AUT merged with another union, NATFHE, to form the University and College Union (UCU).

While the academic boycott has gained increasing support amongst lecturers and teachers, it is fraught with difficulty. When the UCU Congress voted in 2007 for a discussion among its branches regarding a boycott of all Israeli academic institutions, it ignited an intense debate that resulted in a swift retraction of the motion. The union cited "legal advice" stating that an academic boycott would be unlawful and infringe UK discrimination legislation.[50] Much of the criticism centred around the perceived targeting of Jews and attacks on the sanctity of academic freedom. The first accusation is an age-old ploy of Israel used to dismiss as anti-Semitic any criticism of its attack on Palestinians. The second is a farcical notion, considering the occupation's crushing of Palestinian academic freedom and the constraints on Palestinian students' freedom to attend university. This move by UCU, while unsuccessful, brought British action for an academic boycott firmly in line with calls from the Palestinian Academic Boycott Initiative (PACBI), which states:

> "We, Palestinian academics and intellectuals, call upon our colleagues in the international community to comprehensively and consistently boycott all Israeli academic and cultural institutions as a contribution to the struggle to end Israel's occupation, colonization and system of apartheid."

Recent UCU attempts to recognise the negative role of Israeli academic institutions have been watered down to the extent that they fail to adequately address the call issued by PACBI. During its annual congress meeting in May 2011, a motion was passed to instruct the UCU National Executive Committee to circulate information about the academic and cultural boycott calls to members, as well as send a delegation to the Israeli Ambassador to

---

[48]http://corporateoccupation.wordpress.com/2011/05/06/british-universities-links-to-israel-part-one-soas/, *Idem,* [accessed September 2011].
[49]BRICUP (2007), *Why boycott Israeli universities? Idem.*
[50]http://www.ucu.org.uk/index.cfm?articleid=2829, [accessed 26th May 2011].

"raise concerns".[51] The motion did not state a commitment to boycott Israeli academic institutions. With the centralised leadership at UCU shying away from strong support of an academic boycott, some branches have broken rank to support the Palestinian calls. Perhaps the most notable is the solidarity between the UCU and the Students Union at SOAS, which has passed a motion to "campaign for academic boycott of Israeli institutions."[52] Lecturers from SOAS UCU also publicly supported student attempts to force the university to cancel their aforementioned Tel Aviv lecture series.[53]

Similarly, boycott motions have been pursued by students at several higher education institutions in the UK. Following a 2009 referendum at Sussex University, the Students Union (SU) stopped stocking Israeli goods at its outlets, although non-SU cafes and shops were not covered by the ban. In 2011 the University of London Union (ULU), which covers institutions including UCL, Goldsmiths and LSE, voted to initiate university divestment from companies "implicated in violating Palestinian human rights" and to actively support the BDS movement.[54] The National Union of Students (NUS) has also begun to take tentative steps towards supporting the Palestinian fight for justice in the face of strong Zionist opposition. Following its May 2011 National Executive Committee meeting, the body representing students in the UK resolved to support the Palestinian right to education and demand an end to the occupation of the West Bank and blockade of Gaza.[55] While this is a significant development, the notion of an academic boycott was absent and a clause to boycott Israeli goods was overturned.

Where next?

While the boycott of Israeli academic institutions has generated an enormous amount of debate in the UK and across Europe, there is still much to be done to strengthen a large-scale academic boycott. Due to the dependency of Israeli universities on European and American academia, the impact of a wide-ranging academic boycott on Israel could be similar to that of the sporting boycott on South Africa during apartheid. One way to achieve this goal is to build strong partnerships with pro-Palestinian student groups at UK universities linked to Israeli institutions.

The roles and double standards of the European Union and British government need to be addressed. It is laughable that these institutions should support UN resolutions condemning West Bank settlements on the one hand, while supporting institutions that help provide the intellectual and technological tools to legitimise and entrench the occupation on the other. Because the scientific prestige of Israeli universities is both a great source of national pride

---

[51] http://www.bdsmovement.net/2011/ucu-congress-2011-7185, [accessed 26th May 2011].
[52] http://www.thejc.com/news/uk-news/soas-marks-israeli-apartheid per centE2 per cent80 per cent99, [accessed 26th May 2011].
[53] http://www.timeshighereducation.co.uk/story.asp?storyCode=405030&sectioncode=26, [accessed 26th May 2011].
[54] Personal correspondence with authors.
[55] Personal correspondence with authors.

and a generator of foreign direct investment and GDP, targeting EU funding for joint research projects is vitally important.

Students and staff should target their universities' investments in, and contracts with, companies profiting from Israeli apartheid, militarism and colonisation. One way to achieve this would be large-scale replication of the student occupations seen during Israel's 2009 siege of Gaza, when university lecture theatres from Sussex to Edinburgh were occupied in protest at connections between British academic institutions and companies that supply the Israeli war machine. This can be coupled, as it was at Sussex University, with demands that British universities do more to establish connections with their Palestinian counterparts to help forge strong links in the struggle against apartheid. Students could also push the NUS to adopt a stance against the discriminatory treatment of Palestinian students in Israeli universities.

13
Manufacturing

15.6 per cent of the Israeli workforce is engaged in manufacturing.[1] The main Israeli manufacturing industries are computer hardware and software, diamond cutting, medical technologies and pharmaceutical products.[2]

In contrast to these high-tech industries, the settlement manufacturing sector is predominantly low-tech and low-paid. Israeli economist Shlomo Swirski found that 83% of businesses in the Israeli industrial zones were low tech, a far higher figure than in 1948 Israel, which is dominated by high-tech manufacturing.[3] 17 settlement industrial zones in the West Bank[4] host some 220 Israeli companies.[5] The workforce in these industrial zones is predominantly Palestinian, who are paid less than, or at best equal to, the minimum wage and provide a captive workforce for Israeli companies.

In order to have a serious impact on the Israeli economy, the BDS movement needs to target the high-tech, diamond, pharmaceutical and defence sectors. However, the low-tech manufacturing sector has a greater direct impact on the Palestinians and Syrians living under Israeli occupation as they constitute the workforce in this sector and the manufacturing infrastructure is set up on their land.

The traditional Israeli approach to the Palestinian manufacturing industry has been to prevent the setting up of businesses in occupied Palestine that might compete with Israeli manufactured goods.[6] Since the death of Yasser Arafat and the co-option of Mahmoud Abbas' Palestinian Authority, Israel's strategy in the West Bank has been to cautiously encourage the setting up of 'joint enterprises' between Palestinian and Israeli businesses. Israeli corporations and the Israeli state act as gatekeepers, with a Palestinian elite as junior partners managing a captive, subjugated Palestinian workforce. This business model relies on the maintenance of the status quo, ie the occupation, for its continued profitability.

Textiles

The Israeli textile sector is an important source of exports. It is one of the manufacturing industries that has been targeted by the US-promoted Qualified Industrial Zone (QIZ) agreements. The US and Israel have attempted to undermine the Arab states' boycott of Israel by promoting joint manufacturing through allowing duty-free exports to the US of textiles cut in Israel and manufactured in Egypt, Turkey and Jordan. As a result more than 90 per

---

[1] OECD, *Economic survey of Israel 2009, Idem*, p.3.
[2] *Ibid.*
[3] Swirski, S (2008), *The burden of occupation*, p.32.
[4] *Ibid.*
[5] *Ibid.*
[6] *Ibid*, p.18.

cent of Israeli textile manufacturers sell their products using another company's brand.[7] The US is the largest export market for Israeli textiles, followed by the UK and Germany.[8]

Company profiles

Delta Galil (DG), established in 1975, is Israel's largest textile manufacturer.[9] DG, which makes underwear, socks, baby clothes, leisurewear and fabrics, sells its products to **Marks & Spencer, Target, Wal-Mart, Kmart**[10] and through the **Calvin Klein, Nike, Hugo Boss** and **Pierre Cardin** brands. DG also licenses several brands, including **Wilson, Maidenform, Nicole Miller, Barbie, Tommy Hilfiger, Tra La La** and others.[11] The company and its subsidiaries have shops in the settlements of Pisgat Ze'ev and Ma'ale Adumim and a warehouse in the Barkan settlement industrial zone.[12]

DG had $128.5 million in market capital in September 2011.[13] Its products are manufactured in Egypt, Jordan, Turkey and Mexico, taking advantage of the QIZ agreements, and also in Asia and Bulgaria. The company's marketing and logistics departments are based in the US, UK and Israel.[14]

DG has become heavily dependent on Wal-Mart and M&S for a large proportion of its revenues[15] and, as such, campaigns targeting the company's supply to these stores could have a significant impact.

Another Israeli textiles business active in the UK is **Teva Naot,** which trades under the name 'Naot'. The company, which is the 11th largest company in the Israeli textile industry, is a manufacturer of shoes and handbags. It has export revenues of $24.4 million.[16]

Teva Naot has a store in the Gush Etzion settlement industrial zone.[17] The company exports

---

[7] http://www.mfa.gov.il/mfa/mfaarchive/2000_2009/2001/7/facets%20of%20the%20israeli%20economy-%20textiles%20and%20appare, [accessed 26th May 2011].
[8] *Ibid.*
[9] http://www.bdicode.co.il/Rank_ENG/59_0_0/Textile,%20Footwear%20and%20Clothing%20-%20Industry, [accessed 26th May 2011].
[10] http://www.mfa.gov.il/mfa/mfaarchive/2000_2009/2001/7/facets%20of%20the%20israeli%20economy-%20textiles%20and%20appare and http://www.deltagalil.com/company-profile.aspx, [accessed 26th May 2011].
[11] http://www.deltagalil.com/company-profile.aspx, [accessed 26th May 2011].
[12] http://www.whoprofits.org/Company%20Info.php?id=996, [accessed September 2011].
[13] http://www.tase.co.il/TASEEng/General/Company/companyDetails.htm?ShareID=00627034&CompanyID=000627&subDataType=0, [accessed September 2011].
[14] http://www.bdicode.co.il/Rank_ENG/59_0_0/Textile,%20Footwear%20and%20Clothing%20-%20Industry, [accessed September 2011].
[15] http://www.textilesintelligence.com/tistoi/index.cfm?pageid=3&repid=TISTOI&issueid=141&artid=1503, [accessed September 2011].
[16] http://www.bdicode.co.il/Rank_ENG/59_0_0/Textile,%20Footwear%20and%20Clothing%20-%20Industry, [accessed September 2011].
[17] http://www.whoprofits.org/Company%20Info.php?id=568, [accessed September 2011].

to the US, Canada, Germany and the UK. It has a store in London, close to Golders Green.[18]

Cosmetics

Israel's cosmetics industry exports $165 million worth of products annually. $417 million worth of Israeli cosmetics and toiletries were sold in 2009. The main export market is Europe, which accounts for about 60% of total exports.[19] Exports to North America and Asia amount to 26% and 11% respectively.[20] Within this, Dead Sea products are particularly significant. Other major outputs include nappies, feminine hygiene products and shaving products.[21] There is also an increasing demand for Israeli 'natural' and organic products.[22] Many Israeli companies participate in the European Private Label Exhibition in Amsterdam and the COSMOPROF exhibitions in Italy and Asia.[23]

Company profiles

Ahava is the largest Dead Sea cosmetics company. The majority of Ahava's products come from their factory situated in the illegal West Bank settlement of Mitzpe Shalem. In 2004 Ahava was granted a permit to mine mud from the north shores of the Dead Sea in the occupied West Bank.[24]

Intercosma, established in 1949, produces cosmetics, toiletries and Dead Sea mineral products. It has premises in Ashdod and Tel Aviv. Until 2010, the company had premises in Atarot settlement industrial zone. In 2010 the Israeli NGO, *Gush Shalom*, reported that the company no longer worked in the occupied territories.[25]

Avgol, a manufacturer of nappies and tampons, has its main manufacturing plant in Barkan settlement industrial zone. Avgol is an international company with manufacturing facilities in the US, Russia and China.[26] Its main clients include **Procter and Gamble** (US) and **Covidien**.[27] In 2010, the company had revenues of $277.5 million and profits of $60 million.[28] The majority of its revenues came from the US (41%) and Europe (16%), with only 6% coming from the Israeli market.[29]

---

[18] *Ibid.*
[19] http://www.export.gov.il/Eng/_Uploads/600Cosmetics.pdf, [accessed September 2011].
[20] *Ibid.*
[21] http://www.export.gov.il/Eng/_Articles/Article.asp?CategoryID=482&ArticleID=600, [accessed September 2011].
[22] http://www.export.gov.il/Eng/_Uploads/600Cosmetics.pdf, [accessed September 2011].
[23] *Ibid.*
[24] http://twitwall.com/view/?what=0208080F0A50, [accessed September 2011].
[25] http://www.scoop.co.nz/stories/WO1004/S00565.htm, [accessed September 2011].
[26] http://www.avgol.com/upload/pdf/Avgol_acquires_Cleaver%20Associates_29Dec2010.pdf, [accessed September 2011].
[27] http://www.whoprofits.org/Company%20Info.php?id=456, [accessed September 2011].
[28] http://www.avgol.com/upload/pdf/Q1%20First%20Quarter%20Financial%20Results.pdf, [accessed September 2011].
[29] *Ibid*, p.7.

14
Israel's Settlement Industrial Zones

Industrial zones are at the forefront of Israel's occupation of Palestine. Most of Israel's industrial zones in the West Bank are connected to illegal residential settlements and provide an indispensable economic backbone to the local settler economy.

There are approximately 17 Israeli settlement industrial zones in the West Bank.[1] The exact number of active business areas is hard to establish as some are dormant and hold on to the label primarily in order to be able to control the land. The 4 Mishor Adumim, connected to Ma'ale Adumim residential settlement; Barkan and Ariel West, connected to the Ariel residential settlement; Atarot, close to Qalandia checkpoint; and the smaller, but notorious, Nitzanei Shalom (or 'Buds of Peace') industrial zone on the land of Tulkarem.

The smaller and less active settlement industrial areas are Karney Shomrom, Shahak, Bar-On, Ma'ale Efrayim, Binyamin, Maitarim, Alon Moreh, Halamish, Nili, Ptza'el, Kiryat Arba and Gush Etzion.[2] There is also one medium sized and one small industrial zone in the occupied Syrian Golan: Katzrin and Bnei Yehuda respectively.

Because of what they represent and help to achieve, settlement industrial parks in the occupied territories receive all sorts of subsidies and support from the Israeli government. Examples include low rent, special tax incentives and lax enforcement of environmental and labour protection laws.[3] This chapter will provide a brief overview of how these policies affect the Palestinians whose land has been stolen to make way for these zones, as well as highlighting avenues for action that can be taken against them.

Economic factors

According to the Israeli NGO *B'Tselem*, initial government investment in each industrial park stands at about NIS 20 million[4] and between 1997 and 2001, 22% of Israel's total investment in industrial parks went to areas on occupied land.[5] All industrial zones are classified by Israel as economic National Priority Area A[6] (not to be confused with the Area A designation in the Oslo accords). The purpose of the government assigning an area Area A status is so businesses can be offered tax deductions to set up there or to expand.[7] In other words, in the case of West Bank settlement industrial areas, it is a way of rewarding settler

---

[1] Swirski, S. (2008), *The burden of occupation*, Idem, p.32.
[2] Who Profits, Private correspondence with the authors, April 2011.
[3] Who Profits, *Soda Stream: A case study for corporate activity in illegal Israeli settlements*, Available: http://www.scribd.com/doc/49588306/Januar-2011-WhoProfits-Production-in-Settlements-SodaStream, [accessed 20/6/2011].
[4] Swirski, S. (2008), *The burden of occupation*, Idem, p.32.
[5] *Ibid*.
[6] Who Profits, *Soda Stream: A case study for corporate activity in illegal Israeli settlements*, Idem.
[7] *Ibid*.

businesses and facilitating settlement expansion. Inside 1948 Israel, A areas, while encouraged to develop industry, tend to be rural and sparsely populated. However, industrial zones connected to settlements often get the best of both worlds: beneficial economic conditions, close proximity to Israel's cities across the green line and access to cheap labour in nearby Palestinian population centres.[8] Swirski has used the example of Ariel industrial park to illustrate the perks offered to businesses willing to trade from settlement industrial zones. Companies in the park pay NIS 41 per square meter in municipal taxes, while businesses in Rosh Ha'Ain, only 10 minutes drive away, but within the Green Line, pay NIS 87.[9] More examples of the benefits enjoyed by traders from settlement industrial zones can be found on the Mishor Adumim industrial zone's homepage, which uses these benefits as a way of attracting new business.[10]

Research has shown that Israeli companies operating from the West Bank settlement industrial zones, primarily firms involved in construction and industry, are generally not particularly profitable despite these favourable conditions.[11] From this, one can conclude that the settlement industrial zones are fully dependant on state subsidies and the underpaid labour of the exploited Palestinian workforce. It also means that companies in these zones are perfect targets for BDS action.

Workers

Apart from those working in agriculture, most Palestinian settlement workers either work in one of the settlement industrial zones or a connected industry such as construction.[12] At the end of 2007, the Israeli high court ruled that Israeli labour laws should also be applied to Palestinians working for Israelis in settlements in the West Bank. Since then, settlement workers are theoretically entitled to the Israeli minimum wage, holiday pay, payslips and health cover.[13] Although this law is positive in that it is striving to achieve equality for Palestinian workers, it is also problematic, as *Kav LaOved* has pointed out, in that it is incompatible with international law, which states that occupiers are not allowed to enforce their system of law on occupied populations.[14]

During the last few years, workers' conditions in the industrial zones have slightly improved, especially in comparison with the lack of progress for agricultural workers *(see our earlier chapter on agriculture)* and attempts were made to induce employers to implement conditions consistent with the high court ruling. Unsurprisingly, there has been resistance to

---

[8] *Ibid.*
[9] Swirski, S. (2008), *The burden of occupation, Idem,* p.36.
[10] http://www.parkedom.co.il/Edomim/Templates/ShowPage.asp?DBID=1&LNGID=1&TMID=84&FID=317, [accessed September 2011].
[11] Swirski, S (2008), *The burden of occupation, Idem,* p.36.
[12] Alenat, S (2010), *Working for survival: labor conditions of Palestinians working in settlements*, Kav LaOved Available: http://www.kavlaoved.org.il/media-view_eng.asp?id=3048, [accessed 21/6/2011].
[13] *Kav LaOved* (2007), *Precedent setting ruling*, Available: http://www.kavlaoved.org.il/media-view_eng.asp?id=1123, [accessed 21/6/2011].
[14] Alenat, S (2010), *Working for survival, Idem.*

these changes and progress has been slow, with the majority of successes coming about as a result of court cases or media exposure of poor working conditions. *Kav LaOved* believes that a majority of factories in Barkan and Mishor Adumim now pay the minimum wage to their workers, but some still do not. The organisation has also observed many cases where employers try to bypass the high court's decision by claiming that they are subject to Jordanian, not Israeli, law, or that their employees pay matches PA salaries. They also blame Palestinian labour contractors for any breaches of labour law.[15] Another way that Israeli employers avoid paying their employees a living wage is by declaring the wrong amount of hours worked on the now obligatory payslips, making it look like they pay the legal amount when workers have, in fact, worked many more hours than stated.[16] Other aspects of the ruling, such as health and safety issues, holiday pay and healthcare are still largely ignored.

While conditions might be slightly improving for Palestinian workers in industrial zones, most still have to take court cases against their employers to gain their legal rights. This is a risky business for a workforce that is reliant on passing Israeli security clearances on a regular basis and many have been fired in the process. *Kav LaOved* and the Palestinian General Federation of Trade Unions have recently started to jointly manage a project to support the labour rights of Palestinians employed in settlements,[17] a positive step for a workforce that has traditionally lacked union representation.

Environmental issues

Industrial zones can have a devastating effect on Palestinian communities. Apart from the obvious issues arising from settlement takeover of land and resources the zones are also contributors to pollution in the areas where they operate.

Environmental laws and checks are much less rigidly enforced in the occupied territories than inside Israel.[18] As a result the industrial zones house a large number of industries that deal with toxic materials and harmful waste. The proximity of these factories to Palestinian villages and homes has a huge impact on the communities living in the vicinity. The environmental impact of the industrial zones on Palestinian communities is illustrated by the case of Nitzanei Shalom settlement industrial zone in Tulkarem.

Case study: Nitzanei Shalom settlement industrial zone

A horror story even when compared with other Israeli settlement industrial zones, Nitzanei Shalom employs just over 400 workers[19] in eight businesses. The oldest company in Nitzanei Shalom, **Geshuri Advanced Technologies,** established a chemical factory called **Keshet Prima** on a 22 dunam piece of land confiscated by the Israeli military from the Abu Sham'a

---

[15]*Ibid.*
[16]Swirski, S (2008), *The burden of occupation, Idem,* p.34.
[17]Alenat, S (2010), *Working for survival, Idem.*
[18]Who Profits, *Soda Stream: A case study for corporate activity in illegal Israeli settlements, Idem.*
[19]Information from a private meeting between the PGFTU and the authors in Tulkarem, Spring 2010.

family of Tulkarem in 1984.[20] Its move there was a result of a failure to get a licence to operate in the Israeli town of Tel Mond, due to environmental and health concerns.[21] After that, other factories with dubious environmental records and license problems in Israel have moved to the zone. According to the PGFTU **Solor** moved there after Israelis in Netanya took the company to court and forced it out.[22] In 2004, Israeli authorities confiscated more land from citizens of Tulkarem, and razed Palestinian agricultural land in order to build a large wall around the industrial zone, which is now also blocked in by the apartheid wall with all the factories on the Palestinian side.[23] To emphasise just how bad the situation is, the Geshuri factory operates around the clock, except on days when the wind blows west towards Israel. When that happens, work is deemed too damaging to carry out at all.[24] In the evenings the pollution is visible above Tulkarem and there is a constant smell of chemicals in the air.

The view of Nitzanei Shalom settlement industrial zone from the Palestinian town of Tulkarem (Corporate Watch 2010)

The working conditions in most of the factories operating in Nitzanei Shalom are appalling. During interviews workers gave numerous examples of cases where employees had been seriously injured or even died as a result of the hazardous environment.[25] The wider

---

[20] http://www.poica.org/editor/case_studies/view.php?recordID=1114, [accessed 22/6/2011].
[21] Applied Research Institute Jerusalem (2005), *Report on the Israeli colonization activities in the West Bank and the Gaza Strip*, Available: http://www.arij.org/publications(8)/Monitoring%20Report/81.pdf, [accessed 22/6/2011].
[22] PGFTU, Spring 2010, *Idem*.
[23] *Ibid.*
[24] *Ibid.*
[25] There are at least six documented fatalities. See http://www.kavlaoved.org.il/media-view_eng.asp?id=1789, [accessed 22/6/2011].

implications for Tulkarem have also been devastating. A reported 2.5 dunams of fertile farming land are now too polluted to farm as a result of their proximity to the industrial area.[26] The number of cases of cancer and respiratory problems in the city are twice as high as in the nearby city of Nablus.[27] It is claimed that there are increased incidents of skin disease, allergies and asthma close to the settlement industrial zone.[28]

Companies in Nitzanei Shalom settlement industrial zone

Geshuri and Sons Industries' factory in Nitzanei Shalom is called **Keshet Prima** and is privately owned by the Geshuri family. It produces chemicals for construction and additives for agriculture.[29]

Trucks transporting goods manufactured in Nitzanei Shalom settlement industrial zone into 1948 Israel, Tulkarem (Corporate Watch 2010)

The **Solor Group** is a private holding group that consists of **Solor Gas Industries, TreaTec21 Industries, Tezet Gaz** (Poland), **Solmoran, Dixxon Gas, Solopaz** and **Elevating**. Solor's production facility in Nitzanei Shalom is run by Solor Gas Industries and manufactures pressurised air tanks and petrol tanks. **Solmoran** also rents out business space

---

[26] For a full report of health implications of Nitzanei Shalom in Tulkarem see: Al-Khalil and Qasem, *The impact of Israeli industrial zone on environmental and human health in Tulkarm City,* Available: http://bit.ly/mvxg5c, [accessed 22/6/2011].
[27] Private meeting between the authors and the Palestinian Ministry of Health, Spring 2010.
[28] Al-Khalil and Qasem, *The impact of Israeli industrial zone on environmental and human health in Tulkarm City,* Available: http://bit.ly/mvxg5c, [accessed 22/6/2011].
[29] http://www.whoprofits.org/Company%20Info.php?id=765, [accessed 22/6/2011].

in the industrial zone.[30]

Yamit is a company involved in the development and production of water treatment and filtration solutions for both private and agricultural use. The company has subsidiaries in China, Holland and Germany,[31] with further customer sites and installations around the world.[32]

Tal El is a collection, waste removal and recycling company for cardboard, paper and plastic. It is privately owned and has one sister company, **Nitzanei Shalom Paper Industries**.[33]

Lotar is another privately owned company in the textiles industry. It provides knitting services and manufactures knitted cloths.[34] Other companies operating in Nitzanei Shalom settlement industrial zone include **Atzei Shitim**, a privately owned recycled wood company;[35] **Shai Key Metal Trade**, a scrap metal company and **Tagwiri Plastic**.[36]

Industrial zone profiles

There are around 1,400 Israeli companies registered as operating from the West Bank,[37] and a majority of these are located in settlement industrial zones. It is therefore not possible to cover each and every one. These profiles are simply designed to highlight those which might be successfully targeted by BDS campaigners.

Mishor Adumim is one of the largest settlement industrial zones and is located just outside the boundaries of Jerusalem. It covers 1,550 dunams[38] and is connected to the Ma'ale Adumim settlement block, the third largest and quickest growing settlement block in the West Bank, which had a population of 39,000 in 2011.[39] Both the industrial zone and residential areas are part of Israel's controversial East 1 (E1) project.[40] Initiated by Yitzhak Rabin in 1995, the project aims to cut the West Bank off from East Jerusalem through strategic settlement expansion, hence destroying any possibility of a viable Palestinian state. Ma'ale Adumim's mayor, Benny Kashriel, has been very open about the industrial zone's role in colonising Palestinian land, saying that his "dream is to build Adumim all the way to

---

[30] http://www.whoprofits.org/Company%20Info.php?id=774, [accessed 22/6/2011].
[31] http://www.whoprofits.org/Company%20Info.php?id=778, [accessed 22/6/2011].
[32] http://www.yamit-f.com/Contacts.asp, [accessed 22/6/2011].
[33] http://www.whoprofits.org/Company%20Info.php?id=776, [accessed 22/6/2011].
[34] http://www.whoprofits.org/Company%20Info.php?id=779, [accessed 22/6/2011].
[35] http://www.whoprofits.org/Company%20Info.php?id=780, [accessed 22/6/2011].
[36] http://www.whoprofits.org/Company%20Info.php?id=777, [accessed 22/6/2011].
[37] Swirski, S (2008), *The burden of occupation*, Idem, p.32.
[38] http://www.parkedom.co.il/Edomim/Templates/ShowPage.asp?/DBID=1&LNGID=1&TMID=84&FID=267, [accessed 22/6/2011].
[39] http://en.wikipedia.org/wiki/Ma'ale_Adumim, [accessed 22/6/2011].
[40] http://www.timesonline.co.uk/tol/news/world/middle_east/article6031894.ece, [accessed 22/6/2011].

Jerusalem [...] to be a legal part of the land of Israel, but to be economically independent of Jerusalem. That will be accomplished thanks to Mishor Adumim".[41]

The industrial park is managed by **The Ma'ale Adumim Economic Development Company Ltd** which is working closely with the Israeli Lands Administration to encourage expanded settlement industry in the area. The **Ma'ale Adumim Planning and Development Company Ltd**, its subsidiary, also controls a landfill established on the land of Abu Dis. The 430 dunam site receives the waste from Ma'ale Adumim, Jerusalem and surrounding areas.[42]

The settlement was built on land stolen from the Palestinian villages of Abu Dis, Al Izriyyeh, Al Issawiyyeh, Al Tur and Anata[43] and has driven the Jahalin Bedouin off their land.

Mishor Adumim and the Jahalin

The Palestinian Jahalin tribe was ethnically cleansed from the Naqab (Negev) area during the *Nakba*[44] and part of the tribe has lived in the area surrounding the Jerusalem-Jericho highway since the late 1950s. They have been constant victims of Israel's expansionist settlement plans and since the approval of Ma'ale Adumim in 1976 their life in the area has become a constant struggle, with Israel trying to force them on to smaller and smaller pieces of land near Palestinian towns, primarily Abu Dis.[45] After the Oslo accords, Jahalin land was designated as area C and attempts at expulsion were intensified by the Israeli authorities. Numerous forced evictions of Jahalin Bedouin were carried out by the Israeli military throughout the 1990s, with houses being bulldozed repeatedly and hundreds of families made homeless. In 1998, around 35 families were forced against their will to strike a deal with the Israeli Civil Administration and lease some 'Israeli state land', meaning land stolen by Israel from other Palestinian communities, for them to live on.[46] This land is located next to the Municipal Jerusalem rubbish dump. Since then the situation for the rest of the Jahalin has become even more precarious because of the construction of the apartheid wall. Around five families are still living along the road next to Mishor Adumim, and many others are still in 'unrecognised areas', living without water close to Ma'ale Adumim.[47] Several members of the Jahalin community are now working in Mishor Adumim, the construction of which was the reason for their removal from their land.[48]

---

[41] www.jr.co.il/ma/manews03.htm, [accessed 22/6/2011].
[42] http://www.parkedom.co.il, [accessed 22/6/2011].
[43] http://mondediplo.com/1999/11/08israel, [accessed 22/6/2011].
[44] Hunaiti, H (2008), *Arab Jahalin: from the Nakba to the wall, Idem*, p.16
[45] *Ibid*, p.42.
[46] Human Rights Watch (2010), *Separate and unequal: Israel's discriminatory treatment of Palestinians in the occupied Palestinian territories*, Available: http://www.hrw.org/sites/default/files/reports/iopt1210webwcover_0.pdf, [accessed September 2011], p.121.
[47] Hunaiti, H (2008), *Arab Jahalin from the Nakba to the wall, Idem*, p.53.
[48] Based on interviews by Tom Anderson and Therezia Cooper with members of the Jahalin community, April 2010.

Overview of the Israeli Economy: Israel's Settlement Industrial Zones **98**

The hilltop in Abu Dis, next to Jerusalem municipal rubbish dump, that the Jahalin were forced to move to after the construction of Mishor Adumim (Corporate Watch 2010)

Boys from the Jahalin community scavenging amongst the rubbish in Jerusalem municipal rubbish dump (Corporate Watch 2010)

Mishor Adumim company profiles

Like most West Bank settlement industrial zones, Mishor Adumim houses a large number of industries that deal with toxic materials and harmful waste. A majority of the over 170 businesses in the zone work with plastic, cement, leather tanning, detergents, textile dying, aluminium and electro-plating.[49]

---

[49]http://corporateoccupation.wordpress.com/2009/12/02/occupation-industries-the-israeli-industrial-zones/, [accessed 17/8/2011].

Soda Stream is a manufacturer of home carbonation systems and drinks makers. The company is registered in the Netherlands and Israel, has subsidiaries around the world and trades in 39 countries. It operates under the trademarks **Soda Stream, Soda Club, AlcoJet, Sprudelino, Aquabar, Gazoz, Aquafizz, Aquabubbler, Penguin, Sodamaker, Fountain Jet** and **Edition1**,[50] with Soda Club being the most well known. **Soda Stream Industries** is registered in Israel and is responsible for the plant in Mishor Adumim and a plant in Ashkelon, which produces Soda Club flavourings.[51]

According to Who Profits, the facility in Mishor Adumim includes a metal factory, a plastic and bottle-blowing factory, a machining factory, an assembly factory, a cylinder manufacturing facility, a CO2 refill line and a cylinder retest facility,[52] as well as offices and warehouses.

Soda Club has, in the past, been heavily criticised for the poor pay, working conditions and job security for the workers in their factory. In 2009, after international recognition of this, the company seemed to have bowed under the pressure and started to adhere to Israeli labour laws. The workers' rights organisation *Kav LaOved* even published a statement praising Soda Club's "readiness to comply with the Israeli labor law", saying that it was now an exception to the rule amongst settlement businesses employing Palestinians.[53] *Kav LaOved* also pointed out that this improvement would never have happened without the pressure placed on Soda Club by the international media, especially in Sweden.[54] However, in 2010 the company seemed to have returned to its old ways when they dismissed 140 Palestinians working for it through the subcontractor, **Pearl Sol**.[55] Although the company eventually rehired the workers, following pressure from *Kav LaOved*, it did not rehire those workers who had been involved with workplace organising. *Kav LaOved* now has problems obtaining any further information about working conditions inside the plant as workers are afraid of being singled out.[56]

Since 2010, Soda Stream has been publicly traded on the NASDAQ. 31.7 per cent of Soda Stream's shares are held by the private equity fund **Fortissimo** and a further 18.7 per cent is held by the Liberian company **Real Property Investment**, whose shares are, in turn, held in the tax haven of Gibraltar by British businessman Conrad Morris.[57]

Soda Stream products are widely available in the UK. Chain stores which stock Soda Stream products include **John Lewis**, **Comet**, **Argos**, **Lakeland**, some **Asda** stores and

---

[50] Who Profits, *Soda Stream: A case study for corporate activity in illegal Israeli settlements*, Idem, p.9.
[51] *Ibid*, p 14.
[52] *Ibid*, p 16.
[53] http://www.kavlaoved.org.il/media-view_eng.asp?id=2262, [accessed 22/8/2011].
[54] *Ibid*.
[55] *Ibid*.
[56] Who Profits, *Soda Stream: A case study for corporate activity in illegal Israeli settlements*, Idem, p.20.
[57] *Ibid*, p.13.

Sainsbury's, **Harvey Nichols**, **Stamer Trading**, **Robert Dyas**, **Homebase**, **Best Buy**, **The Range** and selected **Maplin** stores.[58]

Extal, another company in Mishor Adumim, is a privately owned company involved with aluminium manufacturing and the development of systems for aluminium production. Its products are used in the construction, manufacturing and agriculture industries.

Approximately 45% of its output is designated for export[59] and the company has subsidiaries in the US (**Extal USA**), Romania (**Tensai Tec**) and Switzerland (**Tensai International**),[60] as well as sales representatives in the UK and Canada.[61] With over 200 employees and office and factory facilities covering 85,000 square metres,[62] Extal is one of the biggest companies in Mishor Adumim.

Mayer's Cars and Trucks is the official representative and distributor for the **Volvo Group** in Israel. They own 50% of Mayer Davidov Garages,[63] a Volvo branded facility located in Mishor Adumim. (*For more information about Volvo, see our chapter on construction equipment*).

There are official signs visible for many other car brands throughout the industrial zone, including **DAF**, **Isuzu**, **Chevrolet** and **Opel**. There is also a **Tzarfati Car Services**[64] garage in Mishor Adumim which is certified by **Nissan** (part of Volvo) and **Renault**. It is often uncertain exactly what the relationship is between international companies and their dealerships and repair centres, but the presence of these international brands in the industrial zone allows settler businesses to profit from the associated brand recognition.

BDS case study: resistance against Soda Club

Since it came to the attention of activists that Soda Stream trades from an illegal settlement industrial zone, campaigns have been mounted against it in various countries. Particular success has come in Sweden, where an estimated one out of every five households owns a Soda Stream machine.[65] After much publicised pressure from the Christian development organisation Diakonia in 2008, **Empire,** the company which oversees the distribution of Soda Club components in Sweden, was forced to request that products made by the company for the Swedish market be manufactured outside of any illegal settlement zone. Soda Club reluctantly agreed. However, it is uncertain how this has been enforced. Requests for information about the location of the new manufacturing sites have so far gone unanswered

---

[58] http://www.sodastream.co.uk/gbretail/default.aspx, [accessed 17/8/2011].
[59] www.extal.com, [accessed 19/8/2011].
[60] http://www.whoprofits.org/Company%20Info.php?id=465, [accessed 19/8/2011].
[61] http://www.extal.com/about-us, [accessed 19/8/2011].
[62] *Ibid.*
[63] http://www.whoprofits.org/Company%20Info.php?id=798, [accessed 19/8/2011].
[64] http://www.whoprofits.org/Company%20Info.php?id=538, [accessed 29/8/2011].
[65] Who Profits, *Soda Stream: A case study for corporate activity in illegal Israeli settlements, Idem*, p.12.

by both Empire's representatives and Diakonia.⁶⁶ As has been proven on numerous occasions, the origin of settlement goods is almost always obscured in the labelling process. In July 2011 the **Swedish Coop** decided to stop selling any Soda Stream products through its stores as they were not provided with any verifiable evidence that production had been moved.⁶⁷

Soda Club's factory in Mishor Adumim settlement industrial zone (Corporate Watch 2010)

In an important ruling in 2010, Advocate General Yves Bot, a senior adviser to the European Court of Justice in Luxembourg, gave the opinion that **Brita**, a German company importing products from Soda Club, should repay the money it had saved by illegitimately importing its stock under the preferential trade agreement that exists between Israel and the EU.⁶⁸ This ruling has been very helpful for the movement against settlement products and the mislabelling of West Bank produce. It has also made it harder to make settlement businesses profitable.

Recent news suggests that Soda Stream is responding to the resistance against its illegal presence in Mishor Adumim. The company opened a new production facility in the Galilee town of Alon Tavor in June 2011 and is building an 850,000 square-foot factory in the Idan

---

⁶⁶http://corporateoccupation.wordpress.com/2009/12/02/occupation-industries-the-israeli-industrial-zones/, [accessed 29/8/2011].
⁶⁷BDS Movement, *Coop Sweden stops all purchases of Soda Stream carbonation devices*, Available: http://www.bdsmovement.net/2011/coop-sweden-stops-all-purchases-of-soda-stream-carbonation-devices-7651, [accessed 29/8/2011].
⁶⁸UPI (2010), *EU court: West Bank, Gaza not Israeli*, Available: http://www.upi.com/Top_News/Special/2010/02/26/EU-court-West-Bank-Gaza-not-Israeli/UPI-95981267206295/, [accessed 29/8/2011].

Hanegev Industrial Park in the Naqab, which is due to open in 2013.[69] It is likely that the manufacturing of products for the Swedish market is being transferred to the Galilee.

Although this might seem like a victory, it is important for the BDS movement not to get complacent. As we have seen from *Kav LaOved's* reports, Soda Stream is quick to go back to its exploitative labour practices when it thinks that the world has stopped looking. The new Soda Stream factories inside 1948 Israel should be considered a wake-up call for activists rather than a success. The company's new plants are to be located in areas where there is a large Palestinian population. Industrial development is likely to be used as a way of taking control of more land and water resources, much like the settlement industrial zones are. If anything, activists should see this as an opportunity to talk about the importance of pushing for a boycott of *all* Israeli produce.

Other companies in Mishor Adumim settlement industrial zone[70]

Company	Product/Service
Adir Plastic Packaging	plastic bags (supplier to **Tesco**)
Adumim Food Additives	food additives
Aluminum Construction CL Israel	aluminium
Amisragas	gas supplier
Arza Wine Cellars T.R	wine
Bar Ami	kitchen and bathroom tiles
Better and Different	food products
BRB Industries, BarBur Laundry	textile treatment services (supplier to the IDF)
Contact International (Kalia Israel Ammunition Co)	military equipment (exclusive Israeli distributor for US company **Taser International**)
Golden Ryd Dyl	paper and cleaning products
H. Wagshal (H. Vagshal)	publisher and bookbinder
Ha'alornim Marble	stone, porcelain and ceramics
Hacormim Vineyard	wine
Irit Printing Inc	stickers and paper products[71]
Maxima Air Separation Center	gases
Maya Foods, the Jerusalem Spice of Life	food products
Menachem Wagshal	food products
Rami Levi, Hashikma Marketing	chain of grocery and clothing shops
Shufersal	supermarket
Tzarfati Metals Industries	metal
Zakai Agricultural Know-How and Inputs	agricultural technology and plant equipment

---

[69] http://www.globes.co.il/serveen/globes/docview.asp?did=1000661143&fid=1725, [accessed 29/8/2011].
[70] All info from www.whoprofits.org [accessed March 2011] except where otherwise stated.
[71] Observed during Corporate Watch visit to Mishor Adumim, April 2010.

Atarot industrial zone

The Atarot industrial park is located in occupied East Jerusalem and is the biggest industrial zone within the Jerusalem Municipality. It is situated on the Jerusalem side of the apartheid wall but close to Qalandia, the huge checkpoint which controls all movement between Ramallah and Jerusalem, and the Qalandia refugee camp. It is only accessible to Palestinians from the West Bank if they have a special permit. The zone hosts around 160 businesses, is protected by an entrance checkpoint and has a police station on site. The area has been designated 'priority area A' status by the Israeli authorities,[72] hence enjoying the same tax breaks and benefits as settlement industries on the other side of the wall.

The view from Atarot settlement industrial zone to the apartheid wall
(Corporate Watch 2010)

Atarot is a settlement entity run by Israel but, unlike in most other industrial zones, there are some Palestinian businesses operating in the area. **The Peres Centre for Peace** has published initial plans to convert the Atarot industrial area into a Joint Israeli-Palestinian economic zone[73] or, in other words, create another harmful normalisation project on occupied land. There are indications that the PA might be supportive of this idea. In 2010, after openly implementing a boycott on all settlement produce, it nonsensically excluded products from Atarot with the excuse that wealthy Palestinians do business there. Abdul Hafiz Nofal, from the the PA's Ministry of National Economy, went as far as stating that Atarot is not considered a settlement by the PA as the estimated Palestinian investment there exceeds $500 million.[74]

Atarot area has an airport, which was established during the British mandate but has not been

---

[72]http://www.biojerusalem.org.il/database_tpi.asp?ID=5, [accessed 23/8/2011].
[73]Houk, M (2008), Atarot and the fate of the Jerusalem Airport, *Jerusalem Quarterly*. http://www.jerusalemquarterly.org/ViewArticle.aspx?id=20, [accessed 23/8/2011].
[74]Ma'an News Agency *PA ministry defends settlement permits*, 29/10/2010, [accessed 23/8/2011].

operating since the outbreak of the Second Palestinian *intifada* in 2000.[75] The IDF took over the use of the airport after an agreement with the Israeli Airports Authority in 2001.[76]

Atarot company profiles

The businesses operating from Atarot are diverse and include factories working with aluminium, cement, food products, plastics and many other industries.

Pillsbury, owned by the American food giant **General Mills**, manufactures frozen dough products through its **Shalgal** factory in Atarot. According to Who Profits, General Mills exports kosher products internationally from its facilities in Atarot.[77] Some brands marketed by General Mills include **Green Giant, Old El Paso, Cheerios, Betty Crocker, Yoplait, Nature Valley, Fiber One** and, outside the US, **Häagen-Dazs**, as well as brands local to specific country markets.[78] General Mills operates in over 100 countries and could make a wide-reaching BDS target. **General Mills UK** is located in Uxbridge, Middlesex.

Auto Chen is one of the leading Israeli car specialists. It distributes, markets, sells and services vehicles across Israel. Its website proudly states that between 1969 and 2003 it was instrumental to the process of establishing the **Mercedes Benz** brand in Israel. Auto Chen run a branded service centre dedicated to Mercedes Benz cars in Atarot. It was built "under the direction of **Daimler-Benz**".[79]

Fermentek Ltd is a manufacturer whose products are used in biological research. The company sells its products to chemical companies which are then resold under a variety of brand names. According to Fermentek's website its main trading partners are medical researchers and pharmaceutical manufacturers.[80]
Shapir Civil and Marine Engineering has an office in Atarot *(See our chapter on construction for more on this company)*. **Superbus**, a company which provides bus services to settlers, also has a garage in Atarot.

Temsa Global is a Turkish manufacturer of buses, trucks and construction machinery that operates a factory in Atarot.[81] The company has an office in the UK and locations across Europe.[82]

---

[75] http://www.jerusalemquarterly.org/ViewArticle.aspx?id=20, [accessed 23/8/2011].
[76] Blumenkrantz, Z, *Jerusalem's Atarot Airport handed over to the IDF*, Available: http://www.kokhavivpublications.com/2001/israel/jul/27/0107272234s.html, [accessed 23/8/2011].
[77] http://www.whoprofits.org/Company%20Info.php?id=669 and http://www.whoprofits.org/Company%20Info.php?id=668, [accessed 23/8/2011].
[78] http://www.generalmills.com/company, [accessed 23/8/2011].
[79] http://www.auto-chen.co.il/about.asp, [accessed 23/8/2011].
[80] Corporate watch photographed the Fermentek factory during a visit to Atarot in April 2010. Fermentek's website is www.fermentek.co.il.
[81] Corporate watch photographed the Temsa Global factory during a visit to Atarot in April 2010. Temsa Global's website is www.temsaglobal.com
[82] http://www.temsaglobal.com/eng/dunyada_temsa_global.aspx, [accessed September 2011].

Bio-Lab Ltd is a manufacturer and distributor of selected high-purity solvents and chemicals for research, laboratories and industries. It exports worldwide, mainly through its Dutch subsidiary, **Bio-solve**. According to its website, the company has recently opened a new facility in Haifa in response to growing demand from Europe and America.

Auto Chen's Mercedes Benz Service Centre in Atarot settlement Industrial zone. The centre was set up up "under the direction of Daimler Benz." (Corporate Watch 2010)

Other companies operating in Atarot settlement industrial zone[83]

Manufacturer	Product/Service
Abadi Bakery	bagels
Bar Man Food Industries[84]	seasoning, spices, coffee and related products
Beton Atarot	cement
Clima Israel Aluminum	windows and sound insulation
Eliyahu Abergil Ltd[85]	construction materials
Em Hachita Ltd[86]	food products

---

[83] Information from www.whoprofits.org unless otherwise specified [accessed 23/8/2011].
[84] Corporate Watch photographed the Bar Man Food Industries factory during a visit to Atarot in April 2010. The company's website is http://www2all.co.il/web/sites4/barman/page20.asp.
[85] Observed during Corporate Watch visit to Atarot, April 2010.
[86] *Ibid.*

Manufacturer	Product/Service
Hanson Israel	concrete
Ofer L Aluminium[87]	aluminium products
Oppenheimer Manufacturing and Marketing	chocolate products (including for export)

Barkan and Ariel West settlement Industrial Parks

The Barkan settlement industrial zone was established in 1982[88] and is connected to the residential settlement of Barkan, which is part of the Ariel settlement block. The Ariel West settlement industrial park was established in 1999.[89] In 2008 the Israeli government approved plans for a further 27 factory units in the Ariel Industrial Park, which will lead to the tripling of its size.[90] Figures regarding the amount of workers in the industrial zones and surrounding settlements vary between 3,000 and 6,000,[91] with roughly 50% estimated to be Palestinians. Most Israeli workers are settlers from Ariel and work in administrative or managerial positions. According to people Corporate Watch interviewed in the area, the Palestinian workers come mainly from villages near Salfit but there are also workers from Ramallah, Qalqilya and Nablus.[92]

The Ariel settlement block was built on land stolen from the city of Salfit, and the Haris, Marda, Iskaka, Qarawert Bani Hasan, Bruqin and Sarta villages in the Salfit area,[93] with land belonging to Haris, Bruqin and Sarta being used for the industrial zones. In Haris for example, 1,417 dunams of land were confiscated for the Barkan industrial zone and a further 1,110 dunams for Ariel West.[94]

Approximately 75% of Salfit's land was designated as area C under the Oslo accords and Palestinians in the area suffer frequent house demolitions as a result of aggressive settlement expansion.[95] Since Ariel is one of the settlements Israel would be least likely to want to give up, Greater Salfit is also in the path of the apartheid wall. The completion of the Ariel and Kedumim 'fingers' (which aim to connect the settlements to Israel by putting them on the western side of the wall, despite the fact they lie over 20 kilometres inside the West Bank)

---

[87] Ibid.
[88] http://www.kavlaoved.org.il/media-view_eng.asp?id=2326, [accessed 23/8/2011].
[89] Ma'an Development Center (2008), *Salfit: from agricultural heaven to industrial ghetto*. Available: http://www.maan-ctr.org/pdfs/Salfeeteb.pdf, [accessed 23/8/2011], p.27.
[90] Ibid.
[91] See for instance http://www.kavlaoved.org.il/media-view_eng.asp?id=2326, [accessed 23/8/2011], and Ma'an Development Center (2008), *Salfit: from agricultural heaven to industrial ghetto*, Idem, p.26.
[92] Personal interviews conducted by Tom Anderson and Therezia Cooper in Deir Istya, April 2010.
[93] POICA (2008), *New Palestinian houses threatened of demolition by the Israeli occupation authorities*, Available: http://www.poica.org/editor/case_studies/view.php?recordID=1677, [accessed 23/8/2011].
[94] Ibid.
[95] Ma'an Development Center (2008), *Salfit: from agricultural heaven to industrial ghetto*, Idem, p.15.

has already split the Salfit Governate into several enclaves isolated from each other,[96] with devastating consequences for Palestinians and their capacity to make a living.

The Salfit area was historically famous for its rich agricultural production and ample water resources, but since the establishment of the settlements the character of the land has changed drastically. 16 artesian wells have been confiscated by Israel since 1967,[97] leaving most of the Palestinians without enough water to consume, let alone to farm.

Not only have the settlements deprived Salfit of their natural water resources, there have also been recurring problems caused by untreated waste water from Ariel and the industrial zones being dumped on Palestinian land. The Al Matwi Valley, next to Barkan, has a river of sewage and industrially contaminated water flowing through it, which has contaminated agricultural land and wells still in use by Palestinians.[98] Al Matwi spring supplies over 30 per cent of the water for Salfit city and the local villages.[99] Furthermore, solid industrial waste is dumped in the valley close to Marda village.[100]

Extension of Ariel West settlement industrial zone under construction
(Corporate Watch 2010)

Just as in Tulkarem, all evidence suggests that the industrial zones have a detrimental effect on people's health in the area. According to the Palestinian Ministry of Health's statistics, 70

---

[96]*Ibid*, p.11.
[97]Alternative Information Center (2007), *Salfit: When occupation is just a business*, http://www.alternativenews.org/english/index.php/topics/news/977-salfit-when-the-occupation-is-just-a-business, [accessed 23/8/2011].
[98]*Ibid*.
[99]Ma'an Development Center (2008), *Salfit: from agricultural heaven to industrial ghetto, Idem,* p.22.
[100]*Ibid*, p.22.

per cent of people with cancer in Salfit live in the areas close to the industrial zones and rivers of sewage from Ariel.[101] Skin diseases and hepatitis A and B are also common, most likely as a result of the mosquito build up around the factory waste dumping grounds.[102]

Barkan and Ariel West: company profiles

Many harmful and polluting industries are located in Barkan and Ariel, with many factories involved in oil, plastic and lead production.[103]

Mul-T-Lock is a lock manufacturer, 80% owned by Swedish company **Assa Abloy**. The Mul-T-Lock facility in Barkan, which makes locks and cylinders for security doors,[104] opened in 1985 and is the company's biggest plant.[105]

At the end of 2008, after a Swedish campaign against Assa Abloy's involvement in an illegal settlement and the publication of a report condemning it,[106] the company announced that it would move the Mul-T-Lock factory out of occupied Palestinian territory.[107] In an announcement, the company acknowledged the inappropriateness of trading from a settlement in the West Bank.[108] However, it also said that this could not be done at once. At the time of writing, Mul-T-Lock is still trading from Barkan.[109] Both Mul-T-Lock and Assa Abloy have offices in the West Midlands.

Beigel&Beigel is a bakery business fully owned by the multinational corporation **Unilever**.[110] The company made the headlines when Unilever announced in 2008 that it would seek to sell its share in the company (which was then 51%) amid growing opposition to settlement produce around the world.[111] After two years of trying to rid itself of the company without success, Unilever decided to buy the rest of the shares instead, allegedly to move the facility out of the West Bank.[112] At the time of writing Beigel&Beigel is still

---

[101] *Ibid.*
[102] *Ibid.*
[103] Ma'an Development Center (2008), *Salfit: from agricultural heaven to industrial ghetto*, Idem, p.27.
[104] http://whoprofits.org/Company%20Info.php?id=489, [accessed 23/8/2011].
[105] http://www.mul-t-lock.co.uk/about_history.aspx, [accessed 23/8/2011].
[106] Diakonia, *Report on Swedish company Assa Abloy's factory in illegal settlement,* Available: http://www.diakonia.se/sa/node.asp?node=2718, [accessed 23/8/2011].
[107] Barghouti, O (2008), Boycotting Israeli settlement products: tactic vs. strategy, *Electronic Intifada*, Available: http://electronicintifada.net/content/boycotting-israeli-settlement-products-tactic-vs-strategy/7801, [accessed 23/8/2011].
[108] http://bestinvest.uk-wire.com/Article.aspx?id=20081020210400H1322, [accessed 23/8/2011].
[109] As confirmed by Who Profits in private correspondence with the authors, 24/8/2011.
[110] http://whoprofits.org/Company%20Info.php?id=579, [accessed 23/8/2011].
[111] O'Loughlin, T (2008), Unilever to sell stake in plant based in West Bank settlement, *The Guardian*, Available: http://www.guardian.co.uk/world/2008/dec/01/israel-palestine-unilever, [accessed 23/8/2011].
[112] Sheizaf, N (2011), Citing anti-settlement pressure Multilock to close W Bank factory, *972 Magazine,* Available: http://972mag.com/major-success-for-the-anti-settlements-campaign-multilock-to-close-west-bank-factory/, [accessed 23/8/2011].

trading from Barkan. Unilever is traded on the New York Stock Exchange and has offices in London.

Beigel&Beigel factory in Barkan settlement industrial zone.
Beigel&Beigel is owned by Unilever (Corporate Watch 2010)

Keter Plastic is a plastics company specialising in the manufacture of garden furniture, household storage and garden products. **Lipski Plastic Industries** is a subsidiary of Keter and also has a factory in Barkan.[113] Keter has 29 other plants in Europe and the United States, and its products are sold in over 90 countries worldwide.[114] It has an office in Birmingham. The company's products are widely available in the UK through major retailers such as **Tesco**, **B&Q**, **Homebase**, **Argos**, **Costco**, **Toys R Us**, **Debenhams** and **Makro**.

EFD Home Design Group is an Israeli company specialising in furniture and home design. The company is a joint venture between **Fishman Retail** and **Eitani Group**. It manages many of the leading brands in the Israeli market, including **Betili, IDdesign, Rich & Taylor, Leather Land, MyHomePage** and more.[115]

Idan Camping imports and markets camping products. The company is the sole representative of international brands such as **Igloo** (USA), **Salewa** (Germany) and **Lorpen** (Spain).[116]

Greenkote is a private company which produces metal, alloy and plastic coatings for use by the construction, military and automotive industries. It has locations in the UK, Germany,

---

[113]http://www.whoprofits.org/Company%20Info.php?id=679, [accessed 23/8/2011].
[114]http://www.keter.com/categories/about-keter/, [accessed 23/8/2011].
[115]http://www.efdgroup.co.il, [accessed September 2011].
[116]http://www.whoprofits.org/Company%20Info.php?id=487, [accessed September 2011].

France, USA, Mexico, Brazil, India and China,[117] as well as in Barkan. In the UK, it is based in Esher, Surrey. **Tension Control Bolts** in Whitchurch, Shropshire, is also a licensed supplier of Greenkote products.

Rolbit is a producer of electronic controllers and thermostats. The company exports to Europe, Canada and the US. According to Who Profits, Rolbit works with **Medal Aircon Distribution** in the UK.[118]

Working in Barkan Industrial zone

As in all industrial zones in the West Bank, the situation for the workers in Barkan is harsh. Although, after outside pressure, conditions are slowly getting better, there is no shortage of horror stories to be heard when you visit the surrounding villages. One of the people Corporate Watch interviewed was a man who had worked for one year for **Shamir Salads**, a food distributor specialising in kosher food, readymade salads and dips. According to the company's website it supplies the Israeli army and exports to Russia, the UK, Holland, Denmark, France, Ukraine, Canada and the US. In 2010, the company was exposed by *Gush Shalom* as having deliberately mislabelled its goods as "Made in Israel" when exported to the Netherlands.[119]

Shamir Salads employee: "I worked at Shamir Salads between 5pm and 7am every day for a year. It was all cash-in-hand work because the company refused to give us contracts. Some people got payslips but, because my hours were too long, I did not. I got paid around 3,000 NIS a month. This would have been about the minimum wage if I had worked full-time day shifts, but I was working long hours during the night and should have got paid more. When I say I worked every day I mean it: I did not have a single day off for one year. At the end, I left voluntarily as I was tired, had worked too hard and felt ill."

---

[117] http://www.greenkote.com/contactus.aspx, [accessed 23/8/2011].
[118] http://whoprofits.org/Company%20Info.php?id=758, [accessed 23/8/2011].
[119] Eldar, Akiva (2010), Israeli West Bank food company fakes address for EU markets, *Haaretz*, Available: http://www.haaretz.com/print-edition/news/israeli-west-bank-food-company-fakes-address-for-eu-markets-1.266671, [accessed 23/8/2011].

Other companies operating in Barkan settlement industrial zone and Ariel West settlement industrial Park[120]

Manufacturer	Product/Service
Ability Computer and Software Industries	computer software and mobile-monitoring and intercepting equipment (including for export)
Ahdut Factory for Tehina Halva and Sweets	tahini and sweets
AL Five Star	food products
AlphaBio Tec	dental solutions, implants and prosthetics
Aridan Printing Productions	printed products
Avgol Nonwoven Industries	non-woven fabrics used in sanitary products and nappies (distributed worldwide)
Ayelet Barkan	synthetic fibres for carpets
AS Cohen Marketing	kosher food products
Balfour Industries M.I.T (Balfour Springs Industry)	springs
Bar Mazon Produce	food produce
Barkan Mounting Systems	mounting systems for consumer electronics
Best Stones	stone supplier for tiling and building work
Caesarea Carpets and Carmel Carpets	stone surfaces and kitchen cabinets
California Shayish and Carpenters	stone and quartz surfaces and kitchen cabinets
Chano Textile	underwear
Chic Design Ltd	furniture
DNM Technical Equipment and Tools	heavy tools (supplier to the Israeli army)
Danshar Holdings	market and distribute cosmetics and cleaning products. shareholder in **Willi Foods**, owners of **Shamir Salads**
David Nona	garments
Delta Textile Marketing	textiles for underwear (Subsidiary of **Delta Galil** whose products are used in garments by **Marks and Spencer, Victoria's Secret, Calvin Klein, Tommy Hilfiger, Nike** and **Hugo Boss**).
Dispobud	disposable fabric products

---

[120] Information from www.whoprofits.org [accessed 23/8/2011] unless otherwise specified.

Manufacturer	Product/Service
Distek	chemicals and equipment for metal surface treatment
Doron Furniture Design	furniture for children
El Ez	aluminium coating and wood colours
Elyahu Zalman & Sons Metal Tubes Industries	structural steel pipe and tubing products. (owns **TOP greenhouses**)
Enercon Ariel	power supply units for military systems
Europal Recycling Ltd	recycling
Evyg Advanced Technology	metal coatings and finishings
Fried Brothers Feather Industries	mattresses, sleeping bags, pillows and other feather based products
Fun Bak Ltd	nut based spreads
Galran SE Industries	aluminium products for windows and doors
Green Oil Energy	oil recycling
Ha'argaz Technopach Metal Industries	metal equipment for the high-tech, communications and security industries, components for unmanned aerial vehicles (UAVs) and UAV weapons systems
IKOO Designs	home furnishings
Impertec Industries	gas masks (part of the **Supergum Group**).
Intellitech Engineering Mechanical and Aviation	military consultancy
IO Solutions Ltd[121]	*no information available*
IRPC. Rubber Products Co	rubber products for the automotive industry
Ishai Zion and Sons	polished stone
Isratoys	board games
Ivgi Morris	furniture
Schleisner Works	metal working, plasma cutting
Katzenstein Adler	electrical goods (manufacturer and importer)
Koralek Almog Sifting Machines and Production Systems	machinery for agriculture and food production
Krashin Shalev Metal Industries	heat exchangers, supplies condensers, evaporators, boilers, cooling towers and pumps. Israeli representative of several international corporations.
Lipski Plastic Industries	plastic sanitary and plumbing products
Mega Print	disposable cloth products (such as hospital wear)

---

[121] Observed during Corporate Watch visit to Barkan industrial zone, April 2010.

Manufacturer	Product/Service
Metal Factory Hamachresha	prefabricated industrial buildings
Neetuv Management and Development Co	swimming pools
Neumann Steel Industries for Construction	steel products for the construction industry
Ofer Carpenters	cabinets
Ofertex Industries	recycled cloth
Paz El Sinun	water filters and irrigation equipment
Plasto Polish	cleaning products (including for export)
Plustic Solutions	moulds for plastic production
Ram Quality Products B.R. (Tip Top Toys Star)	plastic toys (owns the **Interstar** brand name)
Ratek Industries	clutches and break plates
Renaissan	clothes
Romix Mixing Equipment	industrial mixing equipment
Rono Polidan Packaging	packaging (provides packaging to, for example, **Eden Springs** and **Beigel&Beigel**)
Rosentoys, Buba-Li Industries	plastic toys and balls
Royal Life	textiles
Shomron Barkalit Tires	tires
Si Kirsum	metal products
Spiral Glass	glass products
Spray Metal Coatings	metal coating
Spyro Plastics	thermoplastic sheets and plastic products
Star Night Technologies	night vision and safety equipment (supplier to the IDF)
Supergum Industries	rubber, plastic and sealing products for automotive, industrial and military products (supplier to the IDF and the Swedish army among others)
TAC Accessory Corporation Israel	clothes hangers
Tayar Doors	doors and security doors
Teltone Electronics	speakers and amplifiers
The Archivists	archiving
Top Greenhouses Ltd	greenhouses

Manufacturer	Product/Service
Twitoplast	plastic components for air-conditioners (distributed by Medal Aircon in the UK)
Unikowsky Maoz	importer and distributor of home, building and gardening products
Von Roll Transformers	electrical infrastructure products
Yahav Oranit	private security
Ye'ela Quality Furniture	furniture
Yerushalmi Rope Industries	ropes, nets, cloths, bags, military coats
Zeev's Technics	industrial tools supplier
Zriha Hlavin Industries (Dr Byte)	plastic products and communication components

Katzrin industrial zone

Katzrin was established in 1977 and is the biggest settlement in the occupied Syrian Golan, with a population of 6,500.[122] Built on the land of the Syrian area of Fakhura, it is considered the capital of the Golan by Israel. Almost all industry in the Golan, apart from agriculture, is located in the Katzrin settlement industrial zone. As the Golan is frequently forgotten by the boycott movement, Katzrin is rarely included in lists of industrial zone production.

Katzrin company profiles

Readymix Industries is a producer and supplier of raw materials for the construction industry and is heavily involved in the occupation. Readymix is a subsidiary of the Mexican cement and concrete giant **Cemex**. Cemex operate on a large scale in the UK with locations all over the country.[123] The company has facilities in Katzrin, Atarot, Mishor Adumim and the Movo Horon settlements, and its products have been used for the construction of the wall as well as military checkpoints and the Jerusalem light railway project.[124]

Biomor is a manufacturer of organic biocides. It is part of the **Stockton Group** which has its head office in Switzerland and regional offices in 22 countries around the world. Biomor's head office in Israel is in the Katzrin plant.

(Longer profiles of some of the companies trading from Katzrin can be found in our chapter on the occupied Syrian Golan).

---

[122] *Adalah* (August 2009), *Adalah's Newsletter, Volume 63*, Available: http://www.adalah.org/features/land/Position_Paper_on_Land_Reform_and_EJ_and_GH_settlements_English_Final%5B1%5D.pdf, [accessed 29/9/2011].
[123] For locations see http://www.cemexlocations.co.uk/, [accessed 29/08/2011].
[124] http://www.whoprofits.org/Company%20Info.php?id=645, [accessed 29/08/2011].

Other companies in Katzrin settlement industrial zone[125]

Company	Product/Service
Benda Plast	food packaging
Capernaum Vista Olive Farm	olives and olive oil products
Gesher Golan	car rentals and sale
Golan Brewery	beer
Golan Winery	wine
Ionics	cleaning products
Lithotech Medical	devices for the removal of kidney stones.
Maytag High Tech Ventures	technology developer, mainly for the bio-medical industry
Mey Golan	settler cooperative involved in water supply and wind energy
New Noga Light	manufacturer of night vision equipment (supplier to the IDF)[126]
Nistec	arms
Pigmentan	paint
Ramat Hagolan Dairies	dairy products[127]

Bnei Yehuda settlement industrial zone[128]

The Bnei Yehuda settlement industrial area is a business park connected to the Israeli *moshav* settlement of Bnei Yehuda in the occupied Golan. Bnei Yehuda was established on the site of the Syrian area of Scopia which was depopulated when the Israeli military forced most of the Syrian residents of the Syrian Golan out of their homes.[129] The table below lists some of the companies based in Bnei Yehuda industrial zone:

---

[125] All info, except where otherwise stated, from three visits by the authors to Katzrin industrial zone in 2010. See http://corporateoccupation.wordpress.com/2http://corporateoccupation.wordpress.com/2010/03/25/corporations-in-katzerin-industrial-zone-part-three/010/05/04/readymix-in-katzerin-industrial-zone/, http://corporateoccupation.wordpress.com/2010/03/16/businesses-in-katzerin-industrial-zone-part-two/, http://corporateoccupation.wordpress.com/2010/03/16/businesses-in-katzerin-settlement-industrial-zone-part-1/, [all accessed September 2011].
[126] Who Profits http://www.whoprofits.org/Company%20Info.php?id=710, [accessed 29/9/2011].
[127] Who Profits http://www.whoprofits.org/Company%20Info.php?id=711, [accessed 29/9/2011].
[128] All info from Corporate Watch http://corporateoccupation.wordpress.com/2010/07/27/bnei-yehuda-industrial-zone/, [accessed 29/9/2011].
[129] Jonathan Moloney (2009), The illegality of Israeli settlements in the occupied Syrian Golan under IHL Al Maarsad, Available: http://www.golan-marsad.org/pdfs/The_Illegality_of_settlement_products_under_IHL.pdf, [accessed September 2011].

Company	Product/Service
Avanova	cosmetic products
Buffalo	kosher food
BE Machinery	machinery and processing plants for the food, pharmaceutical and cosmetics industries. The company is part of **Beth El** a multi-faceted business engaged in the production of various military and safety equipment, including bomb shelters, filtration systems and vehicle components. The UK is listed as both an importing and exporting partner of Beth El on the Israel Export and International Cooperation Institute's web-site.
Elbit	military aircraft

Karnei Shomron settlement industrial zone[130]

Karnei Shomron is an Israeli settlement in the North-Western West Bank. The table below lists some of the companies based in Karnei Shomron industrial zone:

Company	Product/Service
Fibertech	fiber glass
Gat Shomron Winery	wine
Israphot Industries	printing press and publisher
Palphot	stationery

Kiryat Arba settlement industrial zone[131]

Kiryat Arba is a West Bank settlement established in 1968 close to Al Khalil (Hebron). The table below lists some of the companies based in Kiryat Arba's industrial zone:

Company	Product/Service
Mofet B'Yehuda	technology developer
Trendlines Group	marketing, media and sales

Ma'ale Efraim settlement industrial zone[132]

Ma'ale Efraim is the only industrial zone in the Jordan Valley, situated on the road to Nablus. The industrial area is attached to the residential settlement of Ma'ale Efraim. Ma'ale Efraim was established as a military base in 1978 on land seized by military order. The settlement was civilianised in 1979 and further land was seized as 'state' land.

Ma'ale Efraim industrial zone is largely dormant, a holding exercise to monopolise the land for future development. The table below lists some of the companies there:

---

[130] All company info from www.whoprofits.org [accessed 23/8/2011] except when otherwise stated.
[131] *Ibid.*
[132] *Ibid.*

Company	Product/Service
Atid packaging	packaging
Impertec Industries/Supergum	riot gear and gas masks for biological, chemical and atomic weapons.[133]
Tel Bar Industries for Health Institutions	disposal of medical waste

'Joint' and PA-initiated industrial zones

Apart from the existing settlement industrial zones, there are 10 other zones currently being discussed for the West Bank and Gaza, all of which come with their own set of problems. Firstly, there are four PA (and Israel) approved projects being planned in Jenin, the Jordan Valley, Bethlehem and Tulkarem.[134] These projects, not dissimilar to 'free trade zones' or Qualifying Industrial Zones around the world, are essentially part of the PA's state-building efforts and aim to bring foreign and private investment to Palestine;[135] The Jenin zone is funded by Germany and Turkey; the Jordan Valley project by the Japanese JICA project and the Bethlehem park by France.[136]

Although these zones are still in the early stages of development, what they symbolise is very worrying. Created under the occupation, the zones, if completed, would be harmful normalisation projects tying Palestinian business firmly to the Israeli economy. As Sam Bahour, a Palestinian businessman, put it in his essay *Economic prison zones*: "Because the zones will depend on Israeli cooperation to function, and because they will exist within an Israeli-designed economic system that ensures Palestinian dependence on Israel, they cannot form the basis of a sovereign economy. Relying on them will perpetuate the status quo of dependency."[137] Everything, from new infrastructure to product export routes, would be controlled by Israel, with little benefit for ordinary Palestinians who are not part of the consultation process and can, at most, look forward to a menial, underpaid and polluting job not dissimilar to the ones offered in settlement industrial zones now.[138]

The PA approved zones can be joint projects in their own right. However, as mentioned above, there are several more projects in the offing where Israel might play an even bigger

---

[133] Corporate Watch profile, http://corporateoccupation.wordpress.com/2010/12/02/maale-efraim-impertec-industries/, [accessed 28/8/2011].
[134] Corporate Watch interview with Shir Hever from the The Alternative Information Center, March 2010.
[135] For the PA's economic plan for Palestine see *Ending the occupation, establishing the state: program of the thirteenth government*, (2009). Available from: http://www.mop-gov.ps/web_files/issues_file/090825%20Ending%20Occupation,%20Establishing%20the%20State%20-%20Program%20of%20the%2013%20government.pdf, [accessed 25/08/2011].
[136] Bahour, S (19/11/2010), *Economic prison zones*, Available: http://jfjfp.com/?p=19122, [accessed 25/8/2011].
[137] *Ibid*.
[138] Corporate Watch interview with Shir Hever, 2010, *Idem* and Tabakhna, O (2010), *The effects of joint industrial zones on the Palestinian agricultural sector*, presented to the *Palestinian development among sovereignty and dependency: industrial zones as a model,* workshop given in Al Bireh.

role. Shir Hever argues that 'there is some intentional confusion between the PA-initiated industrial zones: Jenin, Jordan Valley, Tulkarem and Bethlehem, and the offer by Israel to establish "joint" zones in Bethlehem, Tulkarem, Jenin, Erez and Karni, the last two being in Gaza',[139] and details are hard to come by. What is perfectly clear is that the beneficiaries will not be the Palestinian people, who run the risk of being exploited by the occupation and big business simultaneously. One example is that of the people of the Palestinian village of Jayyous, who after years of struggling to win some of their land back from the apartheid wall, were finally successful only to be told that 500 out of the 800 dunams that had been returned would be confiscated for a new industrial zone. It has as yet not been made clear in writing whether or not this was done with PA approval.[140] Instead of working towards a free Palestine with a viable independent economy, all these zones are essentially working towards is the privatisation of the occupation.

The West Bank village of Jayyous. Farmland on the outskirts of the village is earmarked for a new industrial zone (Corporate Watch 2010)

Where next?

It is clear that Israel is doing everything it can to avoid boycott action, which harms the settlement industry. Several workers from Barkan industrial zone told Corporate Watch researchers that their employers try to hide the name of their factories from them, as they count on them not being able to read Hebrew. We were also told on several occasions that clothes being manufactured there were sent on to Tel Aviv to be labelled, a clever way of both preventing the workers from seeing any brand names and cheating the tax laws.[141] It is

---

[139]Tabakhna, O (2010), *The effects of joint industrial zones on the Palestinian agricultural sector*, Idem.
[140]Corporate Watch interview with Stop the Wall, April 2010.
[141]Information from Corporate Watch interviews conducted in Deir Istya, April 2010.

important that activists expand their efforts and keep pressuring companies which operate, or trade with, factories in the industrial zones. But it is also essential that the movement follows up on good work, and does not simply accept vague assurances of relocation as in the cases of Mul-T-Lock and Soda Stream. It is also worth noting that, at the moment, most improvements in workers' conditions are only won after Palestinians take either strike or legal actions against their employers, at great risk to themselves. It is therefore paramount that there is worldwide, vocal support for these actions and against the settlement profiteers.

With more checks being imposed in relation to the EU Israeli Association agreement, the profitability of trading from occupied land is already under threat. Increased BDS action could finally present a real challenge to Israel's economic prison zones.

THE WALL AGAINST THE BEDOUIN

THE 'ARAB JAHALIN' BEDOUIN WERE DISPLACED FROM THEIR LAND IN THE NAQAB (NEGEV) IN 1948 BY ISRAELI FORCES. THE NAQAB WAS ANNEXED TO ISRAEL.

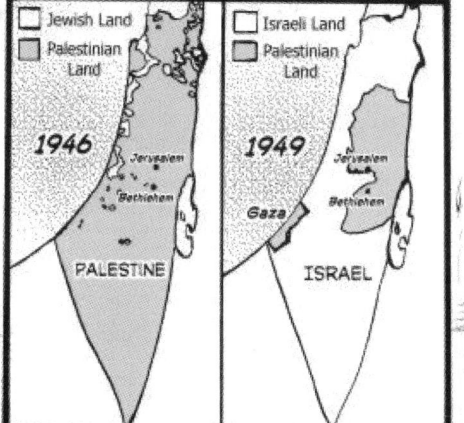

531 CITIES, TOWNS AND VILLAGES WERE DESTROYED OR DEPOPULATED. MORE THAN 750,000 PALESTINIANS WERE EXPELLED AT THAT TIME. THE STATE OF ISRAEL WAS THEREFORE ESTABLISHED ON AROUND 77% OF THE AREA OF HISTORIC PALESTINE.

SOME OF THE ARAB JAHALIN MOVED TO AN AREA BETWEEN JERUSALEM AND RAMALLAH IN THE WEST BANK. THEN IN 1967, THE WEST BANK WAS OCCUPIED BY ISRAEL.

400,000 PALESTINIAN WERE FORCED OUT, SOME BEING EXPELLED FOR THE SECOND TIME.

STILL, THE MAJORITY OF PEOPLE STAYED.

The Jahalin protested against the occupation.

NOT WANTING TO OFFICIALLY ANNEX THE LAND BUT UNWILLING TO RELINQUISH IT, THE ISRAELI AUTHORITIES DECIDED TO SETTLE IT. THE DELIBERATE POLICY OF AGGRESSIVELY INCREASING JEWISH SETTLEMENT ON THESE LANDS, AND THE STRANGLING OF THE EXISTING PALESTINIAN COMMUNITIES THERE.

The Wall Against the Bedouin by Sean Michael Wilson and Rejena Smiley

SO, FROM 1977 ZIONIST GOVERNMENTS PUMPED HUGE RESOURCES INTO SETTLEMENT PROJECTS.
BY 1984, THERE WERE 113 SETTLEMENTS IN THE WEST BANK. TODAY THERE ARE 148 SETTLEMENTS INHABITED BY APPROXIMATELY 470,000 SETTLERS.*

IN THE SEVENTIES, THE ISRAELI KNESSET APPROVED THE BUILDING OF A SETTLEMENT CALLED MA'ALE ADUMIM, AND AN INDUSTRIAL AREA NAMED MISHOR ADUMIM ON THE LAND WHERE THE BEDOUIN WERE FARMING. MISHOR ADUMIM INDUSTRIAL ZONE IS AN INTEGRAL PART OF THE PLANS TO ETHNICALLY CLEANSE THE AREA OF BEDOUINS AND IS STRATEGICALLY PLACED TO PREVENT THE POSSIBILITY OF THE CREATION OF A "VIABLE" PALESTINIAN STATE.

THE GOVERNMENT BUILDING PERMIT COMMENTED THAT THE JAHALIN WOULD NEED TO BE 'RELOCATED' TO MAKE ROOM FOR THE CORPORATE EXPANSION OF COMPANIES AND FACTORIES IN THE AREA.
THE CONSTRUCTION OF THE INDUSTRIAL ZONE AT MA'ALE ADUMIM HAS BEEN USED TO JUSTIFY THE EXPANSION OF THE ROAD SYSTEM, MEANING THAT MORE LAND IS MONOPOLIZED BY THE OCCUPIERS.

*There are now 136 settlements in the West Bank and over 500,000 settlers

IN 1997, MORE OF THE JAHALIN WERE FORCIBLY MOVED TO A HILL IN ABU DIS NEXT TO THE MAIN JERUSALEM RUBBISH DUMP. MANY OF THEM WORK AT THE DUMP FOR BELOW THE ISRAELI MINIMUM WAGE.

OTHER JAHALIN WORK IN FACTORIES IN MISHOR ADUMIM, OFTEN ON LAND WHERE THEY PREVIOUSLY LIVED. WORKERS IN MISHOR ADUMIM SHOULD GET THE ISRAELI MINIMUM WAGE, BUT ARE OFTEN PAID LESS THAN HALF OF IT.

WITH CRUEL IRONY, THEY HAVE TO WORK FOR THE SAME SETTLERS WHO CONTINUE TO HARRASS THEM OUT OF THEIR HOMES.

THE ISRAELI STATE'S 'E1 PLAN' IS TO EXPAND MA'ALE ADUMIM, WITH NEW SETTLEMENTS AND INDUSTRIAL ZONES, TO CONNECT MA'ALE ADUMIM WITH THE ILLEGAL SETTLEMENTS IN EAST JERUSALEM AND ISOLATE THE REST OF THE WEST BANK FROM EAST JERUSLEM. THE PLAN WILL UPROOT THE JAHALIN LIVING AROUND MA'ALE ADUMIM.

FROM 2002 THE ISRAELI AUTHORITIES BEGAN CONSTRUCTING A WALL IN THE WEST BANK. THE PURPOSE OF THE WALL IS TO ANNEX MORE LAND TO ISRAEL AND THE SETTLEMENTS.

NOW THE WALL THREATENS TO UPROOT THE JAHALIN ONCE AGAIN. THIS TIME THE JAHALIN IN THE NORTHWEST OF JERUSALEM ARE BEING DISPLACED. JAHALIN FAMILIES HAVE BEEN ISSUED WITH DEMOLITION ORDERS AND ARE LIKELY TO BE EXPELLED TO ABU DIS.

15
Military Industry

"Israel's largest comparative advantage is in military products, because these demand advanced technology on one hand and military experience on the other... no country in the world is as dependent on arms sales as Israel. The Jaffa orange is fast being edged out of the public consciousness by the Uzi sub-machine gun as Israel's major export. Israel is the largest per capita arms exporter in the world"[1]

Moshe Arens, former Israeli Defence Minister

Two sisters killed by an Israeli airstrike in Beit Hanoun (International Solidarity Movement 2009)

Israel produces a wide range of military products, from ammunition, small arms and artillery pieces to sophisticated electronic systems and tanks. There are approximately 450 defence, aerospace and security firms in Israel,[2] with estimated combined revenues of $3.5 billion.[3] The three largest entities are all government-owned, **Israeli Aerospace Industries (IAI)**, **Israel Military Industries (IMI)** and the **Rafael Arms Development Authority**, although there are ongoing moves towards privatization. Other privately owned companies include **Elbit Systems** and **EMIT Aviation**. Israel's military industry employs around 50,000 people.[4]

---

[1] Stop the Wall (2007), *Exporting occupation: the Israeli arms trade.* Available: http://www.stopthewall.org/downloads/pdf/Exportoccupation.pdf.
[2] http://www.export.gov.il/NewsHTML/economy/Israel'sEconomicReviewFebruary2011.pdf, [accessed September 2011].
[3] http://www.globalsecurity.org/military/world/israel/industry.htm, [accessed September 2011].
[4] http://www.globalsecurity.org/military/world/israel/industry.htm, [accessed September 2011].

Israel has the largest arms exports per capita in the world. It is difficult to estimate the contribution of military industries to Israel's GDP as these figures would include Israeli government purchases of domestic arms. This information does not appear to be publicised.

Arms export figures fall into several headings: aircraft parts, civilian and military, made up 2.1 per cent of Israel's total exports in 2009, according to the Israeli Ministry of Finance;[5] electronic equipment, some of which is military, made up 17.6 per cent;[6] arms and ammunition 0.71 per cent;[7] vehicles (civilian and military), 1.19 per cent;[8] ships and boats (civilian and military), 0.35 per cent.[9] According to *Neged Neshek*, an Israeli anti-arms research group, total arms exports in 2009 amounted to $6.75 billion, roughly 12 per cent of total Israeli exports.[10] 'Non-military' aerospace and 'security' exports came to $3 billion in 2010.[11]

The Israeli 'defence' sector is crucial to the Israeli state's ability to maintain its militarist policies. The Israeli domestic military sector provides a large proportion of the weapons and equipment used by the Israeli military against the Palestinians, as well as the high-tech repression and surveillance technologies used in the apartheid wall, checkpoints and the occupation. The repression, murder and ethnic cleansing of Palestinians have provided a fertile testing ground for the development of increasingly specialised equipment and Israeli military equipment is frequently marketed as combat-proven or battle tested.[12]

The story of the growth of the Israeli military sector is bound up with the myth of 'plucky little Israel', a nation that had to fight on all fronts to survive against insurmountable odds. Globalsecurity.org writes: "having to fight five major wars in its first four decades, Israel built a comprehensive standing army – the Israel Defense Forces (IDF) – and furnished it with an arsenal of highly advanced military hardware. The government, which owns three major defense firms, also encouraged the formation of private companies to equip the IDF.

The development of a sophisticated defense industry inevitably led to exports, which today account for a majority of its revenues and allows the country's defense industry to compete against some of the largest companies in the world."[13] Far from being forced to fight, Israel has far more often chosen to fight, and its history has been one of aggression, ethnic

---

[5] http://www.cbs.gov.il/publications/isr_in_n09e.pdf, [accessed September 2011], p.20.
[6] http://www.intracen.org/appli1/TradeCom/TP_TP_CI.aspx?RP=376&YR=2009, [accessed September 2011].
[7] *Ibid.*
[8] *Ibid.*
[9] *Ibid.*
[10] Private correspondence between the authors and *Neged Neshek*. December 2010.
[11] http://www.export.gov.il/NewsHTML/economy/Israel'sEconomicReviewFebruary2011.pdf, [accessed September 2011].
[12] See, for example, here http://www.defpro.com/news/details/27932/?SID=85968d5ce0f0e26a30d16bead64a59b0, [accessed September 2011].
[13] http://www.globalsecurity.org/military/world/israel/industry.htm, [accessed September 2011].

cleansing and expansionism. Israel is one of the most militarised societies in the world. The country's military expenditure has been steadily rising over the last twenty years, although military spending as a percentage of GDP has been falling slightly. In 2008 Israeli military expenditure stood at 7 per cent of GDP.[14] About 1.5 percentage points of this figure is covered by military aid from the USA[15] but domestic expenditure is still huge, compared to, say, 4.3 per cent total military expenditure in the USA or 2.5 per cent in the UK.[16]

The F16, supplied to Locheed Martin, the IDF's weapon of choice

Israel is the largest recipient of foreign aid in the world.[17] A large proportion of this is in the form of US military aid.[18] Total US aid to Israel between 1973 and 2008 was over $200 billion.[19] Israel is the only recipient of US military aid permitted to use portions of the grant money to invest in domestic, rather than US-made, military equipment.[20] US military aid is therefore a major contributor to the success of Israeli domestic arms and security industries.

Israel buys the majority of its weapons from US prime contractors, such as **Lockheed Martin**, **Boeing** and **Raytheon**.[21] However, Israel's domestic arms sector profits from these purchases through supplying ancillary and upgrade equipment for these US made weapons.

---

[14]http://milexdata.sipri.org/result.php4, [accessed September 2011].
[15]OECD (2009), *Economic survey of Israel 2009, Idem*, p.31.
[16]http://milexdata.sipri.org/result.php4, [accessed September 2011].
[17]Hever, S (2010), *The political economy of Israel's occupation: repression beyond exploitation,* Pluto Press, p.32.
[18]*Ibid*, p.32.
[19]Hanieh, A (2011), Review: the political economy of Israel's occupation, *Journal of Palestine Studies*, 40, 4. Pp. 100-101.
[20]*Ibid*, p.32.
[21]http://imeu.net/news/article0020963.shtml, [accessed September 2011].

For example, IAI provides the armour for US firm **Caterpillar**'s D9 military bulldozers[22] and upgrades for Lockheed Martin's F16s,[23] while Israeli Military Industries works on joint projects with US arms giant Raytheon.[24]

Company profiles

The birth of **Israeli Military Industries** (IMI) is tied up with Israeli militarism and ethnic cleansing. The Haganah, a Jewish militia that carried out the majority of the ethnic cleansing of Palestinians in 1947-9,[25] clandestinely stockpiled weapons and set up secret arms factories, which developed into Israeli Military Industries.[26] The company supplied the majority of basic weapons, such as guns and ammunition, to the nascent Israeli army in the first two decades of the state of Israel. Israeli Military Industries became a state-owned company in 1990,[27] prior to which it was operated by the Israeli MOD.

IMI specialises in upgrades for US-made heavy firearms and is the lead company producing Israel's Merkava tank. The company also manufactures cluster weaponry.[28] In 2008 it generated turnover of $650 million, of which 60 per cent was attributed to foreign exports.[29]

Israeli Aerospace Industries (IAI) was established in 1953 as a state-owned company. IAI has developed some homegrown fighter aircraft, the Kfir and the Lavi. The development of the latter faltered after the US refused to fund the development of an alternative to the F16.[30] As a result, the company's business is still concentrated on contracts with US firms such as Boeing and Lockheed Martin. IAI provides upgrades and ancillary systems for the US-made F15 and F16 aircraft.[31] It also manufactures systems for the F4 aircraft, the Yasur 2000 and CH-53 helicopters, Dvora patrol boats, Gabriel sea-to-sea missiles, Phalcon Early Warning aircraft and the Arrow anti-tactical ballistic missile.[32] IAI also provides the armor kit for the

---

[22] http://www.iai.co.il/23048-31739-en/MediaRoom_NewsArchives_2004.aspx?PageNum=5, [accessed September 2011].
[23] http://www.iai.co.il/17866-23270-en/Business_Areas_Military_Aircraft_Upgrades.aspx?btl=1, [accessed September 2011].
[24] See, for example http://www.iai.co.il/23048-31739-en/MediaRoom_NewsArchives_2004.aspx?PageNum=5, [accessed September 2011].
[25] For a history of the ethnic cleansing of 1947-9 see Pappe, I (2006), *The ethnic cleansing of Palestine,* One World Publications.
[26] http://www.globalsecurity.org/military/world/israel/industry.htm, [accessed September 2011].
[27] *Ibid.*
[28] http://www.haaretz.com/news/human-rights-watch-charges-georgia-used-defective-israeli-made-cluster-bombs-1.256568, [accessed September 2011].
[29] http://www.imi-israel.com/home/doc.aspx?mCatID=63195&mCatID2=0, [accessed September 2011].
[30] http://www.fas.org/man/dod-101/sys/ac/row/3fal90.htm, [accessed September 2011].
[31] http://www.iai.co.il/12019-en/CompanyInfo-IAIandtheSecurityofIsrael.aspx, [accessed September 2011].
[32] http://www.iai.co.il/12019-en/CompanyInfo-IAIandtheSecurityofIsrael.aspx, [accessed September 2011].

IDF's Caterpillar D9 bulldozer.[33]

By the late 1980s IAI was employing 14,000 people.[34] IAI's sales in the first half of 2008 were $1.9 billion.[35] IAI pays dividends to the state of Israel, which in 2007 amounted to $256 million.[36]

Tanks being transported through the Jordan Valley (Corporate Watch 2010)

Rafael Advanced Defense Systems, previously the **Rafael Arms Development Authority**, set up in 1948 as the '**Science Corps**', has essentially been the research and development wing of the Israeli army. It was re-organised as the Rafael Arms Development Authority in 1958. The company boasts that the majority of IDF weapons use Rafael systems, or benefit from Rafael's research.[37] Rafael developed and now manufactures the Python and Popeye 'smart' airborne missiles, both of which have co-production agreements with major US aerospace companies. In addition, its products include unmanned systems, passive armor, naval decoys, observation balloon systems, acoustic torpedo countermeasures, ceramic armor, air-breathing propulsion and air-to-air, air-to-surface and surface-to-surface missiles.[38] The company made $112 million in net profits in 2009.[39]

---

[33] http://en.wikipedia.org/wiki/Israel_Aerospace_Industries#cite_note-1, [accessed September 2011].
[34] *Ibid.*
[35] http://www.iai.co.il/12021-38947-en/CompanyInfo-PresentPastFuture.aspx?pos=10, [accessed September 2011].
[36] http://www.iai.co.il/12021-38947-en/CompanyInfo-PresentPastFuture.aspx?pos=10, [accessed September 2011].
[37] www.linkedin.com/company/rafael, [accessed September 2011].
[38] http://www.globalsecurity.org/military/world/israel/industry.htm, [accessed September 2011].
[39] http://www.rafael.co.il/Marketing/192-1614-en/Marketing.aspx, [accessed September 2011].

Elbit Systems, based in Haifa, is Israel's largest arms and security company. Elbit has absorbed seven companies since 2000 and now employs over 10,000 people, as well as presiding over a considerable network of subsidiaries and affiliated corporations.[40] The company owns a facility in the occupied Golan, on the settlement of Bnei Yehuda.[41]

> Elbit Systems shares are traded on the Nasdaq (NASDAQ) under the symbol "ESLT" and on the Tel-Aviv Stock Exchange.[42] The company's largest shareholders include Blackrock, UBS, Federmann, Bank of America Corporation, Renaissance Technologies, Meitav Investmement House, Generali Assicurazioni, Ganden Holdings, Psagot Investment House, Bank of New York Mellon, Harel Insurance, Banque Degroof, Delek Group, Analyst IMS Investment Management, Epsilon Investment House, the State of Washington and the T Rowe Price Group.[43]

SIBAT: marketing Israeli militarism

Defence exports and procurement for the IDF are administered by SIBAT (Foreign Defense Assistance and Defense Export Organization).[44] SIBAT markets Israeli military products, sells off surplus IDF equipment[45] and arranges Israeli presence at arms fairs, such as the biannual DSEi arms fair in docklands, London.[46]

EU funding

Israel is the main foreign partner for the EU's "framework program" for scientific research (FP7), which has been allocated €53 billion between 2007 and 2013. Using the pretext of fighting terrorism, the EU has decided in recent years that arms companies are eligible to receive funding for 'security research'. Ten of the 45 initial projects described by the EU as 'security research' have involved Israeli companies, academic or state institutions. Israeli projects that have received funding include a **Motorola Israel** surveillance project, an IAI project, **Aeronautics Defence Systems** and an Elbit drone development project.[47] Funding also goes to several Israeli universities, including Haifa's **Technion**, for arms-related research programmes.[48]

---

[40] http://corporateoccupation.wordpress.com/2009/12/02/making-new-markets-parcaberporth-and-the-commercialisation-of-drone-technology/, [accessed September 2011].
[41] http://corporateoccupation.wordpress.com/2010/03/12/businesses-in-bnei-yehuda-settlement/, [accessed September 2011].
[42] http://www.whoprofits.org/Company%20Info.php?id=554, [accessed September 2011].
[43] Bureau Van Dyck, Orbis database, [accessed September 2011].
[44] http://www.sibat.mod.gov.il/sibatmain/sibat/about/overview.htm, [accessed September 2011].
[45] http://www.sibat.mod.gov.il/sibatmain/sibat/about/military.htm, [accessed September 2011].
[46] http://www.sibat.mod.gov.il/sibatmain/sibat/about/export.htm, [accessed September 2011].
[47] http://www.ipsc.ie/pdf/ipsc_factsheet_-_how_israeli_arms_companies_benefit_from_eu_science_funds.pdf, [accessed September 2011].
[48] European Security Research Cooperation with Israelv2.pdf - http://ebookbrowse.com/european-security-research-cooperation-with-israelv2-pdf-d39691800, [accessed September 2011].

In February 2011, the European Commission presented a Green Paper in which it outlined its vision of EU research funding after FP7 expires at the end of 2013. The EU is currently considering directly funding research for explicitly military purposes after 2013, which could tie the Israeli military and security industry even more closely to Europe.[49]

Nuclear weapons

The Israeli state has maintained a position of "nuclear ambiguity": neither confirming nor denying its possession of nuclear weapons, as if it did admit possessing unauthorised nuclear weapons the US would have to break its own policy not to grant military aid to a nuclear state.[50] Israel has never signed the Nuclear Non-Proliferation Treaty.[51]

Israel's nuclear weapons programmes were begun by the Science Corps, the predecessor of Rafael, in 1949. In 1957 Israel signed an agreement with the French government to build a nuclear reactor and chemical reprocessing plant at Dimona, in the Naqab. Israel gave public assurances that the reactor would not manufacture atomic weapons, and the plant began to function in 1964.[52]

In 1986 Mordechai Vanunu, a nuclear weapons technician at Dimona working for the Israeli Atomic Energy Commission, blew the whistle on Israel's secret nuclear weapons programme and leaked photographs of the reactor, which proved it was manufacturing atomic weapons components, to the Sunday Times.[53] Vanunu was lured to Rome by Mossad agents, kidnapped and sentenced to 18 years in prison for treason and espionage. He was released after twelve years but has been subjected to several subsequent periods of imprisonment and his movement continues to be restricted.

Exporting the unmanned occupation

Unmanned aircraft, sometimes known as UAVs, have been developed by Israel through its repression of the Palestinians, and are now a much-sought-after international military commodity. Unmanned planes survey every inch of the Gaza Strip, unmanned vehicles[54] guard the apartheid wall's perimeter, unmanned boats patrol the coast while unmanned bulldozers demolish Palestinian homes.

---

[49] BNC, private correspondence with the authors.
[50] http://www.vanunu.com/nukes/20071120guardian.html, [accessed September 2011].
[51] http://www.nytimes.com/2004/04/21/international/middleeast/21CND-NUCL.html?scp=1&sq=Vanunu%20drugged&st=cse, [accessed September 2011].
[52] http://www.globalsecurity.org/wmd/world/israel/nuke.htm, [accessed September 2011].
[53] http://www.timesonline.co.uk/tol/news/article830147.ece?token=null&offset=12&page=2, [accessed September 2011].
[54] http://whoprofits.org/Company%20Info.php?id=554, [accessed September 2011].

UAVs are one of Israel's key military exports. The most prominent exporters of Israeli drones are **Elbit**, **IAI** and **Aeronautics Defence Systems**.[55] Israel began using US-made UAVs during Israel's occupation of the Sinai.[56] The first Israeli UAVs were developed by IAI and **Tadiran** and, quickly overtaking US drone technology, were used in extra-judicial assassinations during the Israeli occupation of Lebanon in 1992.[57]

IAI produces the following unmanned drones: Pioneer (jointly with the US), Hunter (jointly with the US), Heron, Harpy, Eitan, Ranger, Scout, Searcher, Skylite, Bird-Eye, Panther and Ghost. The company boasts that its drones are used by 48 international customers.[58] Rafael manufactures unmanned boats equipped with lethal firepower.[59]

Israeli companies have reportedly sold UAV technology to the UK, USA, France, India, Vietnam, Uganda, Thailand, Turkey, Switzerland, Sweden, Sri Lanka, Spain, South Korea, Slovakia, Singapore, Serbia, Russia, Poland, Peru, China, Nigeria, Netherlands, Mexico, Kazakhstan, Ireland, Indonesia, Hungary, Greece, Germany, Georgia, Finland, Equatorial Guinea, Ecuador, El Salvador, Czech Republic, Cyprus, Chile, Canada, Brazil, Belgium, Azerbaijan, Australia, Argentina and Angola.[60]

The UAV industry is growing, with the global market expected to be worth up to $13.6 billion by 2014.[61] The use of UAV technology for policing and private security is also growing. UAVs have been used by France and Russia to monitor anti-G8 protests and by **Chevron** to guard its Angolan oil fields.[62] Israeli companies are likely to continue to benefit from this steadily expanding market.

Israeli drones and the UK

Israeli UAV companies, profiting from know-how gleaned from the repression of Palestinians, have penetrated the lucrative UK arms procurement market. **Elbit**, through its British subsidiary **U-TacS**, has been awarded a £44.5 million contract to provide Intelligence, Surveillance, Target Acquisition and Reconnaissance (ISTAR) support capability for the UK armed forces operating in Afghanistan. The contract includes continued supply of the Hermes drone system.[63]

---

[55] http://www.negedneshek.org/exports/uavs/israel-and-the-rise-of-drone-warfare/, [accessed September 2011].
[56] *Ibid.*
[57] *Ibid.*
[58] http://www.iai.co.il/18892-en/BusinessAreas_UnmannedAirSystems.aspx, [accessed September 2011].
[59] http://www.rafael.co.il/Marketing/359-1037-en/Marketing.aspx, [accessed September 2011].
[60] http://www.negedneshek.org/exports/uavs/, [accessed September 2011].
[61] http://www.negedneshek.org/exports/uavs/israel-and-the-rise-of-drone-warfare/, [accessed September 2011].
[62] *Ibid.*
[63] http://corporateoccupation.wordpress.com/2010/11/08/israeli-company-to-supply-british-forces-in-afghanistan, [accessed September 2011].

Overview of the Israeli Economy: Military Industry **132**

Elbit operates a UK subsidiary, **UAV Engines** of Lichfield, whose engines are incorporated into many of the company's drones.[64] Elbit also owns the majority of shares in **U-TACs** in Leicester, along with French arms company, **Thales**.[65] Elbit's drone-testing ground in the UK is at ParcAberPorth in Wales.[66]

EMIT Aviation, another Israeli company specialising in drones, has also made two UAV-related sales to the UK.[67]

Elbit Hermes drones have been sold to the British military

Surveillance and 'security'

Israel's subjugation of its non-Jewish population is a melting pot for the development of surveillance and 'security' technology. **Magal** and **Elbit** are the two companies contracted to provide surveillance equipment for the West Bank apartheid wall.[68]

Israel operates 99 military checkpoints in the West Bank.[69] These checkpoints restrict movement and hamper the development of the Palestinian economy. Five private firms are

---

[64] http://www.guardian.co.uk/world/2009/jan/09/armstrade-gaza, [accessed September 2011].
[65] http://corporateoccupation.wordpress.com/2010/11/08/israeli-company-to-supply-british-forces-in-afghanistan, [accessed September 2011].
[66] http://www.corporatewatch.org/?lid=3470, [accessed September 2011].
[67] http://www.negedneshek.org/exports/uavs, [accessed September 2011].
[68] Swirski, S. (2008), *The burden of occupation*, *Idem*, p.31.
[69] http://www.btselem.org/english/Freedom_of_Movement/Checkpoints_and_Forbidden_Roads.asp, [accessed September 2011].

contracted by the government to provide security services to the checkpoints: **Mikud Security**, **Ari Avtaha**, **SB Security Systems**, **Modi'in Ezrachi** and **Sheleg Lavan**.[70] The involvement of these firms serves to divest the Israeli state of responsibility for actions taken against Palestinians at checkpoints. This was graphically illustrated in 2004 when an employee of **Ari Security** opened fire on unarmed protesters with an Uzi and the state claimed that it was not responsible.[71]

International private security contractors are also creeping into the West Bank security 'marketplace'. US government personnel have bodyguards provided by **International Solutions**, a company closely associated with **Xe** (formerly **Blackwater**).[72]

Electronic security equipment, such as scanners, is provided by **L-3 Communications** and **Rapiscan** through their representative in Israel, **Hashmira** (a subsidiary of British-Danish firm **G4S**)[73] and by **Garrett Metal Detectors (US)**, the Italian company **CEIA** and **Chevrolet**. **Chemonics (US)** has provided cargo scanning equipment to some of the larger checkpoints, designed for the control of the movement of goods and products in and out of the West Bank and Gaza.[74] The equipment was supplied by the American company **AS&E**, and manufactured by the Chinese company **Nuctech**.[75]

G4S

G4S, a multinational British-Danish corporation that provides 'security solutions', owns 90% of G4S Israel (the Israeli security company Hashmira). The company is facing growing criticism of its contracts in the West Bank and the crossings into Gaza. It faces allegations of complicity in Israeli violations of international law due to its role in the maintenance of illegal Israeli settlements and to logistical support for the route of the illegal apartheid wall.

G4S was formed in 2004 through the merger of the British company **Securicor** and the Danish **Group 4 Falck**. The Danish company had purchased 90% of Hashmira in 2002. G4S currently operates in 125 countries and employs over 625,000 people. Its turnover reached $11.7 million in 2010.[76]

At the London session of the Russell Tribunal on Palestine in November 2010 Merav Amir

---

[70] http://www.whoprofits.org/Newsletter.php?nlid=29, [accessed September 2011].
[71] Gutman, M (12th March 2004), Israeli ministry, IDF deny responsibility for 'private' guards at separation fence, *Jerusalem Post*.
[72] http://www.presstv.ir/detail/159620.html, [accessed September 2011].
[73] In 2011 G4S stated that they would exit these contracts. However it is not clear if this has taken place – see http://corporateoccupation.files.wordpress.com/2011/03/g4s-israel-statement-march-11-1-1.pdf, [accessed September 2011].
[74] http://www.whoprofits.org/Newsletter.php?nlid=29, [accessed September 2011].
[75] http://www.whoprofits.org/Newsletter.php?nlid=29, [accessed September 2011].
[76] http://www.g4s.com/en/Investors/Reporting%20Centre/~/media/Files/Corporate%20Files/Annual%20Reports%20and%20CSR/g4s_annual_report_2010.ashx, [accessed September 2011], p.2 and p.10.

and Dr Dalit Baum gave evidence to show that G4S was operating security services at checkpoints and in settlements in the occupied Palestinian territories. Specifically, the company had contracts to provide baggage and body scanners at the Qalandia, Bethlehem, Sha'ar Efraim and Eyal checkpoints; supply equipment to the Erez checkpoint into and out of Gaza; provide security services to businesses operating inside settlements in the West Bank; construct and maintain perimeter defences and a central command room at Ofer prison in the West Bank; and provide the entire security systems for Keziot Prison and a central command room in Meggido Prison inside Israel.[77]

G4S Israel provides services to settlements and Israeli prisons (Danwatch 2010)

The Russell Tribunal concluded that it may be possible to bring a civil claim and a public law action against G4S for its actions in honouring these contracts. The civil claim would be under tort law and based on G4S' supply of equipment to checkpoints that form part of the illegal route of the apartheid wall. The public law action would relate to G4S's support of settlement businesses, which would constitute alleged complicity in violations of international criminal law.[78]

Following these conclusions G4S came under growing pressure to discontinue its business activities in the occupied Palestinian territories. This pressure was especially strong in Denmark where politicians made pronouncements and the public demonstrated against the company. Large pension funds and even the city of Copenhagen began to consider divesting from G4S.[79]

---

[77]http://www.russelltribunalonpalestine.com/en/wp-content/uploads/2011/01/RTOP-London-Session-Findings.pdf, [accessed September 2011], p. 18 and http://english.themarker.com/danish-company-halts-equipment-supply-to-west-bank-in-wake-of-public-protest-1.349239, [accessed September 2011].
[78]http://www.russelltribunalonpalestine.com/en/wp-content/uploads/2011/01/RTOP-London-Session-Findings.pdf, , [accessed September 2011]. p.47-8.
[79]http://electronicintifada.net/content/outcry-denmark-over-firms-involvement-occupation/9142 and http://english.themarker.com/danish-company-halts-equipment-supply-to-west-bank-in-wake-of-

G4S issued a statement on 11 March 2011 announcing its exit from some of its West Bank contracts. This came in the wake of a report by Hjalte Rasmussen, an expert on international law commissioned by G4S to investigate the legality of its contracts in the West Bank and Israel. The report concluded that G4S' contracts did not violate any national or international laws.[80] G4S announced that it would end some contracts for "ethical", reasons even though it had been shown that the "contracts with private enterprises in the area for traditional security and alarm monitoring services are not discriminatory or controversial."[81]

However Rasmussen's suggestion that G4S is beyond legal sanction is far from certain and has been strongly challenged, particularly with regard to his comments on prison services. While conducting his investigation Rasmussen did not visit any Israeli prisons yet felt qualified to argue that the Palestinians detained in Ofer prison are "common criminals", despite the widespread knowledge that Ofer houses Palestinian political detainees and prisoners. Rasmussen's verdict of innocence for G4S was also based on an insistence that there was no evidence of "systematic abuse of prisoners in Israeli jails", directly contradicting the findings of numerous human rights groups.[82] In March 2011 *Adalah*, Physicians for Human Rights-Israel and the *Al Mezan* Center for Human Rights (Gaza) presented evidence to the UN Committee on the Exercise of the Inalienable Rights of the Palestinian People showing that 5,640 Palestinian political prisoners had been imprisoned in Israel by January 2011. Among them were 37 women and 213 minors. Over 2,000 Palestinian children have been charged with security offences between 2005 and 2009. They were held without charge for up to 8 days and prosecuted by military courts.[83]

Moreover, the rights of political prisoners from occupied Palestine are violated by their systematic transfer to prisons in Israel. This contravenes articles 76, 66 and 49 of the Fourth Geneva Convention, which forbid an occupying power from transferring and holding prisoners from an occupied territory in the occupying state. This transfer policy affects sixty percent of the Palestinian child detainees.[84] This is particularly problematic for G4S given the company's role in supporting Israeli prisons and in controlling Palestinian access to controlled areas, including the "Seam Zone".

G4S, hiding behind Rasmussen's verdict, which had been commissioned by the company itself, and its exit from a handful of contracts in the West Bank, has sought to shake off pressure from civil society and political groups over its role in the occupation of Palestine. However it continues to supply security services to illegal West Bank settlements and to

---

public-protest-1.349239, [accessed September 2011].
[80]http://corporateoccupation.wordpress.com/2011/03/27/g4s-delivers-services-to-israeli-prisons-and-illegal-settlements/, [accessed September 2011].
[81]http://corporateoccupation.files.wordpress.com/2011/03/g4s-israel-statement-march-11-1-1.pdf, [accessed September 2011].
[82]http://corporateoccupation.wordpress.com/2011/03/27/g4s-delivers-services-to-israeli-prisons-and-illegal-settlements/, [accessed September 2011].
[83]http://www.mezan.org/upload/11648.pdf, [accessed September 2011].
[84]http://corporateoccupation.wordpress.com/2011/03/27/g4s-delivers-services-to-israeli-prisons-and-illegal-settlements/, [accessed September 2011].

prisons in Israel. As such it remains a key target for BDS campaigners, especially as the UK government's plans to further privatise public services will only result in the expansion of G4S' UK business.[85]

Public demonstrations against G4S have gathered widespread support since the alleged manslaughter of Angolan deportee Jimmy Mubenga by G4S UK security guards in October 2010.[86] On the 19 May 2011 pro-Palestine campaigners were joined by members of the Justice for Jimmy Mubenga campaign at a demonstration outside the G4S AGM at the Barbican in London.

Campaigners have also focused on targeting local councils that have contracts with G4S and requesting that they exclude the company from bidding in future. Freedom of information requests have revealed that a number of councils have had, currently have, or are considering contractual arrangements with G4S.

G4S' contracts with UK local authorities[87]

Local authority	Type of contract	Value
Amber Valley	Cash transit	£14,000 per annum
Antrim	Cash transit	£19,000 per annum
Birmingham	Cash transit	£196,544.91. Contract expires 31 December 2011
Bristol City	G4S may soon bid for a security personnel contract that is being tendered	-
Bromley	Installation of new Access Control systems and additions to existing ones	£120,000
Camden	Employed G4S in the past for one-off activities. Does not currently have a contract with the company	-

---

[85] http://www.thompsonstradeunionlaw.co.uk/information-and-resources/lelr/weekly-233.htm?utm_source=Thompsons+Solicitors&utm_campaign=8b75b87208-LELR-ISSUE-233-1-SEPT-2011&utm_medium=email#just_who_is_running_our_public_services, [accessed September 2011].
[86] http://www.guardian.co.uk/uk/2010/oct/14/security-guards-accused-jimmy-mubenga-death, [accessed September 2011].
[87] Information from UK activist who obtained details through a Freedom of Information request.

Local authority	Type of contract	Value
Sefton	Cash transit	£34,910 per annum. Contract expires March 2012.
Wakefield	Cash transit	£30,000 per annum. Contract runs from 19 November 2008 to 30 September 2011, with an option to extend for another year.
Waltham Forest	Cash transit	£54,000 per annum. Contract expires March 2012 but with an option to extend for another year.

Case study - ISS

ISS provides 'facilities services', ranging from cleaning to catering to security services. It is a Danish company but now has a global presence. It operates in over 50 countries and employs more than 520,000 people. Its revenue for 2010 was 74.073 billion DKK (£13.5 billion) and net profit was 4.367 billion DKK ($773 million).[88] ISS has operated in Israel since 1999 as **ISS Israel Comprehensive Business Services**. **ISS Israel** employs around 13,000 workers and its turnover is more than 1 billion NIS (£170 million).[89]

ISS Israel provides the full range of services offered by its parent company. These include security services, which are provided through **Kfir Protection and Control Solutions**, Israel's leading security company. ISS Israel's own website boasts that it operates a nationwide network of branches that provides security to various 'compounds' and that its directors are all former police, IDF or security forces personnel. ISS Israel/Kfir offers risk surveys, consultations, security systems, and the recruitment and management of local security. It also offers surveillance services including CCTV monitoring and 24 hour, 7 days-a-week patrols linked to a command centre.[90] Who Profits reports that ISS Israel provides manpower services to illegal Israeli settlements in the West Bank.[91]

The website for ISS's UK division states that it provides full facility services for the Ministry of Defence and the Armed Forces.[92] The company also provides services to Camden Council, **London Underground** and University College London. ISS stands to gain further contracts as a result of the UK government's move to privatise public services.

---

[88] http://ipaper.ipapercms.dk/ISS/External/issworld/Investor/Annual_Reports/Annual_Report_2010, [accessed September 2011], p.2.
[89] http://www.issisrael.co.il/?CategoryID=155, [accessed September 2011] and http://duns100.dundb.co.il/ts.cgi?tsscript=comp_heb&duns=532221660, [accessed September 2011].
[90] *Ibid* and http://www.isskfir.com/?CategoryID=156, [accessed September 2011].
[91] http://www.whoprofits.org/Company%20Info.php?id=860, [accessed September 2011].
[92] http://www.uk.issworld.com/our_services/pages/iss_mediclean.aspx, [accessed September 2011].

ISS could be particularly vulnerable to BDS campaigns in light of its reliance on public sector contracts. Targets should include companies, local authorities and universities that employ ISS for their cleaning and security needs.

The National Union of Rail, Maritime and Transport Workers (RMT), the union for London Underground workers, has adopted a pro-BDS stance and has made a number of pro-Palestine statements in the past, condemning Israeli discrimination against Arab workers, Operation Cast Lead and the attack on the Mavi Marmara.[93] As such the RMT may be amenable to working with the wider BDS movement against ISS gaining further contracts.

A high-tech occupation

The occupation fuels Israel's high-technology industries. Much of the weaponry, surveillance and security technology used in the occupation is itself high-tech and the 'civilian' and military high-tech industries operate symbiotically.

Soldiers from IDF combat units receive special concessions to attend Israeli universities under the Absorption of Discharged Soldiers Law (1994).[94] Many take advantage of these to attend institutions like the Technion, many of whose graduates go on to work in high-tech. Several high-tech companies have been set up by ex-IDF soldiers, often benefiting from technical knowledge gained in the military. Military technologies are frequently altered to produce civilian products. The founders of **Given Imaging**, an Israeli company traded on the NASDAQ, took the miniaturised sensing systems from the nose cones of fighter jets to create PillCam, a swallowable surgical camera.[95] The directors of **Compugen**, a successful Israeli high-tech bio-tech company, met through high-tech work for the IDF.[96]

As indicated above, many Israeli high-tech companies provide technology for the checkpoints. For example, **Shamrad**, a civilian company at first glance, supplies technology to Qalandia terminal.[97] Israeli arms companies provide high-tech military technology to the occupation. For example Elbit provide surveillance cameras and electronic fence systems to the West Bank apartheid wall.[98]

Many international high-tech companies are involved in providing technology used in the occupation. The Israeli subsidiary of the American **EDS** (a subsidiary of **Hewlett Packard**)

---

[93] http://www.bdsmovement.net/2009/palestine-the-key-international-issue-at-this-years-trade-unions-congress-552, [accessed September 2011], http://www.rmtlondoncalling.org.uk/node/554, [accessed September 2011], http://www.rmtlondoncalling.org.uk/node/463, [accessed September 2011] and http://www.rmtlondoncalling.org.uk/node/1592, [accessed September 2011].
[94] *Adalah, New discriminatory laws and bills in Israel*, Available: http://www.adalah.org/upfiles/2011/New_Discriminatory_Laws.pdf, [accessed September 2011].
[95] http://www.newsweek.com/2009/11/13/soldiers-of-fortune.html, [accessed September 2011].
[96] *Ibid.*
[97] http://corporateoccupation.wordpress.com/wp-admin/post.php?post=161&action=edit&message=1, [accessed September 2011].
[98] http://whoprofits.org/Company%20Info.php?id=554, [accessed September 2011].

is the prime contractor for the Basel Project, an automatic biometric access control system installed in major checkpoints in Gaza and the West Bank.[99] **Ingersoll Rand**, another international high-tech company, provides fingerprint scanners for checkpoint personnel at several West Bank checkpoints.[100]

MIRS, has been a provider of cellular phone services to the Israeli army since 2005 and will do until at least 2011. The company installs communication units in army vehicles and builds communication facilities in army bases throughout the West Bank and occupied Syrian Golan.[101] The Israeli army also uses Motorola radios.[102]

The deadly experiment

"The Israeli government and its army have been for years now using the West Bank and Gaza as their testing ground. The Palestinians are their guinea pigs. The Israeli army uses tear gas that would probably be banned in any other countries in the world. They shoot tear gas, directly at protesters, once again, an illegal act. But a very rewarding one. Israel's security industry is booming. It's never been this good..."

From the blog, Bil'in: A Village of Palestine, 02/01/11[103]

The above statement was made after Jawaher Abu Rahma, a non-violent demonstrator, collapsed and died from tear gas inhalation during a demonstration in Bil'in on New Year's Eve 2010.[104] Bil'in and villages across Palestine have become testing grounds for the Israeli security industry and for international arms companies that need an arena to try out their wares. Villages engaged in the popular struggle against the occupation are subjected to countless experiments in so-called 'non-lethal', sometimes called 'less-lethal', weapons technology. Non-violent demonstrations have been attacked with bullets, plastic-coated steel bullets, rubber bullets, baton rounds, water cannon firing corrosive chemicals, coloured dye and foul smelling water that makes you vomit, and chemical and noise weapons. Many of these weapons will soon be found on the international market.

---

[99] http://www.whoprofits.org/Newsletter.php?nlid=29, [accessed September 2011].
[100] Ingersoll Rand equipment was seen by Corporate Watch researchers in the Qalandiyah and Bethlehem terminals in March 2010 see
http://corporateoccupation.wordpress.com/2010/02/26/qalandiya-terminal-entering-the-corporate-nightmare/, [accessed September 2011].
[101] http://whoprofits.org/Newsletter.php?nlid=46, [accessed September 2011].
[102] IDF soldiers were seen by Corporate Watch researchers using Motorola radio equipment in Al Khalil (Hebron) in March 2010.
[103] Bil'in, A Village of Palestine (02/11/2011), *Happy New Year from the occupation forces: the story of the Abu Rahme Family.* Available: http://www.bilin-village.org/english/articles/different-look/Happy-New-Year-from-the-Israeli-Occupation-Forces-The-Story-of-the-Abu-Rahme-Family, [accessed September 2011].
[104] http://corporateoccupation.wordpress.com/2011/01/03/1080/, [accessed September 2011].

Spent tear gas canisters collected by demonstrators in Bil'in (Bil'in Popular Committee 2010)

Company profiles

Combined Systems (CSI), based in Jamestown USA, is the prime supplier of tear gas to Israel and flies an Israeli flag outside its US headquarters.[105] A Combined Systems Model 4431 CS Powder Barricade Penetrating Projectile high-velocity shell killed Bassem Abu Rahma, an unarmed protester, in Bil'in in April 2009. The primary purpose of these canisters is to penetrate barriers, with a secondary function of releasing a chemical gas. They clearly should not be used for crowd dispersal.[106]

CSI's customers include the Joint Non Lethal Weapons Directorate, the US State Department, **General Dynamics, Israeli Military Industries**, **Rafael Armament Development Authority** and L3 Communications.[107]

---

[105] http://adalahny.org/press-releases-other/action-alert-end-us-tear-gas-supply-and-military-aid-to-egypt-tunisia-and-israel, [accessed September 2011].
[106] B'Tselem (2010), *Summary of findings on the April 17, 2009 death of Bassem Ibrahim Abu Rahma, Bil'in*, Available: http://www.btselem.org/Download/abu_rahmeh/Abu_Rahma_report_1.pdf, [accessed 04/01/2011].
[107] Kepler, T, *Is Israel using lethal tear gas to disperse demonstrations?* Available: http://www.alternativenews.org/english/index.php/topics/news/3150-is-israel-using-lethal-tear-gas-to-disperse-demonstrations, [accessed 03/01/2011].

Corporate mercenaries

In the 1950s, 60s and 70s, the Mossad overseas intelligence agency was involved in military, political and commercial operations in a number of African countries. Mossad cultivated dictators and generals and helped them by providing advisers. The most well-known examples are its support of Idi Amin in Uganda and Mobuto Sese Seko in Zaire (now the Democratic Republic of Congo). Israeli mercenaries also worked, under the auspices of Mossad, in Central and South America.[108]

To an extent, the Israeli state's role in providing mercenaries has now been corporatised. Israeli companies are involved in supplying private military services around the world. These services are notoriously hard to pin down but it is clear that Israeli companies like the **Golan Group**, **Isrex** and **International Security and Defence Systems (ISDS)** are active in providing training, advice, bodyguard and security services in Central America.[109]

The services of military advisers are often traded with regimes in return for securing access to foreign markets. The UN has noted that military training and expertise was used as a bargaining chip when acquiring diamond concessions for Israeli companies in the Democratic Republic of Congo (*see our chapter on diamonds for more information*).[110]

Israeli mercenaries are also reportedly working on ships sailing off the Somali coastline.[111] In 2008 the **Ares Group,** another Israeli company, was part of a joint project training Indian military contractors.[112]

Resistance

Understandably, the BDS movement has put up considerable resistance to the Israeli military sector. The majority of this resistance has centered around the foreign companies supplying arms to Israel and will be discussed in a later section. There has, however, been some nascent resistance to the Israeli military export industry.

In 2004, several demonstrations and occupations were held at Rafael's office in London. This led to the relocation of the company's offices.[113] During Israel's massacre in Gaza, as the British mainstream media were speculating whether British made engines were incorporated in drones involved in killing civilians, demonstrations were held outside the **UAV engines**

---

[108] http://www.haaretz.com/print-edition/news/despite-recent-case-israelis-never-excelled-as-mercenaries-1.248378, [accessed September 2011].
[109] http://stopthewall.org/downloads/pdf/buy-in2-occ.pdf, [accessed September 2011].
[110] United Nations (December 13th 2001), *Democratic Republic of the Congo (DRC)*. Report Diamond Intelligence Briefs.
[111] http://www.haaretz.com/hasen/spages/1081385.html, [accessed September 2011].
[112] http://timesofindia.indiatimes.com/Mumbai/Private_security_firms_from_India_and_Israel_in_joint_venture/articleshow/3888225.cms, [accessed September 2011].
[113] http://www.indymedia.org.uk/en/2004/04/288502.html?style=screen, [accessed September 2011].

plant in Lichfield, UK (owned by Elbit).[114] Campaign group Bro Emlyn for Peace and Justice is involved in resisting Elbit's drone testing at ParcAberPorth in Wales.[115]

The Irish government recently turned down a tender from Israeli Military Industries to supply bullets to the Irish armed forces after pressure, through protests and lobbying, by the Irish Palestine Solidarity Campaign.[116]

Protesters hurled shoes at Downing Street during mass demonstrations against Israel's 2009 massacre in Gaza (UK Indymedia 2009)

In 2009 the Norwegian government pension fund divested from Elbit after pressure from Norwegian activists.[117] In February 2010, after further pressure from BDS campaigners **Danske Bank** divested from Elbit. Thomas H. Kjaergaard, the staff member responsible for socially responsible investment at Danske Bank said: "We handle clients' interests, and we do not want to put customers' money in companies that violate international standards."[118] The Swedish pension fund followed suit in March 2010.[119]

The death of Jawaher Abu Rahma at New Year 2011 sparked a wave of global protests against CSI, Israeli activists responded to this call by blocking a main street in Tel Aviv[120] and holding a procession to the US ambassador's house to 'return' CSI tear gas canisters, fired at demonstrators in Bil'in.[121] In the US 35 New Yorkers demonstrated outside the

---

[114]http://www.guardian.co.uk/world/2009/jan/09/armstrade-gaza, [accessed September 2011].
[115]http://www.indymedia.org.uk/en/2009/12/442920.html, [accessed September 2011].
[116]http://cosmos.ucc.ie/cs1064/jabowen/IPSC/ipsc/displayRelease.php?releaseID=412, [accessed September 2011].
[117]http://www.bdsmovement.net/2009/norwegian-pension-fund-divests-from-israeli-military-giant-elbit-533, [accessed September 2011].
[118]http://electronicintifada.net/v2/article11084.shtml, [accessed September 2011].
[119]http://www.jpost.com/Israel/Article.aspx?id=172146, [accessed September 2011].
[120]Goldman, S (01/01/2011), Hundreds rally in Tel Aviv to protest Bil'in protesters death, +972. Available: http://972mag.com/hundreds-rally-in-tel-aviv-to-protest-bilin-protesters-death/comment-page-1/#comment-2268, [accessed 03/01/2011].
[121]Rosenfeld, J and Dana, J (03/01/2011), Tears and gas; a call to mobilise, *Al Jazeera*, Available: http://english.aljazeera.net/indepth/features/2011/01/201113870502192.html, [accessed 04/01/2011].

Manhattan offices of **Point Lookout Capital Partners**, a New York investment firm that invest in CSI. Adalah NY instigated a letter writing campaign to the investors in CSI and the state department.[122] In the UK demonstrations in solidarity with the Abu-Rahma family were held at supermarkets selling Israeli goods and in Bil'in, a week after Jawaher's death thousands of Palestinians, Israelis and internationals marched to the apartheid wall. The Israeli army responded with rubber bullets and a water cannon.[123]

The wave of protests in response to the Gaza massacre in the UK saw clashes between activists and the police outside the Israeli embassy
(UK Indymedia 2009)

G4S's statement in March 2011 that they would exit some of their contracts was a preemptive action, in response to increased interest in the company by BDS campaigners, such as a citizen's tribunal into the company in London.[124] This shows that international companies are becoming increasingly aware of the threat posed by the global boycott movement.

Some initial moves have been made to lobby the EU against providing research funding for Israeli arms companies.[125] These are apparently planned to be scaled up as the EU reassesses FP7.

---

[122]http://adalahny.org/press-releases-other/1-21-11-update-tear-gas-death-triggers-mobilization-against-israel-s-lethal-tear-gas, [accessed September 2011].
[123]http://www.youtube.com/watch?v=oTEAHMuHCkM, [accessed September 2011].
[124]http://www.russelltribunalonpalestine.com/en/1089/russell-tribunal-hears-details-of-need-to-end-uk-israel-arms-deals, [accessed September 2011].
[125]See for instance http://www.ipsc.ie/pdf/ipsc_factsheet_-_how_israeli_arms_companies_benefit_from_eu_science_funds.pdf, [accessed September 2011].

In July 2011 the BNC issued a new call, endorsed by a broad coalition of Palestinian groups, for an arms embargo against Israel. The call demands that governments:

1. Cease forthwith any provision to Israel of arms and related material of all types, including the sale or transfer of weapons and ammunitions, military vehicles and equipment, paramilitary police equipment, including dual-use equipment, and spare parts for the aforementioned, and cease as well the provision of all types of equipment and supplies and grants of licensing arrangements for the manufacture of aforementioned or maintenance of the aforementioned;
2. Stop all military and dual-use imports (equipment, assistance and munitions) from Israel;
3. Stop the transfer of military products to and from Israel through national ports, territory and airspace;
4. Stop cooperation with the Israeli army, military companies, and military-related R&D projects, including joint ventures (whether bilateral or multilateral);
5. Halt all military-related training and consultancies involving the Israeli army, military companies and academic research institutions;
6. End all military aid to Israel;
7. Refrain from any cooperation with Israel in the manufacture and development of nuclear weapons and mobilize for a nuclear-free Middle East.[126]

Where next?

Israeli military companies and their subsidiaries have premises internationally. These premises should be the target of direct action aimed at making it impossible for the Israeli arms trade to retain a base outside Israel.

BDS campaigners should focus on preventing the renewal of the FP7 programme and should campaign for the exclusion of Israeli arms companies implicated in war crimes from all current and future EU research funding projects, and take steps to ensure that all companies complicit with Israeli violations of international law are excluded from post-2013 EU research funds. It may be possible to isolate EU research projects, identify the participants in joint projects and campaign for a boycott of these projects until Israeli companies are excluded.

Governments should be pressured to adhere to the BNC call. In particular, not to enter into joint projects with Israeli arms companies, such as the ParcAberPorth programme in Wales, and to exclude the Israeli arms sector from military procurement tendering.

---

[126]http://www.bdsmovement.net/activecamps/military-embargo, [accessed September 2011].

BIL'IN

THE ISRAELI ARMS, 'DEFENCE', AND SECURITY INDUSTRIES ARE BOOMING. NO WONDER -- THEY AND THE INTERNATIONAL COMPANIES WORKING WITH THEM USE THE PALESTINIAN POPULATION AS TEST SUBJECTS!

UNMANNED BULLDOZERS, AIRCRAFT AND BOATS PATROL AND BOMBARD THE BESIEGED GAZA STRIP AND THE LATEST IN CCTV, FINGERPRINT AND BODY SCANNER EQUIPMENT PROLIFERATE AT THE HUNDREDS OF ISRAELI CHECKPOINTS ACROSS THE WEST BANK, THE VILLAGE OF BIL'IN HAS, SINCE 2005, BEEN RESISTING ISRAEL'S APARTHEID WALL AND SETTLEMENTS WHICH ENCROACH ON THE VILLAGE'S LAND.

VILLAGES LIKE BIL'IN ARE SUBJECTED TO COUNTLESS EXPERIMENTS IN SO CALLED 'NON LETHAL' OR 'LESS LETHAL' WEAPONS TECHNOLOGY. THE COMMUNITY'S STEADFAST RESISTANCE HAS WON AN ANNOUNCEMENT IN FEBRUARY 2010, BY THE MILITARY, THAT THE WALL'S ROUTE AROUND THE VILLAGE WOULD BE ALTERED.

BIL'IN HAS BECOME A SYMBOL OF A NEW POPULAR RESISTANCE TO THE ISRAELI OCCUPATION AND HAS ATTRACTED INTERNATIONAL SOLIDARITY IN THE EFFORT FOR BOYCOTT, DIVESTMENT AND SANCTIONS (BDS) AGAINST ISRAELI APARTHEID.

BIL'IN'S SUCCESSES HAVE COME AT A PRICE TO MANY OF ITS OCCUPANTS. SUCH AS THE ABU RAHMA FAMILY.

Bil'in by Sean Michael Wilson and Rejena Smiley 146

2009...
CRICCK!
BASSEM ABU RAHMA, THE BROTHER OF ASHRAF, WAS SHOT AT CLOSE RANGE BY A TEAR GAS CANISTER AND DIED FROM HIS WOUNDS...
MANY OF THESE WEAPONS WILL SOON BE FOUND ON THE INTERNATIONAL MARKET, AFTER BEING TRIED AND TESTED ON THE PEOPLE OF PALESTINE, WHOSE DEATHS, WHOSE SUFFERING AND GRIEF IS VALUED LESS THAN THAT OF THE PEOPLE OF LONDON OR WASHINGTON.

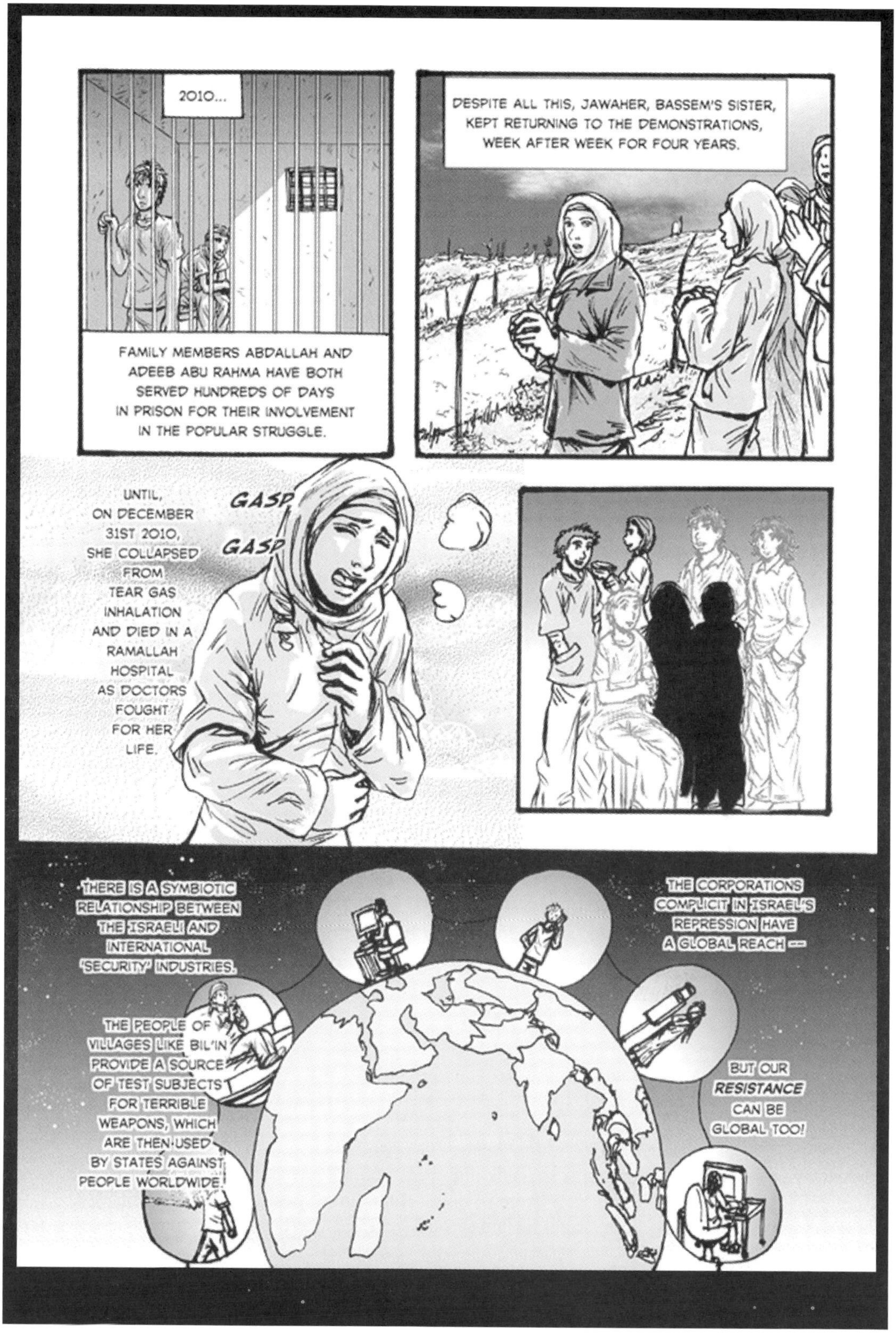
2010...
FAMILY MEMBERS ABDALLAH AND ADEEB ABU RAHMA HAVE BOTH SERVED HUNDREDS OF DAYS IN PRISON FOR THEIR INVOLVEMENT IN THE POPULAR STRUGGLE.
DESPITE ALL THIS, JAWAHER, BASSEM'S SISTER, KEPT RETURNING TO THE DEMONSTRATIONS, WEEK AFTER WEEK FOR FOUR YEARS.
UNTIL, ON DECEMBER 31ST 2010, SHE COLLAPSED FROM TEAR GAS INHALATION AND DIED IN A RAMALLAH HOSPITAL AS DOCTORS FOUGHT FOR HER LIFE.
GASP
GASP
THERE IS A SYMBIOTIC RELATIONSHIP BETWEEN THE ISRAELI AND INTERNATIONAL 'SECURITY' INDUSTRIES.
THE PEOPLE OF VILLAGES LIKE BIL'IN PROVIDE A SOURCE OF TEST SUBJECTS FOR TERRIBLE WEAPONS, WHICH ARE THEN USED BY STATES AGAINST PEOPLE WORLDWIDE.
THE CORPORATIONS COMPLICIT IN ISRAEL'S REPRESSION HAVE A GLOBAL REACH --
BUT OUR RESISTANCE CAN BE GLOBAL TOO!

16
High-Tech

Israel's high-tech sector accounts for around 15 per cent of the country's annual GDP[1] and almost 45 per cent of Israeli exports.[2] According to market analysis by financial services company **Morgan Stanley**, Israel's high-technology goods and services have "developed beyond the wildest projections and now account for about one-third of GDP."[3] With high-tech firms contributing around a third of industrial output, several analysts think the Israeli economy as a whole is "over-reliant" on the sector.[4] A BDS focus on the high-tech sector could therefore present a serious challenge to Israeli apartheid.

The country has the highest number of high-tech start-up companies per capita in the world, although many are eventually bought out by larger international firms. Still, the sale of start-ups has contributed considerably to the $70 billion of foreign direct investment flowing into Israel since 1998.[5] The success of the sector is built on calculated intervention by the Israeli state and any company taking advantage of the state's economic incentives gives tacit support to the Israeli government's apartheid policies. The favour is now being repaid as the presence of **Intel** and other international high-tech giants feeds into the false narrative that presents Israel as an advanced market economy backed by liberal democracy.

Israel's non-military high-tech sector, whilst dating back to the 1960s, took off during the 1990s as part of a targeted government scheme aimed at generating start-ups. The *Yozma* (initiative in Hebrew) programme partnered the government with foreign venture capitalist funds, providing capital for start-ups to take advantage of the Information and Communication Technology (ICT) revolution. As a result, a burgeoning Israeli high-tech cluster developed, in which international and domestic firms became concentrated in particular areas of the country, orienting the sector towards a start-up-intensive ICT model.

The *Yozma* funds, which began in 1993, raised $460 million up until the end of the program in 1998. Yet the capital investment was only part of high-tech's success. A favourable external environment also played a major role, including the deregulation of communications markets, which allowed penetration by foreign capital.[6] Similarly, internal factors such as domestic regulatory reform favouring entrepreneurship, the alleged 'peace dividends' of the

---

[1] Toth, S (2010), Innovative Israel failing to grow high-tech start-ups, *Wall Street Journal*. Available: http://online.wsj.com/article/SB10001424052748703632304575451211403181030.html?mod=google news_wsj, [accessed 09/03/2011].
[2] http://www.state.gov/r/pa/ei/bgn/3581.htm, [accessed 09/03/2011].
[3] http://www.jewishpolicycenter.org/221/israels-high-tech-boom, [accessed 09/03/2011].
[4] Klingler Vidra, R (2011), Insights from Israeli Central Bank [guest post], *Venture Capital Cafe*. Available: http://www.vccafe.com/israel/insights-from-israeli-central-bank-guest-post/, [accessed 16th July 2011].
[5] http://online.wsj.com/article/SB10001424052748703632304575451211403181030.html?mod=googl enews_wsj, [accessed 09/03/2011].
[6] *Ibid*.

Oslo Accords, and the concomitant influx of well-educated Russian immigrants, also played a part.

The phrase 'peace dividends' (economic incentives brought about by perceived conflict resolution) is based on the false premise that business supported the Oslo Accords for altruistic reasons, when, in fact, all that business wanted was a more stable environment to realise greater profit margins.[7] At the beginning of the 1990s Israeli business leaders became more vocal in support for negotiations between their government and the PLO. For example, at the Jerusalem Business Conference held in the run-up to the 1992 Israeli parliamentary elections the president of the Israeli Manufacturer's Association, Dov Lautman, made a statement claiming the major obstacle to foreign investment in Israel was regional instability.[8] The Oslo Accords, whilst consolidating Israel's occupation and Israeli apartheid, created a more favourable investment environment because the agreement was presented to the international community as a sign of reconciliation and future stability.

Economic migration

Israel has benefited greatly from immigration, which has helped create a highly skilled and well-educated workforce. The country has more scientists and engineers, proportional to population, than any country in the world. Yet their salaries, at an average of $62,000 per year,[9] are considerably lower than their counterparts in Silicon Valley (which averaged $99,000 in 2010).[10] This combination has made Israel an attractive site for multinational research and development (R&D) labs.

Importing a highly skilled workforce in itself is a result of stratification within Israel's Jewish population based on ethnic lines. Moshe Machover and Akiva Orr argue that the expansion of the Israeli economy created greater demand for skilled workers, which could be achieved in one of two ways. Either investment in educating the large number of unskilled Middle Eastern and African Jews, or recruiting Jewish skilled workers from abroad.[11] Due to the dynamics of both capitalism and Zionism, the second option was pursued, compounding the inferior position of African and Middle-Eastern Jews in Israel.[12]

---

[7]Ben-Porat, G (2005), Between power and hegemony; business communities in peace processes, *Review of International Studies,* volume 31, p.325-348.
[8]Shafir, G (1998), Business in politics: globalization and the search for peace in South Africa and Israel/Palestine. *Israel Affairs,* 5: 2-3, p. 103-120.
[9]Swirski, S (2011), *Israel's new business elite and the rifts it rests on, Adva Centre,* Available: http://jfjfp.com/?p=23667, [accessed 16th July 2011].
[10]Iwatani Kane, Y (2011), Local technology salaries lead the nation, *Wall Street Journal.* Available: http://online.wsj.com/article/SB10001424052748703439504576116192416198636.ht ml, [accessed 16th July 2011].
[11]Machover, M and Orr, A (2002), The class character of Israel, *International Socialist Review.* Issue 23, May-June 2002.
[12] Machover, M, and Orr, A (2002), The class character of Israel, *Idem.*

Foreign influence has played a big part in the development of Israel's high-tech sector, with **Motorola**, **IBM** and **Intel** opening research labs in the country during the 1970s.[13] This helped to develop a pool of scientists and engineers in Israel even before the influx of Soviet migrants. Universities, such as Haifa and the Hebrew University, also established research labs focusing on high-tech innovation.

Matam high-tech park in Haifa (Corporate Watch 2010)

Today, there are a plethora of high-tech industrial parks littering the country, with the most important centring around Tel Aviv and its suburbs. These include Tel Aviv's Atidim Industrial Park, the MATAM High Tech Park in Haifa, and the Kiryat Weizmann Industrial Park.[14] Many of these parks work in conjunction with neighbouring universities and research institutions. The result is that "most [Israeli] kids dream of high-tech";[15] that is, knowledge work, international travel and public offerings on the NASDAQ stock exchange.[16]

Office of the Chief Scientist (OCS)

Part of the Ministry of Industry, Trade and Labor, the OCS is charged with encouraging and supporting industrial research and developments in Israel, providing a variety of support programmes with an annual budget of around $300 million, spent on 1,000 projects undertaken by 500 companies.[17] OCS' main programme supports Israeli companies in R&D

---

[13] Kose, G and Pedersen, JB (2008/09), Venture capital's effect on formation and development of high-tech clusters: the case of Israel, *Microeconomics of Technical Change,* Available: http://www.scribd.com/doc/38787882/VC-and-High-Tech-Clusters-in-Israel-Final-Version, [accessed 09/03/2011].
[14] http://www.jewishvirtuallibrary.org/jsource/Economy/eco4.html, [accessed September 2011].
[15] Beit-On; cited Avishai, B (2002), Post-Zionist Israel, *The American Prospect*. Available: http://prospect.org/cs/articles?article=postZionist_israel, [accessed 16th July 2010].
[16] *Ibid*.
[17] http://www.investinisrael.gov.il/NR/exeres/E94974C8-983B-4ED6-9E7E-CC7D0EDB1534.htm, [accessed September 2011].

projects, offering grants of up to 50 per cent of the R&D expenditure, which is then repaid should the project be commercially successful.

EU funding

Israel also benefits from being the only non-European state fully participating in the EU's Seventh Framework Program for R&D (FP7). The aim of the FP7 is to strengthen the technological and scientific industries, with monetary contributions coming from the EU, European countries and private-sector participants.[18] The EU is second only to the **Israel Science Foundation** in Jerusalem as a source of research funding Israel.[19] The Israeli government forecasts the return on its involvement in the current EU programme to be worth at least €500 million ($684 million) by its conclusion in 2013.[20]

The EU also makes the Israeli high-tech sector more attractive to other investors. US high-tech companies are attracted by preferential access to lucrative EU markets through the EU-Israel Association Agreement, which came into force in June 2000.[21]

Small pool of big players

Despite this apparent success, the country has just four technology companies worth more than $1 billion.[22] These include **NICE Systems**[23] and **CheckPoint Software Technologies**.[24] The latter is a leading multinational company which, according to the Jewish Policy Centre, provides internet security solutions to each and every company on the Fortune 100 list.[25] CheckPoint's 2010 profits were $452.8 million.[26]

NICE Systems has similar coverage. Over 25,000 organisations utilise NICE, in both business and security, stretching across 150 countries and encompassing more than 80 Fortune 100 companies. Customers include **Air France, American Express, JP Morgan Chase, Lloyds TSB** and **T-Mobile**. NICE security systems are also used at the Eiffel Tower and the Statue of Liberty.[27] NICE Systems' gross profits for 2010 were $451.9 million, up from $371.1 million for the previous year.[28]

---

[18] http://cordis.europa.eu/fp6/fp6_glance.htm, [accessed September 2011].
[19] http://www.silviacattori.net/article1077.html, [accessed September 2011].
[20] *Ibid.*
[21] http://ec.europa.eu/trade/creating-opportunities/bilateral-relations/countries/israel, [accessed September 2011].
[22] Toth, S (2010), Innovative Israel failing to grow high-tech start-ups, *Wall Street Journal.*
[23] http://ycharts.com/companies/NICE/market_cap, [accessed September 2011].
[24] *Ibid.*
[25] http://www.jewishpolicycenter.org/221/israels-high-tech-boom, [accessed September 2011].
[26] http://www.bizjournals.com/sanfrancisco/news/2011/01/31/check-point-software-profit-up-in-2010.html, [accessed September 2011].
[27] http://www.nice.com/company-overview, [accessed September 2011].
[28] http://www.nice.com/content/nice-reports-record-fourth-quarter-and-full-year-2010-results, [accessed September 2011].

Beyond ICT: ISCAR

The Israeli high-tech sector is not confined to software and internet start-ups. It encompasses companies such as **Iscar Metalworking**, a world leader in manufacturing precision metalworking tools. Iscar is part of Israel's metalworking conglomerate **IMC Group**, owned by Israeli billionaire Stef Wertheimer and his family. Wertheimer has established five industrial parks, with Iscar operating from the Tefen industrial park in Western Galilee.[29] Iscar is a conglomerate, with subsidiaries in countries including China, Turkey, Britian and South Korea.

Iscar company made the headlines in 2006 when US investment tycoon Warren Buffet, and his **Berkshire Hathaway Holdings**, paid $4 billion for an 80 per cent controlling stake.[30] In 2008, Iscar became the first Israeli company to take over a Japanese company when it purchased 95 per cent of shares in competitor **Tungaloy**.[31]

International Investment

As highlighted above, many international companies have R&D labs in Israel, while others have bought out small high-tech start-ups. **Motorola** was the first multinational to begin operations in Israel, opening a semiconductor facility at Arad in 1964. The facility produces two-way radios, modems, mobile phones and alarm systems. In total, the company has four R&D centres in Israel. **Motorola Israel** is responsible for engineering, marketing and sales for Eastern European and Central African markets.[32]

One of **Microsoft**'s three 'Strategic Global Development Centre's[33] is based in Ra'anana, north of Tel Aviv. A high-tech park on the northern edge of Ra'anana is also home to **Hewlett Packard**, which has a laboratory on the campus of the **Technion** Israeli Institute of Technology in Haifa.[34] **IBM** runs an R&D lab on Haifa University campus, employing over 500 staff and students.[35] The lab collaborates with other multinational companies, including **Samsung**.[36] IBM also has facilities in Tel Aviv, Herzliya, Rehovot, Jerusalem and Matam business park in Haifa. The latter employs over 2,000 people.[37]

---

[29] http://www.iscar.com/Section.asp/CountryID/17/SectionID/813/SectionFatherID/14, [accessed September 2011].
[30] http://newstopics.jpost.com/topic/ISCAR_Metalworking, [accessed September 2011].
[31] http://www.haaretz.com/print-edition/business/iscar-buying-japanese-competitor-for-1b-1.254275, [accessed September 2011].
[32] *Ibid.*
[33] http://www.microsoft.com/Israel/rnd/, [accessed September 2011].
[34] www.hpl.hp.com/israel, [accessed September 2011].
[35] http://www.israel21c.org/technology/ibm-israel-and-samsung-develop-software-reuse-technology, [accessed September 2011].
[36] *Ibid.*
[37] http://palestinechronicle.com/view_article_details.php?id=15722, [accessed September 2011].

In 2003, American software manufacturer **Marvell Technology Group** acquired one of the successful Yozma start-ups, **RADLAN,** which supplies intranet network services.[38] The company was renamed **Marvell Software Solutions Israel (MSSI)** and supplies components to, among others, **Intel**, **Apple**, **Dell** and **Cisco**.[39] Marvell also merged with another start-up, **Galileo**, to create a subsidiary, **Marvell Semiconductor Israel Ltd**.[40] The company is located at Atidim business park in Tel Aviv.

Company profile: Intel

Intel Israel produces computer processors and other hardware components, operating a billion-dollar export business. These products are used in PC's, Apple Macs and smart phones. The company has been operating in Israel since 1974, in fact the country was the site of Intel's first development centre outside the US.[41] The company now has five facilities: microprocessor plants in Har Jotzim (Jerusalem) and Qiryat Gat, and research and development centres in Haifa, Yakum and Tel Aviv district.

Intel's Fab 28 plant in Kiryat Gat, on the land of Al-Faluja and Iraq-al-Manshiya (In Minds 2002)

According to US-based journalist Henry Norr the Qiryat Gat plant, called Fab 28, lies on the land of two villages, Iraq al Manshiyya and al-Faluja, located in an area designated within the Palestinian territories by the 1947 UN partition plan.[42] Whilst Egyptian troops ensured

---

[38]http://investing.businessweek.com/research/stocks/private/snapshot.asp?privcapId=515437, [accessed September 2011].
[39]http://www.ivc-online.com/G_info.asp?objectType=1&fObjectID=9irgcbaw2en&CameFrom=GoogleSearch&utm_source=google&utm_medium=google_pages&utm_campaign=google_pages, [accessed September 2011].
[40]http://investing.businessweek.com/research/stocks/private/snapshot.asp?privcapId=28813, [accessed September 2011].
[41]http://www.intel.com/jobs/israel, [accessed September 2011].
[42]http://electronicintifada.net/content/nakba-intel-and-kiryat-gat/7625, [accessed September 2011].

Jewish forces did not capture the villages during the 1948-49 war, Israel finally gained control of the area after agreeing an armistice with Egypt in February 1949.[43] Over 2,000 Palestinian villagers and 1,100 refugees were then expelled from Iraq al Manshiyya and al-Faluja.[44]

(Above and below) The expulsion of Palestinians from Al Faluja by Jewish forces in 1949. Intel's facility was established there in 1999 (Palestine Remembered)

---

[43] *Ibid.*
[44] *Ibid.*

Intel is hugely important to the Israeli high-tech sector. The company is Israel's largest private employer, with over 7,000 employees[45] which is more than Intel's Silicon Valley workforce.[46] It also holds the dubious honour of being Israel's largest private exporter.[47] The Fab 28 plant produces more than $10 million worth of advanced microprocessors every day. Intel exports from Israel totalled $2.7 billion in 2010, down from a record $3.4 billion in the previous year.[48] The company is expected to invest over $2 billion in upgrading Fab 28 between 2011 and 2013.[49] An additional 1,000 people will be hired to support the expansion. The Israeli government is so desperate to keep Intel operating in the country that Finance Minister Yuval Steinitz offered the company a $110 million grant in 2010 for long-term commitments to Israel.[50]

Intel's next generation of nano-chips, code-named Sandy Bridge, have been developed between labs in Haifa and the US. They are expected to generate about a third of Intel's revenue in 2011. The Haifa centre is working on advancing other next-generation processors.[51] The Intel Centrino microchip was designed and developed at the Petach Tikva facility just outside Tel Aviv.[52]

Blurring the Borders

The lines between where the Israeli military sector ends and the civilian high-tech sector begins are sketchy at best. There is a huge amount of crossover, due to the symbiotic relationship between high-tech companies, arms manufacturers and the academic institutions providing engineers, scientists and R&D labs. As the Israeli economy moved towards a high-tech intensive model, the country's universities became valuable tools in building the required knowledge base.[53] They have also helped foster Israeli military technology.

---

[45] http://www.reuters.com/article/2011/01/18/intel-israel-idUSLDE70H0NI20110118, [accessed September 2011].
[46] http://www.palestineremembered.com/Gaza/al-Faluja/Story10915.html, [accessed Sept 2011].
[47] http://www.vosizneias.com/74263/2011/01/25/jerusalem-intel-to-invest-2-7-bln-in-israel-chip-plant, [accessed September 2011].
[48] http://www.reuters.com/article/2011/01/18/intel-israel-idUSLDE70H0NI20110118, [accessed September 2011].
[49] http://www.reuters.com/article/2011/01/18/intel-israel-idUSLDE70H0NI20110118, [accessed September 2011].
[50] Coren, O (2010), Israel offers Intel $110 million for commitment to stay in the country, *Haaretz*.
[51] http://www.vosizneias.com/74263/2011/01/25/jerusalem-intel-to-invest-2-7-bln-in-israel-chip-plant, [accessed September 2011].
[52] http://www.israel21c.org/technology/intel-develops-the-eco-chip-with-israeli-help, [accessed September 2011] and http://www.jewishvirtuallibrary.org/jsource/Economy/israelchip.html, [accessed September 2011].
[53] Yacobi Keller, U (2009), The economy of the occupation: academic boycott of Israel, *Alternative Information Center* (AIC) Bulletin No. 23-24. Available: http://kanan48.wordpress.com/2009/10/23/the-economy-of-the-occupation-academic-boycott-of-israel-by-uri-yacobi-keller, [accessed 12/03/2011].

The **Technion** in Haifa has "all but enlisted" itself in the military,[54] helping develop high-tech instruments used in the daily grinding-down of the Palestinian people. For example, the remote-controlled D9 bulldozer, used to demolish Palestinian homes, was designed at the university.[55]

Intel has a very close relationship with the Technion and takes advantage of the human capital the institution produces. Thus, Technion trains engineers for Intel, while Intel nurtures a research environment at the university, providing labs, grants and directions for research into the new technologies.[56]

Likewise, there is cross-fertilisation between military and civilian high-tech research, with the latter benefiting greatly from military know-how. The biggest benefit came from the restructuring of the defence industries during the late 1980's and early 90's, in which hundreds of engineers were made redundant.[57] Similarly, research is being carried out by arms manufacturers that has seemingly civilian purposes. **Israel Aerospace Industries** (IAI), whose warplanes are used in the occupied territories, is benefiting from the EU-financed "Clean Sky" project, aimed at developing environmentally-friendly aircraft engines.[58] Many software and electronics companies, both Israeli and international, also manufacture high-tech military products.

Benefits from discriminatory laws

International high-tech companies have benefited from Israeli laws which, whilst encouraging foreign direct investment, are also designed to crush the Palestinians economically – both inside 1948 Israel and in the OPT. Areas deemed as 'National Priority Areas' (NPAs) include the Naqab, where the Israeli government is currently operating a calculated policy of ethnic cleansing against Bedouin communities.

The 2009 Economic Efficiency Law grants government powers to classify towns, villages and areas as NPAs and allocate enormous state resources without criteria. These classifications are overwhelmingly given to Jewish towns, a practice that led to a landmark Israeli Supreme Court ruling in 2006 that a government decision classifying 553 Jewish towns and only 4 small Arab villages as NPAs was unconstitutional.[59]

This law is an amendment to the Encouragement of Capital Investments Law, passed in the

---

[54]*Ibid.*
[55]Yacobi Keller, U (2009), The economy of the occupation, *Idem.*
[56]http://technionlive.blogspot.com/2011/02/technion-intels-sandy-bridge-chip.html, [accessed 12/03/2011].
[57]Avnimelech, G (2009), *VC policy: Yozma Program 15-year perspective,* paper presented at the Summer Conference 2009 at Copenhagen Business School.
[58]Cronin, D (2009), How Israeli arms companies benefit from EU science funds. Available: http://www.silviacattori.net/article1077.html, [accessed 14/03/2011].
[59]*Adalah* (2010), New discriminatory laws and bills in Israel, Available: http://www.old-adalah.org/eng/, [accessed 14/03/2011].

1950s, which splits the country into three 'priority areas' – A,B,C with A being of highest priority. Intel's original $1.6 billion plant at Qiryat Gat, which began operations in 1999, benefited from a $600 million grant from the Israeli state as part of this law.[60] Motorola has similarly benefited from the scheme, building an R&D centre at Ashdot Yaakov in the part of the Jordan Valley inside 1948 Israel.[61]

Yoneam Industrial Zone is in 'National Priority Area A', and state approved enterprises enjoy the highest level of tax breaks and investment grants. It benefits from it's close proximity to the Technion in north eastern Haifa, which also means there is a cross over between high-tech companies and the institute through Israeli NPA policies. Domestic businesses that have benefited from tax breaks and other economic incentives through NPA include **3DV**, which was purchased by Microsoft in 2009.[62] 3DV developed the Project Natal technology which **Microsoft** is now using to rival the **Nintendo** Wii in sensory gaming technology.[63].

Other International high-tech companies with R&D investments in Israel include **PayPal, Google, Siemens, Cisco, AOL, Philips, Texas Instruments, Nortel** and **AT&T**.[64]

Google's facilty in Haifa

---

[60] http://archive.globes.co.il/searchgl/Haviva%20Cohen,%20director%20of%20the%20Investment%20Promotion_s_hd_0L3CqE3SqN3GrC3GsDIveT6ri.html, [accessed 12/03/2011].
[61] http://www.globes.co.il/serveen/globes/docview.asp?did=1000324592, [accessed 15th July 2011].
[62] http://www.vccafe.com/3dv-systems/3dv-systems-and-primesense-are-the-israeli-firms-behind-microsofts-project-natal/, [accessed 15th July 2011].
[63] http://www.engadget.com/2009/06/03/microsofts-project-natal-roots-revealed-3dv-systems-zcam/, [accessed 15th July 2011].
[64] http://www.slideshare.net/IsraelExport/new-mediaisrael-export-institute, [accessed 15th July 2011].

Outsourcing the occupation

A recent phenomenon in Israel's high-tech sector is the outsourcing of work to Palestinian companies in the West Bank. As with peace dividends, this is not based on an inherent desire among businesses to build bridges towards a political solution, but purely on economics. Palestinian engineers and programmers are cheaper, work within the same time zone and more often than not speak Hebrew or English, allowing for easier communication.[65] Around 10 start-up and international companies with a base in Israel have become involved in this type of outsourcing since 2007, including Cisco, Intel, Hewlett Packard and Microsoft.[66] Unsurprisingly, projects are conducted without recourse to the political situation and represent a new dimension to the paradigm of denial that exists amongst multinational companies operating in Israel. It normalises a situation in which people working on the same project cannot meet as they could in the UK or US, because of the restriction of movement imposed on Palestinians.

Resistance

There is a lot of work to be done in terms of targeting international high-tech companies complicit in the cross-fertilisation and symbiosis between military, software and academic R&D. Motorola has been targeted by the Hang Up on Motorola campaign, although more for the company's military high-tech involvement. The most concerted targeting of Intel has come from the Connecticut based Palestine Right to Return Coalition, which has been encouraging Palestinians and international activists to write to the media about Fab 28's location on an evacuated village.[67] The coalition is also trying to contact the original villagers of Iraq-al-Manshiyya and neighbouring Al-Faluja and their descendants (around 15,000 people). The chief demand of the group is that Intel divests from Israel.

In 2009, Hampshire College at Amherst, Massachusetts, became the first US college to divest from companies involved in propping up the occupation.[68] The move came after a concerted effort from Students for Justice in Palestine (SJP). Among the six multinationals divested from was Motorola. A similar campaign could easily be pursued by students and trade unionists in the UK. Any local authority or university pension fund with investment in Intel, Microsoft and the myriad of other high-tech firms benefiting from apartheid are ripe targets. Similarly, whenever procurement contracts are issued, or computer suits need renewing, concerted pressure is needed to frame the terms on which this is achieved, freezing out any company with links to businesses investing in Israel.

---

[65] Associated Press (2010), Israeli high-tech companies outsourcing to Palestinians, *Haaretz*. Available: http://www.haaretz.com/news/national/israeli-high-tech-companies-outsourcing-to-palestinians-1.331256, [accessed 15th July 2011].
[66] *Ibid*.
[67] http://www.inminds.com/boycott-intel.html, [accessed 15th July 2011].
[68] http://pulsemedia.org/2009/02/12/hampshire-college-becomes-first-college-in-us-to-divest-from-israeli-occupation/, [accessed 15th July 2011].

Where next?

Because Israeli high-tech companies and research labs generate so much revenue, and their services permeate a huge number of multinational companies, they are an important target for the BDS movement. Yet, it can also make them harder to avoid. Without doubt, if the boycott is going to achieve its aim of ending occupation and apartheid, it needs to move beyond settlement industries and target the Israeli economy as a whole. Because Israel's economy is so reliant on high-tech, a BDS focus on this sector represents a chance to seriously damage Israel's ability to continue funding the occupation.

The obvious target is Intel, although purchasing a computer without an Intel microprocessor is difficult. Non-Israeli alternatives include **ADM** and **VIA**. However, the former has entered into a distribution contract with Israeli company **Commex**.[69] As with boycotts aimed at agricultural goods, it is important to express a desire to avoid buying a computer with an Intel chip or other Israeli components to shop assistants and explain why.

Targeting high-tech companies like Intel offers a chance for the boycott movement to move beyond consumer actions. The Zionist logic thrives on the fact that it is near-impossible to buy a computer or even mobile phone without an Israeli component. As such, it is necessary to attack the high-tech sector on all fronts, particularly in forcing multinational companies to divest from the country. This means moving beyond individual consumer actions and towards targeted divestment campaigns and direct action.

---

[69] http://www.globes.co.il/serveen/globes/docview.asp?did=1000292708&fid=1725, [accessed 15th July 2011].

17
Diamonds

"Contrary to claims by the diamond industry and jewellers that all diamonds are now conflict-free, they are not. Israel's dominant position in the industry means that diamonds crafted in Israel are interspersed globally with diamonds crafted in other countries. Consumers who purchase diamonds that are not laser-inscribed to identify where they were crafted run a significant risk of purchasing a diamond crafted in Israel, thereby helping to fund gross human rights violations."

Israel's Blood Diamonds, Sean Clinton, Electronic intifada, 2010[1]

Israeli businesses play a significant role in the global diamond industry, cutting, polishing and selling diamonds from around the world. Israel is the largest global exporter of cut diamonds.[2] Polished diamonds account for a significant share of Israeli export trade, amounting to some 31 per cent of Israel's total exports in 2009.[3] Around half Israel's polished diamonds are consistently exported to the US. Other important markets are China, Singapore, Japan, India, Hong Kong and Switzerland.[4] The sector, however, accounts for only a relatively small share of GDP.[5] Israel's net polished diamond exports were worth $1.45 billion in the first quarter of 2010.[6] In 2009, diamonds accounted for 14.4 per cent of Israel's imports.[7]

Israel's diamond sector is divided between a small number of diamond magnates, or corporate oligarchs, who vie for a bigger slice of the lucrative supply of African rough diamonds. Two of these oligarchs are Lev Leviev, who imports rough diamonds from Angola and Namibia and Dan Gertler, scion of Israel's 'King of Diamonds', who has attempted to achieve a monopoly on the supply of rough diamonds from the Democratic Republic of Congo (DRC). For decades the Israeli diamond industry relied on a supply of rough diamonds from **De Beers**. Gertler and Leviev penetrated the West African diamond market after De Beers pulled out of Angola and DRC.[8]

The Ramat Gan Diamond Exchange in Tel Aviv is, according to its chairman, the most secure place in Israel. Entrance is strictly forbidden for the general public and the exchange

---

[1] Clinton, S (2010), Israel's blood diamonds, *Electronic intifada*, Available: http://electronicintifada.net/v2/article11170.shtml, [accessed February 2011].
[2] *Ibid*.
[3] http://www.cbs.gov.il/publications/isr_in_n09e.pdf, [accessed February 2011], p.20.
[4] http://www.israelidiamond.co.il/english/ImportExpport.aspx?id=94&boneid=1472, [accessed February 2011].
[5] OECD (2009), *Economic survey of Israel 2009, Idem*, p.29.
[6] http://af.reuters.com/article/topNews/idAFJOE64N0L720100524?pageNumber=2&virtualBrandChannel=0, [accessed February 2011].
[7] http://www.cbs.gov.il/publications/isr_in_n09e.pdf, [accessed February 2011], p.20.
[8] Berger, S (2001), Diamonds in the rough, *Jerusalem Post*.

strictly limits its membership to benefit its existing members.[9]

The Israeli diamond industry promotes itself at a range of international trade shows. During March 2011 20 Israeli diamond companies exhibited at BASELWORLD 2011, an annual jewelry trade fair in Basel.[10]

Diamond exchange district in Ramat Gan, Tel Aviv

Blood diamonds from Israel

In July 2000, players in the global diamond industry set up the World Diamond Council (WDC). The WDC was established as a response to public outrage about the use of diamonds to fund bloody conflicts in West African countries.[11] In 2003, the WDC introduced a system of self-regulation, called the Kimberly Process Certification Scheme, to stem the flow of 'conflict' or 'blood diamonds'. The concerns of the WDC and the Kimberley Process are confined to scrutinising the trade in rough diamonds from source, not investigating the ethics of the entire diamond trade. This definition allows Israel, a nation engaged in an illegal occupation and regularly accused of war crimes, to head the Kimberley Process, which it chaired in 2010.[12]

Despite Israel's prominence in the Kimberley Process its diamond trade is by no means squeaky clean. In 2007 a security company contracted by Lev Leviev was accused by an Angolan human rights monitor of participating in practices of "humiliation, whipping, torture, sexual abuse, and, in some cases, assassinations."[13]

---

[9] *Ibid.*
[10] http://www.baselworld.com/en-US/The-Show/Key-Facts-And-Figures.aspx, [accessed February 2011].
[11] Clinton, S (2010), Israel's blood diamonds, *Electronic intifada, Idem.*
[12] http://www.israelidiamond.co.il/english/news.aspx?boneid=2889, [accessed February 2011].
[13] http://nymag.com/news/intelligencer/31549/, [accessed February 2011].

Dan Gertler: Trading conflict for diamonds

Israeli Diamonds International (IDI), owned by Dan Gertler, agreed, in 2000, to pay Laurent Kabila, President of the Democratic Republic of Congo, $20 million for a monopoly on the purchase of Congolese diamonds. The UN received information that the deal included unpublished clauses, in which IDI agreed to arrange, through its connections with high-ranking Israeli military officers, the delivery of undisclosed quantities of arms, as well as training for the Congolese armed forces.[14]

The UN noted in 2001 that Israeli businesspeople were becoming prominent in Congo and Angola, where diamonds were exchanged for "money, weapons and military training" and that Israeli Air Force pilots flew the diamonds to Tel Aviv for cutting and selling at Ramat Gan Diamond Centre.[15]

IDI's 2000 contract soon fell apart but Gertler negotiated another 88 per cent monopoly on DRC diamonds through a Canadian firm he controlled, **Emaxon Finance Corporation**. The Emaxon deal gave Gertler access to diamonds from **MIBA**, the DRC's state diamond company, at a highly discounted rate.[16] These contracts were undoubtedly facilitated by Gertler acting as an emissary on behalf of Kabila to Washington in 2002. As part of this delegation, Gertler asked Jendayi Frazer of the US National Security Council to reduce the pressure Kabila was under from human rights organisations.[17]

Dan Gertler at the wedding of Joseph Kabila

---

[14]United Nations (13/12/2001), Democratic Republic of the Congo (DRC) Report, *Diamond Intelligence Brief*.
[15]*Ibid*.
[16]Melman, Y and Carmel, A (24/03/2005), Diamond in the rough, *Haaretz*, Available: http://www.haaretz.com/diamond-in-the-rough-1.153919, [accessed February 2011].
[17]*Ibid*.

Overview of the Israeli Economy: Diamonds **164**

> **Profile: Lev Leviev**
>
> Lev Leviev has a net wealth of $2.6 billion,[18] gleaned from investment in the diamond industry, real estate and prisons. Leviev was a 'sight-holder', buying diamonds from De Beers until 1995. Since then he has developed a comprehensive diamond empire, controlling everything from extraction, to polishing to sale.[19] He is the owner of **LLD Diamonds Ltd**, which was the largest Israeli exporter of diamonds in 2010.[20] Leviev also owns **Africa-Israel**, which owns diamond mines in Russia, Angola and Namibia.[21] Leviev partnered with the Angolan government to set up **Sodiam International** in order to export Angolan diamonds to Israel.[22] LLD has several international shop-fronts including in New York and London. Leviev has recently sold some of his stakes in Angola[23] and begun investing in Alaskan diamonds.
>
> **Africa-Israel Investments**, also owns the swimsuit maker **Gottex**, 1,700 **Fina** gas stations in the south-westernn United States and a stake in Israel's first toll road (*see our chapter on construction later in this book*).[24] He is also the largest franchisee for **7-Eleven** in the US.[25]

Diamonds fuelling the occupation

Both Dan Gertler and Lev Leviev have been involved in the construction of West Bank settlements. Leviev, through a diverse array of companies, has been linked to the construction of the Matittyahu East,[26] Har Homa[27], Zufim[28], Ariel,[29] Adam[30] and Ma'ale

---

[18] http://www.blid-international.com, [accessed February 2011].
[19] See, for instance, Jones, A (2008), Lev Leviev's empire built on diamonds and real estate, *Muckety*. Available : http://news.muckety.com/2008/02/04/lev-levievs-empire-built-on-diamonds-and-real-estate/582, [accessed February 2011]. This article includes a diagram showing Lev Leviev's network of companies.
[20] http://www.israelidiamond.co.il/English/news.aspx?boneId=918&objid=8574, [accessed February 2011].
[21] http://www.forbes.com/lists/2006/10/XUR9.html, [accessed February 2011].
[22] Globes (2005), Alrosa confirms it will market $250m of Angolan diamonds a year in Israel with DGI; Lev Leviev was supposed to market Katoka mine rough diamonds, *Globes*.
[23] http://pearlre.wordpress.com/2011/06/11/if-diamonds-are-forever-why-not-invest-in-them, [accessed September 2011].
[24] http://www.blid-international.com, [accessed February 2011].
[25] Lev Leviev's empire built on diamonds and real estate, *Idem*.
[26] See, for example, http://www.bilin-village.org/english/articles/press-and-independent-media/Presse-Release-Palestinians-Sue-Boymelgreen-Companies-for-War-Crimes-Leviev-Implicated, [accessed February 2011].
[27] *B'Tselem* and BIMKOM, *Under the guise of security*, Available: http://www.btselem.org/downl oad/200512_under_the_guise_of_security_eng.pdf, [accessed February 2011].
[28] *Ibid*.
[29] http://adalahny.org/land-developer-bds-leviev/land-developers-bds/page-12, [accessed February 2011].
[30] http://adalahny.org/land-developer-bds-leviev/land-developers-bds/page-8, [accessed February 2011].

Adumim[31] settlements.

Dan Gertler Israel (DGI) owns, through **FTS Worldwide Corporation** and **Lexinter Management**, two Canadian registered firms, **Green Park** and **Green Mount**, which are involved in the building of condominiums in the settlement of Mod'iin Illit, on the land of the village of Bil'in.[32] Leviev and Gertler's diamond business undoubtedly helps bankroll their settlement building activities in the West Bank.

Other key players in the sector

Leo Schacter imports diamonds from Botswana to be polished in Tel Aviv and sold worldwide, principally in New York. Schacter owns **Schacter Diamonds Complete** and the **William Goldberg Centre** in New York and outsources some diamond polishing to Mumbai, India.[33] Benny and Yossi Meirov own **MID House of Diamonds**, the third largest exporter of diamonds from Israel.[34]

Companies supplying the Israeli diamond trade with rough diamonds:

- **International Diamond Industries (IDI)** – Dan Gertler's company exporting from the DRC
- **Sodiam International** – Leviev's company in Angola
- **Sakawe Mining Corporation (Samicor)** – Leviev's company in Namibia[35]
- **Sakawe Mining Corporation (Samicor)** – Leviev's company in Namibia[36]
- **Dan Gertler Israel (DGI)**

The top exporters of diamonds from Israel in 2010 were:[37]

1   LLD Diamonds Ltd
2   Leo Schachter Diamonds Ltd

---

[31] Roth, S and Sheffer, S (09/08/2007), Hapoalim: Heftsiba is lying in its motion to halt legal steps, *Haaretz,* Available: http://www.haaretz.com/print-edition/business/hapoalim-heftsiba-is-lying-in-its-motion-to-halt-legal-steps-1.227160, [accessed February 2011].
[32] Gordon, S and Oakland, R (July 11th 2008), Palestinian villagers sue Montreal firm, *Toronto Star*, http://www.thestar.com/comment/columnists/article/458375, [accessed February 2011] and 'Andrew' (15th January 2011), Conflict diamonds, Israeli settlements and the Lieberman-Gertler connection, *Current Events Enquiry*, http://ceinquiry.us/2011-01-15-us-israel-diamonds-gertler-lieberman, [accessed February 2011].
[33] http://www.youtube.com/watch?v=az0zyMXtuBo&feature=player_embedded, [accessed February 2011].
[34] http://www.middiamonds.com/Family_History.aspx, [accessed February 2011].
[35] Manor, H (10/02/04), Leviev obtains 36 Namibian diamond mining concessions, *Globes*, Available: http://www.globes.co.il/serveen/globes/docview.asp?did=770067, [accessed February 2011]
[36] Manor, H (10/02/04), Leviev obtains 36 Namibian diamond mining concessions, *Globes*, Available: http://www.globes.co.il/serveen/globes/docview.asp?did=770067, [accessed February 2011]
[37] http://www.israelidiamond.co.il/English/news.aspx?boneId=918&objid=8574, [accessed February 2011].

3   MID House Of Diamonds Ltd
4   AA Rachminov Diamonds (2000) Ltd
5   EZ Diamonds Ltd
6   Yoshfe Diamonds International Ltd
7   Ofer Mizrahi Diamonds Ltd
8   Sahar Atid Diamonds Ltd
9   Arabov Group Ltd
10 Niru Diamonds Israel (1987) Ltd
11 Rosy Blue Sales Ltd
12 A Schwartz & Sons Diamonds Ltd
13 Kuperman Brothers Diamonds Ltd
14 Royal Gem (Israel) Ltd
15 Segaldiam Ltd
16 Eran Diamonds-Yehuda Sayag
17 Beta Diamonds Ltd
18 Jogdiam (Israel) 1988 Ltd
19 Waldman Diamonds (WDC) Israel Ltd
20 Yoram Dvash Diamonds Ltd
21 Eshed-Diam Ltd
22 Katz Chaim Precious Stones 1992 Ltd
23 ABT Diamonds Ltd

Resistance

Resistance to Israel's diamond industry has focused on its links to settlement building. Adalah NY, a New York based campaign for the boycott of Israel, along with the Popular Committee of Bil'in, have launched a campaign against Lev Leviev's settlement building activities. Activists have also focused on Leviev's philanthropic activities, often held up by the billionaire in the face of criticism. As a result, UNICEF, has announced that it would no longer accept donations from Leviev.[38] Street theatre and protests have been held outside Leviev's flagship store in Bond St,[39] London, his new store in New York's Madison Avenue[40] and in Tel Aviv.[41]

In 2010, the Norwegian Pension fund divested from Africa Israel and **Danya Cebus**, a Leviev-owned construction firm, over the companies' links to settlement building. This was a result of concerted grassroots campaigning.[42] The BNC has called for global solidarity with

---

[38]Trotta, D (20/6/2008), UNICEF cuts ties to Israeli billionaire Leviev, *Reuters*, Available: http://www.reuters.com/article/2008/06/20/us-un-israel-leviev-idUSN2047885820080620, [accessed February 2011].
[39]See, for instance, http://www.youtube.com/watch?v=FrEb4DxBzIk, [accessed February 2011].
[40]See, for instance, http://www.youtube.com/watch?v=y-1c9xN8BBU, [accessed February 2011].
[41]International Solidarity Movement (2007), *Anti-Leviev protest at Tel Aviv Critical Mass,* Available: http://palsolidarity.org/2007/12/2867/, [accessed February 2011].
[42]http://bdsmovement.net/?q=node/765, [accessed February 2011].

striking workers at LLD's diamond polishing plant in Windhoek, Namibia.[43]

There has been some resistance against Dan Gertler linked companies. Residents of the village of Bil'in who have lost land as a result of the development of Modi'in Illit, took the Canadian representatives of Green Park and Green Mount, companies linked to DGI, to court in 2009. A Quebec court ruled the case '*forum non conveniens*', meaning it had to be adjudicated in Israel.[44] An appeal is planned.

Protesters outside Lev Leviev's diamond store in Old Bond Street, London, (ISM London 2008)

The Irish Palestine Solidarity Campaign (IPSC) has launched a campaign to have Israeli diamonds ruled as conflict diamonds. They have also challenged **Blue Nile**, the largest global online diamond retailer, over its sale of Israeli diamonds.[45]

Where Next?

It is of paramount importance for the global BDS movement to challenge the Israeli diamond industry. The export of diamonds clearly bankrolls the maintenance of Israel's occupation. BDS action so far has focused, primarily, on one protagonist in the industry, Lev Leviev. To be effective a broader resistance is necessary, and one that moves from lobbying and letter writing to a true challenge to the industry's profits.

Lev Leviev's store in Bond Street should be a key target of the BDS movement, particularly now that Ahava, just down the road in Covent Garden, has closed after years of protests.

---

[43] http://www.bdsmovement.net/?q=node/18, [accessed February 2011].
[44] http://corporateoccupation.wordpress.com/2009/10/16/bilin-vs-green-park-round-2, [accessed February 2011].
[45] http://www.ipsc.ie/campaigns_diamond_boycott.php, [accessed February 2011].

18
Pharmaceuticals

The total market value of the Israeli pharmaceutical sector is NIS 6.36 billion ($1.8 billion), but is projected to rise to NIS 7.67 billion ($2.06 billion) by 2015[1] (around one per cent of Israeli GDP). In 2010 Israeli medicine exports totalled $5 billion (out of a total of $80.5 billion of exports),[2] the majority of which headed to the United States and Europe.[3]

The Israeli pharmaceuticals sector is split between the research, development and marketing of drugs and therapeutic cosmetics, and the research, development and marketing of active pharmaceutical ingredients. Like the high-tech sector, Israeli pharmaceutical companies have benefited hugely from the migration of scientists both before and after the *Nakba*. This knowledge base lead multinational companies, including **Pfizer**, **AstraZeneca** and **GlaxoSmithKline**, to invest in the country. The sector now boasts more than 60 companies, employing over 28,000 people, and patents for a variety of drugs used to treat cancer, Alzheimers and Multiple Sclerosis.[4]

In 1999, there were 24 pharmaceutical plants registered in Israel, with the five leading plants (**Teva**, **Agis**, **Dexxon**, **Taro** and **Rakah**) producing over 80 per cent of locally produced pharmaceuticals.[5] The manufacturing of drugs is part of the wider life sciences industry in Israel, which has grown rapidly in the first decade of the new millennium. According to Israeli Embassy data, between 1996 and 2010 the number of life sciences companies jumped from 186 to 1,000, with around 80 new companies starting up annually.[6]

Company profiles

Teva Pharmaceutical Industries Ltd (*Teva* is 'nature' in Hebrew) is Israel's largest company, and a global pharmaceutical conglomerate specialising in development, production and marketing of generic and branded pharmaceutical products, as well as active pharmaceutical ingredients.[7] Its net profits in 2009 were $13.9 billion,[8] with 80 per cent of

---

[1] http://www.bizreportshop.com/product/bmi/Israel-Pharmaceuticals-and-Healthcare-Report-Q2-2011_177850.html, [accessed September 2011].
[2] http://www.israelnationalnews.com/News/News.aspx/144061, [accessed September 2011].
[3] *Ibid*.
[4] The Embassy of Israel to the United States (2011), *Lifescience in Israel*. Available: http://www.israelemb.org/index.php/en/latest-news/429-life-sciences-in-israel, [accessed 10th June 2011].
[5] Monitor Inc. (2001), The pharmaceutical industry in Israel, *Business briefing: Pharmatech*, Available: www.touchbriefings.com/pdf/17/pt031_r_8_blay.pdf, [accessed 16th March 2011].
[6] http://www.israelemb.org/index.php/en/latest-news/429-life-sciences-in-israel, [accessed 10th June 2011].
[7] http://www.investinisrael.gov.il/NR/exeres/CAEAA95D-CDE2-41F8-952F-712C94E81770.htm, [accessed 10th June 2011].
[8] http://www.tevauk.com/news/view/111, [accessed 10th June 2011].

sales in North America and Europe.[9] The company sold over $16 billion worth of drugs during 2010 and in the first quarter of 2011, sales were up 12 per cent to $4.1 billion, with the strongest sales growth in Europe.[10] This growth is what has made Teva the biggest generic pharmaceutical company in the world.[11] It was once reported that if the company left Israel, the Tel Aviv Stock Exchange would contract almost 25%.[12]

Teva's production facility in Jerusalem, Teva is the largest company on the Tel Aviv Stock Exchange

In addition to the manufacture of generics, Teva also has a small portfolio of branded and patented drugs. The company owns the exclusive license to develop Copaxana (glatiramer acetate) for the treatment of Multiple Sclerosis, which is marketed and sold in 47 countries. Its other patented product is Azilect, used to treat Parkinson's disease.

The company, with a long history dating back further than Israel's creation, was founded in 1901.[13] It's first major new drug, Copaxone, originated during the 1960s in the laboratories of the Weizmann Institute.[14]

Teva's incumbent CEO and president, Shlomo Yanai, took the post in 2007 after a three-year-long stint at agro-chemical conglomerate **Makhteshim-Agan Industries**. Prior to that, Yanai served as a high-ranking officer in the Israeli army, reaching the office of Major General. During his 32 years in the army, he also held the position of Commanding Officer of the Southern Command, and was head of the Israeli security delegation at the Camp David, Shepherdstown and Wye River peace talks.[15]

---

[9]http://www.tevauk.com/corporate/global, [accessed 10th June 2011].
[10]http://www.tevapharm.com/pr/2011/pr_1010.asp, [accessed 10th June 2011].
[11]http://www.tevauk.com/corporate/global, [accessed 10th June 2011].
[12]Shir Hever, personal correspondence with the authors, April 2011.
[13]http://www.biojerusalem.org.il/database_company.asp?ID=76, [accessed 10th June 2011].
[14]Mogenstern, J (2010), Teva: the origin's of Israel's pharmaceutical industry, *Israel High-Tech and Investment Report*. Available: ishitech.co.il/israelat60.pdf, [accessed 8th June 2011].
[15]http://people.forbes.com/profile/shlomo-yanai/78055, [accessed 9th June 2011].

Never shying away from expansion, Teva has been busy buying up global competitors as it seeks to reach deeper into international markets. In a deal completed in August 2010, Teva purchased German company **Ratiopharm Group International** for $5 billion. In May 2011 Teva acquired US company **Cephalon**[16] and leading Japanese generics manufacturer **Taiyo**.[17]

Teva UK, a subsidiary of Teva, is one of the largest pharmaceutical companies in Britain, specialising in generic and respiratory medicines, manufacturing over seven billion tablets annually.[18] According to its own estimates, over 200 tablets or capsules supplied by the company are taken every second by patients around the UK.[19] One in seven packs dispensed by the National Health Service (NHS) is made by Teva UK, meaning the company supplies more packs of medicine to the NHS than any other manufacturer.[20]

Teva UK is also the main producer of Qvar asthma inhalers,[21] which Teva Group acquired upon its purchase of US multinational **IVAX Pharmaceuticals** in January 2006.[22] In July of the same year a successful application was made to the National Institute for Health and Clinical Excellence (NICE) for approval of Qvar as a cost-effective drug for supply on the NHS. Since the phasing out of CFC-based inhalers under the Montreal Protocol, Qvar has become the preferred prescription for adult asthma sufferers in many areas of the UK.[23] In March 2011, Teva UK secured the exclusive rights to supply the British market with generic Lacidipine film-coated tablets, which are used to treat hypertension.[24]

Dexcel Pharma is a fully owned subsidiary of **Dexxon**, and the second largest manufacturer and provider of branded and generic drugs in Israel, holding around 25 per cent of the market.[25] Dexcel has a 40 per cent share of the UK market with its six best-selling products and has long-standing relationships with leading chain pharmacy stores, including for the provision of 'own-brand' generics. UK products include Nifedipress® MR 10, designed to tackle high blood pressure and prevent angina attacks. Both Teva and Dexcel UK provide own-brand generics for **Lloyds Pharmacy**, including propanolol, atenolol and diazepam.[26] Dexcel UK also branches off into **Dexcel Dental**, which manufactures PerioChip and

---

[16]http://www.tevapharm.com/pr/2011/pr_1008.asp, [accessed 9th June 2011].
[17]http://www.tevapharm.com/pr/2011/pr_1011.asp, [accessed 9th June 2011].
[18]http://www.tevauk.com/your-medicines, [accessed 9th June 2011].
[19]http://www.tevauk.com, [accessed 9th June 2011].
[20]http://consumerhealth.tevauk.com/consumer, [accessed 9th June 2011].
[21]http://www.dailymail.co.uk/news/article-1295610/NHS-doesnt-care-cost-medicine-Drugs-firms-accused-profiteering-raising-prices-ONE-THOUSAND-cent.html, [accessed 9th June 2011].
[22]http://www.pharmaceutical.org.uk/ivax/index.html, [accessed 9th June 2011].
[23]www.lmsg.nhs.uk/LMSGDocs%5CGuidelines%5CFC_BDP_Discontinuation_200807.pdf, [accessed 9th June 2011] and www.worcestershire.nhs.uk/file_download.aspx?id=1a80a516, [accessed 9th June 2011].
[24]http://www.tevauk.com/news/view/112, [accessed 9th June 2011].
[25]http://www.dexcel.com/English/Local_Activities/General, [accessed September 2011].
[26]http://dotpharmacy.cmpi.biz/c/portal/layout?p_l_id=259751&CMPI_SHARED_articleId=3036445&CMPI_SHARED_ImageArticleId=3036445&CMPI_SHARED_CommentArticleId=3036445&CMPI_SHARED_ToolsArticleId=3036445&CMPI_SHARED_articleIdRelated=3036445&start=20&end=40, [accessed September 2011].

Acloclair,[27] and **Dexcel Pharma Laboratories Ltd**, a Dexcel affiliate situated in Derbyshire, where it owns a lab dedicated to testing tablets and capsules for their release within the EU.

Insightec is a company set up specifically to develop MR-guided Focused Ultrasound technology. It was founded in 1999 through a merger between **GE Healthcare** (then **GE Medical Systems**) technology and Israel's **Elbit Medical Imaging**.[28] Whilst Elbit Imaging split from defence manufacturer Elbit Systems in 1996, the company uses camera technology originally designed for missiles to create miniature cameras used to view internal organs. The ExAblate 2000, a combination of Magnetic Resonance imaging and Focused Ultrasound technology, was created when members of the company's management, Jacob Vortman and Shuki Vitek combined their know-how and experience after developing night-vision systems and the Black Anchor, the target missile used in trials of the Arrow missile at Rafael.[29]

While the positive healthcare benefits cannot be denied, it is important to contextualise how exactly these research breakthroughs developed, that is via defence industry crossover. It is also important to realise that a more benign research environment aimed at civilian technology would have still been able to achieve these things. Insightec has clinical collaborations with leading hospitals and medical research institutions around the world, including the Women's Hospital of Harvard, the Mayo Clinic, Johns Hopkins Hospital, St. Mary's Hospital of Imperial College, Germany's Charite Hospital and Japan's IseiKai Hospital.[30]

Kamada Ltd is a biopharmaceutical company, developing, producing and marketing speciality therapeutics using patented chromatographic purification technology.[31]

Fermentek is a small company founded in 1994, specialising in providing mycotoxins and other bioactive compounds for medical research. It sells a line of mycotoxin products under the brand name **FermaSol**. The company operates out of the Atarot settlement Industrial zone north of Jerusalem, in an area which was annexed into the greater Jerusalem Municipality following Israel's military incursions in 1967.[32]

Most of Fermentek's products are sold to major chemicals trading companies, which then resell under their own trade names, but a small amount are purchased by universities and government bodies for research purposes.[33] According to Dutch research organisation Profundo some of the products are exported to unnamed sources in the UK.[34]

---

[27] http://www.dexceldental.co.uk, [accessed September 2011].
[28] http://www.investinisrael.gov.il/NR/exeres/95D438B0-0293-4ACB-9F06-51CACD0B0641.htm, [accessed September 2011].
[29] *Ibid.*
[30] *Ibid.*
[31] http://www.investinisrael.gov.il/NR/exeres/6336EB45-A786-436D-A626-B5E1DDF47046.htm, [accessed September 2011].
[32] http://en.wikipedia.org/wiki/Atarot#cite_ref-Michaeli_3-0, [accessed September 2011].
[33] http://www.fermentek.co.il/index.html, [accessed June 2011].
[34] http://electronicintifada.net/v2/article10402.shtml, [accessed June 2011].

Taro Pharmaceuticals Industries Ltd is the brainchild of Israeli pharmacists and American physicians, who created the company in 1950 with the aim of helping the nascent Israeli state develop a world-class pharmaceutical industry.[35] Eleven years later Taro became a public company through an Initial Public Offering (IPO) in the US. By 1982 it was listed on the NASDAQ stock exchange. It entered the Canadian and US markets in the 1980s, initially supplying generics.[36] Taro has an active pharmaceutical ingredients (API) arm, which it manufactures at chemical plants in Israel. Taro UK products include Etopan XL tablets; Metformin 500 mg and 850 mg Tablets; Teril Retard 200mg and 400 mg tablets; and Warfarin 0.5, 1, 3 and 5 mg tablets.[37]

Perrigo is an American company that was listed on both the NASDAQ and Tel Aviv Stock Exchange (TASE) after it bought Israeli drug company **Agis Industries**. Its flagship drug, Omprezol, is a non-prescription version of heartburn medication Prilosec. Perrigo's UK subsidiary supplies the British market with generics of paracetamol and ibuprofen.

SuperPharm, a chain of chemists, was started in the 1970s by Leon Koffler, a member of the Koffler family, which owns the Canadian drugstore chain **Shoppers Drug Mart**. There are now more than 120 SuperPharm stores in Israel, in addition to 14 in Poland and a few in China, with sales of approximately $500 million. The company also owns a stake in the Israeli **Toys-R-Us** franchise.[38]

Occupation Therapy

Israeli pharmaceutical companies benefit from the illegal occupation of the West Bank and the siege of Gaza in two ways. Firstly, high import tariffs and other economic restrictions mean that the small Palestinian pharmaceutical industry poses no threat to the Israeli market, despite it being cheaper to manufacture these goods in the OPT. Secondly, the dependency of the Palestinian economy on Israel and the lack of a Palestinian currency means that the OPT are highly dependent on aid. According to some estimates, almost half of the money donated to the OPT ends up in the Israeli economy. This includes the drugs needed to treat Palestinians, which are bought from Israeli companies.

In 2000, around 32 per cent of the drugs consumed in the West Bank and Gaza were from Israel, with around the same amount distributed by a small nucleus of Palestinian pharmaceutical manufacturers.[39] The latter has since risen to around a 50 per cent share of market volume,[40] whilst Israeli companies now supply between 20-30 per cent.[41] Yet, any

---

[35]http://www.taro.com/Corporate/CompanyHistory/Page.html, [accessed June 2011].
[36]*Ibid*.
[37]http://www.taropharma.co.uk/Products/Rx/ProductsByAlpha.html, [accessed June 2011].
[38]http://www.forbes.com/lists/2006/81/biz_06israel_Leon-Koffler_Y6RP.html, [accessed June 2011].
[39]USAID (2002), *Sector report: pharamceutical industries in West Bank/Gaza*. Available: pdf.usaid.gov/pdf_docs/PNACU078.pdf, [accessed 16th March 2011].
[40]http://www.paltrade.org/Paltrade/business/pharma.htmhttp://www.paltrade.org/Paltrade/business/pharma.htm, [accessed June 2011].
[41]World Bank (2008), *Reforming prudently under pressure*, Available:

statistic on the number of pharmaceuticals consumed in the West Bank and Gaza tells only half the story. Many Palestinian patients have to be transferred to Israeli hospitals for treatment and will, therefore be given Israeli pharmaceutical products instead.[42] The occupation is the single determinant behind this fact, because without the crippling of the Palestinian economy, hospitals in the West Bank and Gaza would be better placed to treat patients. Medical costs for Palestinian patients are then paid for by the Palestinian Authority,[43] which by extension, means that international donor money is lining the pockets of Israeli pharmaceutical companies instead of helping to stimulate the Palestinian economy.

According to a 2001 report by the Ramallah based Health, Development, Information and Policy Institute (HDIP), the Israeli policy of closing all borders during the second *intifada* seriously hindered the production and marketing of pharmaceuticals by Palestinian companies.[44] Severe restrictions on the movement of both goods and people meant workers could not get to laboratories, and the raw materials needed to manufacture drugs were denied entry into the West Bank.

Sales dropped by 40 per cent and companies were functioning at only a quarter of their full productive capacity.[45] The situation was similar with aid. According to Physicians for Human Rights, Israel tightly controls the imports of medicines and medical equipment donated or purchased abroad.[46] This includes the insidious barrier of bureaucracy, which allows Israel to create a façade of normality while hampering Palestinian health care workers.

Expensive discriminatory bureaucracy is equally obvious in Israel's use of the 1993 Paris Protocol trade agreements to stifle competition and allow Israeli pharmaceutical companies to benefit from a mark-up in price.[47] Industry representatives interviewed by the World Bank argue: "Israeli authorities rely on certain stipulations in the Paris Protocol to require that all pharmaceutical goods entering the Palestinian Territories need to comply with Israeli process standards. This requirement means that all medicines not produced in Israel and not being

donated in kind by international organisations such as the UN are required to pre-register in Israel."[48]

---

http://siteresources.worldbank.org/INTWESTBANKGAZA/Resources/WBGHealthPolicyReport.pdf, [accessed 1st July 2011] and Azza Shoaibi, personal correspondence with the authors, 2011.
[42]Shir Hever, personal correspondence with the authors, 2011.
[43]Kraft, D (2009), Lifeline cut as Palestinians vacate Israeli hospitals, *Jewish Chronicle*. Available: http://thejewishchronicle.net/view/full_story/1993421/article-Lifeline-cut-as-Palestinians-vacate-Israeli-hospitals-, [accessed 1st July 2011].
[44]www.graduateinstitute.ch/palestine/pdf/intifada/intifada_report_II_v5.0.pdf, [Accessed 30th June 2011].
[45]*Ibid.*
[46]Physicians for Human Rights (2002), *A legacy of injustice: a critique of Israeli approaches to the right to health of Palestinians in the occupied territories*. Available: http://reliefweb.int/node/114709, [accessed 30th June 2011].
[47]World Bank (2008), *Reforming prudently under pressure, Idem.*
[48]*Ibid*, p. 78.

The situation is similar with products leaving the West Bank. All pharmaceutical manufacturers wishing to export to Israel must register with the Israeli Ministry of Health. The Palestinian Trade Centre (Paltrade) claims that many firms are yet to initiate the medicine registration process because a facility inspection would be required.[49] It is argued that this is impossible due to the unwillingness of Israeli Ministry of Health inspectors to visit the West Bank. Difficulties have come to a head in the case of East Jerusalem, which is recognised as occupied under international law, yet falls under the jurisdiction of the Israeli Ministry of Health. Therefore, the same restriction on exports applies to an area which is legally part of the West Bank. Paltrade notes that there is no official documented policy "that bans or restricts the entry of these products into East Jerusalem; banning of entry has been communicated only verbally so far."[50]

Other restrictions are secondary. The prime example is that Palestinian firms do not comply with international patent laws due to the unique situation that the industry operates within. Because of the strict controls on imports many pharmaceutical companies are producing generic versions of drugs that companies in World Trade Organisation (WTO) member countries hold patents for.[51] So, although the West Bank and Gaza need to comply with these rules as non-members of the WHO, Israel is a member and so therefore "has a responsibility to prohibit the import or sale of these drugs within its borders."[52] This means that hospitals in East Jerusalem cannot use Palestinian manufactured pharmaceuticals and are forced to use more expensive Israeli and international drugs. Equally, Palestinian pharmacies say that Israeli health insurance companies would stop dealing with them it was discovered they were selling uncertified Palestinian pharmaceuticals.[53]

Military crossover

Israel is involved in the EU's research activities on nanotechnology. Following Israel's war against Lebanon in 2006, Shimon Peres, now Israel's president, expressed a desire to see nanotechnology yielding the weapons of the future. Although Israel has more recently conveyed the impression that most of its nanotechnology activities are medical in nature, Israel's interest in this area of science cannot be separated from the occupation of Palestine. Israel's national strategy on nanotechnology is being implemented with advice from representatives of the Israeli ministry of defense and a former president of Israeli weapons manufacturers, **Rafael**.[54]

---

[49]Paltrade (2010), *Movement of goods from West Bank to East Jerusalem and Israel*. Available: www.lacs.ps/documentsShow.aspx?ATT_ID=2486, [accessed June 30th 2011].
[50]*Ibid*, p. 13.
[51]*Ibid.*.
[52]*Ibid*. (p. 14).
[53]*Ibid*.
[54]http://www.silviacattori.net/article1077.html, [accessed 23rd July 2011].

Resistance

In May 2010, a protest organised by the umbrella group Rome Palestine Solidarity Network targeted the COSMOFARMA expo held at Rome's exhibition centre. The Network called on physicians, pharmacists and healthworkers, among the thousands of health professionals attending, not to purchase products manufactured by Teva.[55].

Anti-Teva street theatre in Paris (Paris BDS activists 2011)

Other European activists have also targeted Teva, with boycott initiatives particularly strong in France. The French BDS movement is targeting Teva's generic drugs, which can easily be substituted for other generics with no effect to the medial benefits. For example, on 5th March 2006 the *Union Juive Francaise Pour la Paix* (French Jewish Peace Union) voted in a recommendation that its members refuse the purchase of Teva-branded generics from chemists if other generic brands are on sale, and to encourage friends and family to act in the same way.[56]

Medical boycott

Perhaps the largest campaign against Israel's occupation relating to healthcare are the British calls for a boycott of the Israeli Medical Association (IMA). The call was first expressed in an April 2007 Guardian letter, signed by a number of UK physicians led by Dr. Derek Summerfield and Professor Colin Green. It was written in response to a leader article in the same newspaper criticising the National Union of Journalists' (NUJ) decision to boycott Israeli goods.[57] The signatories argued that, whilst the Guardian claimed the NUJ had strayed

---

[55] http://mondoweiss.net/2010/05/bds-activists-target-israeli-pharma-at-italy-expo.html, [accessed 23rd July 2011].
[56] http://www.jai-pal.org/content.php?page=285, [accessed 23rd July 2011].
[57] Lyons, R (2007), Israeli boycotts: gesture politics or a moral imperative?, *The Guardian*. Available: http://www.guardian.co.uk/world/2007/apr/21/israel.comment, [accessed 23rd July 2011].

too far from its legitimate business, "We do not think such arguments apply to our grave concerns as doctors about the health-related impact of Israeli policy on Palestinian society. Persistent violations of medical ethics have accompanied Israel's occupation."[58] The call builds on appeals from leading Palestinian health organisations that fellow professionals in the international community recognise how the IMA is complicit in the oppression of Israel's occupation and, thus, "forfeited its right to membership of the international medical community."[59]

The UK campaigners are calling for the expulsion of the IMA from the World Medical Association (WMA), a notion the WMA has consistently made a mockery of – firstly by appointing former long-time IMA President Yoram Blachlar to the position of WMA President between 2008-2009, and secondly, in appointing current IMA chairman Leonid Eidelman as chair of the WMA Finance and Planning Committee.[60] In doing so, the WMA is tacitly supporting the open flouting of international medical standards, both by Israeli physicians working within the IDF and by the Israeli state in its denial of even basic medical treatment to Palestinians living in the West Bank and Gaza.[61] Former President Blachlar has even defended an Israeli professor who claimed that "a couple of broken fingers" during the interrogation of Palestinians was worthwhile for the information that could be obtained.[62]

In a letter to the British Medical Journal, Dr. Summerfield outlined the two basic premises of the call for an IMA boycott: complicity in torture and Israeli violations of the rights of civilian population and heath professionals under the fourth Geneva Convention.[63] In one rather grotesque case an Israeli physician had told Dr. Summerfield that a medical colleague had confessed to her that he had "removed the intravenous drip from the arm of a seriously ill Palestinian prisoner, and told the man that if he wanted to live, he should co-operate with his interrogators."[64] Needless to say, upon writing to the IMA requesting an investigation, Dr. Summerfield received no reply.

Where next?

Israeli pharmaceutical companies are yet to be targeted in a concerted way by any boycott but there is scope to affect, at the very least, the international subsidiaries of the major companies. There is an argument that we should be careful in targeting the manufacturers of drugs used to treat sick people, but we also have to treat the greater illness of military occupation and colonialism. What makes boycotting Israeli pharmaceutical companies easier is that the biggest players, Teva and Dexcel, generate the bulk of their revenue through

---

[58] Ibid.
[59] Ibid.
[60] http://www.wma.net/en/60about/40leaders/, [accessed March 2011].
[61] Summerfield, D (2009), Letter by Dr Derek Summerfield to the British Medical Journal. Available: http://www.boycottima.org/article-categories/6-torture/7-letter-by-dr-derek-summerfield-to-the-british-medical-journal, [accessed 23rd July 2011].
[62] Ibid.
[63] Ibid.
[64] Ibid.

generics, which can easily be supplied by other manufacturers. The first goal in the UK should be changing the statistic of one in seven medicine packs on the NHS coming from Teva UK. Building on the campaign in France, BDS campaigners in the UK, when given Teva or Dexcel generics, could ask for alternatives and explain to the pharmacy why they are making this choice.

Similarly, BDS campaigners outside of the medical profession can support the calls for both the British Medical Association and the World Medical Association to take a tough line against their Israeli counterpart. Additionally, perhaps the BMA can be pressed to endorse a boycott of Teva and Dexcel generic drugs when an alternative is available.

19
Construction and Real Estate

Part one - Overview

To examine the Israeli construction sector it is necessary to look at the following industries in detail:

- Real Estate and housing construction
- Infrastructure projects
- Construction materials
- Israel's Walls and
- Construction equipment

The Israeli construction industry is primarily a domestic one. According to the Israeli Ministry of Finance, the gross domestic capital generated from building in 2008 was NIS 59.4 billion ($16.2 billion).[1] The construction sector contributes about 5 per cent of Israeli GDP.[2]

Construction and real estate, along with agriculture, are the industries which cement Israel's colonialism most directly. Israeli construction and real estate companies finance and profit from property development within the context of Israel's apartheid system, which systematically marginalises non-Jewish communities in the land and property market.

Construction firms involved in building Israel's settlements in the West Bank and occupied Syrian Golan are the foremost example of companies profiting from the occupation. Without the occupation the land for construction and real estate projects in these territories would simply not exist. Without the state policy of encouraging migration into the settlements, state subsidies for individual settlers and building projects, and the protection provided to the settlements by the Israeli military, the market for construction and real estate would be much smaller. Construction and real estate developments directly challenge the ability of Palestinian and occupied Syrian communities to remain on the land. Property development is facilitated by land seizures, closed military zones, and house demolitions. In short, ethnic cleansing.

---

[1] Israeli Central Bureau of Statistics, *Israel in figures: 2009*, Available: http://www.cbs.gov.il/publications/isr_in_n09e.pdf, [accessed September 2011], p.22.
[2] http://www.mfa.gov.il/MFA/Facts+About+Israel/Economy/ECONOMY-+Sectors+of+the+Economy.htm, [accessed September 2011].

Land

Companies within the Israeli construction and real estate sector reap the rewards of the ethnic cleansing of 1947-9 and the apartheid system that was consolidated after 1948. From 1947-9, 800,000 Palestinians were forcibly expelled from 531 villages and 11 urban centres.[3] Their homes were destroyed and their lands transferred, predominantly to the **Jewish National Fund** (JNF).[4]

After the establishment of the Israeli state the Israeli government consolidated Jewish control of the lands ethnically cleansed in 1948. Only 7 per cent of land in Israel is privately owned,[5] the remainder being under the control of state or parastatal organisations.

Crane looming over the ever expanding settlement of Mod'in Illit, Mod'in Illit is built on the land of the Palestinian village of Bil'in (Corporate Watch 2010)

The JNF directly owns 13 per cent of the land in Israel and has direct influence over a further 80 per cent of Israeli land managed by the **Israeli Lands Administration** (ILA). ILA policy is set by the **Israeli Lands Council**, comprised of 12 government ministers and 10 JNF representatives.[6] The JNF strives to permanently preserve the land for the Jewish people and leases the 13 per cent of land which it owns directly to Jews only.

The 93 per cent of land under the control of the JNF/ILA is apportioned through private

---

[3]For a history of the ethnic cleansing of 1947-9 see Pappe, I (2006), *The ethnic cleansing of Palestine, Idem.*
[4]*Ibid.*
[5]OECD (2009), *Economic survey of Israel 2009, Idem,* p.31.
[6]White, B (2009), *Israeli apartheid: a beginner's guide,* Pluto Press, p.49.

trading in the ILA's leases. These are typically for either 49 or 98 years.[7] Palestinians, and other non-Jewish residents of Israel, are massively disadvantaged in obtaining these leases. Israeli-Jewish construction and real estate firms operate within this discriminatory context and profit from it.

Israel's colonisation of Palestinian land did not stop after 1948. Ethnic cleansing has been carried out within the state of Israel ever since its foundation. Nazareth, for example, was the largest majority-Palestinian town in Israel after 1948.[8] In 1957, David Ben-Gurion's government gave permission for the establishment of a new Jewish settlement, Upper Nazareth (Nazareth Illit).[9] Today, its 53,000 Jewish residents live on 48,000 dunams (a dunam is roughly a fourth of an acre) of land, 19,330 dunams of which were confiscated from Nazareth and surrounding Arab villages. In contrast, Nazareth's population of 70,000 live in an area of 14,200 dunams.[10] Nazareth's municipality receives only a quarter of the state funding received by Nazareth Illit.[11] Nazareth Illit is a priority development area and industrial development is encouraged through generous governmental subsidies and tax breaks for investors. Nazareth has none of these benefits and has a very small industrial area, limiting the opportunities for Palestinian industrial and real estate development.

In 1967, Israel occupied the West Bank, the Gaza Strip, the Syrian Golan and East Jerusalem. During the 1990s, Netanyahu and Barak's Likud and Labour governments approved more and more settlement housing units in these areas. Israel's post-1967 settlement policy follows, although more aggressively, the same discriminatory colonial model established inside Israel since 1948. Israeli real estate companies and construction companies have benefited from this rush to colonise the occupied territories. According to Israeli economist Schlomo Swirski,[12] there is no way to quantify the amount of residential units built by each company. In the following chapters we will profile the companies involved.

Labour

As in other Israeli industries, workers in the construction sector are divided into four classes who receive different levels of wages and social benefits: Jewish-Israeli labourers, Palestinian-Israeli labourers, migrant labourers and Palestinian labourers from the territories occupied in 1967.

Construction and agriculture have traditionally been the largest areas of employment for Palestinian citizens of Israel.[13] In 2004, 50,000 Palestinian-Israelis made up 25 per cent of

---

[7]OECD (2009), *Economic survey of Israel 2009, Idem*, p.31.
[8]http://www.arabhra.org/HRA/SecondaryArticles/SecondaryArticlePage.aspx?SecondaryArticle=1438, [accessed September 2011].
[9]*Ibid.*
[10]*Ibid.*
[11]*Ibid.*
[12]Swirski, S (2008), *The burden of occupation, Idem*, p.28.
[13]http://www.labournet.net/world/0406/isrdeleg1.html, [accessed September 2011].

the construction industry workforce.[14] Wages for Palestinian citizens of Israel working in construction have always been lower than those of Jewish Israeli citizens.[15] After 1967, there was a large influx of low-paid workers from the West Bank and Gaza Strip to Israel.[16] In the early 1990s Israeli military closures of the West Bank and Gaza prevented Palestinians from the territories occupied in 1967 from accessing the Israeli labour market. As a counterbalance the state facilitated the migration of hundreds of thousands of migrant workers, primarily Chinese,[17] who by 2001 made up 12.5 per cent of the construction workforce (300,000 people).[18] By 2002, this consensus was reversed and the state began limiting migration and set up a migration police force.[19]

Despite this, migrant labour has continued to form a prominent part of the Israeli construction labour force due to the low wages employers are able to pay. It has been estimated that a migrant worker within Israel engaged in basic construction work costs her/his employer on average $5 per hour, while a local worker costs $7.[20] In the course of a year, that amounts to a saving of $4,800 per worker. Furthermore, a collective agreement concerning construction workers, signed by the Israeli contractors' association (ACBI) and the **Histadrut**, contains a separate article reducing pension payments to migrant workers from 18 per cent of their salary to 4 per cent.[21]

Palestinian Workers on a West Bank settlement construction site (Corporate Watch 2010)

---

[14] *Ibid.*
[15] OECD (2009), *Economic survey of Israel 2009, Idem*, p.43.
[16] http://www.labournet.net/world/0406/isrdeleg1.html, [accessed September 2011].
[17] OECD (2009), *Economic survey of Israel 2009, Idem*, p.126.
[18] http://www.labournet.net/world/0406/isrdeleg1.html, [accessed September 2011].
[19] *Ibid.*
[20] *Ibid.*
[21] *Ibid.*

During the second Palestinian *intifada* the Israeli state granted permits to workers in the construction industry but the wall and the checkpoints made it impossible to provide a regular workforce. As a result Palestinian citizens of Israel, who had been pushed out of the workforce during the 1990s, became the principal labour provider.[22]

ACBI has consistently lobbied for a larger migrant workforce in the construction industry as well as a larger quota of West Bank Palestinian labourers.[23] Companies engaged in construction in the West Bank settlements benefit from the fact that the majority of labour is carried out by Palestinian residents of the West Bank who are paid below the Israeli minimum wage. West Bank Palestinians are paid less than Israeli workers and less than Palestinians with Israeli IDs.[24] Furthermore, Israelis who have completed their military service receive a NIS 8,000 ($2,182) grant when entering work in the construction industry.[25] This gives Jewish workers (who are eligible for military service) a distinct advantage in the industry.

The Israeli government department responsible for construction is the Ministry of Construction and Housing (MOCH). According to Schlomo Swirski, a department of the MOCH, the Rural Construction Administration, is heavily involved in the planning and administration of settlements, including settlement outposts that the Israeli state has declared publicly are illegal.[26]

Building continues in the West Bank settlement of Mod'in Illit despite the construction ban (Corporate Watch 2010)

---

[22]*Ibid.*
[23]http://www.ynetnews.com/articles/0,7340,L-4011203,00.html, [accessed September 2011].
[24]Swirski, S (2008), *The burden of occupation, Idem,* p.29.
[25]OECD (2009), *Economic survey of Israel 2009, Idem,* p.99.
[26]Swirski, S (2008), *The burden of occupation, Idem,* p.59.

Part Two – Construction

Many of Israel's largest construction companies are involved in projects in the occupied territories. Here are brief profiles of two of them:

Company profiles

Africa Israel was set up in 1934 as **Africa-Palestine Investments Ltd** by "a group of Jewish investors from South Africa, with the purpose of engaging in acquisition and development of real estate for Jewish settlement in Israel."[1] Africa-Palestine became Africa Israel (AFI) in 1967.[2] In the early 1970s the company was acquired by **Bank Leumi**.

In 1996 AFI was bought by the diamond cutter, and owner of **LLD Diamonds**, Lev Leviev,[3] often described as the richest person in Israel.[4] AFI is now ranked fourth in the sector by business website BDI Code and second in terms of construction holdings.[5] AFI owns **Danya Cebus**, a construction company involved in building housing, infrastructure, rail and PFI projects.

Africa Israel companies have been involved in settlement construction in Mattityahu East and Modi'in Illit, close to the Palestinian village of Bil'in, as well as in Zufim, Maale Adumim and Har Homa.[6] However, in October 2010, in an official letter to the Israeli NGO Who Profits, Africa-Israel stated: "Neither the company nor any of its subsidiaries and/or other companies controlled by the company are presently involved in or has any plans for future involvement in development, construction or building of real estate in settlements in the West Bank."[7] AFI also owns a mall in Nazareth Illit.[8]

---

[1] http://adalahny.org/land-developer-bds-leviev/land-developers-bds/page-4, [accessed May 2011].
[2] *Ibid*
[3] http://pqasb.pqarchiver.com/jpost/access/64139565.html?FMT=ABS&FMTS=ABS:FT&date=Mar+5,+1997&author=Nehemia+Strasler&pub=Jerusalem+Post&edition=&startpage=03&desc=The+Ayatollah+of+Ramat+Aviv, [accessed May 2011].
[4] Swirski, S (2008), *The burden of occupation, Idem*, p.29.
[5] http://www.bdicode.co.il/Rank_ENG/101_0_0/Construction%20Holdings and http://www.bdicode.co.il/Rank_ENG/102_0_0/Construction, [accessed May 2011].
[6] http://www.bdsmovement.net/files/2011/02/Palestine_CW_report.pdf, [accessed May 2011].
[7] http://www.whoprofits.org/Company%20Info.php?id=706, [accessed May 2011].
[8] http://www.afigroup-global.com/africa_israel_properties_malls.htm, [accessed May 2011].

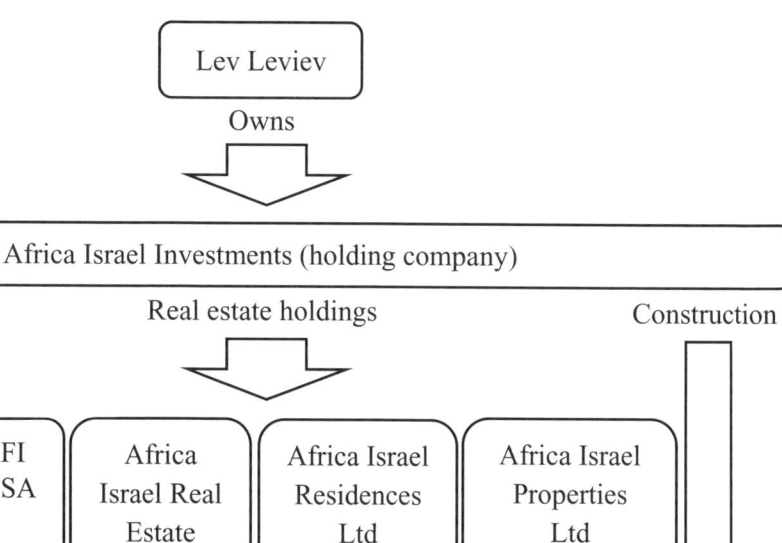

Overview of the Israeli Economy: Construction and Real Estate: Construction

```
                        Lev Leviev
                           │ Owns
                           ▼
        Africa Israel Investments (holding company)
           │ Real estate holdings        │ Construction
           ▼                              ▼
  ┌──────────┬──────┬──────────┬──────────┬──────────┐
  │   AFI    │ AFI  │  Africa  │  Africa  │  Africa  │
  │Development│ USA  │ Israel   │  Israel  │  Israel  │
  │   Plc    │      │   Real   │Residences│Properties│
  │          │      │  Estate  │   Ltd    │   Ltd    │
  └────┬─────┴──────┴──────────┴──────────┴──────────┘
       │                                          │
       ▼                                          ▼
  Registered on the London Stock Exchange      Danya
  Concerned with AFI's Russian projects        Cebus
```

Construction in Mod'In Illit, below the Palestinian village of Bil'in (Corporate Watch 2010)

Shikun&Benui (Arison Group) is the leading Israeli real estate and infrastructure company.[9] The first S&B companies were established in the 1920s. The company boasts that it has "played a major role in the establishment of the Jewish 'settlement' in Israel by leading the construction and building of the young state."[10]

Solel Boneh (the office for public works) was set up in 1923 by the Histradrut, the **General Federation of Laborers in the Land of Israel**, which had been established in 1920.[11] The company assisted the IDF in 1948 and, in 1961, the first shares in the company were traded on the TASE. In 1989, control of Solel Boneh was passed on to the **Housing & Construction Holding Company Limited (Shikun U'Binui)**. In 1996, control of that holding company, including Solel Boneh, was passed on to the **Arison** family. Solel Boneh is now a division of Shikun&Benui and has supplied construction materials for the checkpoints and built parts of the cross-Israel highway, including a wall separating this road from the Palestinian town of Qalqiliya, which was later incorporated into the apartheid wall. The company has built, as a subcontractor, housing projects and infrastructure in West Bank settlements, including Homat Shmuel, Ariel, Imanuel and Modi'in Illit.[12]

Solel Boneh and Shikun&Benui are part of the Arison group of companies controlled by the Arison and Nechama families. Political economists Nitzan and Bichler, in 2002, estimated that the Arison Group holds the fifth largest concentration of capital in Israel.[13]

Case study: Rawabi – building the occupation economy through 'joint projects'

In 2008, the Palestinian Authority's Higher Planning Council approved the construction of a new Palestinian town, Rawabi. The construction of Rawabi, close to Jerusalem, will be administered by developer Bashar Masri, chairman of the board of the **Bayti Real Estate Investment Company**, jointly owned by **Qatari Diar Real Estate Investment Company** and **Massar International**.[14]

The bulk of the Rawabi development site was private land purchased by developers from the Bayti Real Estate Investment Company. The remainder, however, was sequestered by Presidential decree, taking approximately 1,537 dunams of lands from the neighbouring village of Ajjul, 122 dunams from Attara and 118 dunams from Abwin.[15]

---

[9]http://www.bdicode.co.il/CompanyTextProfile_ENG/1021_857_0/Shikun%20%20Binui%20Lt d, [accessed May 2011].
[10]http://en.shikunbinui.co.il/category/history, [accessed May 2011].
[11]Nitzan, J and Bichler, S, (2002), *The global political economy of Israel, Idem,* p.97.
[12]http://whoprofits.org/Company%20Info.php?id=787, [accessed May 2011].
[13]Nitzan, J and Bichler, S (2002), *The global political economy of Israel, Idem,* p.98.
[14]http://www.maannews.net/eng/ViewDetails.aspx?ID=358002, [accessed May 2011].
[15]*Ibid.*

In 2009, the JNF donated thousands of trees to the Rawabi development, in a clear attempt to 'green' its image.[16] Masri initially accepted the donation, then bowed to Palestinian criticism and agreed to uproot the trees (though, at the time of writing, the trees are still there).

In 2011, Masri announced that Rawabi would be built by 12 Israeli companies.[17] The use of Israeli contractors that will, undoubtedly, take advantage of cheap Palestinian labour consolidates the occupation economy, where occupied Palestinians are junior partners to the Israeli business class. The proposed tree donation from the JNF further illustrates this inequality.

In a bizarre twist, Masri, in line with the Palestinian Authority's 2010 policy to boycott settlement goods, required the Israeli contractors not to use building materials sourced from the settlements.[18]

A Palestinian child from the village of Bil'in looking toward the settlement of Mod'iin Illit (Bil'in Popular Committee 2010)

---

[16]*Ibid.*
[17]http://www.israelnationalnews.com/News/News.aspx/141579, [accessed May 2011].
[18]*Ibid.*

List of companies involved in construction in Israeli settlements in the West Bank and occupied Syrian Golan:[19]

Ahim Hasid;	Ahim Uzan;
Ahudat Adi Construction Company;	Allied Holdings;
Almog CDAI;	Amos Hadar Properties and Investments;
Ashdar;	Avisror Moshe and Sons;
B Yair Building Corporation;	Barad Company for Landworks Developments and Roads;
Binyanei Bar Amana Construction and Development;	C Refael Projects;
CIM Lustigman;	D Rotshtein;
Dalia Eliasfor;	Danya Cebus;
Dekel Acher Group;	Digal Investments and Holdings;
Dona Engineering and Construction;	Efgad Engineering and Construction Works;
Electra Construction;	Eli Yohanan Engineers;
Euro Israel;	Eyal Itzkhin;
G Infinity Promotion and Investment/Shalaf Hasharon;	Haim Zaken Construction and Investments;
Industrial Buildings Corporation – Mivney Taasiya;	Isra Marine Manufacture of Structures;
Kal Binyan;	Kiryat Sefer;
Kotler Adika Building Company;	Leader Management and Development (owned by Africa Israel);
Maoz Daniel Construction Contractors Company;	Mei-Tal Engineering and Sevices;
Meshulam Levinstein Group Contracting and Engineering;	Metal Factory Hamachresha;
Minrav Group;	Mishab Building and Development;
Mishkan Eliyahu Construction and Investment Company;	Mitzpor Adumim;
Mordechai Aviv Construction Industries;	Neot Hapisga;
Neumann Steel Industries for Construction;	NOA Management and Consulting;
NRS Consulting and Engineering;	Om Brothers Construction Works Investment and Development Company;
Peled - Klein Civil Engineering;	Peretz Bonei Hangev;
Peretz Louzon Construction & Development;	Ramet;
Rami Levi - Hashikma Marketing;	Rubin Landsman Building Engineering;
S ADR Construction Works Co;	Sasi Building Earth and Road Contractors;

---

[19] Company information in this list from www.whoprofits.org, [accessed June 2011].

Shapir Civil and Marine Engineering;	Shikun Dayarim;
Shlomo Cohen Construction Company;	Solel Boneh;
Stern Group;	The Metrontario Group (Canada);
Tzifha International;	Tzifha International;
Yael Hill;	YD Barazani;
Yehezkel Morad and	YH Dimri Construction and Development;
ZF Building Company.	

Resistance

"Bil'in has become the graveyard of Israeli real estate empires. One after another, these companies are approaching bankruptcy as the costs of building on stolen Palestinian land are driven higher than the profits."
Abdullah Abu Rahmah, in a letter written from his prison cell, January 1st 2010.[20]

The BDS movement has put up strong resistance to Lev Leviev's real estate empire and, lead by the Bil'in Popular Committee, to the companies involved in settlement building close to the village of Bil'in. The announcement that AFI companies will no longer work on settlement projects is clearly due to BDS pressure. It remains to be seen, however, whether the company will stay true to its word.

For a summary of resistance against Africa Israel, Danya Cebus, **Green Park** *and* **Green Mount** *see the chapter on the Israeli diamond sector earlier in this book.*

Construction Companies – Where next?

The Israeli construction sector is dominated by indigenous Israeli companies. The BDS movement should target the international businesses of these companies, isolate them from investors through divestment campaigns and, ultimately, make it impossible for them to operate internationally.

It is strategically important to target those companies involved in construction in the settlements. However, excluding companies whose business lies purely in 1948 Israel would ignore the Palestinian BDS call and the apartheid nature of the Israeli state. As such, all parts of Lev Leviev's construction empire should continue to be targeted.

---

[20] http://www.indymedia.org.uk/en/2010/03/446969.html, [accessed September 2011].

Part three – Infrastructure construction

Israeli infrastructure projects reflect the apartheid state that carries them out. Prior to the ethnic cleansing of Palestinians in 1947-9 and the establishment of the state of Israel the labour Zionist trade union, the Histradrut, established the Office of Public Works (**Solel Boneh** now controlled by the **Arison Group**), which carried out infrastructure projects for the nascent Zionist movement.

After 1948, the development of infrastructure was engineered to benefit Israel's Jewish population and has been used as a tool for the further marginalisation of non-Jewish communities. Road projects have been designed to expropriate land from Palestinian communities while benefiting Jewish communities. Recent rail projects have sought to consolidate Israel's settlements by connecting them to Israel's post-1948 borders.

Rail

Rail infrastructure projects are an area where Israeli and international companies frequently collaborate.

The Jerusalem Light Railway

The Jerusalem Light Rail (JLR) project has long been a focus for the international BDS movement, primarily due to the involvement of two French companies, **Veolia** and **Alstom**. The JLR will link West Jerusalem with East Jerusalem settlements, such as Pisgat Ze'ev and French Hill, while bypassing Palestinian communities. This will consolidate Israel's grip on East Jerusalem. Part of the line is being built on occupied territory.[1]

The **Citypass** consortium was specially set up for the JLR project and includes **Harel** (20%), **Polar Investments** (17.5%) and the **Israel Infrastructure Fund** (10%), constructors **Ashtrom** (27.5%) and engineers **Alstom** (20%), plus service operators **Connex** (now **Veolia Transport**) (5%).[2] The contract was awarded to CityPass for 30 years, after which time ownership of the entire project will revert to the Israeli state.[3]

The JLR is a discriminatory project. A TV advert for staff on the light railway in August 2010 required applicants to speak Hebrew and to have undertaken military service. The spokesperson for Citypass, in an ill-advisedly candid moment, told a Belgian researcher that the life patterns of Jews and Palestinians were "so different" that they would not use the same services.[4]

---

[1] http://electronicintifada.net/v2/article11488.shtml, [accessed September 2011].
[2] http://www.calcalist.co.il/local/articles/0,7340,L-3408127,00.html, [accessed September 2011].
[3] *Ibid.*
[4] See Adri Nieuwhoef's presentation to the Russell Tribunal (2010), Available: http://www.russelltribunalonpalestine.com/en/sessions/london-session/video-of-proceedings, [accessed September 2011].

Company profiles

The **Ashtrom Group** is Israel's largest private construction company.[5] Established in 1963, it has annual revenues of $778 million and a workforce of 1,170.[6] The company has recently completed the construction of a port in Ashdod and a traffic tunnel in Haifa.[7] Ashtrom has a 27.5% stake in the Citypass consortium[8] and is constructing housing units in the East Jerusalem settlement of Nof Zion.[9] Ashtrom's subsidiary, **Ashdar**, has building projects in the settlements of Oranit, Alfeii Menashe and Beitar Illit.[10]

Ashtrom group is privately owned while **Ashlad**, its subsidiary, is traded on the TASE. **Ashtrom international** is active in the USA, Eastern Europe, Africa and the Caribbean. One of Ashtrom's major shareholders is **Allied Holdings**,[11] whose shares are controlled by **Trust AG** in Jersey.[12]

The A1 train project

The A1 project, a high-speed train from Jerusalem to Tel Aviv, is one of the biggest infrastructure projects that the Israeli government has undertaken in the last decade,[13] with an estimated cost of $1.67 billion.[14] The A1 route crosses into the West Bank in 2 places.

The overall plan includes what would become the longest, highest bridge in Israel, as well as the longest tunnel, requiring the use of tunnel boring machines never used in the country before. As the skills are not available within the country the Israeli contractors for these sections have had to partner with foreign contractors with the relevant know-how and experience. The machinery for the tunnels is also unavailable in Israel and has to be built specially for this project by international suppliers.[15]

The project is being carried out in conjunction with several European state-owned and private firms, including **Moscow Metrostoy** (Russia) and **Pizzarotti** (Italy). As of October 2010, the construction of most of the route is well under way, but the main tunnelling has not

---

[5] http://www.bdicode.co.il/CompanyTextProfile_ENG/733_132_0/Ashtrom%20Group%20Ltd, [accessed September 2011].
[6] *Ibid.*
[7] *Ibid.*
[8] http://corporateoccupation.wordpress.com/2010/03/12/walking-the-route-of-veolias-tramline-in-east-jerusalem/, [accessed September 2011].
[9] http://www.whoprofits.org/Company%20Info.php?id=480, [accessed September 2011].
[10] *Ibid.*
[11] http://www.whoprofits.org/Company%20Info.php?id=733, [accessed September 2011].
[12] *Ibid.*
[13] Who Profits (2010), *Crossing the line: the Tel Aviv-Jerusalem fast train, a new Israeli train line through West Bank areas*, Available: http://www.whoprofits.org/articlefiles/WP-A1-Train.pdf, [accessed May 2011], p.4.
[14] Who Profits (2010), *Crossing the line, Idem*, p.23.
[15] *Ibid*, p.24.

yet begun. The deadline for completion has been postponed to 2016-7.[16]

Israeli companies contracted to build sections of the A1 line include the **Minrav Group**,[17] **Shapir**,[18] **Yugan Engineering**,[19] **Eldad Spivak Engineering**[20] and **Hofrey Hasharon**.[21]

Shapir, rated as the number 1 firm in Israeli infrastructure construction in 2009,[22] has formed a partner company with the Italian firm Pizzarotti, called **Shapir Pizzarotti Railways (SPR) Construction**.

In the 2 cases where the planned route for the train line enters the West Bank, Israeli planners have been careful to avoid confrontation with Israeli residents.[23] The complaints, of which there have been many, by Palestinian residents are much easier to ignore.[24]

Roads

Road building in Israel is designed to consolidate the Jewish monopoly over land both in 1948 Israel and the occupied Palestinian territories (OPT).

In the West Bank, since the signing of the Oslo Accords, Israel has built a system of bypass roads serving the settlements. These roads have formed part of Israel's settlement expansion agenda, monopolising as much land as possible. Palestinians are excluded from some of these roads.[25] Israeli settlers are able to drive on these roads without so much as a reminder that there are Palestinians living nearby.

Siemens traffic control systems are installed by the company's Israeli representative, **Orad Group**, on apartheid roads; roads in the West Bank on which only Israelis are allowed to travel, including road 5 and road 443.[26] Siemens is a multinational company with its UK headquarters in Surrey and locations across the UK.[27]

Cross Israel Highway project (Highway 6)

The Cross-Israel highway, is a major toll road that began operating in the 2000s. The

---

[16] *Ibid*, p.4.
[17] *Ibid*, p.24-25.
[18] http://www.whoprofits.org/Company%20Info.php?id=699, [accessed May 2011].
[19] Who Profits (2010), *Crossing the line, Idem*, p.27.
[20] *Ibid*.
[21] http://www.whoprofits.org/Company%20Info.php?id=700, [accessed May 2011].
[22] http://www.bdicode.co.il/Rank_HEB/103_0_0/%D7%AA%D7%A9%D7%AA%D7%99%20D7%AA-%20%D7%91%D7%A0%D7%99%D7%94, [accessed May 2011].
[23] Who Profits (2010), *Crossing the line, Idem*, p.20.
[24] *Ibid*, p.14.
[25] Swirski, S (2008), *The burden of occupation, Idem*, p.31.
[26] http://www.whoprofits.org/Company%20Info.php?id=877, [accessed May 2011].
[27] http://www.siemens.co.uk/en/contact/contact_details.htm, [accessed September 2011].

southern extension of the Cross-Israel Highway is still being completed. Part of the highway, a wall separating the road from the Palestinian town of Qalqiliya, was later incorporated into the apartheid wall.[28]

Company profiles

Derech Eretz is the contractor for the Cross Israel Highway project and operator for Highway 6.[29] The company is owned, in three equal parts, by Solel Boneh (a division of Shikun&Benui); Danya Cebus (an Africa Israel company) and **Canadian Highways Investment International Corporation**.[30]

Ramet has been involved in the construction of the Beit Safafa bridge, the Ramot bridge, the French Hill bridge and the Mount Scopus portal, which are all in East Jerusalem. The company has also constructed sewage systems in the old city in East Jerusalem. It was also involved in the construction of the Strings Bridge, part of the light rail project in Jerusalem. In January 2011, the company started building a bridge over the Atarot Stream, which will connect to the 443 road in the West Bank. Ramet is partly controlled by a Dutch corporation.[31]

Minrav Group is currently contracted by the Jerusalem Municipality to build a sewage treatment plant for the settlements of Pisgat Ze'ev and French Hill, providing water for settlements in the occupied Jordan Valley.[32]

The Citypass tramline in East Jeruslem (Corporate Watch 2010)

---

[28]http://www.whoprofits.org/Company%20Info.php?id=787, [accessed September 2011].
[29]http://duns100.dundb.co.il/ts.cgi?tsscript=comp_eng&duns=532642592, [accessed May 2011].
[30]http://whoprofits.org/Company%20Info.php?id=787, [accessed May 2011].
[31]http://www.whoprofits.org/Company%20Info.php?id=948, [accessed May 2011].
[32]http://www.whoprofits.org/Company%20Info.php?id=755, [accessed May 2011].

List of companies involved in infrastructure projects in the occupied territories[33]

Company	Infrastructure project
Ashtrom **Alstom** **Veolia** **Ramet**	Citypass tramline
Nesher **Yehuda welded mesh** **New Way Traffic** **Readymix**	equipment for Citypass tramline
Baran **Egis Rail** **Eldad Spivak Engineering Co** **HBI Haerter** **Hofrey Hasharon** **Moscow Metrostoy** **Parsons Brinckerhoff** (owned by Balfour Beatty. Provided support to the A1 Train project prior to its purchase by BB in 2009) **Pizarotti/SPR Construction** **Shapir Civil and Marine Engineering** **YD Barazani** **Yugan engineering**	A1 Train
Solel Boneh	Cross-Israel Highway
Peretz Sela Civil Engineering	road projects in Ma'ale Adumin and Alfei Menashe settlements
Salit	infrastructure projects in settlement of Beitar Illit
Yatz-Ar	constructed the main water pumping station in the Modi'in Illit settlement
Yehezkel Morad	building the Ofer checkpoint on route 443 and the road around Beqa'ot settlement
YD Barazani	paved roads in Talpiyot East settlement and pavements in East Jerusalem
Minrav	East Jerusalem sewage treatment plant
Ramet	Beit Safafa bridge, Ramot bridge, French Hill bridge, Mount Scopus portal, sewage systems in the old city in East Jerusalem

---

[33] All company info from www.whoprofits.org, [accessed September 2011].

Resistance

One of the most successful BDS campaigns to date has been the campaign against Veolia. Campaigners have attempted to persuade public bodies all over Europe to exclude Veolia from public tenders on the grounds that it is complicit in grave breaches of the Geneva Convention.

The campaign against Veolia has led to the company losing millions of pounds worth of public contracts across Europe and in Australia,[34] and to legal cases in France against Veolia and Alstom.[35] Careful and expert lobbying that made Veolia's complicity in war crimes clear led to pension funds in the Netherlands, Sweden and Denmark excluding Veolia from their investment portfolios.[36] In August 2011, the company **announced that it would pull out of half of the 77 countries it operates in due to financial difficulties.**[37] Veolia is seeking to sell its stake in Citypass to an Israeli company, Egged, once "it has fulfilled its contractual obligations". It is clear that no international company is willing to buy Veolia's stake because of fears of becoming a target of the BDS movement.[38]

In 2011, **Deutsche Bahn**, a German state-owned company, pulled out of the A1 train project after BDS pressure.[39]

Infrastructure construction companies – Where next?

Veolia and Alstom should continue to be key targets of the global BDS movement until they pull out of all their Israeli projects. European activists should target Pizarotti, who work in France, Switzerland and Romania, for their involvement in the A1 train project.

---

[34]http://www.corporatewatch.org/?lid=3433, [accessed September 2011].
[35]http://electronicintifada.net/content/veolia-and-alstom-continue-abet-israels-rights-violations/8550, [accessed September 2011]
[36]Deas, M (2011), Palestine solidarity: Hitting corporations where it hurts, *Corporate Watch*.
[37]http://www.zawya.com/story.cfm/sid20110804_18369_112, [accessed September 2011].
[38]http://www.russelltribunalonpalestine.com/en/sessions/london-session/video-of-proceedings, [accessed September 2011].
[39]http://www.ft.com/cms/s/0/4b6b59fc-7a4b-11e0-bc74-00144feabdc0.html#axzz1MikZCkx4, [accessed September 2011].

Part four - Israel's walls

Israel has built walls and fences along its borders with Jordan and Lebanon and has several ongoing separation wall projects in the West Bank, at Rafah in Gaza, and at Eilat. These huge infrastructure projects offer substantial opportunities to a vast array of construction, security and high-tech companies.

The West Bank apartheid wall

The West Bank apartheid wall is Israel's largest infrastructure project,[1] with costs estimated at $13 billion.[2] The project involves 53 construction firms,[3] 22 of which are currently working on the wall.[4] The wall - in some places a wire fence, in others a 12 meter high concrete wall incorporating stone barriers, checkpoints and terminals - is planned to span 790 kilometres.[5] The project will utilise 600,000 square meters of wire fence and 3 million meters of barbed wire.[6]

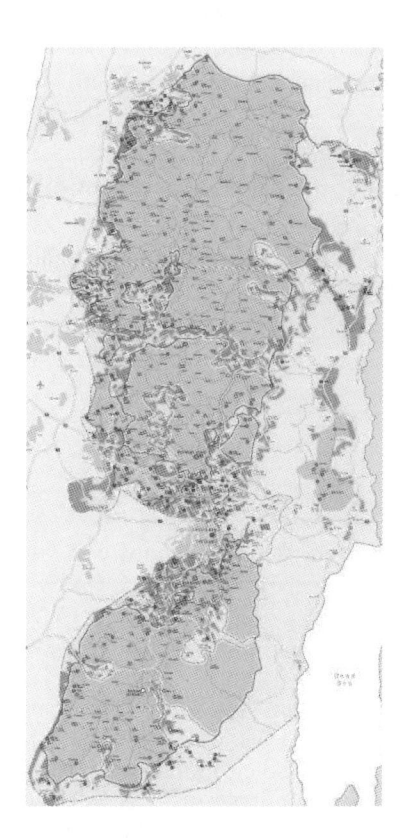

---

[1] http://www.securityfence.mod.gov.il/Pages/ENG/execution.htm, [accessed September 2011].
[2] Swirski, S (2008), *The burden of occupation, Idem,* p.31.
[3] *Ibid.*
[4] http://www.securityfence.mod.gov.il/Pages/ENG/execution.htm, [accessed September 2011].
[5] Swirski, S (2008) *The burden of occupation, Idem,* p.31.
[6] http://www.securityfence.mod.gov.il/Pages/ENG/execution.htm, [accessed May 2011].

Company profiles

Tyco Electronics is a global provider of electronic parts based in Switzerland. In 1999, Tyco merged with **Raychem**. Raychem components were found on pieces of the wall close to the West Bank village of Jayyous. Raychem has premises in the UK in Swindon, Wiltshire.[7]

Barad Company for Landworks Developments and Roads is contracted to construct the infrastructure for the West Bank wall.[8] The company has a British subsidiary, **Horizon Development**.

Cement Roadstone Holdings (CRH), the largest company on the Irish stock exchange, owns controlling shares in **Nesher**, through **Mashav**, an Israeli holding company. Nesher has admitted that "in all probability" its cement is used in the construction of the apartheid wall.[9] 2 out of 8 of the directors on the board of Nesher are from CRH.

CRH had sales of over €17 billion and returned profits of €598 billion in 2009. The company operates in 35 countries.[10] Nesher have a monopoly on the supply of cement in Israel.

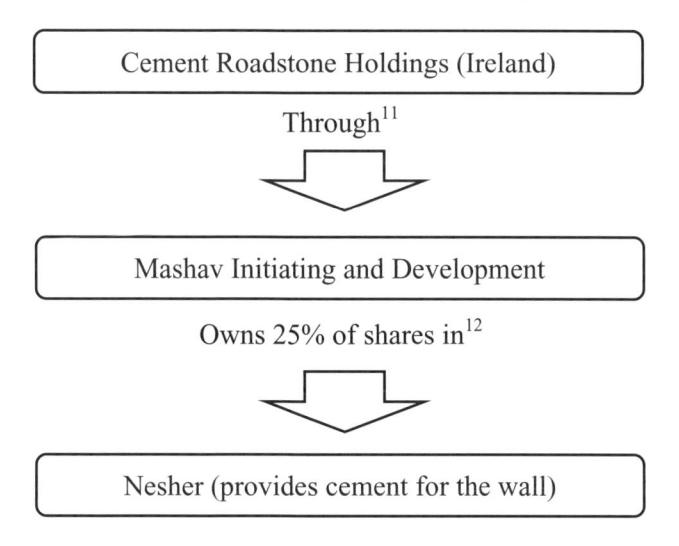

```
Cement Roadstone Holdings (Ireland)
        Through[11]
           ↓
Mashav Initiating and Development
    Owns 25% of shares in[12]
           ↓
Nesher (provides cement for the wall)
```

Mashav recently acquired **Hanson Israel**, the second-largest building materials company in Israel, which owns a quarry in the West Bank.[13]

---

[7] http://www.applegate.co.uk/all-industry/tyco-electronic-0007130.htm, [accessed May 2011].
[8] http://www.whoprofits.org/Company%20Info.php?id=726, [accessed May 2011].
[9] http://www.whoprofits.org/Company%20Info.php?id=614, [accessed May 2011].
[10] Evidence given by John Dornan to the Russell Tribunal (2010), http://www.russelltribunalonpalestine.com/en/sessions/london-session/video-of-proceedings, [accessed June 2011].
[11] http://www.stopthewall.org/downloads/pdf/companiesbuildingwall.pdf, [accessed May 2011].
[12] http://electronicintifada.net/content/heidelbergcement-tries-sell-west-bank-mines-legal-boycott-pressures-grow/8340, [accessed May 2011].
[13] http://www.stopthewall.org/downloads/pdf/companiesbuildingwall.pdf, [accessed June 2011].

The top 50 shareholders in CRH are:

Affiliated Managers Group,	Allianz SE,
Allied Irish Banks,	Altrinsic Global Advisors,
American Century Companies,	Artio Global Investors,
Artio Global Management,	AXA,
Bank of New York Mellon,	BNP Paribas,
BPCE SA,	Brandes Investment Partners,
Capital Group International Inc,	Concerned Parents and Teachers of Wycocomagh and Area,
Covea,	Credit Suisse,
CRH Plc's Employees Benefit Trust,	Danske Bank,
Dekabanke Deutsch Girozentrale,	Deutsche Bank,
Dimensional Fund Advisors,	Edinburgh Partners Ltd,
European Investment Trust.[14]	F&C Asset Management,
Federated Investors,	FMR,
Government of Norway,	Grantham,
Groupe CM,	Henderson Group,
ING Group,	Invesco,
Irish Life Investment Managers Ltd,	J O Hambro Capital Management,
Jupiter Fund Management,	Legg Mason Inc,
Mandarine Gestion,	Manning and Napier Advisors,
Mayo,	Morgan Stanley,
Norges Bank,	Northern Cross,
PGGM Vermogensbeheer,	Polaris Capital,
Province De Quebec,	Regeringskansliet,
SAS Rue la Boetie,	Schroders,
State Street Corporation,	Stichting Pension Funds ABP,
Swedbank,	Teachers Insurance and Annuity Association of America,
Templeton Global Advisors Ltd,	UBS AG,
Unicredit, Spa,	Union Asset Management Holding,
Van Lanschot NV,	Van Otterloo and Co,
Vanguard Group,	Wellington Management

---

[14] Orbis database, Bureau Van Dijk, [accessed 19/08/2011].

List of Companies involved in the West Bank Apartheid wall:

Company	Country of origin	Involvement with the West Bank apartheid wall
Ackerstein Industries	Israel	concrete slabs[15]
Avi Cranes	Israel	cranes and maintenance equipment (Avi Cranes is the Israeli representative of **Manitou, Snorkel, Beka Max, CASAR** and **Faymonville**)[16]
Barad Company for Landworks Developments and Roads	Israel	infrastructure construction[17]
Biri Barashi Land Works, Development Infrastructure and Roads	Israel	infrastructure construction
Bobcat	US	construction equipment[18]
Cape Gate	South Africa	supplies wire for fencing[19]
Caterpillar	US	construction equipment[20]
Magal	Israel	fencing and detection systems[21]
Elbit	Israel	surveillance systems[22]
Nesher – provides cement for the wall	Israel (owned by Irish company, CRH)	Cement
Controp Precision Technologies	US	Electro Optical Scanning Radar (SPIDER)
EDIG Construction management	Israel	generators[23]
Eli Yohanan Engineers	Israel	construction[24]
Solel Boneh	Israel	construction[25]
Volvo	Sweden	construction equipment[26]

---

[15] http://www.whoprofits.org/Company%20Info.php?id=476, [accessed May 2011].
[16] http://www.whoprofits.org/Company%20Info.php?id=723, [accessed May 2011].
[17] http://www.whoprofits.org/Company%20Info.php?id=726, [accessed May 2011].
[18] http://www.stopthewall.org/downloads/pdf/companiesbuildingwall.pdf, [accessed May 2011].
[19] http://www.whoprofits.org/Company%20Info.php?id=483, [accessed May 2011].
[20] http://www.stopthewall.org/downloads/pdf/companiesbuildingwall.pdf, [accessed May 2011].
[21] *Ibid.*
[22] *Ibid.*
[23] http://www.whoprofits.org/Company%20Info.php?id=502, [accessed May 2011].
[24] http://www.whoprofits.org/Company%20Info.php?id=829, [accessed May 2011].
[25] http://www.whoprofits.org/Company%20Info.php?id=787, [accessed May 2011].
[26] http://corporateoccupation.wordpress.com/2010/12/06/volvo-machines-used-to-demolish-

Company	Country of origin	Involvement with the West Bank apartheid wall
Liebherr	Germany	construction equipment[27]
Manitou	France	construction equipment[28]
Olenik Transportation Earth Work and Road Constructions	Israel	construction[29]
Peretz Sela Civil Engineering	Israel	planning[30]
Readymix	Owned by Cemex (Mexico)	cement[31]
Raychem	Switzerland	electronic parts[32]
Riwal	Holland	cranes and mounted platforms[33]
Orad	Israel	detection systems[34]
Tamam	Israel	surveillance technology (owned by **Israel Aerospace Industries**)[35]
Terex	US	trucks and floodlight systems[36]
Yehezkel Morad	Israel	construction.[37]
Yehuda Welded Mesh	Israel	fencing[38]

---

palestinian-homes/, [accessed May 2011].
[27] http://www.stopthewall.org/downloads/pdf/companiesbuildingwall.pdf, [accessed May 2011].
[28] *Ibid.*
[29] http://www.whoprofits.org/Company%20Info.php?id=862, [accessed May 2011].
[30] http://www.whoprofits.org/Company%20Info.php?id=716, [accessed May 2011].
[31] http://www.whoprofits.org/Company%20Info.php?id=645, [accessed May 2011].
[32] http://www.stopthewall.org/downloads/pdf/companiesbuildingwall.pdf, [accessed May 2011].
[33] Salma Karmi, evidence to the Russell Tribunal (2010), Available: http://www.russelltribunalonpalestine.com/en/sessions/london-session/video-of-proceedings, [accessed May 2011].
[34] http://whoprofits.org/Company%20Info.php?id=641, [accessed May 2011].
[35] http://www.stopthewall.org/downloads/pdf/companiesbuildingwall.pdf, [accessed May 2011].
[36] http://www.whoprofits.org/Company%20Info.php?id=916, [accessed May 2011].
[37] http://www.whoprofits.org/Company%20Info.php?id=891, [accessed May 2011].
[38] http://www.whoprofits.org/Company%20Info.php?id=492, [accessed May 2011].

Israeli soldiers fire on Palestinian activists who are demonstrating against the apartheid wall (Bil'in Popular Committee 2010)

The Gaza Walls

Israel began building a 60 kilometre fence around the Gaza Strip after the Oslo Accords in 1994. According to the Oslo interim agreements, the wall was never supposed to constitute a border. Israel used the pretext of the Palestinian *intifada* to justify fortifying the fence, now predominantly a concrete wall, erect surveillance posts and impose a one-kilometre 'buffer zone'.[39]

Since 2001, Israel has destroyed thousands of houses in the buffer zone.[40] Some 2,500 Gazan homes were destroyed during the second Palestinian *intifada*, the majority in Rafah in the border area, referred to by Israel as the *Philadelphi* route or *Philadelphi* Corridor.[41] Demolitions during the *intifada* resulted in the clearance of 10% of the land in Gaza.[42] These clearances were carried out using explosives, aerial strikes and **Caterpillar** D9 military bulldozers.[43] The *Philadelphi* Corridor was further attacked by Israel during the 2009 massacre in Gaza.[44]

---

[39]http://www.jcpa.org/brief/brief004-12.htm, [accessed June 2011].
[40]http://www.jcpa.org/brief/brief004-12.htm, [accessed June 2011].
[41]http://icahd.dolphin.nethost.co.il/wordpress/wp-content/uploads/2010/05/Obstacles-2009.pdf, [accessed June 2011]. p.42.
[42]*Ibid,* p.43.
[43]War on Want (2005), *Caterpillar: the alternative report,* Available: http://www.waronwant.org/attachments/Caterpillar-%20The%20Alternative%20Report.pdf, [accessed September 2011].
[44]See interview with Jenny Linnell of the International Solidarity Movement, Available: http://www.youtube.com/watch?v=9g74j4HMMSg (from 3:57 in recording) and Locke, S (2010), *gaza beneath the bombs*, Pluto Press.

The part of Gaza close to the Israeli wall has become a no-go zone for Palestinians, an area policed and patrolled remotely by unmanned aircraft and vehicles. Palestinians living or farming in the area close to the wall's buffer zone are constantly harassed, injured and killed by the Israeli military.[45]

In 2009, the Egyptian government, at Israel's behest, began building a 100 foot deep underground steel wall.[46] The wall has reportedly been designed and constructed by US army engineers but private contractors are also clearly involved. For example, the Egyptian government-owned company **Arab Contractors** has been accused of involvement in building the Rafah wall.[47] Since the 2011 uprising in Egypt, there is evidence that suggests construction of this wall has been suspended.[48]

The Gaza steel wall

---

[45]See http://farmingunderfire.blogspot.com, [accessed May 2011].
[46]http://apjp.org/wall-of-shame-egypts-barrier, [accessed May 2011].
[47]http://www.almasryalyoum.com/en/node/9804, [accessed May 2011].
[48]http://www.tehrantimes.com/index_View.asp?code=238547, [accessed May 2011].

Companies involved in the construction of the Gaza walls:

Company	Country of origin	Involvement with the Gaza walls
Alper	Israel	electronic sensors[49]
Arab Contractors	Egypt	construction (Gaza underground steel wall)[50]
Caterpillar	US	construction/demolition machinery[51]
Yehuda Welded Mesh	Israel	built the fence around the Gaza Strip[52]

The Eilat Wall

Israel is building a new security fence around the Red Sea city of Eilat, close to the border with Egypt. Companies known to have tendered for stakes in the $270 million project include: **Motorola Israel**; **Ortek**, a subsidiary of Israeli arms manufacturer **Elbit**; **Magal Security Systems**; **D-Fence;** and **El-Far**.[53]

Resistance

Since the death of American activist Rachel Corrie in 2003 there has been a global campaign against Caterpillar because of its complicity in the demolition of Palestinian homes, often to make way for the Gaza wall. Corrie was killed on 13th March 2003 while attempting to prevent the demolition of houses in the *Philadelphi* Corridor, close to the Gaza wall buffer zone. She was crushed to death by a Caterpillar D9 military bulldozer.

The campaign against CAT has included global demonstrations, direct action and sabotage, including arson attacks against Caterpillar dealerships.[54] The campaign groups SUSTAIN[55] (Stop US Tax Funded Aid to Israel Now) and Stop Caterpillar campaigned against CAT's supply of D9s in the US, while the Caterkiller campaign, War on Want and the Palestine Solidarity Campaign focused on CAT's UK activities. In the US, CAT AGMs saw large protests and blockades, while Caterpillar factories and dealerships were targeted in the UK. Many campaigners focused on CAT's footwear and clothing range, staging protests and street

---

[49] http://www.whoprofits.org/Company%20Info.php?id=492, [accessed May 2011].
[50] http://www.almasryalyoum.com/en/node/9804, [accessed May 2011].
[51] War on Want (2005), *Caterpillar: the alternative report*, [accessed September 2011].
[52] http://www.whoprofits.org/Company%20Info.php?id=492, [accessed May 2011].
[53] http://corporateoccupation.wordpress.com/2010/01/28/israel-to-fortify-the-prison-walls-around-eilat, [accessed May 2011].
[54] For a report of the arson attacks see http://gipfelsoli.org/Home/Heiligendamm_2007/G8_2007_english, [accessed May 2011].
[55] http://electronicintifada.net/content/activists-demand-immediate-halt-caterpillar-bulldozer-sales-israeli-defense-forces/207, [accessed May 2011].

theatre outside high street stores. As a result, the Methodist Church and the Church of England divested millions of pounds worth of shares in CAT.[56]

In 2007, a case was brought in the US by the Corrie family against Caterpillar, charging the company with complicity in the death of Rachel and of Palestinians killed or injured by Caterpillar bulldozers demolishing their homes, causing them to collapse on top of them. The case was dismissed on the grounds that any ruling would intrude on US foreign policy decisions.[57] However, in 2010 Caterpillar temporarily suspended deliveries of D9s in response to a civil suit against the IDF brought by the Corrie family in an Israeli court.[58]

A Caterpillar D9 bulldozer painted red by activists (Active Stills 2006)

There has been a campaign against Cement Roadstone Holdings (CRH) in Ireland since 2004, which has seen pickets of the company's premises, shareholder actions and a divestment campaign that led to questions being asked in the Irish parliament about the company's role in the building of the wall[59] and to **ASN** bank and the New England United Methodist Church divesting shares in the company.[60] CRH says that it cannot control the end users of its products and is not responsible for the use of its cement in the wall.[61] BDS

---

[56] http://www.waronwant.org/campaigns/fighting-occupation/palestine/inform/16455-divestment-campaign-builds-as-companies-profiteering-from-the-occupation-come-under-pressure, [accessed May 2011].
[57] http://ccrjustice.org/ourcases/current-cases/corrie-et-al.-v.-caterpillar, [accessed May 2011].
[58] http://www2.pslweb.org/site/News2?page=NewsArticle&id=14733&news_iv_ctrl=1007, [accessed May 2011].
[59] John Dornan, evidence to the Russell Tribunal (2010), Available: http://www.russelltribunalonpalestine.com/en/sessions/london-session/video-of-proceedings, [accessed May 2011].
[60] http://www.stopthewall.org/downloads/pdf/companiesbuildingwall.pdf, [accessed May 2011], and John Dornan, evidence to the Russell Tribunal (2010), *Idem*.
[61] John Dornan, evidence to the Russell Tribunal (2010), *Idem*.

campaigners have also waged several successful divestment campaigns against Elbit *(see our earlier chapter on the Israeli military sector)*.

On 14th October 2010, after pressure from BDS campaigners, the Dutch equipment hire company, **Riwal**, had its offices raided and documents seized after a Palestinian human rights group, Al Haq, complained that it was complicit in the building of the apartheid wall.[62] Questions about Riwal's involvement in the building of the wall had first been asked in the Dutch parliament in 2006 after a Dutch television crew filmed cranes active in construction of the apartheid wall, and of settlements, which bore the Riwal company logo. As a result, in 2008, the Dutch Government warned Riwal not to engage in activities in the occupied territories. When it became clear that Riwal had continued supplying the equipment, Dutch prosecutors initiated a case against them.[63]

Israel's Walls – Where Next?

The dismantling of Israel's apartheid walls should be a fundamental goal of the BDS movement. The ruling of the International Court of Justice that "all states are under an obligation... not to render and/or assist" the construction of the West Bank wall is helpful to campaigners. There is a clear legal case to be made that companies involved in building the wall should be prosecuted for complicity in war crimes. Campaigners may be able to initiate court cases against companies involved in the building of the wall. Those who take direct action against these companies may be able to argue, in their legal defence, that they acted out of 'necessity'.

CRH should be a major focus of the BDS movement and campaigners should consider legal action against the company. The investors in CRH, for example the Government of Norway and **Capital Research and Management Company** could be divestment targets. The Bank of Norway seems a soft target as divestment campaigns have already had significant success with the Norwegian pension fund. **The Capital Group**, the parent company of **Capital Research and Management**, has offices worldwide, including in London.[64]

---

[62] http://www.oikoumene.org/en/programmes/public-witness-addressing-power-affirming-peace/churches-in-the-middle-east/pief/news-events/a/article/7313/dutch-police-raided-the-o.html, [accessed May 2011].
[63] Salma Karmi, evidence to the Russell Tribunal (2010), *Idem.*
[64] see http://www.capgroup.com/about_us/office_locations.html, [accessed May 2011].

Part Five – Real estate

The Israeli real estate sector has been largely overlooked by the BDS movement. However, businessmen operating in the UK have a substantial stake in the settlement industry

Company profiles

"Israel is our shining star among the investments outside the UK"

Leo Noe, 2007[1]

Leo Noe is a British real estate tycoon. He controls 75% of shares in the **REIT** group and has purchased the Israeli real estate firm, **Azorim Properties**, which he renamed **British-Israel Investments Ltd**, from the Israeli conglomerate the **Dankner Group**.[2] REIT merged with **F&C Asset Management** in 2008, forming **F&C REIT Asset Management,** which is registered at Companies House in the UK.[3] F&C Reit is one of the top 5 real estate companies in the UK.[4] Leo Noe is the executive chairman of the company.[5] F&C is a major investor in companies complicit in Israeli war crimes, including CRH and **G4S**.

Mall belonging to British Israel Investments in the West Bank settlement on Ma'ale Adumim (Corporate Watch 2010)

---

[1] http://www.british-israel.co.il/en/media-cover/4, [accessed May 2011].
[2] http://real-estate-entrepreneur.com/index.php?option=com_content&view=article&id=384:leo-noe-uk&catid=34:united-kingdom&Itemid=64, [accessed May 2011] and http://wck2.companieshouse.gov.uk/c75ac40f39e73ce891a33d75d7cd0799/compdetails, [accessed May 2011].
[3] http://www.propertyweek.com/news/fc-asset-management-to-merge-with-leo-noe%E2%80%99s-reit-asset-management/3118749.article, [accessed May 2011].
[4] Orbis database, Bureau Van Dyck, [accessed September 2011].
[5] http://www.fandcreit.com/default.aspx?id=86296, [accessed May 2011].

British Israel Investments (BII) Ltd is a real estate company that boasts that it is the leader in the construction of shopping malls and commercial centres in Israel.[6] Amir Biram, CEO of BII Israel,[7] told the New York Times that BII's investments were "Zionism, but business all the same."[8] REIT owns, through BII, the Adumim shopping mall in the settlement of Ma'aleh Adumim, 50% of the Israeli **Ikea** Trade area in Netanya, and shopping malls in Haifa, Ramat Gan and elsewhere.[9]

A major BII shareholder is the **Zabludowicz Trust**, registered in Lichtenstein and controlled by British real estate tycoon Poju Zabludowicz. Zabludowicz is a London based billionaire, whose fortune derives from his father's arms company. He is a major donor to the British Conservative party and the Conservative Friends of Israel. He is also the chairman of the British-Israel Communications and Research centre (BICOM).[10] **Tamares**, Zabludowicz's real estate company, has offices in central London.[11]

Top investors in F&C Reit:

Pershing Nominees	Sherbourne Investors (Guernsey)
Eureko	Aviva
FMR	Artemis Strategic Asset Management
Fidelity International	Bank Sarasin
Prudential	Legal&General
Cazenove Capital Holdings	Dimensional Fund Advisers
Cantor Fitzgerald Europe	Black Rock
Ameriprise Financial	Franklin Resources
Henderson Group	JP Morgan
Government of Norway	Lloyds
Liverpool Victoria Friendly Society	Legg Mason
Barclays	HSBC
AXA	The Universities Superannuation Scheme
West Yorkshire Pension Fund	Aberdeen Asset Management
Teachers Insurance and Annuity Association of America	Deutsche Bank
Investec	

---

[6] http://www.british-israel.co.il/en/, [accessed May 2011].
[7] http://www.british-israel.co.il/en/management, [accessed May 2011].
[8] http://www.nytimes.com/2006/09/12/realestate/12iht-reisrael.2785157.html?_r=1, [accessed May 2011].
[9] http://www.british-israel.co.il/en/media-cover/4, [accessed May 2011].
[10] http://www.powerbase.info/index.php?title=Poju_Zabludowicz, [accessed May 2011].
[11] http://www.tamares.com/contact.html, [accessed May 2011].

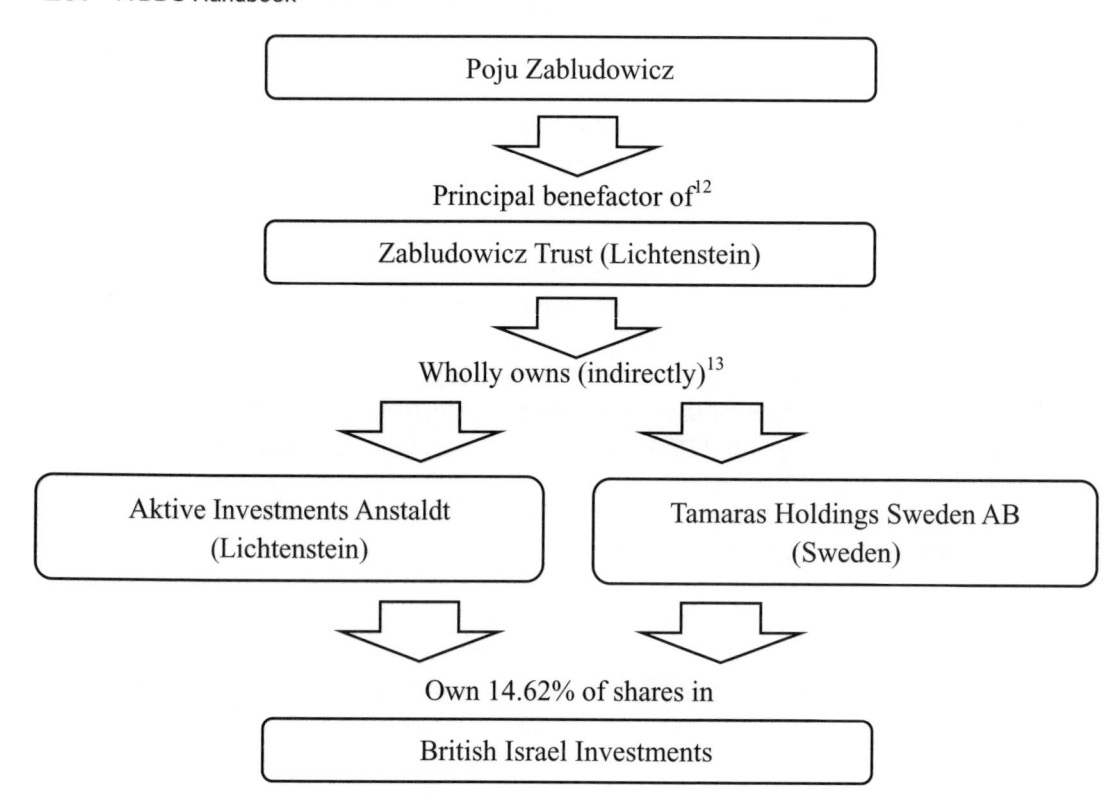

```
┌─────────────────────┐
│   Poju Zabludowicz  │
└─────────────────────┘
           ⇓
   Principal benefactor of[12]
┌─────────────────────────────┐
│ Zabludowicz Trust (Lichtenstein) │
└─────────────────────────────┘
           ⇓
   Wholly owns (indirectly)[13]
   ⇓                    ⇓
┌──────────────────┐  ┌──────────────────────┐
│ Aktive Investments│  │ Tamaras Holdings     │
│ Anstaldt         │  │ Sweden AB            │
│ (Lichtenstein)   │  │ (Sweden)             │
└──────────────────┘  └──────────────────────┘
           ⇓                    ⇓
       Own 14.62% of shares in
┌─────────────────────────────┐
│ British Israel Investments  │
└─────────────────────────────┘
```

Meshulam Levinstein, established in 1964, is one of Israel's leading development, construction and real estate companies.[14] The company, publicly traded on the Tel Aviv Stock Exchange, has constructed a housing development in the Jerusalem settlement of Homat Shmuel and a cement factory for Nesher, a company which supplies cement for the apartheid wall.[15] **Levinstein Assets Ltd**, the real estate arm of Meshulam Levinstein, owns several large properties including Discount Tower in Tel Aviv, home of **Israel Discount Bank, Apax Partners** and several foreign embassies. **Faber**, another arm of the company is concerned with infrastructure construction.[16]

Meshulam Levinstein operates in Eastern Europe, Panama, India (through **Lev India**)[17] and the UK. In the UK Meshulam Levinstein has received backing from British banks to build housing projects in Hornsey, Mayfair, Paddington and Battersea and is preparing to tender for further construction projects in Battersea.[18]

---

[12] http://maya.tase.co.il/bursa/report.asp?report_cd=523524, [accessed March 2010].
[13] *Ibid.*
[14] http://www.bdicode.co.il/CompanyTextProfile_ENG/870_827_0/Meshulam%20Levinstein%20Contracting%20Engineering%20Group%20Ltd, [accessed May 2011].
[15] http://www.whoprofits.org/Company%20Info.php?id=833, [accessed May 2011].
[16] http://www.bdicode.co.il/CompanyTextProfile_ENG/870_827_0/Meshulam%20Levinstein%20Contracting%20Engineering%20Group%20Ltd, [accessed May 2011].
[17] *Ibid.*
[18] http://www.levinstein.co.il/index.php?page_id=12, [accessed May 2011].

Israeli real estate – Where Next?

The Israeli real estate sector has not been targeted as a separate entity to the construction sector. Owners of Israeli real estate benefit from the apartheid policies of the Israeli state. The BDS movement should target the owners of Israeli real estate companies, with a focus on the owners of settlement real estate. Companies owning property in the settlements should be divestment targets and prosecutions should be considered against their directors.

REIT/British Israel Investments should be major targets for the British BDS movement. F&C REIT, a British registered company, owns a major Israeli real estate developer, BII. BII is a self-proclaimed Zionist company and owns property in the settlement of Ma'aleh Adumim.

The possibility of bringing a legal case against BII/REIT should be seriously explored in the light of Bil'In's case against the Canadian **Green Park** companies *(for details of this case see our chapter on the Israeli diamond industry earlier in this book)*. BII's ownership of the Ma'aleh Adumim shopping mall raises possibilities of a case against it for complicity in war crimes. Alongside legal action, grassroots campaigns should target these British companies, their British owner, Leo Noe, and shareholder Poju Zabludowicz.

Part six - Construction equipment

Any company providing Israel with services and equipment, such as diggers and bulldozers, will be aware that its products are likely to be used as tools in the occupation. Indeed, there is frequent crossover between construction, transport and military equipment. By supplying equipment to Israel, companies such as **Volvo**, **Caterpillar** and **JCB**, support the government's policies - building the apartheid wall one day and demolishing Palestinian homes in the Naqab or the Jordan Valley the next.

International construction equipment companies have been trying to distance themselves from the ways their products are used to displace Palestinians and build the infrastructure of occupation. As we have seen, Caterpillar has experienced sustained campaigns, leading to large-scale divestment in the case of CAT. However, very little real action has been forthcoming from the companies themselves. More often than not attempts are made to hide behind 'codes of conduct' with little practical implications. One good example is the response from M Wikforss, the vice president of the media relations and corporate news department of **Volvo Group**, to accusations of occupation profiteering by his company. Wikforss claimed that Volvo "do not have any control over the use of our products, other than to affirm in our business activities a Code of Conduct that decries unethical behavior,"[1] and the company's code of conduct does indeed state: "Within its sphere of influence, the Volvo Group supports and respects the protection of internationally proclaimed human rights and ensures that it is not complicit in human rights abuses."[2] It is up to the BDS movement to make such companies realise that decrying unethical behaviour while aiding a brutal occupation is never going to be good enough.

Company profiles:

Volvo Construction Equipment is part of the Swedish Volvo Group. Its other subsidiaries are **Volvo Buses**, **Volvo Trucks**, **Volvo Penta**, **Volvo Aero**, **Volvo Financial Services**, **Renault Trucks**, **Mack** and **Nissan Diesel**.[3] The Volvo Group is represented in Israel by **Mayer Cars and Trucks** which also imports and distributes **Jaguar** and **Honda** cars, **Mitsubishi** trucks, and heavy machinery from **Honda** and **Atlas Copco** in Israel.[4]

Bulldozers manufactured by Volvo Construction Equipment are frequently used during the construction of checkpoints and settlements in the West Bank.[5] During 2010 there were documented incidents of Volvo machinery demolishing Palestinian houses in Abu Al Ajaj in

---

[1] Adri Nieuwhof for Corporate Occupation, http://corporateoccupation.wordpress.com/2010/06/16/volvo-equipment-effective-tool-in-the-israeli-occupation-of-palestine/, [accessed 114/6/2011].
[2] Statement from Volvo's code of conduct, http://www.volvogroup.com/GROUP/GLOBAL/EN-GB/RESPONSIBILITY/COMMITTED_CSR/CODE_OF_CONDUCT/HR_WORKPLACE/PAGES/HUMAN_RIGHTS.ASPX, [accessed 114/6/2011].
[3] http://www.whoprofits.org/Company%20Info.php?id=799, [accessed 114/6/2011].
[4] *Ibid*.
[5] *Ibid*.

the Jordan Valley, Al Araqib in the Naqab, Wadi Qadum, Silwan, Beit Hanina, Atir, Um Hayran and Walaja.[6] These demolitions take place in order to cleanse the area of Palestinians and facilitate settlement expansion in the West Bank and East Jerusalem, and Jewish takeover of land in the Naqab. In the case of Walaja, land was cleared to make room for the apartheid wall. Corporate Watch researchers have also observed Volvo machines at work on illegal settlement projects in Ariel, Givat Hamivtar and Mod'iin Illit in the West Bank,[7] as well as at a quarry in the occupied Syrian Golan.[8]

Demolitions using Volvo machinery in the Jordan Valley village of Abu al Ajaj (Jordan Valley Solidarity 2009)

Volvo Buses, another part of the Volvo Group, is supporting the occupation through its 26.5% share in **Merkavim.** Merkavim is an Israeli company that provides buses for the Israeli prison authority. It regularly transports Palestinian political prisoners from the 1967 occupied territories to prisons inside Israel. It also provides armoured buses for the Israeli bus company **Egged** to serve settlements in the West Bank. They are also the main body builder for Volvo in the Middle East.[9] A distributor of Volvo generators, **Orcal Industries and Mechanization**, trades from the illegal settlement of Atarot.[10]

---

[6]http://www.corporatewatch.org/?lid=3844, [accessed 114/6/2011].
[7]*Ibid*.
[8]http://corporateoccupation.wordpress.com/2010/04/03/digging-up-the-golan-heights, [accessed 114/6/2011].
[9]http://www.whoprofits.org/Company%20Info.php?id=801, [accessed 114/6/2011].
[10]http://www.whoprofits.org/Company%20Info.php?id=678, [accessed 114/6/2011].

JCB (JC Bamford Excavators) is the world's third largest construction equipment manufacturer[11] and produces equipment used in the agriculture, defence, and construction industries. As with Volvo and Caterpillar, its machinery is used by the Israeli military in the occupied territories. JCB is a British company with a head office in Rochester and is privately owned by the Bamford family. The chairman is Sir Anthony Bamford, a major donor to the British Conservative Party.[12] It has 2 subsidiaries, **JCB Finance** and **JCB Insurance Services**.[13] JCB's partner and distributor in Israel is **Comasco Construction Machinery and Systems Ltd**,[14] which is located in Mitzpe Sapir Industrial Park inside 1948 Israel and about 1 kilometre from Qalqilya, a Palestinian town of over 40,000 people completely surrounded by the apartheid wall.

Goat killed during the demolitions in Abu al Ajaj (Jordan Valley Solidarity 2010)

JCB equipment has been used for construction in the illegal settlements of Alfei Menashe and Zufin, and at the checkpoints in Qalandia, near Ofer prison and in the Ariel West settlement industrial zone.[15] JCB machinery is also used in both the A1-train line project between Tel Aviv and Jerusalem, which crosses Palestinian land,[16] and in work on the East Jerusalem tram line.[17]

---

[11]http://www.yorkshirepost.co.uk/business/business-news/jcb_reaps_reward_for_tough_action_as_profits_show_a_rise_1_2581349, [accessed 114/6/2011].
[12]http://www.guardian.co.uk/politics/2011/may/25/labour-party-donors-unions, [accessed 114/6/2011].
[13]JCB http://customer.jcb-finance.co.uk/insurance/insurance.jhtm, [accessed 114/6/2011].
[14]http://www.whoprofits.org/Company%20Info.php?id=915, [accessed 114/6/2011].
[15]*Ibid.*
[16]*Ibid.*
[17]http://corporateoccupation.wordpress.com/2010/03/12/walking-the-route-of-veolias-tramline-in-

On the 30th of April 2010 a Corporate Watch researcher observed the Israeli army using a militarised digger bearing a JCB logo to dig up the garden of a Palestinian family in the occupied Jordan Valley. According to the American website Army Technology, Israel has purchased the JCB High-Mobility Engineer Excavator via the foreign military sales provisions.[18]

Terex is an American truck and construction equipment company whose machinery has been used in the construction of the wall on the land of Nil'in and Ras A-Tira and on the A1-train line. Floodlights manufactured by **Amida Industries**, a company owned by Terex, are used at checkpoints and construction sites along the wall as well as in quarrying in the occupied Syrian Golan. Terex subsidiary **Terex Demag Cranes** is leased in Israel through **Riwal**, a major equipment supplier in the construction of the wall.[19] The company previously owned a controlling stake in **TATRA**, which supplies the Israeli army with trucks used to mount artillery systems.[20] Terex is publicly listed on the New York Stock Exchange. The company has many subsidiaries and trades globally.[21] Terex has a UK office in Coventry.[22]

Liebherr, a company with head offices in Germany, is privately owned by the Swiss family of the same name. Its machinery has been used in the construction of the apartheid wall.[23]

The Japanese conglomerate **Mitsubishi** distributes generators through the Israeli company **Orcal Industries**, which operates from the Atarot settlement industrial zone.[24] Mitsubishi trucks are imported by Mayer Cars and trucks *(see above)*.[25]

Ashtrom is an Israeli construction and engineering company that supplies construction materials for checkpoints. The company owns a quarry in the settlement of Beithar Illit and a concrete plant in the Atarot settlement industrial zone.[26] **Bobcat** is a US based manufacturer of construction vehicles. It supplies tools used for settlement construction and checkpoints.[27]

Nesher Israel Cement Enterprises Ltd is an Israeli cement giant involved in supplying cement to all Israeli construction projects in the West Bank. The company has a monopoly on the supply of cement in the Israeli market, claiming on its website to be the sole producer of cement in the country. It is 25% owned by Cement Roadstone Holdings.[28] Nesher itself

---

east-jerusalem, [accessed 114/6/2011].
[18] http://www.army-technology.com/projects/jcbhighmobilityengin, [accessed 114/6/2011].
[19] http://www.unitedmethodistdivestment.com/CompaniesInvolved.html, [accessed 114/6/2011].
[20] *Ibid*.
[21] Information from Who Profits: http://www.whoprofits.org/Company%20Info.php?id=916, [accessed 114/6/2011].
[22] http://www.terex.co.uk/about_contact.php, [accessed 114/6/2011].
[23] http://www.whoprofits.org/Company%20Info.php?id=560, [accessed 114/6/2011].
[24] http://www.whoprofits.org/Company%20Info.php?id=678, [accessed 114/6/2011].
[25] http://www.whoprofits.org/Company%20Info.php?id=798, [accessed 114/6/2011].
[26] http://www.whoprofits.org/Company%20Info.php?id=480, [accessed 114/6/2011].
[27] http://www.whoprofits.org/Company%20Info.php?id=744, [accessed 114/6/2011].
[28] http://www.whoprofits.org/Company%20Info.php?id=637, [accessed 114/6/2011].

jointly owns **Taavura Holdings Ltd**, which specialises in road haulage, logistics, heavy lifting and earth moving. Its **Tashtit Division** imports construction equipment and is the sole importer and distributor of trucks and buses for Dutch company **DAF** within Israel.[29]

Emcol is a supplier of construction tools and is the Israeli representative of **Swedish SKF** and **Bobcat**.[30]

Neuman Steel Industries for Construction is an Israeli steel product manufacturer and supplier. The company is currently building a new factory in the Ariel West settlement industrial zone.[31]

Bobcat machinery in use in the settlement of Katzrin, occupied Syrian Golan (Corporate Watch 2010)

New Way Traffic is an Israeli company which installs traffic safety equipment and supplies equipment for the checkpoints and the East Jerusalem tram line.[32]

Readymix is the largest supplier of raw materials for construction in Israel. It has provided the concrete for buildings such as the Weizmann Institute of Science and the Diamond Exchange tower in Ramat Gan.[33] It operates in several settlement industrial zones and owns a 50 per cent stake in the Yatir quarry next to the illegal settlement of Teneh Omarim in the West Bank's south Hebron hills.[34] Readymix is a subsidiary of Mexican building conglomerate **Cemex**.[35]

---

[29] http://www.taavura.com/244.html, [accessed 114/6/2011].
[30] http://www.whoprofits.org/Company%20Info.php?id=745, [accessed 114/6/2011].
[31] http://www.whoprofits.org/Company%20Info.php?id=953, [accessed 114/6/2011].
[32] http://www.whoprofits.org/Company%20Info.php?id=638, [accessed 114/6/2011].
[33] http://www.bdicode.co.il//CompanyTextProfile_ENG/465_143_0/Readymix%20Industries%20%28Israel%29%20Ltd, [accessed 114/6/2011].
[34] http://www.newsfrommiddleeast.com/?new=77836, [accessed 114/6/2011].
[35] http://www.whoprofits.org/Company%20Info.php?id=645, [accessed 114/6/2011].

Resistance

The campaign against CAT is discussed above. There have been initial steps toward targeting Volvo Group, mainly in the form of divestment campaigns. The United Methodist Church has already placed the company on their divestment list.[36]

UK activists occupy Caterpillar equipment at a trade fair (UK Indymedia 2004)

Construction equipment – Where Next

Considering that JCB is a private, British owned company with well documented links to occupation projects, action against it is long overdue and a sustained campaign in the UK would be welcomed. There has already been some activity around Volvo but this has primarily involved research and awareness raising.[37] The efforts around Volvo should intensify and diversify to include direct action. International construction equipment companies exporting to Israel tend to trade globally so there is plenty of scope for coordinated worldwide pressure to be effective.

Pressure against Caterpillar should continue and international companies such as Mitsubishi, that distribute goods in Israel through settlement companies, should be pressured to drop these distributors. There is also a strong case for targeting companies like DAF that supply trucks and other vehicles to Israeli construction companies.

---

[36] http://www.quakerpi.org/QAction/ECON-SURVEY-Version2.html, [accessed 114/6/2011].
[37] See for instance http://www.bdsmovement.net/2009/volvo-providing-armored-buses-for-israeli-settlements-569, [accessed 114/6/2011].

20
Franchises

Many international companies have franchisees operating in Israel, the West Bank and the occupied Syrian Golan. Below are profiles of a selection of them.

Ikea the Swedish furniture giant has a franchisee, **Northern Birch Ltd**, which runs Ikea stores in Netanya and Rishon LeZiyon and is planning to open a third store in Haifa next year.[1]

Ikea Israel delivers to Israeli settlements in the West Bank but not to Palestinian addresses.[2] Shortly after IKEA Israel's delivery policy was revealed, a campaign was launched in Sweden and soon spread to other countries including Canada. Letters were written to IKEA, pickets organized outside its stores and its management contacted. Much of the campaign material can be found on the blog: bdsikea.wordpress.com.

In 2010, **Inter IKEA Systems BV**, which administers the franchise agreement, wrote to Canadians for a Just Peace in the Middle East, stating: "there are restrictions set by the government in Israel on crossing the border between the state of Israel and territories controlled by Palestinian Authorities. Such restrictions prevent people living in these territories to visit the IKEA Stores in Israel and prevent transportation companies from delivering hereto. We as well as our Israeli franchisee regret any limitations preventing any customer from visiting the IKEA stores or from using the services offered by the IKEA partners."[3]

In 2010 Corporate Watch researchers photographed a **Lee Cooper franchise** trading in the settlement of Ma'ale Adumim.[4] The Lee Cooper brand of denim fashionwear is currently controlled by **Sun Capital Partners**, an international private investment firm which, along with its affiliate and two unrelated equity sponsors, purchased the Lee Cooper Group in June 2011.[5] **Lee Cooper Group Limited** was liquidated on 13 September 2011 and, according to Sun Capital Partners PR, all that remains is the brand.[6] Sun Capital Partners controls the

---

[1] http://www.cjpme.org/DisplayDocument.aspx?DocumentID=1579, [accessed 114/6/2011].
[2] Radio Sweden, 23 June 2010, Available:
http://sverigesradio.se/sida/gruppsida.aspx?programid=3304&grupp=6251&artikel=3803017, [accessed 114/6/2011] and Cecilia Uddén for Radio Sweden, 23 June 2010, Available:
http://sverigesradio.se/diverse/appdata/isidor/images/news_images/83/1134815_520_292.jpg, [accessed 114/6/2011].
[3] http://bdsikea.wordpress.com/, [accessed 114/6/2011].
[4] http://corporateoccupation.wordpress.com/2010/03/15/evidence-of-british-company-lee-cooper-trading-in-illegal-israeli-settlement/#more-253, [accessed September 2011].
[5] http://www.prnewswire.co.uk/cgi/news/release?id=148345, [accessed September 2011].
[6] http://wck2.companieshouse.gov.uk/afc7986a9918a9f982bd57cb62090eab/compdetails, [accessed September 2011].

rights to the Lee Cooper trademark. The company has offices worldwide and an enormous portfolio of investments.[7]

The Lee Cooper store at Ma'ale Adumim serves to support the economy and viability of the settlement, which is the third largest in the West Bank. Established in 1976, it now has a population of around 35,000 and is rapidly growing. The settlement is at the heart of the controversial E1 project, which aims to cut the West Bank off from East Jerusalem and to facilitate further settlement expansion. Ma'ale Adumim was established on land stolen from the Palestinian villages of Abu Dis, Al Izriyyeh, Al Issawiyyeh and Anata.[8]

The liquidation of the Lee Cooper Group points to its weakness as a brand. The brand is a legitimate boycott target as Sun Capital Partners continue to profit from the occupation through the sale of Lee Cooper clothing from the store in Ma'ale Adumim.

H&M is a Swedish clothing retailer. In 2008, H&M entered into an agreement with **Match Retail**, an Israeli company controlled by the Horesh family, to open several stores in Israel.[9] In March 2010 various organizations, from Belgium, Sweden, Britain, Ireland, Denmark, Palestine and Israel called on H&M to postpone the establishment of seven planned stores in Israel "until Israel respects international law in line with the UN resolutions." Pickets of H&M stores were held across Europe and the Tel Aviv store was occupied by hundreds of activists.[10]

Protest outside H&M in Copenhagen, Denmark (In Minds 2010)

---

[7]See: http://www.suncappart.com/portfolio.php, [accessed September 2011].
[8]http://corporateoccupation.wordpress.com/2010/03/15/evidence-of-british-company-lee-cooper-trading-in-illegal-israeli-settlement/#more-253, [accessed September 2011].
[9]http://about.hm.com/gb/__prfinance.nhtml?pressreleaseid=398255, [accessed 114/6/2011].
[10]http://www.haaretz.com/news/pro-palestinian-groups-urge-h-m-boycott-after-israel-branch-opens-1.264655, [accessed 114/6/2011].

H&M promoting itself in Tel Aviv (Corporate Watch 2010)

Blockbuster Video is a US-owned company which has been trading since 1985.[11] Blockbuster's franchise in Israel is owned by **NMC United Entertainment**, a publicly traded company whose main shareholders (75%) are owned by Moshe and Leon Edri.[12] Blockbuster stores and vending machines can be found across Israel. Blockbuster vending machines are present in Modi'in Illit, Pisgat Ze'ev, Ariel,[13] and Givat Ze'ev.[14]

Blockbuster has video rental stores across the UK and franchises in most countries in Europe. However, it has yet to encounter resistance from the BDS movement. The company could be a soft target as it is already nearing bankruptcy due to the growing popularity of downloaded movies.[15] Blockbuster advertises it franchises on the basis that franchisees will be able to utilise assistance from Blockbuster in management and operations, as well as benefiting from its well-known brand name. Blockbuster charges a fee to its franchisees,[16] thus profiting from NMC's business on illegal Israeli settlements.

Pizza Hut and **Kentucky Fried Chicken** are subsidiaries of **Yum Brands**, the world's largest restaurant company.[17]

---

[11] http://www.blockbuster.com/corporate/news, [accessed 114/6/2011].
[12] http://www.whoprofits.org/Company%20Info.php?id=500, [accessed 114/6/2011].
[13] Corporate Watch personal observation, march 2010, [accessed 114/6/2011].
[14] http://www.whoprofits.org/Company%20Info.php?id=500, [accessed 114/6/2011].
[15] http://online.wsj.com/article/SB10001424052748704129204575506443334512852.html, [accessed 114/6/2011].
[16] http://www.thefranchisemall.com/franchises/details/11149-0-Pizza_Hut.htm, [accessed 114/6/2011].
[17] http://www.yum.com/company/ourbrands.asp, [accessed 114/6/2011].

KFC and Pizza Hut have restaurants across Israel. In 2010 Pizza Hut was operating a restaurant in the East Jerusalem settlement of Pisgat Ze'ev but this has closed down.[18] Pizza Hut and KFC both charge fees to their franchisees, while KFC also charge royalties.[19] The KFC and Pizza Hut franchises are owned by the **Alon Group**, which owns **Blue Square**, a retail chain with outlets on settlements, and **Dor Alon**, an energy company with a monopoly on the supply of petroleum to the Gaza Strip.[20]

Where next?

The BDS movement has not yet tackled the issue of international franchises operating in Israel in any serious way, save for the wave of protests against H&M *(see above)* and a nascent campaign against **France Telecom** (owner of the **Orange** brand name) and its franchise agreement with **Partner Communications** *(see our earlier chapter on telecommunications)*. However, it would be wrong to ignore these agreements as they make the international franchises complicit in the actions of their franchisees.

---

[18] http://corporateoccupation.wordpress.com/2010/04/11/businesses-in-the-east-jerusalem-settlement-pisgat-zeev/, [accessed 114/6/2011]. A Corporate Watch researcher visited Pisgat Ze'ev in 2011 and confirmed that the store was no longer there.
[19] http://www.thefranchisemall.com/franchises/details/11149-0-Pizza_Hut.htm, [accessed 114/6/2011].
[20] http://www.whoprofits.org/Company%20Info.php?id=452, [accessed 114/6/2011].

Part Two

Geographical Case Studies

21
The Syrian Golan

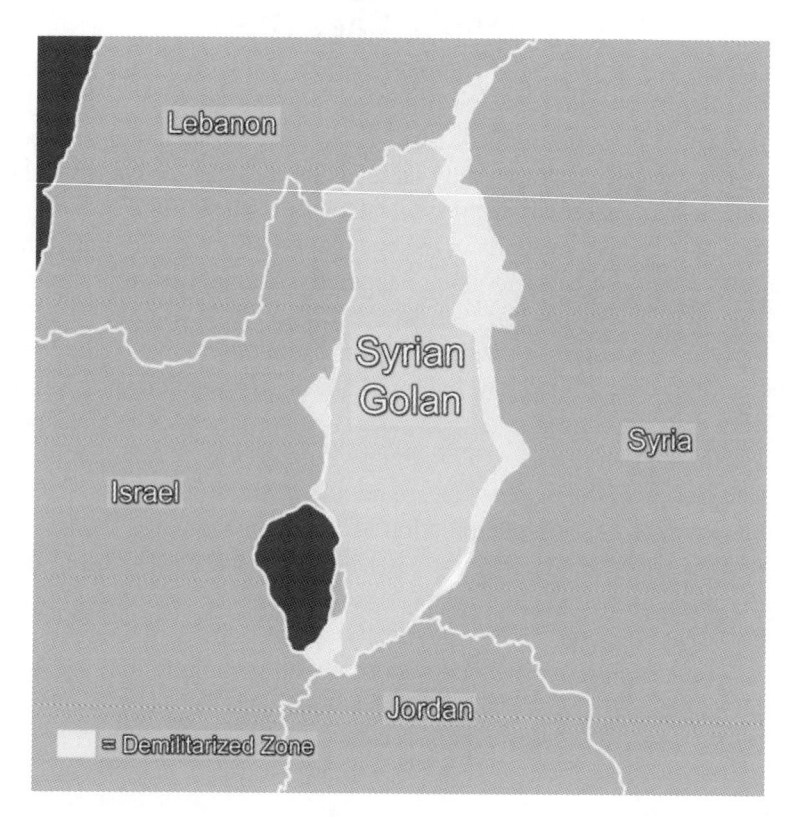

The Syrian Golan, referred to as the Golan Heights by Israel,[1] is located in south-western Syria and was occupied by the Israeli military in 1967. It was annexed by Israel in 1981, to great international condemnation. The area borders Israel to the west, Lebanon to the north and Jordan to the south. The overall landmass of the Golan is 1,860 square kilometres, out of which 1,500 square kilometres remain under Israeli military control.[2] There are at least 33 illegal settlements in the occupied Golan[3] and 20,000 settlers live there.[4]

The area has a mountainous landscape and the top of Mount Hermon (*Jabal al-Shaykh* in Arabic), its highest point, provides clear views of southern Syria, southern Lebanon and

---

[1] The region will here be referred to as the Syrian Golan or the occupied Golan rather than the Golan Heights.
[2] Permanent Mission of the Syrian Arab Republic to the United Nations *The Syrian Golan*, Available: http://www.un.int/syria/golan.htm, [accessed 9/5/2011].
[3] Official figures vary, but are never less than 33. A detailed list of the settlements and their population can be found at http://www.fmep.org/settlement_info/settlement-info-and-tables/stats-data/settlements-in-the-golan-heights, [accessed 9/5/2011].
[4] Molony, Stewart and Tuohy (2009), *From settlement to shelf: the economic occupation of the Syrian Golan*, Al-Marsad, 2009, p.17.

northern Israel.[5] As a result, it has always been considered of huge strategic and military importance for the Israeli state, which can monitor movements deep into Syria from its bases on the mountain.

The Syrian Golan has the richest water sources in the region with one-third of Israel's water supply originating there.[6] Its rainwater feeds directly into the Jordan River and Israel harvests all of the water from the Banias River.[7] Part of the Syrian Golan also borders Lake Tiberias, whose water resources are used by Israel as far away as the Naqab.[8] The Golan is a rich volcanic plateau with extremely fertile soil.[9] Israel's control of the water resources there has been one of their strongest weapons in the occupation, as it has facilitated the expansion of agricultural settlements whilst suffocating occupied Syrian agricultural development.

The occupation of the Syrian Golan manifests itself differently to that of the West Bank and Gaza. The area has received limited international interest and publicity, even from pro-Palestine and BDS activists, throughout the years. However, the lack of checkpoints and more 'normalised' interaction between the indigenous and settler population can be deceiving, and the results of the occupation are no less devastating here than in Palestine. Before 1967, the Golan had a Syrian population of 140,000, compared to just 20,000 today. During Israel's conquest of the area 2 cities, 130 villages and 112 agricultural farms were completely razed to the ground,[10] with the remaining Syrian communities now concentrated in just 5 villages. Israel's occupation has drastically changed the demographics of what used to be a religiously diverse Syrian area. Today virtually all remaining Syrians are Druze, a minority group which equalled just 6 per cent of the total population before 1967.[11]

The JNF take over land in the Golan through the planting of trees (Corporate Watch 2010)

---

[5]*Ibid*, p.10.
[6]http://news.bbc.co.uk/1/hi/world/middle_east/country_profiles/3393813.stm, [accessed 10/5/2011].
[7]Murphy, R and Gannon, D (2008), *Changing the landscape: Israel's gross violations of international law in the occupied Syrian Golan*, Al-Marsad, p.15.
[8]The Arab Association for Development (1993), *Twenty-five years of Israeli occupation of the Syrian Golan Heights*, p .26.
[9]*Ibid*, p.15.
[10]Report from the London international conference on the Golan, 2007.
[11]Murphy, R and Gannon, D (2008), *Changing the landscape, Idem*, p 21

Some brief history

As mentioned above, the Syrian Golan is strategically important for Israel, both from a military perspective and in relation to control of resources. There have been complex border disputes between Syria and Israel ever since the creation of Israel in 1948. In 1949, as a result of UN-supported negotiations, demilitarised zones were created in the border areas experiencing conflict. But in 1951, Israel began asserting control over these zones. The biggest factor in confrontations between Syria and Israel that followed was the struggle for the areas' water resources and access to the headwater of the Jordan River.[12] Water is one of the main issues of the conflict to this day.

In 1967, the Syrian Golan was occupied by Israeli troops, completely destroying all but 5 Syrian villages and cities. Israel immediately began to establish settlements in the Syrian Golan, taking over areas from which the indigenous population had been forcefully displaced from.

In 1973, Syria launched a surprise attack on Israel with the aim of regaining the Golan, but the attempt ultimately failed. In 1974 Syria and Israel signed an armistice agreement.[13] The ceasefire line is still under observation by the UN.

In 1981, the Israeli Knesset passed the Golan Heights Law, which extended Israeli law to the Syrian Golan, resulting in a *de facto* annexation[14] not recognised by the international community or by the majority of Syrian residents of the Golan.

Business in the occupied Golan

Most settler businesses operating in the Golan are agricultural, with a particular focus on grapes, wineries and apples, as well as dairy products distributed to the Israeli market. Another important part of the Golan settler economy is the tourism industry, which works in tandem with the wineries located there. There is a small amount of settlement industry located in the Golan, mostly in the Katzrin and, to a limited extent, the Bnei Yehuda industrial zone. An estimated 20 per cent of Golan's settlement produce is exported abroad.[15]

Corporate control of water

Agriculture has always been the main economic activity of the local population in the Golan[16] but the Israeli occupation has created huge changes in the area. In 1967, Israel took control of 90 per cent of the landmass and the remaining Syrian villages were left with just

---

[12] *Ibid*. A good overview of these issues can be found on p.16-17
[13] *Ibid*, p.18-19.
[14] http://www.mfa.gov.il/MFA/Peace+Process/Guide+to+the+Peace+Process/Golan+Heights+Law.htm, [accessed 17/5/2011].
[15] Murphy, R and Gannon, D (2008), *Changing the landscape, Idem*, p55
[16] The Arab Association for Development (1993), *Twenty-five years of Israeli occupation of the Syrian Golan heights*, p 26.

100 square kilometres of land. Out of this, 30 per cent is inaccessible to them as a result of various Israeli government orders.[17] Israel has also stolen most of the water resources from the Syrians. Whereas water from the Golan is used in great quantities by the settlement farms, or piped into Israel, springs in the Syrian villages have largely dried up as a result of Israel's water exploitation.[18] The Syrian Golan's water resources are primarily controlled by the Israeli national water company **Mekorot** and **Tahal**. The latter is a multinational engineering company with headquarters in Amsterdam. Tahal has 2 Israeli subsidiaries, **Tahal Consulting Engineers Ltd** and **Water Planning for Israel Ltd.** Tahal boasts about how its technology "played a key role in the legendary blooming of the country's desert."[19] There is also a water company called **Mei Golan** operating in the area set up exclusively for the settlers and controlling several reservoirs in the area.[20]

Agricultural companies in the occupied Syrian Golan

Despite obstacles such as lack of access to water and cold storage facilities, agriculture still provides the main source of income for Syrians in the Golan.[21]

Beresheet is the largest Israeli agricultural company operating from the Golan. The company was founded in 2005 after a merger between 2 major fruit packing houses and is owned by 4 kibbutzim in the Galilee and 7 illegal settlements in the occupied Golan. It also works with independent growers in the area. The company's main focus is apples but it also markets pears, kiwifruit, cherries, peaches, nectarines, apricots, plums and berries. Beresheet claims to have a 30 percent share of the fruit export market and its website states that it is exporting to England.[22]

An apple plantation belonging to Beresheet in the settlement of Ein Zivan in the occupied Syrian Golan. (Corporate Watch 2010)

---

[17]*Ibid*, p 26.
[18]Murphy, R and Gannon, D (2008), *Changing the landscape, Idem,* p15.
[19] http://www.tahal.com/general.aspx?FolderID=168&lang=en, [accessed 24/5/2011].
[20]Molony, Stewart and Tuohy (2009), *From settlement to shelf*, p.57.
[21]*Ibid*, p 26.
[22]http://www.pri-beresheet.co.il/template/default.aspx?CatId=6, [accessed 24/5/2011].

There is an **Agrexco** packing house in the illegal settlement of Bnei Yehuda and signs for the company have been spotted close to the settlement of Alonei HaBashan. It is unclear what the fate of Agrexco's assets in the occupied Syrian Golan will be following the company's liquidation.[23]

Mehadrin is involved in the occupied Syrian Golan through its 50 per cent ownership of **Miriam Shoham** which owns a mango packing house in the area.[24]

Wineries

There are 14 settlement wineries located in the occupied Syrian Golan, including the large **Golan Heights Winery.** According to Who Profits, 40 per cent of the grapes used in wine by Israeli producers are grown in the occupied Syrian Golan and Galilee regions.[25] The **Carmel**, **Barkan**, **Binyamina** and **Tishbi** wineries also own vineyards in the Golan.[26]

Although exports to Britain from Israeli wine companies are very small, the wine industry punches above its weight when it comes to impact on the indigenous population, as its vineyards take over Syrian land because of the tourism industry created around it.

Odem is one of the fourteen settlement wineries in the occupied Golan (Corporate Watch 2010)

---

[23]http://www.bdsmovement.net/2011/palestinian-civil-society-welcomes-agrexco-liquidation-calls-for-celebration-of-this-bds-victory-8010, [accessed September 2011].
[24]http://www.whoprofits.org/Company%20Info.php?id=967, [accessed 24/5/2011].
[25]Who Profits (2010), *Forbidden fruit: the Israeli wine industry and the occupation*, http://www.whoprofits.org/articlefiles/WhoProfits-IsraeliWines.pdf, [accessed 23/5/2011], p.5.
[26]*Ibid*, p.30-39.

Case Study: Golan Heights Winery

The Golan Heights Winery was founded in 1983 in the illegal settlement of Katzrin, where the company also hosts a visitors' centre. It maintains vineyards across the occupied Golan and all grapes used for its wines are grown there. Cooperatively owned by 7 different settlements in the area, plus 1 *moshav* in Galilee,[27] it sells wine under the labels **Yarden**, **Gamla** and **Golan**.[28] The company's website states that it has an 18 per cent share of the domestic Israeli wine market and a 38 per cent market share of Israel's wine export market. In Israel, the winery is credited with "leading the development of the whole wine industry in Israel to its present state."[29]

Golan Heights Winery currently has 2 distributors in the UK: **Allot & Associates** and **Hatov Distribution**.

Tourism

The Syrian Golan is an area of outstanding natural beauty and this is something the Israeli state is using to its full advantage. An estimated 2.1 million tourists, primarily Israeli, visit the region every year[30] and great efforts are being made to increase this number. Through tourism, Israel hopes to both normalise the occupation of the Golan and make the settlements economically viable. All tourist destinations in the area are controlled by a settlement, with the most profitable being the ski and hiking resort Mount Hermon. All of its business is run by the Neve Ativ settlement, which was built on the ruins of the Syrian village of Jubata ez-Zeit that was razed by the Israeli military after the Six Day War.[31]

All settlement businesses in the Syrian Golan are trying to cash in on, and expand, the tourist industry. There are visitors' centres in all the wineries and many of the settlements have small guest houses for tourists. The Ein Zivan settlement illustrates how the industry is expanding – when Corporate Watch visited it in 2010 it was in the middle of launching a children's park and petting zoo to accompany its pick-your-own-fruit service and winery.[32] Many settlers also provide horse riding and other outdoor activities.

Most settlements in the Syrian Golan are very small and currently get most of their tourists from inside Israel. A good strategy for the BDS movement would be to challenge travel agents who are offering holidays to the occupied Golan, or tours which include the area, to prevent an increase in foreign tourism. Most of these advertise through internet travel websites.

---

[27] *Ibid*, p 32.
[28] http://www.golanwines.co.il/General_eng.asp, [accessed 24/5/2011].
[29] Who Profits (2010), *Forbidden fruit, Idem*.
[30] Molony, Stewart and Tuohy (2009), *From settlement to shelf*, p.55.
[31] http://corporateoccupation.wordpress.com/2010/07/26/empowering-the-occupiers-elin-seilbahntechnik/, [accessed 24/5/2011.
[32] http://corporateoccupation.wordpress.com/2010/10/26/tourism-fruit-picking-and-occupation-ideology-ein-zivan-settlement-in-the-golan-2/, [accessed 24/5/2011].

Obviously internet information changes all the time but at the time of writing, the following websites advertise trips to or accommodation in the occupied Golan: **Booking.com**, **Longwood Holidays** and **Venere.com**.

The slopes of Mount Hermon are popular with tourists. The area is controlled by the settlement of Neve Ativ (Corporate Watch 2010)

Campaign spotlight: Eden Springs

Eden Springs is an Israeli water company which has been based in the Syrian Golan since 1982. It extracts water from a spring in the illegal settlement of Slokia, then bottles it in a settlement facility in Katzrin.[33] The company has distributors in 15 European countries,[34] where it works with the **Danone Group**. In the UK, Eden Springs is located in Scotland, where it provides bottled water and water coolers to office environments. Although **Eden Springs UK** has been very reluctant to admit its Israeli connections, it is managed and controlled by the Israeli mother company and hence complicit in profiting from the occupation of the Golan.

There has been a BDS campaign in Scotland against Eden Springs which has achieved considerable success. In 2008 the company was forced to close its East of Scotland depot after "losing hundreds of contracts across Scotland"[35] as a result of the campaign against its complicity with Israeli colonisation.

---

[33] Molony, Stewart and Tuohy (2009), *From settlement to shelf, Idem*, p.122.
[34] For locations of Eden Springs in Europe, see http://www.edensprings.com/our-locations.html, [accessed 24/5/2011].
[35] http://www.scottishpsc.org.uk/index.php?option=com_content&view=article&id=2759:spsc-closes-israels-eden-springs-depot-as-part-of-boycott-campaign&catid=255&Itemid=100345, [accessed 24/5/2011].

The company in charge of procurement for the National Health Service in the UK, **Buying Solutions**, currently lists Eden Springs as a preferred provider of water coolers. So far, Buying Solutions has been unresponsive to concerns raised by campaigners and MPs about Eden Springs.[36]

Israel Aerospace Industries/Golan Industries is part of the military airport division of Israel Aerospace Industries and is located in the illegal settlement Bnei Yehuda. Golan Industries' main product line is the Crashworthy Airborne Seat for military aircraft.[37] Its mother company has 6 more divisions in other locations which work on everything from civilian aircraft parts and UAVs to upgrades of F16 and F15 fighter jets. (*See the military section of this book for more info on IAI*).[38] In other words, the settlers have stolen the land from the Syrians and then are using it to set up businesses which manufacture equipment used to repress those living under occupation. The Bnei Yehuda settlement was established in 1972 by workers from IAI.[39]

Profiles of other companies operating in the Katzrin and Bnei Yehuda settlement industrial zones can be found in our earlier chapter on the Israeli manufacturing sector.

Resistance

Due to the different context in the occupied Syrian Golan compared to the rest of the occupied territories resistance there has taken a different shape. Due to the mass expulsions of 1967 there are approximately the same number of illegal settlers as there are Syrians living in the Golan, so the indigenous population cannot rely on mass movements or demonstrations as a form of resistance. The goal of the occupied Syrians is not independence but an end to the occupation and reunification with their Syrian homeland. Indeed, they have retained a strong sense of identity against the odds.

During the 1980s, in an attempt to ease annexation, the Israeli state began a campaign that encouraged Syrians to accept Israeli citizenship.[40] This attempt was met with strong opposition by Golan residents, who came together to resist the occupiers by refusing to cooperate and insisting on keeping their Syrian nationality. After the Israeli annexation in 1981, the people of the Golan started a widespread general strike, which lasted 5 months, in protest against Israeli occupation.[41]

There are frequent events and protests around the border between the occupied Golan and the rest of Syria, involving people from both sides, separated by the occupation, In May

---

[36]Correspondence between Caroline Lucas (who was an MEP at the time) and Buying Solutions, 2009.
[37]http://www.iai.co.il/17838-en/Groups_Military_Aircraft_Golan.aspx, [accessed 24/5/2011].
[38]http://www.iai.co.il/Templates/homepage/homepage.aspx#, [accessed 24/5/2011].
[39]http://en.wikipedia.org/wiki/Bnei_Yehuda,_Golan_Heights, [accessed 24/5/2011].
[40]The Arab Association for Development (1993), *Twenty-five years of Israeli occupation of the Syrian Golan heights, Idem.* p.20.
[41]*Ibid*, p 21.

2011, many Syrians, including Palestinian refugees, were killed as they tried to cross the border back to the occupied Golan during a demonstration to mark *Nakba* day.[42]

In terms of the boycott, the focus has so far been on the bottled water company Eden Springs. Increased boycott activity around the Syrian Golan would be a welcome development particularly against UK distributors of wine from the Golan settlements. It would also be easy and effective to monitor the travel websites offering guest-rooms in the Israeli settlements in the Syrian Golan and to campaign against those sites which refuse to remove them.

---

[42] http://electronicintifada.net/blog/ali-abunimah/new-video-shows-israeli-soldiers-firing-mass-marchers-enter-golan, [accessed 25/7/2011].

22
The Jordan Valley

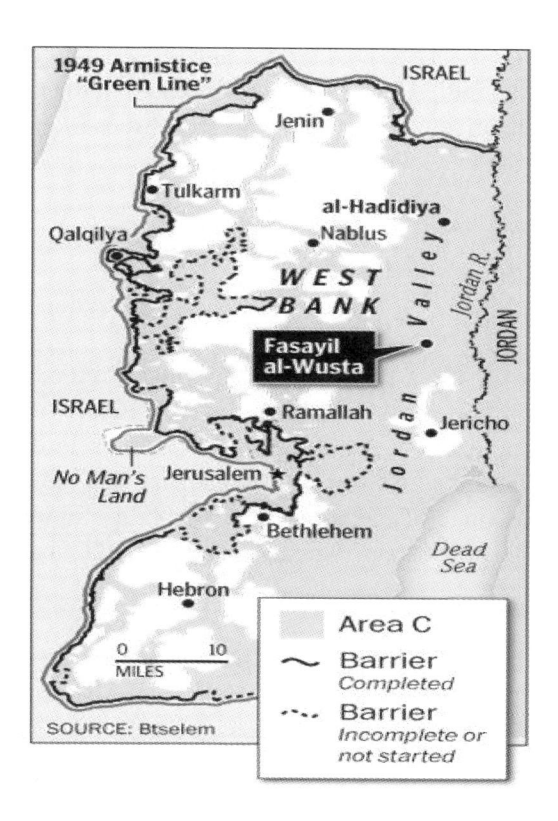

The Jordan Valley is located in the eastern part of the West Bank, with the southern parts bordering the Dead Sea and the eastern parts bordering the Jordan River. The Valley comprises 28.5 per cent of the entire West Bank and has the most fertile land in the region. It was occupied by the Israeli army in 1967 and is now home to 30 illegal Israeli settlements, around 9 settlement outposts[1] and 24 military bases of varying sizes.

The Palestinian population of the Jordan Valley stood at 320,000 in the period between 1948 and 1967, and has fallen to just 56,000 today. Despite the large number of settlements, the settler population is only around 9,000, with most of them being economically rather than ideologically motivated farmers who oversee the agricultural exploitation of the Valley. The last few years have seen an influx of ideologically motivated Zionist settlers since the 2008 establishment of Maskiot, the first new settlement to be approved in the West Bank for a decade.[2]

---

[1] Peace Now, *A new Jordan Valley settlement: facts, background and analysis* Volume 4, issue 4.
[2] For the background to Maskiot's approval see http://www.guardian.co.uk/world/2008/jul/25/israelandthepalestinians.middleeast, [accessed 29/3/2011].

Israel is carrying out a slow but certain programme of ethnic cleansing of the mainly Bedouin population in the Valley. The Israeli government's stated aim is to formally annex the Jordan Valley to 1948 Israel.[3]

Settlements and closed military zones make up around 95 per cent of the Jordan Valley, leaving it inaccessible to the indigenous Palestinian population. Israel also controls 98 per cent of the area's water resources,[4] most of which is used by the agriculture industry.

Some history

"Israel will never cede the Jordan Valley"

Benjamin Netanyahu, March 2010[5]

The Jordan Valley is an area of massive strategic importance to the Israeli state. If retained by Palestine in any peace deal it would constitute the West Bank's only international border. It is the most fertile land in historical Palestine and includes the Jordan River, the Dead Sea and several underground aquifers.[6] Both these factors mean that the Jordan Valley holds the key to the viability and sustainability, as well as the possibility for trade and economic prosperity, for a future Palestinian state. All of this has meant that Israel has always been desperate to control the Valley.

Israel's aim to hold onto the Jordan Valley, come what may, was made clear immediately after the occupation in 1967, when the Israeli minister Yigal Allon presented the then prime minister Levi Eshkol with a template for what has come to be known as the Allon Plan. The plan implemented concepts that had, according to Israeli sources, been part of Israel's military doctrine since 1948.[7] These included retaining total control of the Jordan Valley in order to maintain military control over the West Bank, as well as annexing East Jerusalem.[8]

Although the plan itself now belongs to history, the ideas it articulated are as alive as ever. In 2006, Ehud Olmert stated that any permanent borders of the state of Israel must include the Valley as "It is impossible to abandon control of the eastern border of Israel."[9] These sentiments were reiterated by Netanyahu in 2010[10] and he continues to make high profile visits to the Valley on a regular basis.

---

[3] http://www.btselem.org/english/Settlements/Jordan_Valley.asp., [accessed 3/3/2011].
[4] Brighton Jordan Valley Solidarity *An introduction to the Jordan Valley*, February 2011.
[5] http://www.haaretz.com/news/netanyahu-israel-will-never-cede-jordan-valley-1.266329, [accessed 30/3/2011].
[6] Brighton Jordan Valley Solidarity, *An introduction to the Jordan Valley, Idem.*
[7] http://www.mideastweb.org/alonplan.htm, [accessed 1/4/2011].
[8] *Ibid.*
[9] http://www.nytimes.com/2006/02/07/international/middleeast/07cnd-mideast.html, [accessed 1/4/2011].
[10] http://www.haaretz.com/news/netanyahu-israel-will-neve]./r-cede-jordan-valley-1.266329, [accessed 30/3/2011].

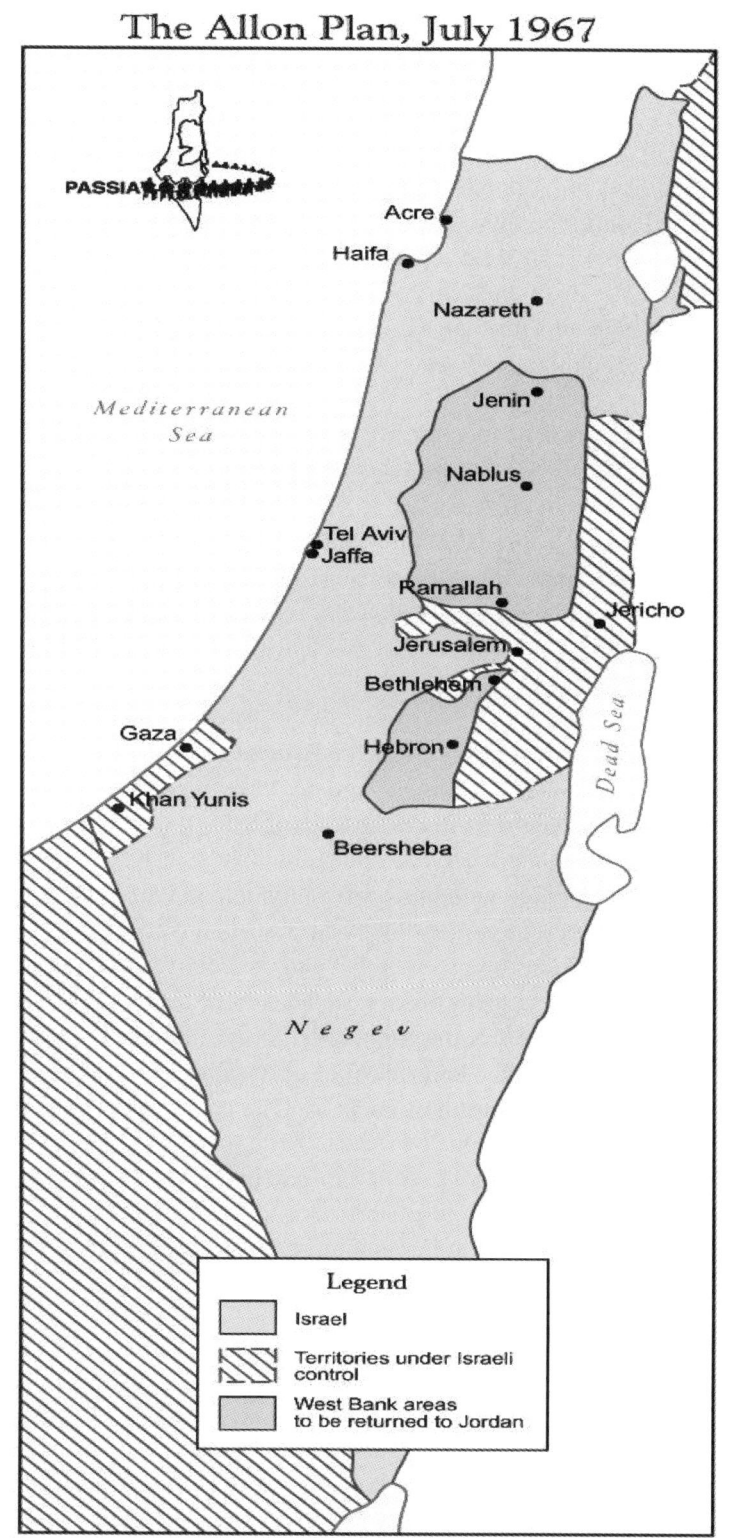

Geographical Case Studies: The Jordan Valley **232**

The Allon Plan, July 1967

Legend
- Israel
- Territories under Israeli control
- West Bank areas to be returned to Jordan

Palestinian Academic Society for the Study of International Affairs (PASSIA)

The Jordan Valley has been hit particularly hard by the 'peace negotiations' of the last few decades. During the negotiations which led to the 1993 Oslo Accords, Israel managed to broker a deal whereby the vast majority of the Valley fell into the area C category and hence came under its direct jurisdiction. Only 4.5 per cent of the Jordan Valley (Jericho and Al Awja) was classified as area A and under Palestinian Authority (PA) control. A further 5 villages (Bardala, Ein el Beida, Marj al Naja, Zbeidat and lower Fasayil) were designated as area B, and are under Palestinian civil, but Israeli military, control.[11] Palestinian movement within the Jordan Valley is heavily restricted by the Israeli military, and checkpoints control all entrances and exits. The main ones are Al Hamra, which isolates the Jordan Valley from the road to Nablus; Tayasir, which isolates the northern Valley from the road to Tubas; Ma'ale Efrayim; Bisan checkpoint and the Jericho checkpoint.

Business, exploitation and ethnic cleansing in the Jordan Valley

From a BDS perspective, economic activities in the Jordan Valley can be separated into 5 categories: settlement industries (mainly large-scale agriculture); nature tourism; foreign companies facilitating the ethnic cleansing of Palestinians; and, finally, plans for normalisation projects in the area.

Agriculture

The industrial agricultural production by illegal settlements in the Jordan Valley has had a huge impact on Palestinian communities. While many Palestinians used to be able to either farm their own land or graze their animals close to their homes, the occupation has made this almost impossible. Instead the landscape is a contrast between lush settler fields and greenhouses on one side compared with dry, barren land where Palestinians do not receive enough water to tend to their crops on the other. The settlements receive subsidised water from the Israeli state, whilst Palestinians often have to collect over-priced water by tractor. Palestinians, barred from utilising local water resources, have no choice but to buy water from Israeli company **Mekorot**. Since the occupation, 162 agricultural water projects that were developed under Jordanian rule have been out of reach to Palestinians, as they are now within one of Israel's closed military zones.[12] The Valley's resources, which are rich enough to provide for its Palestinian population, are instead being used almost solely to help the settlement industry bloom. Agricultural production also has a devastating impact on Palestinian livelihoods as agricultural expansion leads to more and more settlement expansion, ever wider closed military zones and more house demolitions in the surrounding areas.

For the few Palestinians who have some land and manage to grow vegetables and fruit farming is a constant challenge, as they are often held up at checkpoints with time-sensitive fresh produce whilst trying to get it to the markets in Jenin or Jericho. To overcome this,

---

[11]Brighton Jordan Valley Solidarity, *An introduction to the Jordan Valley*, February 2011
[12]Bil'in Popular Committee, *Khalas! We are winning: The 5th annual Bil'in international conference on Palestinian popular resistance*, p 62.

Palestinian fruit stalls have been set up along Road 90, the main route through the Valley, but these are frequently demolished by the army.[13]

Company profiles

Most Israeli agricultural companies have got some kind of presence in the area. **Agrexco**, before the company's liquidation in September 2011,[14] marketed between 60 and 70 per cent of all agricultural produce grown in Israeli settlements,[15] controlling most of the market. Almost all agricultural settlement produce originates in the Jordan Valley. Other companies with established links to the European export market include **Ada** (sold in the UK as **Adafresh**),[16] **Mehadrin (MTEX)**,[17] **Hadiklaim**,[18] **Bickel Group**,[19] **Arava**,[20] **Flora Holland**,[21] **EDOM UK**,[22] **Avniv**[23] and **TBP Export** (an agricultural marketing company).[24] Corporate Watch researchers have also seen herbs being packaged and (wrongly) labelled as Israeli produce in an Agrexco packing house in the Israeli settlement of Mehola[25] for the British company **Fresh Direct**.

Arava Export Growers is the third largest agricultural export company in Israel, with export sales of about €60 million. It is 50 per cent owned by **B. Gaon Holdings** and 50 per cent by farmers in the Arava region of Israel. Arava advertise that its products comply to organic **EUREPGAP** and **British Retail Consortium** standards, suggesting a focus on exports to Europe. The company has a sales office in the UK run by **Mill Associates**. It has

---

[13] Information collected by Corporate Watch and The Brighton Jordan Valley Solidarity Group through interviews with stall holders in the Jordan Valley on several occasions between 2008-2011.
[14] http://www.bdsmovement.net/2011/palestinian-civil-society-welcomes-agrexco-liquidation-calls-for-celebration-of-this-bds-victory-8010, [accessed September 2011].
[15] Chris Osmond, defendant in the 2006 case at Uxbridge Magistrates Court, personal notes, *Idem*.
[16] http://corporateoccupation.wordpress.com/2010/09/14/argaman-organic-goods-grown-on-land-seized-by-military-force/, [accessed 28/4/2011].
[17] http://corporateoccupation.wordpress.com/2010/05/18/mehadrins-business-in-beqaot-settlement-and-tescos-complicity/, [accessed 28/4/2011].
[18] http://corporateoccupation.wordpress.com/2010/08/12/hadiklaim-in-the-jordan-valley/, [accessed 28/4/2011].
[19] http://corporateoccupation.wordpress.com/2010/08/03/companies-trading-from-roi-settlement-in-the-jordan-valley/, [accessed 28/4/2011].
[20] http://corporateoccupation.wordpress.com/2010/04/13/corporations-in-tomer-settlement-part-2/, [accessed 28/4/2011].
[21] http://corporateoccupation.wordpress.com/2010/08/03/companies-trading-from-roi-settlement-in-the-jordan-valley/, [accessed 28/4/2011].
[22] http://corporateoccupation.wordpress.com/2010/06/26/why-the-only-way-to-trade-ethically-is-to-divest-from-israel-%E2%80%93-an-update-on-edom-and-valley-grown-salads/, [accessed 28/4/2011].
[23] http://corporateoccupation.wordpress.com/2010/04/18/netiv-hagdud-and-gilgal/, [accessed 28/4/2011].
[24] http://corporateoccupation.wordpress.com/2010/04/13/corporations-in-tomer-settlement/, [accessed 28/4/2011].
[25] http://corporateoccupation.wordpress.com/2010/03/23/%E2%80%9Cproduce-of-israel%E2%80%9D-british-company-found-in-breach-of-labelling-guidelines/, [accessed 25/7/2011].

subsidiaries in the US and Holland, with head offices in New York and Bleiswijk respectively.

> **Case study: settlement workers in the Jordan Valley**[26]
>
> According to *Kav LaOved* there are an estimated 10,000 'illegal' Palestinian settlement workers in the Jordan Valley.[27] These are workers who lack official Israeli work permits. These workers generally get paid between 60-80 NIS a day, around half of the legal Israeli minimum wage. They have no contracts, get no holiday pay, no health insurance and have no right to join a trade union. Some of the workers live in the Jordan Valley, but a large number commute from afar. For Valley residents, working on a settlement often means being exploited by Israeli companies on land that used to belong to their own communities.
>
> The working day of a settlement worker begins at 3am, in order to make it to work for 6 or 7am. For many workers the commute will involve crossing a checkpoint, where workers are often strip searched or outright refused entry by the soldiers on duty. Because of this many workers choose to get through as soon as the checkpoints open. Workers can often be seen sleeping in the fields around the settlements in the early morning. Settlement workers in the Jordan Valley have no guarantee that their job will still be there the next day as they are not contracted.
>
> Despite the fact that so many Palestinians are 'employed' in the settlements, most workers interviewed by Corporate Watch support a boycott of Israel and see it as the only way they can eventually regain control of their land.
>
> *(For an overview of conditions for agricultural workers in the Jordan Valley and elsewhere see our earlier chapter on agriculture)*

Tourism

Tourism is a small, mainly ideologically driven area of Israeli business in the Jordan Valley. There are some bed-and-breakfasts inside settlements but, as it is entirely possible to take a bus straight from inside Israel and along the Israeli-controlled Road 90, most tourists end up experiencing the Valley as part of a day trip. This ensures that visitors are unlikely to come across any Palestinians on their travels.

A visit to the Jordan Valley Meeting Point, essentially a rest stop along Road 90, highlights the grim reality of Israel's plans for the Valley. The project is proudly sponsored by the **Jewish National Fund (JNF)**, whose sign at the entrance openly states that the site is a part of its "Land Reclamation" project. Information points for tourists describe historical and

---

[26] The information in this section is based on experiences of around 50 Jordan Valley settlement workers interviewed by Corporate Watch March-May 2010.
[27] Alenat, S (2010), *Working for survival, Idem,* [accessed 10/3/2011].

archaeological sites, attractions and tour routes, 'state-of-the-art' agricultural technologies and Israel's "battle legacies" in the area. Inviting tourists to join settler-organised Jeep trips and walking tours, they highlight the possibilities to follow migrating birds and appreciate blossoming wild flowers in a stunning landscape.

Palestinian working on a settler sculpture of a Jordan Valley without Palestinians at the JNF funded Jordan Valley meeting point (Corporate Watch 2010)

What they fail to mention, however, is that no Palestinian has the freedom to enjoy any of these things as their villages are surrounded by closed military zones. In the middle of the Meeting Point stands a sculpture of the Jordan Valley with all the Israeli settlements represented, but with the Palestinian villages literally wiped off the map.[28] In short, the aim of Israeli tourism in the valley is to airbrush the Palestinians out of existence with the help of the JNF. The Meeting Point is a clear example of the use of tourism by both the Israeli state, and settler organisations, to reposition the Jordan Valley as a geographic and historical part of the state of Israel, and perpetuate the idea that the Palestinian population of the Valley have no claim to their own land.

House demolitions, settlement services and foreign complicity

With almost all of the Jordan Valley being designated as area C, Palestinians residing there are especially easy for the Israeli occupation forces to harass. Since they live under total military control, they have no right to build or even repair houses, roads or any infrastructure. Hundreds of houses, animal sheds and water tanks in the area are threatened with demolition orders, which can be implemented at any time, leaving whole communities

---

[28] http://corporateoccupation.wordpress.com/2010/08/11/the-jordan-valley-meeting-point-the-jewish-national-funds-racist-alternative-reality/, [accessed 6/4/2011].

homeless. During the last few years, Israel has tightened its grip on the Jordan Valley and house demolitions are on the increase. In July 2010, virtually the whole village of Al Farisiya was demolished.[29] There have also been recent demolitions in Abu Al Ajjaj[30] and residents in villages such as Al Hadidya have had their homes destroyed by the army over and over again for years.[31] These are just a few of many examples.

House demolitions facilitate expansion of the surrounding settlements and consolidation of Israeli control of the land. For instance, Al Farisiya is close to the new settlement of Maskiot; Abu Al Ajjaj is next to the expanding Massu'a settlement and Al Hadidya is precariously located in-between the big agricultural settlements of Ro'i and Beqaot. There is no doubt that the Israeli state's policies in the area are intended to orchestrate the gradual removal of Palestinians from the valley. There is also no question that land confiscation, ethnic cleansing and Israeli agricultural exports go hand in hand.

Apart from agricultural importers of settlement produce such as supermarkets, there are several international companies that are complicit in the destructive military occupation of the Valley. These include **Volvo**, **Caterpillar** and **JCB**, whose bulldozers and diggers have repeatedly been observed gutting Palestinian houses both in the Valley and elsewhere.[32] By allowing their equipment to be used to destroy people's homes, these companies are complicit in ethnic cleansing.

The French company **Veolia** operates in the Valley through its subsidiary **Veolia Environmental Services Israel**, which runs the Tovlan landfill site located on Palestinian land. Veolia also provides rubbish collection services to the settlements. Corporate Watch researchers have observed Veolia trucks making collections from Tomer, Beqaot and Massu'a settlements.[33] The company does not provide services to Palestinian communities.

Veolia has also met international resistance due to its involvement in the Jerusalem light railway, an apartheid project that aims to connect West Jerusalem to illegal settlements in East Jerusalem[34] as well as running several bus services connecting the Israeli settlements in the West Bank, some of which run on segregated roads. *(See our previous chapters on the public transport sector and the construction Industry).*

---

[29]http://www.jordanvalleysolidarity.org/index.php?option=com_content&view=article&id=62:dwg-revised-information-alfarisiya-demolitions&catid=15:2010&Itemid=21, [accessed 19/4/2011].
[30]http://www.middleeastmonitor.org.uk/news/middle-east/1830-israel-increases-=, [accessed 19/4/011].
[31]http://brightonpalestine.org/2011/node/82, [accessed 28/4/2011].
[32]http://corporateoccupation.wordpress.com/2010/06/16/volvo-equipment-effective-tool-in-the-israeli-occupation-of-palestine/, [accessed 19/4/2011]. For a fact sheet on Caterpillar in Palestine see http://michiganpeaceteam.org/CATDestroysHomesAAF.pdf, [accessed 19/4/2011].
[33]For evidence relating to Veolia's operations in the Jordan Valley see http://corporateoccupation.wordpress.com/2010/01/28/veolias-dirty-business-the-tovlan-landfill/ and http://corporateoccupation.wordpress.com/2010/03/31/veolia-taking-out-israels-trash/, [accessed 19/4/2011].
[34]http://www.corporatewatch.org.uk/?lid=3400, [accessed 19/4/2011].

At the time of writing, the future of the Tovlan landfill is uncertain, with Veolia claiming that it is dropping the project and possibly handing over the business to the nearby settlement of Massu'a. However, this has not yet been independently verified and Veolia signage is still up at the entrance to the facility.[35]

Trucks dumping settlement rubbish at the Tovlan landfill in the Jordan Valley (Corporate Watch 2010)

Normalisation projects

Apart from agriculture, there is currently little in the way of business in the Jordan Valley. There is one industrial zone connected to the settlement of Ma'ale Efrayim, but most of the units there are dormant, with only limited business taking place. Instead, the zone is a way for the settlement to hold on to land with the stated support of the Israeli Ministry of Industry and Trade and the Jewish Agency Settlement Department.[36]

The Jordan Valley has been selected as the location for new industrial zones, essentially aimed at normalising the occupation through the illusion of creating joint Palestinian/Israeli business opportunities. The plan for the Jordan Valley is an agro-industrial park which would provide space for Israeli, Palestinian and, potentially, international companies involved in large-scale agricultural exports. The agro-industrial park is supported by the Japan International Cooperation Agency (JICA). However, for Palestinian farmers, cooperation with Israeli agribusiness would mean a complete reliance on the very companies that are operating on land stolen from Palestinian communities to export their goods to the international market. As the Palestinian organisation Stop the Wall has pointed out "JICA's

---

[35]Observed by Corporate Watch researchers, August 2011.
[36]See http://corporateoccupation.wordpress.com/2010/12/01/some-notes-from-maale-efraim-industrial-zone/, [accessed 19/4/2011].

agro-industrial proposals will facilitate the building of economy and infrastructure that is inextricably bound up with the presence of the occupation, effectively cementing the most serious barrier to long-term development."[37]

Preparing mud bricks for guerilla building projects in Area C
(Brighton Jordan Valley Solidarity 2009)

Resistance

The Palestinians of the Jordan Valley have a motto: "To exist is to resist". The area is quickly gaining a reputation for its creative grassroots spirit. By simply refusing to leave their land despite the overwhelming odds stacked against them, the communities are fighting back against a brutal military machine. Recently the Jordan Valley Solidarity campaign have started building mud brick houses for their villages, ignoring the Israeli ban on any building work. During the last year, several Bedouin communities have been connected to water supplies through a number of guerilla pipe-laying actions. If and when they are destroyed by the Israel occupation forces, they will simply be rebuilt over and over again.[38] The communities in the Valley are endorsing and encouraging increased BDS action abroad, including the campaign against Agrexco, which contributed to the company's liquidation.[39]

The people of the Valley are taking a brave stance - with so much at stake it is of paramount importance that the international solidarity movement stands with them.

---

[37] Stop the Wall (2007), *The Japan International Cooperation Agency's development proposals for the Jordan Valley*, p.15, Available: http://stopthewall.org/enginefileuploads/jica_30_nov_07, [accessed 19/4/2011].
[38] See www.jordanvalleysolidarity.org, [accessed 19/4/2011].
[39] http://www.bdsmovement.net/2011/palestinian-civil-society-welcomes-agrexco-liquidation-calls-for-celebration-of-this-bds-victory-8010, [accessed September 2011].

23
East Jerusalem

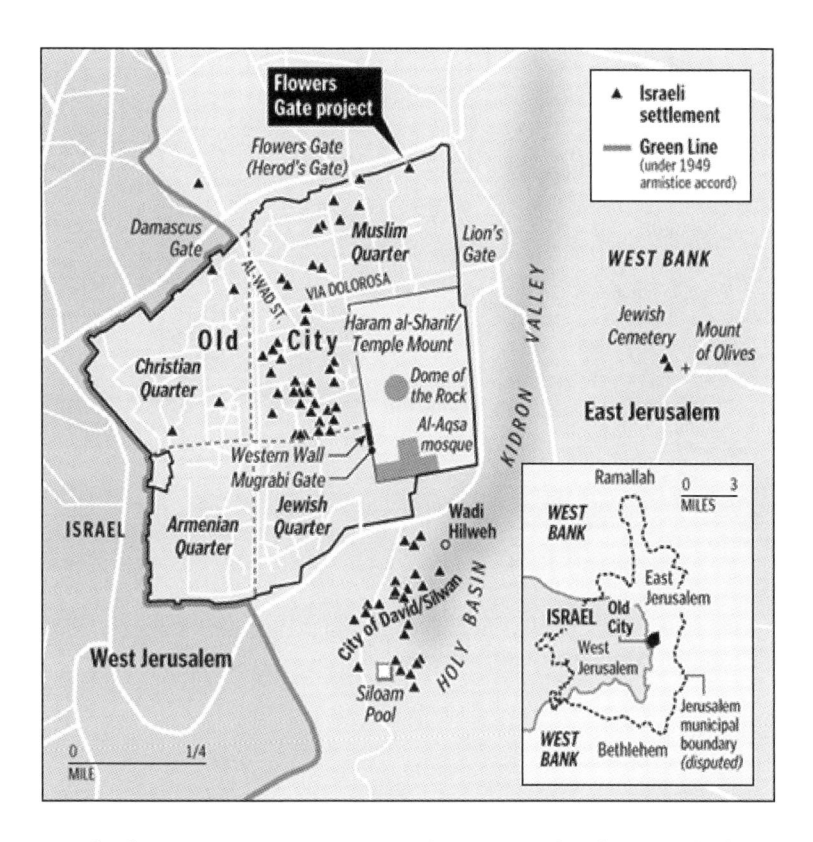

"all legislative and administrative measures and actions taken by Israel, the occupying Power, which purport to alter the character and status of the Holy City of Jerusalem have no legal validity and constitute a flagrant violation of the Fourth Geneva Convention."

UN Security Council Resolution 476 (passed in 1980)[1]

The following chapter is an attempt to summarise the discriminatory policies pursued by the Israeli authorities and settler organisations in East Jerusalem. These policies, designed to ethnically cleanse Palestinian areas of the city and irrevocably change the demographic balance in favour of Israeli Jews, are causing immense suffering to Palestinian residents. These include a calculated program of neglect at every level of social provision, despite East Jerusalem falling under the remit of the Israel-controlled Jerusalem Municipality. Wide-ranging house evictions and demolitions; arbitrary arrests; restrictions on movement and residency and violence take place routinely. As with all of Israel's apartheid policies, these are carried out with the help of private companies.

The manifestation of these problems in each suburb of East Jerusalem is beyond the scope of

---

[1] http://daccess-ods.un.org/TMP/406825.1.html, [accessed September 2011].

this chapter, but 2 areas in which settler organisations and the Israeli authorities are combining to have a devastating effect, Silwan and Sheikh Jarrah, are examined in detail and are indicative of the daily acts of discrimination.

The Silwan neighbourhood of East Jerusalem, where extreme right-wing Jewish settlers run a vicious campaign aimed at evicting Palestinians from their homes (Active Stills)

Some Background

Palestinians living in East Jerusalem inhabit a different legal space to those who live in the rest of the West Bank or Gaza or 1948 Israel. Following the 1967 war, East Jerusalem was annexed by Israel, changing the status of its Palestinian citizens, who had lived under Jordanian rule since Israel's creation in 1948. Thus, unlike Palestinian citizens of Israel, they do not have Israeli citizenship and, unlike Palestinians living in the West Bank or Gaza, they do not have Palestinian citizenship. Instead, Palestinians living in East Jerusalem have what is termed 'permanent residency'. This means that if they study abroad, move to the West Bank, or move to a neighbouring country they could lose their right to live in East Jerusalem forever.

Permanent residency status is not always transferred through marriage. If a Palestinian from East Jerusalem marries a Palestinian from the West Bank or Gaza, they must apply for family unification if they wish to reside in Jerusalem.[2] This, as with other bureaucratic hurdles designed to punish Palestinians, is an expensive and time-consuming process. Similarly, permanent residency is not automatically passed on to children.[3] Where one parent is from East Jerusalem but the other is from the West Bank it can be extremely difficult to register a

---

[2] European Union, EU head of mission report on East Jerusalem, January 2011. Available: news.bbc.co.uk/2/../hi/../10_01_11_eu_hom_report_on_east_jerusalem.pdf
[3] *Ibid.*

child, hindering the ability of these children to access education and health provision. Around 5,000 Palestinian children in East Jerusalem do not attend school. Coupled with the stifling of local business, this has led to a staggering 75 per cent unemployment rate amongst those below the age of 24.[4] Unsurprisingly, drug abuse and poverty has skyrocketed.[5]

Israel's residency policy is designed to alter the demographics in Palestinian areas of the city and allow for the slow transfer of property and land from Palestinians to Jewish Israelis. For example, during 2008, a record 4,577 Palestinians lost their East Jerusalem residency.[6] The logic behind these expulsions can be traced back to a 1973 decision by the Israeli Ministerial Committee for Jerusalem Affairs, which vowed to maintain a population ratio of 22-27 per cent Palestinians within the boundaries of the entire Jerusalem Municipality.[7] This has since been reiterated in the Local Outline Plan for Jerusalem 2000, stating the desired balance of 70 per cent Jews to 30 per cent Palestinians.[8] Palestinians, with birth rates higher than their Jewish counterparts, currently form over a third of the city's total population.[9] The vulnerable residency status of Palestinians constitutes part of a wider policy matrix which the Israeli government is now intensifying to administratively bring the population ratio back in line. These include confiscation of land, discriminatory urban planning policies and house demolitions.[10]

Case study – Silwan

Following its annexation in 1967, Silwan's population grew rapidly as refugees from villages in what is now the Israeli state moved to East Jerusalem. Located to the south of the Old City, it is split into 9 neighbourhoods. Silwan is one of East Jerusalem's poorest areas. Whilst its inhabitants pay the same taxes as all other citizens of Jerusalem, they receive less than 5 per cent of the services.

A major obstacle to development is the Israeli controlled Jerusalem Municipality, which denies permission to virtually all Palestinian construction in East Jerusalem. Despite Palestinians making up over 60 per cent of the population, only 13 per cent of land has been designated for Palestinian development. Thus, whilst it is technically possible for a Palestinian to obtain a building permit, it is virtually assured that such a permit will not be

---

[4] http://english.aljazeera.net/indepth/features/2011/06/201162874544676539.html, [accessed 10th July 2011].
[5] *Ibid.*
[6] Sherwood, H (11/05/2011), Israel stripped 140,000 Palestinians of residency rights, document reveals, *Guardian*.
[7] http://www.middleeastmonitor.org.uk/resources/fact-sheets/1333-israels-judaisation-of-jerusalem, [accessed 10th July 2011] and http://www.israeli-occupation.org/2011-04-14/jonathan-cook-israel-steps-up-jerusalem-expulsions/, [accessed 10th July 2011].
[8] http://www.hrw.org/en/news/2009/11/06/israel-stop-east-jerusalem-home-demolitions, [accessed 10th July 2011].
[9] *Ibid.*
[10] http://www.jadaliyya.com/pages/index/507/jerusalems-protracted-demographic-transformation-, [accessed 11th July 2011].

granted as not a single new building has been approved for construction in Silwan since 1967.[11]

As a result the neighbourhood suffers from a chronic lack of amenities, particularly schools. Yet, families continue to grow and the population increases. Many Palestinians have been forced to build extensions on existing properties, or to construct new homes illegally to accommodate family members. According to UN estimates, around 60,000 Palestinians in East Jerusalem live in buildings designated illegal by the Israeli government.[12] This means homes are under constant threat of demolition by the Israeli state.

Three generations of the Siam family sit amongst the rubble of their demolished home in Silwan. Between 1994-2006, 678 houses were demolished in East Jerusalem alone (Active Stills)

Al-Bustan is a neighbourhood of Silwan located slightly south of Wadi Hilweh.[13] Since 2004 all 88 houses in al-Bustan have had demolition orders against them, which were issued to make way for the expansion of the King's Valley Archaeological Park, a plan which will lead to the forced eviction of more than 1,000 Palestinians. The park is said to represent the ancient gardens of King David, which King Solomon visited 3,000 to 4,000 years ago.[14] In 2005, the Jerusalem Municipality began to carry out the directive and residents received demolition orders by post notifying them of charges against them for building without a permit. However, due to international pressure, the then mayor Uri Lupolianski agreed to suspend demolition plans and allow residents to present an alternative Town Plan Scheme.[15]

---

[11]BRICUP (2007), *Why boycott Israeli universities? Idem.*
[12]*European Union (2011), EU Head of Mission report on East Jerusalem. Idem.*
[13]Al-Bustan Coalition (2009), *Severe threat to al-Bustan-Silwan neighbourhood,* Available: *www.ir-amim.org.il/eng/_../AlBustanCoalitionSummaryEng.doc, [accessed September 2011].*
[14]http://electronicintifada.net/content/israeli-bill-give-settler-group-authority-silwan/9916, [accessed 19th May 2011].
[15]*Al-Bustan* Coalition (2009), *Severe threat to al-Bustan-Silwan neighbourhood. Idem.*

It was rejected 3 years later and Palestinian homes are still under threat. Despite US government opposition, the King's Valley project has been promoted vociferously by Jerusalem's incumbent right-wing mayor Nir Barkat since his election in 2008.[16]

As with many of the excavations in East Jerusalem, archaeologists are sceptical about the validity of claims regarding the planned park's ancient heritage. Israeli archaeologist, Yonathan Mizrahi, told Electronic Intifada that the **Israeli Antiquities Authority (IAA)** has never conclusively stated the King's Garden is even located in the area of Al-Bustan,[17] and maps prepared by the Authority show no archaeological findings in the area.[18] The story is familiar across Silwan and a point of contention within the Antiquities Authority.

Wadi Hilweh is another neighbourhood of Silwan close to the Old City and considered the front-line in the area against settlers. The main settler group operating in Silwan is **El Ad (Ir David Foundation)**, a registered not-for-profit organisation that runs the **City of David** tourist centre in Wadi Hilweh and all archaeological excavations across the district. El Ad operates with a tight group of sympathetic archaeologists, hand-picked for their Zionist bias. The most prominent are Dr. Gabriel Barkay, who lectures at **Bar-Ilan University**, and Dr. Ronny Reich, from **Haifa University**. Reich is also chairman of the **Archaeology Council**, the most senior archaeological body in Israel and advisor to the Director of the Antiquities Authority[19] while Barkay also serves as a member of the council, along with Dr. Eilat Mazar, another regular at El Ad-sponsored digs.

El Ad itself is headed by ex-Israeli commando David Be'eri, who served in the Duvdevan Special Forces Unit that conducts undercover operations in the West Bank.[20] It has been reported that Be'eri used to disguise himself as an Arab to infiltrate Palestinian areas. Be'eri, using his skills of deception, began the process of settling Zionists into the homes of Silwan. He, for instance, passed himself off as a fake tour guide to befriend Musa Abbasi, to whose house he brought groups posing as tourists.[21] He collected information during the visits and used it as evidence to secure the confiscation of the house under the Absentee Property Act.[22]

Absentee Property Act

The Absentee Property Act was passed by the Israeli *Knesset* (parliament) in 1950 and amended in 1967 to include East Jerusalem following its annexation by Israel. The Act ruled that any persons who lived outside the boundaries of the Israeli state any time between

---

[16] http://www.jnews.org.uk/commentary/crunchtime-for-silwan, [accessed September 2011].
[17] *Ibid.*
[18] http://settlementwatcheastjerusalem.wordpress.com/2010/03/02/barkat%E2%80%99s-plan-for-silwan-is-a-political-plan-for-the-settlers-only/, [accessed 19th May 2011].
[19] http://www.haaretz.com/print-edition/news/archaeologists-right-wing-culture-minister-making-appointments-based-on-politics-1.372567, [accessed July 11th 2011].
[20] http://electronicintifada.net/content/israeli-bill-give-settler-group-authority-silwan/9916, [accessed 19th May 2011].
[21] http://silwanic.net/?page_id=106, [accessed 19th May 2011].
[22] *Ibid.*

November 27th 1947 and 1st September 1948 were to have their property automatically transferred to the tenure of the Israeli custodian for Absentee Property without compensation. The law singles out those Palestinians living in so-called enemy states during that time period. As all countries surrounding Israel in 1947 and 1948 were opposed to the Jewish state's establishment on Palestinian land and Palestinians had fled to these countries as refugees, there is little to protect the families affected. The reason for their flight was the calculated policy of ethnic cleansing by Jewish forces.[23]

In 1991, the state of Israel transferred all Palestinian holdings that met the provision of the Absentee Property Act to the **Jewish National Fund (JNF),** which had signed an unwritten agreement with El Ad during the late 1980s allowing the settler group to obtain protected tenancy contracts in return for paying compensation to the Palestinian tenants of JNF property.[24] As part of the understanding, David Be'eri would identify property previously owned by Jewish families in the early 20th century and the JNF would evict the Palestinians currently living in them. Ironically, this is in contravention of the Absentee Property Act itself, which stipulates that the property should be held by the Custodian until a political solution on the status of refugees can be resolved. This point was highlighted by Arab-Israeli human rights organisation *Adalah*, which also argues that the sale of properties belonging to Palestinian refugees is in breach of international law which "explicitly prohibits the expropriation of private property following the termination of warfare."[25]

In 1991, without the Abbasi family's knowledge, the settlers entered their house during the dead of night to evict them. El Ad followers also occupied a further 10 properties owned by the extended Abbasi family. The case went to the Israeli Supreme Court but the then Housing Minister Ariel Sharon, himself a former IDF officer, came to the settlers' defence, claiming that "..it is the policy of the government of Israel to encourage Jewish residence in Jerusalem." Due to intense pressure from right-wing cabinet members, settlers were allowed to stay until their status was clarified. Most of them currently remain in these properties.[26]

Upon stealing the Palestinian homes El Ad settlers build fortresses complete with CCTV, barbed wire and armed private security guards. The security contractor used by El Ad is **Modiin Ezrachi** (meaning Civilian Intelligence), an Israeli firm that is also employed by the Ministry of Defence to operate check-points in the Jerusalem area[27] In 2006, Israel's Minister of Housing directed General Uri Or to head a 'Public committee to examine the security and guarding of compounds in East Jerusalem', which recommended the scrapping of privately hired companies and the transferring of security back to the police.[28] Although the Israeli government adopted these recommendations in January 2007, within 3 months the decision

---

[23] For a history of the ethnic cleansing of 1947-9 see Pappe, I (2006), *The ethnic cleansing of Palestine, Idem.*
[24] *Ir Amim (2009), Shady dealings in Silwan.* Available: www.ir-amim.org.il/eng/_Uploads/dbsAttachedFiles/Silwanreporteng.pdf
[25] http://www.adalah.org/eng/pressreleases/pr.php?file=09_06_22, [accessed 11th July 2011].
[26] Ir Amim (2009), *Shady dealings in Silwan. Idem.*
[27] http://www.whoprofits.org/Company%20Info.php?id=562, [accessed 11th July 2011].
[28] http://www.acri.org.il/en/?p=768, [accessed 11th July 2011].

was scrapped and private guards continue to act with impunity. On 22nd September 2010, for example, a guard working for Modiin Ezrachi shot dead Samer Sarhan, a Palestinian from Silwan.[29]

El Ad leader David Be'eri is flanked by Israeli police officers outside the City of David Visitors Center in Wadi Hilweh, Silwan, as Israeli activists stage a demonstration, (Silwanic)

A distinct lack of transparency surrounds El Ad's funding, which comes predominantly from 'unnamed private donors'.[30] Israeli newspapers have reported that the owner of Chelsea football club, Roman Abramovitch attended a 2005 El Ad fundraiser, along with a number of other Russian business figures including Lev Leviev.[31] Israeli newspaper *Haaretz* cites government sources claiming businessmen originally from Russia are among the main donors to El Ad.[32] Russian-American oil tycoon Eugene Shvidler, for instance, who is a business partner of Abramovitch through **Millhouse LLC**, helped finance the City of David Visitors Center.[33]

A British registered charity, Alliance Family Foundation, donated £9,000 to El Ad in 2003 and 2004.[34] *(see our later chapter on charities for more information on charitable donations to settler organisations).*

---

[29]http://www.jpost.com/Israel/Article.aspx?id=189247, [accessed 17th July 2011].
[30]http://www.time.com/time/magazine/article/0,9171,1957350,00.html, [accessed 16th July 2011].
[31]http://adalahny.org/land-developer-bds-leviev/land-developers-bds/page-4, [accessed 16th July 2011].
[32]Rapoport, M (2007), Group Judaizing East Jerusalem accused of withholding donation sources, *Haaretz,* 21/11/2007.
[33]http://www.bloomberg.com/apps/news?pid=newsarchive&sid=aSiB6pijo7_I, [accessed 16th July 2011].
[34]Alliance Family Foundation annual accounts for 2004 and 2005.

Records cited by *Haaretz* show that, in 2005, a quarter of El Ad's NIS 41 million (approx. $11 million) revenue came from 5 sources. This included a $2 million sum from **Farleigh International IT**, formerly a British investigations firm called **Farleigh Consultants**.[35] When contacted by *Haaretz*, company manager David Bowen claimed Farleigh did not donate any funds to El Ad. Another source of funds, **Ovington Worldwide Limited** is a holding company registered in the tax haven of the British Virgin Islands.[36] The group's funding has since increased astronomically. Its 2009 report to the Israeli authority for not-for-profit organisations shows that El Ad received NIS 72.5 million (approximately £12 million) in donations over the course of 2008.[37] United States tax-deductible donations also come via the Brooklyn-based **American Friends of Ir David**.[38]

Since El Ad began operating in Silwan, Wadi Hilweh has found itself sandwiched between the settler movement and the Municipality. The **City of David** tourist park has devoured over a quarter of all public land. The 11555 Town Planning Scheme designates around 70 per cent of the neighbourhood for the establishment of car parks, archaeological sites and 'open areas'.[39] El Ad was heavily involved in the designing and funding of the plan, passed in 2007, with input also coming from the office of Israeli-American architect **Moshe Safdie**.[40]

Eradication of Palestinian and Islamic history

El Ad has controlled most of Jerusalem's archaeological excavations since 2003, when it was handed the privilege by the Israeli Nature and National Parks Protection Authority, despite a 1998 indictment issued against El Ad for damaging antiquities. It can be argued, however, that El Ad is indeed protecting Israeli national parks, just ignoring all other forms of heritage associated with Jerusalem. The organisation is interested in finding only Jewish history so as to justify the eviction of Palestinians. As a 2010 EU report notes, El Ad's control of the archaeology in Silwan "has resulted in a strong monopolisation of the historical narrative, exploiting the biblical and Jewish-Israeli connotations of the area while effectively disenfranchising Arab/Muslim claims of the historic-archaeological ties to the very same place."[41]

Archaeological experts say El Ad's claim that the biblical palace of King David was built in the vicinity of Wadi Hilweh is dubious. They are also worried that the settler organisation ignores key archaeological practices, such as compiling regular reports. To date, no comprehensive report has been published. These fears came to a head in 2008, when an El Ad-sponsored dig near the Western Wall discovered what was thought to be an ancient

---

[35]Rapoport, M (2007), Group Judaizing East Jerusalem accused of withholding donation sources, *Idem*.
[36]http://www.manta.com/coms2/dnbcompany_9kdqd6, [accessed 17th July 2011].
[37]Shir Hever, personal correspondence with the authors, Summer 2011.
[38]http://www.cityofdavid.org.il/support_eng.asp, [accessed 17th July 2011].
[39]http://www.alternativenews.org/english/index.php/topics/jerusalem/3552-plan-for-national-park-threatens-to-strangle-east-jerusalems-issawiya-neighbourhood-, [accessed 17th July 2011].
[40]*Ibid*.
[41]*European Union (January 2011), EU Head of Mission Report on East Jerusalem, p. 7.*

Muslim graveyard. The skeletons were removed without being documented properly and have now disappeared.[42] Whilst the Antiquities Authorities acknowledges El Ad's glaring faults, it has turned a blind eye to them because El Ad is a major funder of the Authority. As the settler group runs all the excavations in Silwan it decides where and when to dig and hires the IAA to do the work.

In July 2011, as thousands of Israelis took to the streets in protest at the rising cost of living, the *Knesset* approved the first reading of a bill that would see the privatisation of National Parks across the country.[43] The bill is essentially an amendment to the National Parks Law, and is being pushed predominantly by *Knesset* members from the political right.[44] Under the bill's terms, management of the parks can be transferred to non-profit organisations or companies whose goals include "perpetuation of values that have historical, archaeological, architectural or natural importance."[45] Whilst it is being framed as a way to ensure more efficient running of the parks, MK Israel Hasson, a backer of the bill, admitted that one of the main motivating factors behind it is a desire to counter a High Court petition submitted by NGO *Ir Amim* challenging the transfer of the Jerusalem Walls National Park to El Ad.[46]

Case study - Sheikh Jarrah

North of the Old City is the Palestinian neighbourhood of Sheikh Jarrah, another community which has suffered at the hands of the settler movement. Unlike Silwan, however, there is no archaeological premise for the removal of people from their homes and El Ad has little presence. The focus of settler movements in Sheikh Jarrah is proof of ownership, and the perceived right of Jews to return to land they claim was owned by Jews prior to 1948. As with the Absentee Property Act, these claims can be legitimately pursued through the Israeli apartheid legal system. So, while the right of return for Palestinian refugees is categorically denied, alleged Jewish owners are given the full backing of the Israeli legal and security apparatus.

Palestinian families in Sheikh Jarrah are descendants of refugees who lived in West Jerusalem and other areas of Palestine prior to Israel's creation. The neighbourhood fell under Jordanian control following the events of 1948 and an agreement between Jordan and the United Nations Relief and Works Agency (UNRWA) 8 years later led to the building of 28 houses for Palestinian refugees. Whilst it was recognised that the houses were to be erected on "[former]. Jewish property leased by the Custodian of Enemy Property to the Ministry of Development, for the purpose of this project", it was also stipulated that families should pay token rents for 3 years until ownership of the properties would transfer to their

---

[42]http://www.time.com/time/magazine/article/0,9171,1957350,00.html, [accessed 16th July 2011].
[43]http://eslkevin.wordpress.com/2011/08/08/3-articles-on-israeli-government-should-be-spending-more-time-focusing-on-taking-care-of-its-citizens-and-less-time-on-prolonging-the-occupation-of-the-palestinian-territories/, [accessed 17th July 2011].
[44]http://www.haaretz.com/print-edition/opinion/stop-privatizing-national-parks-1.357824, [accessed 20th August 2011].
[45]*Ibid.*
[46]*Ibid.*

names.[47] As a precondition, they also had to relinquish their refugee status and the humanitarian assistance that it affords. However, ownership was never formally bestowed upon the families.[48]

After Israel annexed East Jerusalem, 2 Jewish groups, known as **'the Committees'**, started a process to register the land in their names through the Israeli Land Authority, using what critics argue was dubious Ottoman documentation.[49] Whilst initial attempts at eviction failed, legal proceedings were brought in 1982 by the Committees against 23 families. A lawyer representing the Palestinians reached an agreement in which those living in Sheikh Jarrah were given 'protected tenant' status, completely ignoring the issue of the validity of Jewish ownership claims. As a result, Palestinian families were required to pay rent to the Committees and were not allowed to carry out building renovation.[50] Because they still contested ownership, most of the families refused to pay.

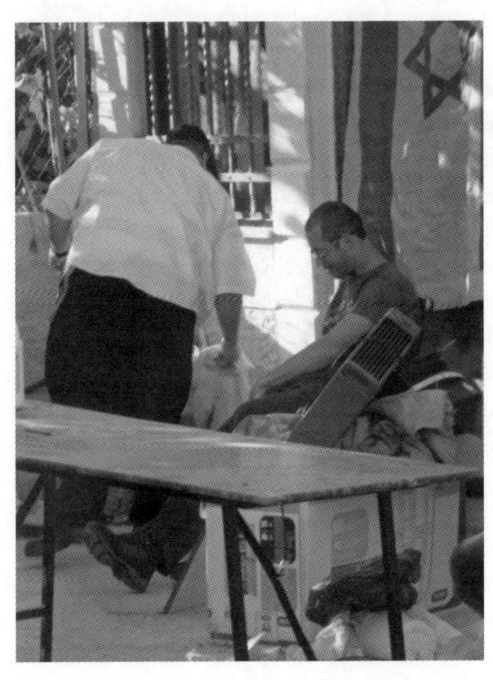

Two members of the rotating group of settlers in the front garden of the house owned by the Al-Kurd family in Sheikh Jarrah (Corporate Watch)

The dispute appeared dormant until settler activity gathered pace and in 1999 families found themselves fighting eviction once again. The Committees began suing for unpaid rent. One family, Al-Kurd, was also alleged to be in breach of the protected tenancy agreement after

---

[47]http://www.csmonitor.com/World/Middle-East/2009/0804/p06s12-wome.html/%28page%29/2, [accessed 12th July 2011].
[48]*Ibid.*
[49]http://www.alternativenews.org/english/index.php/topics/jerusalem/2466-press-conference-about-ongoing-situation-in-sheikh-jarrah, [accessed 12th July 2011].
[50]*Ibid.*

building an extension to accommodate their son Raed.[51] In 2001, settlers broke into the now dormant extension while the Al-Kurds were away and rotating groups of settlers have been living there ever since.

The development of underdevelopment

The Jerusalem Local Planning Commission is currently examining Local Town Plan Scheme 12705, which was submitted in August 2008 by a settler-related company, **Nahalat Shimon International**. If successful 28 Palestinian homes would be demolished, making around 500 people homeless, and 200 settler housing units would be constructed as part of a new settlement called Shimon HaTzadik.[52] Nahalat Shimon has now bought the rights to land in Sheikh Jarrah from the Committees and has begun working with the **Settlers of Zion Association**, led by Israeli *Knesset* member Rabbi Benny Elon.[53] In 2009, however, documents were found in the Ottoman archives in Ankara confirming that Palestinians are the historical owners of a large swathe of the disputed land.[54]

Sheikh Jarrah is also home to some of Jerusalem's most famous hotels, the most prominent of which are the American Colony and the Shepherd Hotel. The latter was seized by Israel following the 1967 war, and transferred to the Israeli Custodian of Absentee Property. In 1985, Jewish-American bingo and hospital magnate **Irving Moskowitz** acquired the hotel and rented it to the Israeli Border Police. He now leads a consortium, along with settler group **Ateret Cohanim** and **C&M Properties**, that recently submitted Town Plan Scheme 11536 to construct 90 apartments, a synagogue and kindergarten on the site.[55] This updates the approved Plan 2591, passed in July 2009, which allows for the destruction of most of the existing buildings in order to establish residential apartments.[56] Permits were issued in March 2010 and, at the time of writing, sections of the Shepherd Hotel had already been demolished.

Much of the money Moskowitz funnels into the settler movements of East Jerusalem comes from proceeds from his bingo hall in Hawaiian Gardens, California. The hall, run as a not-for-profit under a provision in Californian state law, is staffed by volunteers and takings are tax-deductible, representing another American tax-payer subsidy to Israel.[57] These are then

---

[51] http://www.csmonitor.com/World/Middle-East/2009/0804/p06s12-wome.html/%28page%29/2, [accessed 12th July 2011].
[52] http://www.middleastpost.com/1306/evictions-settlement-plans-sheikh-jarrah/, [accessed 12th July 2010].
[53] http://home.al-maqdese.org/en/2/9/626/?tn=Palestinian_Neighborhoods, [accessed 12th July 2010].
[54] http://www.haaretz.com/print-edition/news/turkish-documents-prove-arabs-own-e-jerusalem-building-1.272385, [accessed 12th July 2010].
[55] http://home.al-maqdese.org/en/2/9/626/?tn=Palestinian_Neighborhoods, [accessed 12th July 2011].
[56] http://www.mfa.gov.il/MFA/About+the+Ministry/Behind+the+Headlines/Behind-the-Headlines-Background-information-regarding-the-Shepherd-Hotel-building-19-Jul-2009, [accessed 12th July 2010].
[57] http://www.guardian.co.uk/commentisfree/cifamerica/2009/aug/06/irving-moskowitz-israel-obama-settlements, [accessed 9th July 2010].

channelled via the **Irving I Moskowitz Foundation** into projects in East Jerusalem and the West Bank that would appear to be aiding the Judaization of Palestinian towns, suburbs and neighbourhoods.[58] In recent years, the bingo hall has been making $30-40 million in revenues. The Foundation is also a big contributor to groups supporting settlers, for example donating $5 million to **American Friends of Ateret Cohanim**[59] and a $405,000 contribution to **Friends of Ir David** in 2007.[60]

Institutional neglect

The supply of basic utilities in the whole of Jerusalem falls on the municipality. However, despite being taxpayers many Palestinians are denied access to essential services. East Jerusalemites do not receive services from the Palestinian Authority. In fact, many human rights organisations working in East Jerusalem note that the municipality's tax system [known as *arnona*]. is inherently discriminatory as Palestinian residents pay some of the highest rates in the city.[61]

What follows is a brief outline of the way in which 3 main services - sewage and water, telecommunications and electricity - are carried out within the Jerusalem Municipality. Another public service, transport, is covered in detail in the first section of the book but will also be summarised here.

Sewage, drainage and water provision in Jerusalem is the remit of **Hagihon Water Ltd**, also known as **Gihon**, a privately held company owned by, but operating independently of, the Jerusalem Municipality.[62] The company also owns controlling shares in the Jerusalem **Company for Wastewater Treatment Ltd. (MAVTI)**, a subsidiary operating Israel's largest sewage treatment plant in Nahal Sorek.[63] However, Israeli human rights NGO *B'Tselem* reports that entire Palestinian neighbourhoods remain unconnected to sewage systems,[64] while the Association for Civil Rights in Israel (ACRI) notes that East Jerusalem lacks around 50 kilometres of main sewage lines and that "approximately 160,000 Palestinian residents have no suitable and legal connection to the water network."[65]

Energy in the Palestinian areas of Jerusalem and the Muslim, Armenian and Christian quarters of the Old City is provided by the **Jerusalem District Electric Company**

---

[58] http://stopmoskowitz.org/article0045.shtml, [accessed 9th July 2011].
[59] *Ibid.*
[60] http://www.bloomberg.com/apps/news?pid=newsarchive&sid=asAHh1UQP_jo, [accessed 9th July 2011].
[61] http://electronicintifada.net/content/palestinians-silently-transferred-east-jerusalem/9851 and http://www.jcser.org/index.php?option=com_content&view=article&id=6&Itemid=9, [accessed 1st September 2011].
[62] http://www.hagihon.co.il/eng/odot.asp, [accessed 2nd September 2011].
[63] http://www.hagihon.co.il/eng/biyuv.asp?cat=257&in=256, [accessed 2nd September 2011].
[64] http://www.btselem.org/jerusalem/infrastructure_and_services, [accessed 2nd September 2011].
[65] http://www.acri.org.il/en/?p=722, [accessed 21st August 2011].

(JDEC),[66] which was established in 1914. Following the 1967 occupation, JDEC's concession rights to generate electricity were seized by the state-owned **Israeli Electric Corporation (IEC)**, which has retained control until this day.[67] This has led to the Israeli state applying pressure on JDEC to stop developing sources of power and, instead, to purchase electricity from the Israeli Electric Corporation. As a result JDEC pays around 85 per cent of its monthly income to its Israeli counterpart.[68]

Land-line and internet services in East Jerusalem and the Old City are provided by the Israeli telecommunications company **Bezeq**.[69] There are a number of small Palestinian-owned internet service providers (ISPs), such as **Alquds Network**, but they are merely "resellers of connectivity" and a "last-mile distributor of internet services"[70] as they have to go through an Israeli service provider.[71] In the case of Alquds this means receiving basic infrastructure from Bezeq. However Israeli telecommunications companies refuse to send technicians into East Jerusalem without security, despite the guarantee of 24-hour service.[72] Overall, Israeli telecommunications companies offer Palestinian customers low levels of support.[73]

The Jerusalem light railway is a tram system that is being built by a consortium including French companies **Veolia** and **Alstom** to link West Jerusalem with settlements in East Jerusalem. Many Palestinians argue that, even if they wanted to use the tram system, their incomes are so low that they would not be able to afford it.[74] 2,000 square metres of land belonging to Mahmoud al-Mashni, a resident of the East Jerusalem neighbourhood of Shuafat, was confiscated to make way for the railway and more of his land is to be taken for a station car park.[75]

Jerusalem is an important site for 3 of the world's biggest religions and a place of mystique for archaeologists and historians. The city attracts hundreds of thousands of tourists each year and generates a huge amount of revenue. However, El Ad's City of David operates as a one-sided information hub when it comes to the plight of Palestinians and the fact that East

---

[66] http://middleeastprogress.org/bulletin-viewer/?pid=4249, [accessed 21st August 2011].
[67] http://www.thisweekinpalestine.com/details.php?id=1661&ed=113&edid=113 and http://www.jpost.com/topic/Israel_Electric_Corporation, [accessed 21st August 2011].
[68] http://www.thisweekinpalestine.com/details.php?id=1661&ed=113&edid=113, [accessed 21st August 2011].
[69] http://www.haaretz.com/print-edition/news/as-phones-go-dead-east-jerusalem-residents-lament-bezeq-service-1.332599, [accessed 21st August 2011] and http://middleeastprogress.org/bulletin-viewer/?pid=4249, [accessed 22nd August 2011].
[70] http://www.ebusinessforum.com/index.asp?layout=rich_story&channelid=4&categoryid=31&title=Tough+tests+in+east+Jerusalem&doc_id=11277, [accessed 24th August 2011].
[71] http://www.merip.org/mer/mer213/www-palestine, [accessed 24th August 2011].
[72] http://www.ebusinessforum.com/index.asp?layout=rich_story&channelid=4&categoryid=31&title=Tough+tests+in+east+Jerusalem&doc_id=11277, [accessed 24th August 2011].
[73] *Ibid.*
[74] http://electronicintifada.net/content/veolia-whitewashes-illegal-light-rail-project/9001, [accessed 8th September 2011].
[75] *Ibid.*

Jerusalem is a city under occupation. Tour operators offering East Jerusalem packages, such as the US company **Viator**[76] should be targets for the BDS movement.

Equally, when the OECD decided to hold its annual tourism conference in Jerusalem in 2010, the Israeli Tourism Minister heralded the move as a recognition of the city as Israel's undivided capital. Although many countries, including Britain, Mexico and Sweden, refused to send a representative because of the controversial venue, those who did attend were hosted by settlers. Delegates were seen arriving in a bus owned by the **Mateh Binyamin Regional Council**, which has jurisdiction over 42 settlements in the West Bank.[77]

Since the beginning of the second Palestinian *intifada* in 2000, revenue from tourism in East Jerusalem has declined considerably. The Israeli state has attempted to ameliorate the effects of this decline in West Jerusalem but not in East Jerusalem. In March 2002 the Israeli government approved a tax break which, among other things, provided businesses in downtown West Jerusalem with up to 50 per cent reductions in property tax (*arnona*) over 6 months.[78] Businesses in East Jerusalem were not entitled to this financial aid and many hotels in the area have closed down, many due to accumulation of *arnona* tax debt.[79]

Resistance

The Wadi Hilweh Information Center is situated just a few hundred metres down the street from the City of David tourist site in Silwan. Here tourists are offered talks correcting the false claims made by El Ad, explaining the true meaning behind the archaeological digs. The centre posts alternative news on the web giving constant coverage of problems in the area.[80] In addition, the centre offers music and art classes for Palestinian children denied proper access to education and other social provisions in Silwan.

During the 2011 Passover holiday, activists from the Israeli Sheikh Jarrah Solidarity movement, along with internationals, handed out leaflets to tourists. The leaflets, entitled '5 Facts about the City of David you might not hear from your tour guide', was coupled with alternative guided tours through Silwan led by Palestinians at the Wadi Hilweh Information Center.[81] In response, plain clothes security guards from El Ad filmed activists as they handed out leaflets. El Ad filed a libel suit against several activists contending that activists had claimed that the settler group employs armed guards involved in violent incidents

---

[76] http://www.viator.com/tours/Jerusalem/City-of-David-and-Underground-Jerusalem-Day-Tour/d921-5209CIDAVJ, [accessed 21st August 2011].
[77] http://www.bdsmovement.net/2010/oecd-hires-services-from-extremist-jewish-settler-organization-4781, [accessed 21st August 2011].
[78] http://www.jcser.org/index.php?option=com_content&view=article&id=6&Itemid=9, [accessed 7th September 2011].
[79] *Ibid.*
[80] See www.silwanic.net.
[81] Authors personal observation. March 2011.

against Silwan residents, when the guards, they claimed, are, instead, employed by the Israeli Ministry of Housing.[82]

The success of Wadi Hilweh Information Center has made its director, Jawad Siyam, a constant target of the Israeli authorities. Siyam was arrested on 4th January 2011, while giving classes to children at the centre,[83] and has been in prison or under house arrest ever since. A similar policy has been pursued against Adnan Gheith, who set up a protest tent against house demolition plans in al-Bustan. Like the centre in Wadi Hilweh the tent was a vehicle for al-Bustan residents to tell their story and offer tourists, and other visitors to East Jerusalem, including ex-US president Jimmy Carter, an alternative take on the situation.[84] In November 2010, after months of repeated arrests and interrogation Gheith was served with a notice that he would be expelled from Jerusalem for a period of 4 months.[85]

A settler watches as Sheikh Jarrah Solidarity activists converse at the front of the Al-Kurd house after a Friday demonstration in East Jerusalem (Corporate Watch 2011)

Where Next?

It is of paramount importance that the BDS movement challenges El Ad. In the UK campaigners could investigate Roman Abramovich's attendance at El Ad fundraisers and target British charities which donate to the settler movement. Alliance Family Foundation's donation to El Ad, although small, may be the tip of the iceberg *(see our later chapter on UK charities for a discussion of how to take action).*

---

[82]http://www.en.justjlm.org/458, [accessed 7th September 2011].
[83]http://theonlydemocracy.org/2011/01/east-jerusalem-update-1-palestinian-organizer-drops-his-appeal-another-arrested/, [accessed 7th September 2011].
[84]http://972mag.com/israel-ramps-up-repression-of-non-violence-in-east-jerusalem/, [accessed 7th September 2011].
[85]*Ibid.*

24
The Dead Sea

The Dead Sea coast (Corporate Watch 2011)

The Dead Sea is 68 kilometres long and 11 miles wide, bridging Israel and Palestine's 2 most fertile regions, from the Jordan Valley in the north to the Arava in the south.

The northern part of the Dead Sea was illegally occupied by Israel in 1967 and includes the settlements of Beit Ha'Arava, Kibbutz Kalya and Mitzpe Shalem. The tourist industry sustains these settlements, which also manufacture cosmetics sold to the international market, as well as growing dates for international export.

In the south, the landscape is dominated by upmarket hotels and the **Dead Sea Works**, owned by **Israel Chemicals Ltd**, whose exploitation of the Dead Sea is ruining the environment forever. Palestinians living in this area were expelled to the West Bank by the nascent Israeli state in the late 1940s and early 1950s.[1]

Palestinians, the indigenous inhabitants of the region, derive none of the considerable economic and environmental benefits from the Dead Sea, while both Israel and Jordan exploit the area.[2]

The companies benefiting from exploiting the resources of the Dead Sea region are examined in detail in our earlier chapter on extractive industry.

---

[1] Hunaiti, H (2008), *The Arab Jahalin; from the Nakba to the wall,* Stop the Wall, Available: http://stopthewall.org/activistresources/1720.shtml, p.50-51, [accessed September 2010].
[2] For a breakdown of the economic benefits from the tourist and extractive industries in the region see Friends of the Earth, Middle East, http://foeme.org/uploads/publications_publ68_1.pdf, [accessed February 2011].

Tourism

Tourism is an important industry in the Dead Sea region. Tourists arrive by bus to swim at Ein Gedi, stolen from the Bedouin during the *Nakba*, before dousing themselves with mud at Kalya beach and browsing at the Qumran gift shop, the site of the discovery of the Dead Sea scrolls. Both the shop at Qumran and Kalya's private beaches are owned by the settlement of Kibbutz Kalya and the money spent there helps to sustain the settlement.

There are over 5,500 hotel rooms in the Dead Sea region,[3] catering for a steady flow of tourists. Some tourists stay in the upmarket hotels south of Ein Gedi but guest rooms are also available at Kalya and Almog, both illegal settlements on land occupied in 1967. These rooms are marketed in the UK by several websites and by package tour companies, such as **Longwood Holidays**, which include them in its itineraries.

> ### Case study - Kibbutz Kalya
>
> Kibbutz Kalya is an Israeli settlement on the north coast of the Dead Sea. It offers 'bed-and-breakfast' and a private beach, tapping into the steady flow of tourists to the area.
>
> Visitors to the area could be forgiven for not realising that Kibbutz Kalya lies in occupied territory. It's a straight drive from Tel Aviv along Route 90 which bypasses Palestinian communities almost entirely. The north coast of the Dead Sea, although only a few kilometres from Jericho, is completely devoid of Palestinian areas. Only when you go inside the date packing houses will you see Palestinians. Visible workers on Kibbutz Kalya's settlement farms are Thai migrants.
>
> Kalya advertises rooms at its guest-house on a number of websites including **www.booking.com, www.venere.com, www.agoda.com, www.travelbyclick.net** and **www.webtourist.net**. None of these websites makes it clear that Kalya is in occupied Palestine or that it is an illegal Israeli settlement.

---

[3]*Ibid.* p.21.

Companies selling Dead Sea products in the UK

There are hundreds of companies selling Dead Sea products. None of them are too keen on saying where their products come from, and that they are from stolen land. Although some say 'Made in Israel' others say 'Made in the UK', or nothing at all. It's possible that some of these products don't contain any minerals extracted from the Dead Sea at all.

Ahava is the largest exporter of Dead Sea Products. It sources minerals, extracted from the south coast of the Dead Sea, from Dead Sea Works[4] and mud extracted from the West Bank coastline for its products.[5]

Ahava sold its goods in the UK at its flagship store in Covent Garden, which has closed after pressure from BDS campaigners.[6] Ahava products are also sold in a handful of independent shops and through a mail order business.

Read more about Ahava in our earlier chapter on extractive industries.

Israeli Dead Sea products are packaged by **Finder's Health** in Kent, under the **Dead Sea Magik** brand-name, and marketed by **Kent Cosmetics**. Dead Sea Magik products are currently sold at **Debenhams** and **Holland and Barrett**.[7]

Montagne Jeunesse packages Dead Sea products in Swansea. The minerals and salt are sourced from **Ahava Dead Sea Laboratories**,[8] while the mud and clay products are not sourced from the Dead Sea.[9] Montagne Jeunesse Dead Sea products can be found in **Asda, Boots, Morrison, Sainsburys, Superdrug, Tesco, Savers** and **Wilkinson**.[10]

Dr Fischer/Genesis Dead Sea Minerals package Dead Sea products in a laboratory in Brussels, Belgium.[11]

Dead Sea products are also sold under the **Kedem, Paloma, Sea of Spa** and **Premiere** brand-names. Stalls selling these goods are often found in malls and railway stations.

---

[4]ITN Solicitors, lawyers for the Ahava 4, personal correspondence with the authors.
[5]http://www.whoprofits.org/Company%20Info.php?id=575, [accessed February 2011].
[6]http://www.jta.org/news/article/2011/09/21/3089506/ahava-london-flagship-to-close-over-demonstrations, [accessed February 2011].
[7]Corporate Watch established this through correspondence with Kent Cosmetics and Finder's Health.
[8]Personal Correspondence with Nicola Pugh of Montagne Jeunesses, August 2011.
[9]*Ibid.*
[10]http://www.montagnejeunesse.com/ustorelocator/location/index, [accessed February 2011].
[11]http://corporateoccupation.wordpress.com/2010/03/23/dr-fischer-pharmaceuticals-exploiting-the-dead-sea, [accessed February 2011].

Where next?

The BDS movement should put concerted pressure on Israel Chemicals Ltd and the plethora of cosmetics companies profiting from the exploitation of the Dead Sea. In the UK, BDS campaigners, after the success against Ahava, should turn their attention to the companies selling Dead Sea products to High Street stores. Action should also be taken against the companies advertising accommodation at hotels based on settlements in the Dead Sea region.

Boxes of Dead Sea products being packaged for export at Ahava's factory in the settlement of Mitzpe Shalem (Corporate Watch 2010)

25
The Naqab

The vast expanse of the Naqab desert ('*Negev*' in Hebrew) stretches across 60 per cent of Israel's land mass. It is, however, home to less than 10 per cent of the population, approximately 160,000 Bedouin Palestinian Israeli citizens and 379,000 Jewish Israelis.[1] Located in the southern part of the country, it hugs the border with Egypt, from Gaza to Jordan, and north to the Dead Sea and the West Bank. More than three-quarters of the desert is used by the Israeli Defence Force (IDF) for military training exercises. It is also the site of Ben-Gurion University, the Dimona nuclear facility and a number of agricultural settlements and industrial zones.

The Judaization of the Naqab was a priority among Zionist leaders even before Israel's formation, holding particular allure for David Ben-Gurion, who mused: "Negev land is reserved for Jewish citizens whenever and wherever they want. We must expel Arabs and take their place."[2]

---

[1] http://www.bustan.org/subject.asp?id=25, [accessed 12th July 2011].
[2] http://english.aljazeera.net/indepth/opinion/2011/06/20116238174269364.html, [accessed 12th July 2011].

A brief history

Prior to Israel's creation in 1948, the Naqab was home to a large majority of Palestine's Bedouin population. According to Rebecca Manski of the NGO *Bustan*, by the turn of the 20th century, most of the Bedouin residents of the Naqab were semi-nomadic pastoralists, engaged in agriculture.[3] The ethnic cleansing operations begun in the north of Palestine by Jewish forces in 1947 extended to the Naqab, the last district to be invaded, in the summer of 1948.[4] At that time the Naqab was home to around 90,000 Bedouin, divided between 96 tribes. Jewish troops quickly expelled 11 of the tribes, starting with the Jubarat tribe, which was forcibly transferred to Al-Khalil (Hebron) and Gaza by mid-October 1948.[5] Cleansing operations continued until 1959 following an all-too-familiar pattern including continuous death threats, confiscations and killing of animals, house demolitions and murder.[6] The new Israeli state declared most of the region a closed military zone and designated 85 per cent of the desert 'state land'. Thus, all Bedouin settlements were, from then on, deemed illegal and 'unrecognised'.[7] As a result, only 19 tribes remained of the original 96 that inhabited the area; of these, 12 were forcibly displaced and confined to an area in the north-eastern Naqab known as the *Siyag*.[8] Restriction on movement was achieved by introducing a permit system as the only channel through which the Bedouin could leave the *Siyag*, making it harder for them to continue shepherding and growing crops.[9]

The state passed the Black Goat Law in 1950. Draped in the façade of environmental protection, the law curbed grazing to allegedly prevent land erosion by prohibiting migration of goats outside each herder's recognised land holding.[10] As few Bedouin land claims were recognised, most grazing was thereby rendered illegal.[11] As a result, many Bedouin were forced into wage labour.

Planning authorities ignored the existence of the Bedouin villages when they drafted Israel's first development master plan in the late 1960s, laying the foundations of discriminatory policies that continue to this day.[12] As a result, all buildings in these communities are considered illegal according to Israel's Planning and Building Law, giving the Israeli

---

[3] Manski, R (2007), *The nature of environmental injustice in Bedouin urban townships: the end of self-subsistence, Environmental Injustice Report*. Available: www.bustan.org/admin/my../CD3_manski.natureofenviroinjustice.pdf, [accessed 12th July 2011].
[4] See Pappe, I, *The ethnic cleansing of Palestine*. Idem.
[5] *Ibid*, p.173.
[6] http://stopthewall.org/activistresources/1720.shtml, [accessed 12th September 2011].
[7] Manski, R (2007), The nature of environmental injustice in Bedouin urban townships: the end of self-subsistence, *Environmental Injustice Report*. Idem.
[8] http://english.aljazeera.net/indepth/opinion/2011/06/20116238174269364.html, [accessed 12th July 2011].
[9] *Ibid*.
[10] Manski, R (2007), The nature of environmental injustice in Bedouin urban townships: the end of self-subsistence, *Environmental Injustice Report*. Idem.
[11] *Ibid*.
[12] http://www.hrw.org/en/news/2008/03/30/israel-end-systematic-bias-against-Bedouin, [accessed 12th July 2011].

authorities a legal excuse not to connect unrecognised villages to national electricity and water grids or provide even the most basic infrastructure.[13]

During the 1970s, the Israeli government tried to force the Bedouin into planned townships, which, according to Human Rights Watch, constitute 7 of the 8 poorest communities in Israel.[14] The policy was overtly racist, although couched in altruistic terms: "Bedouins must be brought into the 21st century.. They will now have access to proper schools and medical care."[15] While a significant number of *hamulas* (extended family groupings) relocated to these urban towns, many Bedouin spurned the government and began a long struggle to reclaim their land.

Faced with a non-compliant indigenous population, the then minister of agriculture, Ariel Sharon, declared everything south of the 50-degree latitude a protected nature reserve, effectively freezing Bedouin herders out of a major portion of the Naqab.[16] To enforce this, Sharon also created an environmental paramilitary unit called the **Green Patrol**, notorious for its attacks on Bedouin livelihoods and its efforts to prevent the Bedouin from consolidating their hold on the land through settlement and grazing.[17] The Green Patrol removed 900 Bedouin encampments during Sharon's tenure as Minister of Agriculture between 1977 and 1981.[18] The 1970s also saw the Israeli government beginning a prolific policy of demolishing Bedouin homes - a policy which, according to the NGO *Pax Christi* International, has intensified since 2008.[19] More than 400 structures were destroyed over the course of 2008 and 2009. In January 2010, the **Israeli Land Administration (ILA)**, the Ministry of Interior Affairs, and the southern district of the Israeli Police jointly decided to triple the demolition rate for 'illegal constructions' in the Bedouin communities of the Naqab.[20]

The structures in the 'unrecognised village' of al-Araqib have been demolished an estimated 28 times in 2010 and 2011.[21] On top of that, the residents of the village are facing a 1.8 million NIS (over $500,000) lawsuit for the cost incurred by Israeli government agencies repeatedly destroying their homes.[22] During the first demolition on July 27th 2010, in which

---

[13] Written statement submitted by NGO *Pax Christi* International to the Fifth Session of the UN Human Rights Council, 17/08/2010. Available: www.unhcr.org/refworld/pdfid/4d2d9e492.pdf, [accessed 2nd September 2011].
[14] Ibid.
[15] http://electronicintifada.net/content/Bedouins-negev-israeli-ctizens-or-punishable-trespassers/4411, [accessed 2nd Septembetr 2011].
[16] Manski, R (2007), The nature of environmental injustice in Bedouin urban townships: The End of Self-Subsistence, *Environmental Injustice Report. Idem.*
[17] Ibid.
[18] Ibid.
[19] Written statement submitted by NGO *Pax Christi* International to the Fifth Session of the UN Human Rights Council. Idem.
[20] Ibid.
[21] http://www.amnesty.org/en/news-and-updates/israel-sues-Bedouin-villagers-cost-repeated-evictions-2011-07-29, [accessed 2nd September 2011].
[22] Ibid.

at least 46 homes were razed to the ground, more than 1,000 police officers entered the village alongside Israeli Lands Administration officials.[23]

A Palestinian-Bedouin man from the un-recognised Naqab village of al-Araqib walks towards an Israeli police line before his community is demolished. The disproportionate use of force by the Israeli authorities is designed to intimidate Palestinians, (Active Stills)

Economy

The economy of the Naqab is split between 3 main sectors: chemical industries, high-tech and agriculture. A considerable amount of state and quasi-state investment has been directed to the area, offering incentives in order to attract foreign and domestic capital. The following section will deal with these 3 main sectors in turn, in addition to profiling a number of the region's industrial zones.

Agriculture

Growing crops on a large scale in the arid desert environment requires a lot of capital-intensive research and development in order to discover the required techniques. There is very limited rainfall in the Naqab, ranging between 250 and 500 millimetres annually depending on the area, yet the Israeli state is determined to develop intensive agriculture. To achieve this, farmers in the western Naqab irrigate their fields with reclaimed waste water from urban centres of the country.[24] Haim Levi, head of the Eshkol Regional Council, noted at an agricultural exhibition in the western Negev that: "We are dependent on purified water that is piped here from Israel's central region and on the KKL-JNF reservoirs, and without

---

[23] *Ibid.*
[24] http://www.haaretz.com/news/state-to-compensate-farmers-for-crops-lost-over-negev-arava-drought-1.237665, [accessed 13th July 2011].

water, no one could live here."[25] Yet, that is exactly what the Israeli state expects the Bedouin to do: live in the Naqab without proper access to water.

As a result of targeted investment, both by the government and bodies like the Jewish National Fund, the Naqab has become an important area for agricultural exports. In the Arava Valley, to the north-west of the Naqab, farming families produce almost 60 per cent of Israel's fresh vegetable exports, including 90 per cent of melon exports,[26] and 10 per cent of cut flower exports. This is partly because of the JNF-funded Zohar and Yair R&D stations.[27] In 2004, the sale price per flower stem grown in the Naqab had a profit margin 5 times higher than the growing cost.[28]

Kibbutz Hatzerim, around 8 kilometres west of Be'er Sheva, has cornered 20 per cent of the world jojoba oil market and, due to advanced techniques, can harvest much more per hectare than the world average. Jojoba is a desert plant, the fruit of which produces an oil used in the cosmetics industry for shampoo, creams and soaps.[29] The oil is produced through industrial venture **Jojoba Israel**, established in 1988, and exported to cosmetic manufacturers in the US, China, France, Germany and Japan.[30] Companies supplied include **Laserson** of France and **Shanghai Yikuan Industry Co.** in China, both of which provide wholesale ingredients for international cosmetics production.

Negev Advanced Technology Park

The Negev Advanced Technology Park (ATP) is currently under construction. The ATP is a public-private partnership between **Ben-Gurion University**, Beersheba Municipality and US development firm **Kud International**. Kud is involved in a number of construction projects across the UK, including the new stadium of **Liverpool Football Club** and **Silvertown Quays**, a regeneration project in London's Royal Docks.[31] According to the Israeli Ministry of Foreign Affairs, the ATP will be a "city within a city", complete with recreational facilities and adjacent to what will be the biggest shopping centre in the country, the 'Grand Canyon Mall'.[32] The project is being developed with strong government support and tenants will be able to take advantage of economic incentives including tax breaks, salary subsidies for employers and low-cost development loans. Due to its close proximity to Ben-Gurion University's main campus, the ATP aims to develop R&D relationships between the

---

[25]http://www.jpost.com/GreenIsrael/PEOPLEANDTHEENVIRONMENT/Article.aspx?id=210041, [accessed 13th July 2011].
[26]http://negev.org/Partners/arava.html, [accessed 13th July 2011].
[27]http://issuu.com/jewishnationalfund/docs/byachad_fall_10, [accessed 13th July 2011].
[28]http://www.israelforum.com/board/archive/index.php/t-5451.html, [accessed 23rd September 2011].
[29]http://www.kkl.org.il/kkl/english/main_subject/kkl%20-%20jnf%20in%20the%20press/water%20from%20kkl-jnf%20negev%20reservoirs%20irrigates%20jojoba%20plantations.x, [accessed 14th July 2011].
[30]http://www.jojobaisrael.com/, [accessed 14th July 2011].
[31]http://www.kudllc.com/projects/silvertown-quays.html, [accessed 8th September 2011].
[32]http://www.mfa.gov.il/MFA/InnovativeIsrael/Negev_high-tech_haven-Jan_2011, [accessed 14th July 2011].

University and international high-tech companies.[33] This will be accompanied by a 2-million-square-foot IDF telecommunications research centre housed next to the park, which is also expected to attract collaborations with private contractors.[34] As we have already seen, the boundaries between military, academic and high-tech capital are increasingly blurred in Israel. Senior project leaders claim they already have commitments from some large international companies, although they have so far refused to divulge who these companies are.[35]

Bio-Negev

In March 2010, the Negev 2010 conference was held in Beir al-Saba (Be'er Sheva), drawing hundreds of politicians and business people with the aim of attracting 300,000 new residents to the area.[36] It was at this conference that the minister for the Development of the Negev and Galilee, Silvan Shalom, launched Bio-Negev, a venture to encourage cooperation between different bodies involved in the bio-medical sector in southern Israel.[37] The main premise of Bio-Negev is to mediate between companies and research institutions to provide support for the biotech industry. It is set-up as a not-for-profit organisation.[38] In March 2011, its founders announced a plan to raise between $40-50 million for a new fund to finance companies within its portfolio. They also formed the Bio-Negev science and technology cluster, an industrial park focusing on a range of innovations, including regenerative medicine and nanotechnologies.[39] The Bio-Negev park has signed a cooperation pact with French counterpart **Sophia Antipolis Science Park** in Nice.[40] The agreement is to jointly establish and nurture life-science companies.[41] Companies operating within Sophia Antipolis include **Bayer Cropsciences**[42] and **Dow Agrosciences**.[43]

No'am Industrial Zone

In 2006, the then Prime Minister, Ehud Olmert, signed off a plan to move 60 factories from the centre of Israel to the No'am Industrial Park in the western Naqab. The park is located between the development towns of Netivot, Sderot, Ofakim and Rahat. The last is the first

---

[33] http://www.atp-israel.com/, [accessed 14th July 2011].
[34] *Ibid.*
[35] *Ibid.*
[36] http://english.aljazeera.net/focus/2010/04/20104592655951622.html, [accessed 14th July 2011].
[37] http://www.globes.co.il/serveen/globes/docview.asp?did=1000549159, [accessed 4th September 2011].
[38] http://www.globes.co.il/serveen/globes/docview.asp?did=1000632027&fid=1725, [accessed 4th September 2011].
[39] http://investincotedazur.com/en/newsletter/sophia-antipolis-israel-s-bionegev-very-interested-by-science-park-potential&artid=act8877, [accessed 4th September 2011].
[40] *Ibid.*
[41] http://www.nature.com/nbt/journal/v27/n11/full/nbt1109-959.html, [accessed 4th September 2011].
[42] http://www.bayercropscience.fr/bayer-cropscience/implantations-france.aspx, [accessed 4th September 2011].
[43] http://investincotedazur.com/en/newsletter/sophia-antipolis-canon-inc-and-median-technologies-enter-into-agreement-to-devel&artid=act10186, [accessed 4th September 2011].

recognised Bedouin city in Israel. Netivot, Sderot and Ofakim were essentially constructed to absorb new immigrants from Russia, Eastern Europe and North Africa, and have particularly high rates of poverty compared to other Jewish towns in the country.[44] It is an often overlooked fact that, in addition to discriminating against Palestinians, Israel's elite, who are of mainly Western European descent, discriminates against Jews from other areas of the world, such as the Middle East and North African Sephardi Jews. It is these migrants who have settled in development towns lacking the amenities and education systems found in Mediterranean urban centres like Tel Aviv and Haifa. One of the latest enterprises to move to No'am is **Tara Dairy**, the second-largest milk processor in the country, owned by **Coca Cola Israel**, and a strategic partner of German yoghurt giant **Muller**.[45]

Blueprint Negev

Governmental drives to settle more of Israel's population in the Naqab would be impotent if it were not for the help of the Jewish National Fund. At the 2003 Herzliya Conference, the JNF presented "Blueprint Negev", its future vision for the Naqab, an initiative it claimed would revitalise the region by "[increasing]. the area's population and improve living conditions for all its inhabitants."[46] This includes creating new Jewish communities and expanding existing ones. However, in the 8 years since its unveiling, and despite promises to also work with Bedouin communities, the project has come under intense criticism for what many perceive to be a blatant policy of ethnic cleansing aimed at forcing the Bedouin off their land.

Both the Naqab and the Galilee, where a large majority of Israel's Palestinians live, have been targeted with the specific goal of changing the demographic in favour of Israeli Jews. A quarter of the 4,000 or so Jewish immigrants arriving in Israel in 2010 were settled in these regions, and the Israeli government harbours plans to ensure the numbers keep rising. According to Silvan Shalom, Negev and Galilee Development Minister, the Israeli government will, by 2011, "double the amount of absorption packages for those who are interested in settling the Negev and Galilee. These people are modern pioneers who are manifesting the Zionist vision."[47]

The Blueprint project has been taken up by many JNF-KKL sister organisations across the globe, including **JNF-US** and by the **JNF-UK** under the name the 'Negev Challenge'. One of the communities supported by the latter is Halutzit, which JNF-UK labels as "a remarkable community of pioneers".[48] Based in the Northern Naqab, the community had previously resided at Atzmona, Gush Katif, in Gaza prior to Ariel Sharon's 'disengagement' in 2005.

---

[44] http://www.haaretz.com/print-edition/features/robots-enliven-negev-desert-community-1.337244, [accessed 13th July 2011].
[45] http://www.en.kor-az.com/index.php?go_shop2&data_id=11, [accessed 13th July 2011].
[46] http://www.jnf.org/work-we-do/blueprint-negev/, [accessed 13th July 2011].
[47] http://www.jewishagency.org/JewishAgency/English/About/Press+Room/Jewish+Agency+In+The+News/2011/1/jan27jp.htm?WBCMODE=PresentationUnpublished.htm, [accessed 4th September 2011].
[48] http://www.jnf.co.uk/negev_halutzit.html, [accessed 4th September 2011].

Now the community is being aided by the JNF and is growing sweet peppers and lettuces for export to the UK.[49] The local Rabbi, Eli Adler, teaches at Ometz, a religious school established by the community at Yated and headed by Rafii Peretz, who was named as Chief Rabbi of the IDF in January 2010.[50] The fact that this group of settlers see the Naqab as the next Zionist frontier is telling.

A Caterpillar bulldozer emblazoned with Jewish National Fund (JNF-KKL) flags ploughs land ready for afforestation on the outskirts of al-Araqib. The NGO, whose sister organisation JNF-UK has charitable status in Britain, has been accused of complicity in the ethnic cleansing of Palestinian Bedouin from the Naqab (Alternative Information Center)

This, of course, stands alongside the JNF's complicity in the demolition of and discrimination against the 'unrecognised' Bedouin communities. The JNF has begun planting a forest on the land of al-Araqib. The project is portrayed to the international community as an ecologically sound project aimed at 'greening' the desert. Trees funded by the Anglo-American Christian evangelical channel **God TV** have already been planted on land belonging to the Aturi tribe that lives in al-Araqib.[51] A 2011 Amnesty International delegation to the village witnessed JNF bulldozers levelling land on the village perimeter in preparation for afforestation.[52]

The JNF's involvement is far more than that of a mere benefactor. The Alternative Information Centre reports that **Caterpillar** bulldozers, complete with JNF-KKL flags, have been entering al-Araqib alongside Israeli forces to destroy structures,[53] and that **Volvo**

---

[49] *Ibid.*
[50] http://www.israelnationalnews.com/News/News.aspx/135714, [accessed 4th September 2011].
[51] *Ibid.*
[52] Amnesty International, personal correspondence with the authors. February 2011.
[53] http://www.alternativenews.org/english/index.php/topics/news/3384-el-araqib-destroyed-for-21st-time-jnf-changing-facts-on-ground, [accessed 4th September 2011].

equipment has been used during demolitions in the same village.[54] Additionally, the JNF is deep-ploughing the soil so that rebuilding becomes harder.[55] Thus, while the JNF's public face is that of an ecologically benign organisation attempting to combat desertification and climate change, the reality is that homes, fruit trees and olive groves belonging to the Bedouin are being uprooted and livelihoods destroyed.

A Volvo bulldozer demolishes a structure in the Bedouin village of al-Araqib (Active Stills)

IDF training in the Naqab

While the desert has long been a soldier's playground, the Israeli army began plans to actually move military bases inside the Green Line to the Naqab just under a decade ago. The first of these was a training complex near the Negev Junction, between Be'er Sheva and Yeruham, called Ir Habahadim (City of the Training Bases) or the Bahad City complex.[56] The foundation stones were laid in 2003 but building has been consistently thwarted by environmental problems. Pollution originating from a hazardous waste disposal facility at Ramat Hovav, which has been operating for over 30 years, posed potential health threats and the stench could be smelt for around 9 kilometres.[57] Nonetheless, an environmental risk survey conducted in 2009 found the site to be "safe" and building is expected to be completed by 2012.[58] According to the Ministry of Defence this is the largest-ever IDF base

---

[54] http://electronicintifada.net/content/photostory-volvo-equipment-used-house-demolitions-part-2/9161, [accessed 12th September 2011].
[55] http://www.alternativenews.org/english/index.php/topics/news/3384-el-araqib-destroyed-for-21st-time-jnf-changing-facts-on-ground, [accessed 13th July 2011].
[56] http://www.jewishtoronto.com/page.aspx?id=106778, [accessed 13th July 2011].
[57] *Ibid.*
[58] http://www.israelnationalnews.com/News/News.aspx/138969, [accessed 13th July 2010].

transfer, with the complex expected to house 20,000 personnel on over 3,000 dunums (750 acres) at a cost of more than NIS 1 billion.[59]

The hazardous waste can be used as a prime example to highlight the discriminatory policies of Israel against the Palestinian Bedouin. Even before the decision to transfer soldiers to the area was taken, there were 23,000 Bedouin living in Wadi Naim, Wadi Mashash, Tarabin al-Sanaa and Segev Shalom. All of these villages are closer to Ramat Hovav than Bahad City. But the impact of the waste on these communities was never of concern to the Israeli authorities. According to a study led by the Department of Epidemiology and Health Services at Ben-Gurion University, exposure to pollution from the disposal site has led to increased birth malformations amongst Bedouin women living in close proximity to Ramat Hovav.[60] This has been backed up by the Ministry of Health's own study, which hypothesised that Ramat Hovav was to blame for highly elevated rates of cancer in the region.[61]

Resistance

Bedouin resistance in the Naqab is focussed on remaining in the unrecognised villages regardless of Israeli state policy. In 1997 Bedouin in the Naqab formed the Regional Council of the Unrecognised Villages of the Naqab to address Israeli state discrimination, denial of services and home demolitions against the residents of the unrecognised villages.

The international Stop the JNF Campaign, works to highlight the JNF's role in the ethnic cleansing of Bedouin communities. In the UK, Stop the JNF plans to challenge the charitable status given to JNF-UK, which affords them tax breaks on donations. An Early Day Motion was tabled in parliament seeking an investigation into the JNF's activities, claiming that "there is just cause to consider revocation of the JNF's charitable status in the UK."[62] The wider Stop the JNF campaign has scored a number of notable victories, including the May 2011 decision by Prime Minister David Cameron to relinquish his role as honorary patron to the charity. Cameron claimed this was not due to political pressure but this seems unlikely as the JNF has been able to count on such support from every British prime minister since its inception more than 100 years ago. There are still a number of people within the British political elite listed as patrons of the JNF, such as the ex-Conservative leader Lord Michael Howard,[63] Gordon Brown and Tony Blair.

---

[59] http://www.globes.co.il/serveen/globes/docview.asp?did=888220, [accessed 13th July 2011].
[60] Sarov, B. *et al.* (2006), Major congenital malformations and residential proximity to a regional industrial park including a national toxic waste site: An ecological study, *Environmental Health: A Global Access Source*, 5:8.
[61] http://www.bustan.org/subject.asp?id=25, [accessed 12th September].
[62] http://www.stopthejnf.org/greatbritain_campaignnews_pressrelease30may2011.html, [accessed 12th September 2011].
[63] http://www.jnf.co.uk/about_executive.htm, [accessed 12th September 2011].

Where next?

A groundswell of support is needed to push forward the bid to have the Jewish National Fund's charitable status revoked in the UK. Pressure should be put on British policy makers and MPs, as well as on the JNF-UK itself, in order to challenge the distorted idea that the organisation is 'greening' the desert. Following on from this, a coalition between environmental and Palestinian solidarity groups needs to be forged to extend the campaign into new territories. As members of the Stop the JNF Campaign have highlighted, environmental groups should be outraged at the 'greenwashing' of the JNF's activities. Action should also be taken against God TV, a registered charity based in Sunderland, for its funding of JNF trees on Bedouin land.

Caterpillar and Volvo should continue to be pressured to ensure that their equipment is not used in house demolitions in the Naqab. *(See the construction chapter of this book for a summary of the campaigns against Volvo and Caterpillar).*

THE JEWISH NATIONAL FUND
HERE IT IS, IBRAHIM...
THIS IS WHERE I LIVED WHEN I WAS YOUR AGE.
BUT IT'S ALL PINE TREES, GRANDFATHER!

Jewish National Fund by Sean Michael Wilson and Rejena Smiley

A BDS Handbook

LATER, IN ANOTHER AREA...
THIS IS AL ARAQIB. IT WAS DESTROYED BY THE ISRAELI MILITARY IN 1951.
BUT LOOK - THERE ARE PEOPLE THERE AGAIN!
IS THERE ANY ELECTRICITY ?
NO. OR RUNNING WATER. THE ISRAELI AUTHORITIES REFUSE TO RECOGNIZE THIS PLACE. YET THE PEOPLE CAME BACK.
AMAZING!
BUT THE JNF PLANS TO PLANT A FOREST ON TOP OF AL ARAQIB. IN 2010, IT WAS DEMOLISHED DOZENS OF TIMES.
YET, THE PEOPLE THERE ARE DETERMINED TO REMAIN, DESPITE ALL THIS!

Part Three

The UK - Bringing the Fight Home

26
Arms Companies in the UK

The British state's policy on arming Israel in the last 10 years has been simple; to allow, as much as possible, the unfettered export of weapons components bound for Israel from British companies and, in the face of growing public opposition and resistance, to create the false impression that arms exports are subject to strict controls.

The UN has stated that Israel "violates humanitarian law", and the UK Foreign Office flags Israel as a country of "major concern" regarding human rights abuses.[1] The UK's own 'Consolidated EU and National Arms Export Licensing Criteria' are supposed to assess the impact on regional peace and security and the recipient's human rights record.[2] Yet despite this, the UK has "consistently sold arms to Israel".[3]

The UK government granted export licences for the selling of arms to Israel to the tune of £23.7 million in 2010.[4] For the first quarter of 2011, the figure stood at £4.3 million.[5] As well as providing arms directly to Israel, the UK provides licenses for the export of components to the US which are then incorporated into weaponry and defence equipment that is shipped to Israel. In this way the UK government allows arms companies to circumvent its own arms controls.

As Amnesty International's report 'Fuelling Conflict' described, "the introduction in 2002 of revised UK guidelines for the control of exports of components for incorporation in military systems were specifically intended to allow the export of UK components to the USA for incorporation in military equipment such as F16 combat aircraft and Apache combat helicopters." These were known to be exported to Israel but, conveniently, "details contained within UK government reports do not allow for a meaningful assessment of the end-user of this equipment."[6]

After the devastation of Israel's 2009 Gaza massacre these shadowy deals momentarily hit the spotlight. Then Foreign and Commonwealth Secretary, David Miliband, had to admit that some of the arms used in Gaza "almost certainly" contained UK-supplied components.[7]

The resultant public outcry led the Labour government to make some media-friendly concessions: 5 out of 182 outstanding export licenses were revoked.[8] However British arms,

---

[1] http://www.caat.org.uk/issues/israel.php, [accessed September 2011].
[2] *Ibid.*
[3] *Ibid.*
[4] http://www.caat.org.uk/resources/countrydata/?country_selected=Israel, [accessed September 2011].
[5] *Ibid.*
[6] http://www.amnesty.org/en/library/asset/MDE15/012/2009/en/278d5cfc-0b39-4409-bd68-4c6f44d99a64/mde150122009en.pdf, [accessed September 2011] p.30.
[7] http://www.caat.org.uk/issues/israel.php, [accessed September 2011].
[8] http://www.corporatewatch.org/?lid=3412, [accessed September 2011].

such as weaponry found in F-16s and Apache helicopters, continue to be exported to the US before being dispatched to Israel and direct export licenses, for some equipment, continues to be granted.[9]

While the Labour government had the decency, at least, to squirm when questioned on its own complacency, the new Coalition government is even more flippant about the trade – to the point of denying a policy on selling arms to Israel for use in Palestine even exists.

The parliamentary body for examining government policy and the arms trade is the Committees on Arms Export Controls (CAEC). The CAEC report of April 2011 stated that: ".. the present Government's policy on exporting arms or components of arms that could be used in the Occupied Palestinian Territories appears to be confused. Given that the Government in its response to the previous Committees' last Report stated: 'That the UK Government does not have a policy that UK arms exports to Israel should not be used in the Occupied Palestinian Territories', we recommend that the Government re-states what specific arms or components of arms it is willing to approve for export to Israel that could be used in the Occupied Palestinian Territories. We further recommend that if the Government is unable to identify any such arms or components of arms, it formally withdraws the statement of policy quoted in this paragraph."[10] The Government has yet to respond to the CAEC's concerns.[11]

The government's handling of the issue makes one thing clear: the interests of rich and powerful arms companies are held above the lives of Palestinians and the upholding of international humanitarian law.

Company profiles

BAE Systems is the UK's biggest security and defence company, and the second largest defence company in the world with 2010 sales of £22.4 billion.[12]

No stranger to controversy, BAE Systems has been investigated by the Serious Fraud Office concerning claims of political corruption in arms deals with Chile, Czech Republic, Romania, Saudi Arabia, South Africa, Qatar and Tanzania.[13] The company manufactures a whole catalogue of instruments of death. Those known to be used by Israel in the oppression of Palestinians include 'Head Up Displays' (HUDs) for some F16 aircraft, parts of the 'navigation suite' and elements of the 'self-protection suite' for all of Israel's F16 jets.[14] In providing these parts BAE Systems has a close commercial relationship with US company

---

[9] *Ibid.*
[10] http://www.caat.org.uk/issues/israel.php, [accessed August 2011].
[11] *Ibid.*
[12] http://www.baesystems.com/AboutUs/FactSheet/index.htm, [accessed August 2011].
[13] http://www.guardian.co.uk/world/interactive/2007/jun/07/bae.global.investigations, [accessed August 2011].
[14] http://www.corporatewatch.org/?lid=3395, [accessed August 2011].

Lockheed Martin which manufactures F16s. F16s are Israel's main air attack weapon; more than 200 F16s had been supplied to the Israeli Defence Forces by 2006.[15]

The extent to which the government is willing to protect these commercial relationships became apparent when, in 2002, the then Foreign Secretary Jack Straw defended the granting of an export licence for components made by BAE to the US for Lockheed Martin F16s arguing: "Defence collaboration with the US is also key to maintaining a strong defence *industrial* capacity" (emphasis added).[16]

BAE Systems' headquarters are located in Farnborough, Hampshire, UK. The company has premises across the UK.

> Top shareholders in BAE include Capital Group, Blackrock, Franklin Resources, AXA, Invesco, Barclays, Legal&General, Silchester, UBS, Prudential, State Street Corporation, Bank of New York Mellon, Majedie Asset Management, Lloyds, Standard Life, Henderson Group, Government of Singapore, Ameriprise, Jupiter, HSBC, Deutsche Bank, Affiliated Managers, Aviva, F&C Asset Management, Province of Ontario, Vanguard Group, Mercator Asset Management, Allianz SE, LSV Asset Management, Artisan Partners, Northern Trust, Pzena Investment Management, FMR LLC, Ackermans En Van Haaren, BPCE SA, Public Institution For Social Security, Marathon Asset Management, BP PLC, Universities Superannuation Scheme, NCH Pumpkin, TT International, Charger Corporation, Goldman Sachs, Rathbone Brothers, Real Return, Brewin Dolphin, Marathon Asset Management, Royal London Mutual Insurance Society, JO Hambro, Government of Saudi Arabia, Toronto Dominion Bank, Toronto Dominion Bank, Credit Suisse, Government of Great Britain, BNP Paribas, West Yorkshire Pension Fund, Investec, NFU Mutual Insurance, National Australia Bank, Lazard, State of California, Aberdeen Asset Management, Grupo Entrecanales, Stichting Pension Funds, Grantham Mayo Van Otterloo&Co, Power Corporation of Canada, Morgan Stanley, Societe Generale, Cazenove Capital, Wesleyan Assurance Society, Citigroup, State of Texas, Sumitomo Mitsui Trust, Santander, SAS Rue La Boetie and Liberty Square Asset Management.

UAV Engines Ltd (UEL) is a Staffordshire-based subsidiary of Israeli Elbit Systems. Elbit is one of the world's leading manufacturers of engines for drones, notably the Hermes drone. The company hit the headlines in 2009 when it became apparent that its engines were utilized in the assault on Gaza in 2009.[17] Numerous civilians have been killed in drone attacks: One drone attack during Israel's 2009 massacre killed 16 Palestinian civilians as they

---

[15] Jabarin S (October/November 2006),Stop Arming Israel. *CAAT News* (Campaign Against Arms Trade), Available: http://www.caat.org.uk/issues/IsraelPostcard.pdf, p.8–9.
[16] http://www.caat.org.uk/issues/israel.php, [accessed August 2011].
[17] Pallister (9 January 2009), British link with drone aiding the Israeli war effort, *The Guardian* http://www.guardian.co.uk/world/2009/jan/09/armstrade-gaza

prayed in a Mosque along with the two Hamas targets who were standing outside the building.[18] The company's address is Lynn Lane, Shenstone, Lichfield, WS14 ODT.

Brighton-based arms company **EDO MBM/ITT** is a wholly-owned trading unit of US arms multinational ITT.

The EDO factory in Brighton produces components of bomb racks and release mechanisms for F-16 war planes.[19] It also produces release mechanisms for the Paveway bomb system, under contract with the US company **Raytheon** and the UK Ministry of Defence. Records also show EDO MBM have exported parts to **General Dynamics** (*see below*) in the US.[20]

MBM Technology, originally called MB Metals, was a British company, bought out first by US company **EDO Corporation** and then by US arms giant **ITT**. MBM had acquired the intellectual property rights for the VER-2, the bomb rack for the Israeli F-16 along with the Ejector Release Unit (ERU) 151, the component inside the VER-2 which propels the missile clear of the plane. It also acquired the rights for the Zero Retention Force Arming Unit (ZRFAU), the trigger unit used in the ERU 151. EDO MBM/ITT exports F-16 components to the US,[21] however the company deny that Israel is the ultimate recipient. Grassroots campaigners are convinced that they are lying due to the weight of contradictory evidence.[22]

EDO MBM/ITT also owns the intellectual property rights for the Field Replaceable Connector System (FRCS), a component patented in Israel.[23] The FRCS is manufactured in Brighton and sold to US company **Lockheed Martin** (*see below*) for incorporation into the F-35.[24] In 2010 Israel ordered scores of F-35s from Lockheed Martin.[25]

EDO's US parent company, ITT Corporation, manufactures several components for the Israeli military including the ALOFTS sonar system.[26]

---

[18]Pfeffer A (2 September 2011), 'Wikileaks: IDF uses drones to assassinate Gaza millitants, *Haareetz* http://www.haaretz.com/news/diplomacy-defense/wikileaks-idf-uses-drones-to-assassinate-gaza-militants-1.382269, [accessed September 2011].
[19]Corporate Watch, 2009, *Profiting from occupation*. Available: www.corporatewatch.org/download.php?id=90, [accessed October 2011].
[20]Information from the Import Genius website, [accessed March 2010].
[21]See, for instance, https://www.dibbs.dla.mil/Awards/AwdRecs.asp contract number SPM4A610C0078, [accessed September 2010].
[22]See http://corporateoccupation.wordpress.com/2010/07/29/edo-decommissioners-victorious/, [accessed September 2011].
[23]Israeli State Records, *Patents and designs Journal July 20th 2009, [54], Electrical Connector*.
[24] http://www.defenseworld.net/go/defensenews.jsp?n=Lockheed%20Martin%20has%20awarded%20 contract%20to%20ITT%20for%20F-35%20JSF%20weapon%20release%20systems%20&id=3714, [accessed September 2011] and http://es.is.itt.com/pr2009/pr09_1012.htm, [accessed September 2011].
[25]See, for example, http://www.haaretz.com/news/diplomacy-defense/israel-to-purchase-20-lockheed-martin-f-35-fighter-jets-1.308177, [accessed September 2010].
[26]See http://uss.es.itt.com/scs/sonar.asp, [accessed September 2011] and http://www.edotso.com/clients.htm, [accessed September 2011].

The factory can be found on Home Farm Road, Moulsecoomb, Brighton. ITT also have premises in Basingstoke.[27]

> ITT's top shareholders include Barrow Hanley Mewhinney&Strauss Inc, Old Mutual, Black Rock, State Street Corporation, BPCE SA, Vanguard, Invesco, T.Rowe Price, Gamco, Schafer Cullen, LSV Asset Management, Pictet ET CIE, Deutsche Bank, Prudential, Select Equity, Northern Trust, BNP Paribas, Rabobank, Swedbank, UBS, Credit Suisse, Bank of New York Mellon, Westchester Capital, Eton Park Capital, Government of Norway, State of New York, Bank of America Corporation, Capital Group, Perry Capital, Taconic Capital, Gedde Capital, AXA, Teachers Insurance and Annuity Association of America, JP Morgan, Wells Fargo, PNC, Clovis, City National Corporation, Schroders, State of California, Atlantic Investment, Guggenheim, Neuberger Berman, Minneapolis Portfolio, Legal&General, Allianz SE, Unicredit Spa, MFP Investors, Windy City, Karsch, State of Ohio, Bowen Hanes, Mizuho, Phillipine Investment Management, Honeywell, Morgan Stanley, Aberdeen Asset Management, HSBC and Bank of Canada.

General Dynamics UK (GDUK) is a subsidiary of the US company **General Dynamics**. The company boasts on its website of being "a leading prime contractor and complex systems integrator working in partnership with government, military and civil forces and private companies around the world".[28] GDUK is the 4th largest defence company in Britain with 8 separate UK facilities.[29]

GD, as a global company, has a long history of selling weapons to the Israeli arms company Elbit Systems.[30] In 2010, General Dynamics in the US was awarded a massive tender to produce 600 'Namer' tanks for the IDF over eight years; the contract was worth $400 million in its first phase.[31] GD also produces F-16 jet components, and the bodies of US Paveway bombs, which are then exported to Israel.[32]

GD's UK sites are at Bicester, Hastings, Ashchurch and Pershore, Oakdale and Newbridge and London.[33]

---

[27] See http://www.ittdefence.co.uk/careers/index.html, [accessed September 2011].
[28] http://www.generaldynamics.uk.com/about-gduk, [accessed September 2011].
[29] http://www.generaldynamics.uk.com/about-gduk/economic-benefits-to-the-uk, [accessed September 2011].
[30] http://narcosphere.narconews.com/notebook/brenda-norrell/2009/01/obamas-silence-and-israels-ownership-general-dynamics, [accessed September 2011].
[31] http://www.jpost.com/Israel/Article.aspx?id=192508, [accessed September 2011].
[32] http://www.generaldynamics.com/news/press-releases/detail.cfm?customel_dataPageID_1811=6439, [accessed September 2011], http://bristol.indymedia.org/article/692528 [accessed September 2011] and http://www.defenseindustrydaily.com/israel-looks-to-replenish-bomb-stocks-03590/ [accessed October 2011].
[33] http://www.generaldynamics.uk.com/contact-us, [accessed September 2011].

Boeing is the world's largest aerospace and defence company, with a presence in 70 countries.[34] **Boeing Defence UK** is a wholly owned subsidiary of the US Boeing company. Boeing's trade with Israel has included helicopters, fighter planes and missiles, including the AH-64 Apache Attack Helicopter, used to kill Palestinian civilians.[35] Boeing's UK headquarters are located in central London.

> Boeing's shareholders include Evercore Partners, The Capital Group, Blackrock, State street Corporation, Vanguard Group, T Rowe, FMR, UBS, Prudential, Northern Trust, Goldman Sachs, Allianz SE, Deutsche Bank, Legal&General, Mitsubishi, Morgan Stanley, AXA, State of Wisconsin, Royal Bank of Canada, Bank of Montreal, HSBC and Aberdeen Asset Management.

Israel's Apache Helicopter, supplied by Boeing

---

[34] http://www.corporatewatch.org/?lid=3192, [accessed September 2011].
[35] World Policy Institute (May 2002), Report: US arms transfers and security assistance to Israel, Available: http://www.worldpolicy.org/projects/arms/reports/israel050602.html, [accessed September 2011].

Raytheon is the one of the US' largest arms manufacturers and the fifth largest military contractor in the world.[36] Its UK subsidiary is **Raytheon Systems Ltd**, which has facilities across the UK. Raytheon manufactures missiles used by Israel in the occupied territories, including the AGM 65, Maverick, Patriot and AIM 9 Sidewinder.[37] The company has a number of facilities across the UK.[38]

> Raytheon's shareholders include Barclays, Old mutual plc, Black Rock, Axa, Prudential, HSBC Holdings, Schroders, Aberdeen Asset Management, Aviva, Legal&General, Marathon Asset Management and BNP Paribas.[39]

Brimar is a small company based near Manchester which produces a range of screens and viewing equipment used by the US, UK and Israeli forces, including those of Apache helicopters known to be used by the Israeli military.[40] The components are dispatched to the US, where the helicopters are made, and then sold to Israel.

Meggitt PLC is a UK arms company with headquarters in Dorset, which produces a range of weaponry including cooling systems for tanks, helicopter flight display systems, target systems and UAVs.[41] Meggitt has a sales office in Israel.[42]

Rolls-Royce is an arms manufacturer producing engines for combat aircraft and UAVs.[43] The company embarked on a joint venture with Israeli companies manufacturing compressor blades.[44] The company is also involved in making components for F-35s, which Israel is currently purchasing to replace their F16s.[45] It also owns a stake in the Israeli company **Repair and Overhaul Techjet Aerofoils**. Rolls-Royce has its UK headquarters in London,[46] and branches in Bristol, Coventry, Hucknall, Derby and Scotland.[47]

Further information on other UK companies known to have supplied Israel can be found at the Stop Arming Israel campaign website.[48]

---

[36] http://www.corporatewatch.org/?lid=3192, [accessed September 2011].
[37] World Policy Institute (May 2002), Report: US arms transfers and security assistance to Israel, *Idem*.
[38] See the list on the company website at http://www.raytheon.co.uk/ourcompany/locations/index.html, [accessed September 2011].
[39] Orbis Database, Bureau Van Dijk, [accessed September 2011].
[40] http://electronicintifada.net/content/targeting-britains-war-industry/8444, [accessed September 2011].
[41] http://www.meggitt.com/?OBH=555 and http://www.caat.org.uk/resources/publications/companies/meggitt.php, [accessed September 2011].
[42] http://www.meggitt-avionics.co.uk/about_us/doing_business_with_meggitt_av.aspx, [accessed September 2011].
[43] http://www.caat.org.uk/resources/publications/companies/rolls-royce.php, [accessed June 2011].
[44] http://www.prnewswire.co.uk/cgi/news/release?id=15074, [accessed June 2011].
[45] http://corporateoccupation.wordpress.com/2011/06/19/1230/, [accessed June 2011].
[46] http://www.caat.org.uk/resources/publications/companies/rolls-royce.php, [accessed June 2011].
[47] http://www.rolls-royce.com/about/heritage/branches/index.jsp, [accessed June 2011].
[48] www.stoparmingisrael.org/info/companies.php, [accessed June 2011].

Resistance

The direct link between the products these companies produce and the violent military repression of Palestine has made them targets of concerted campaigns for many years. These campaigns have been a meeting point between Palestine solidarity activism and the wider anti-militarist movement.

In Brighton, EDO MBM/ITT has been the target of the direct action campaign group Smash EDO since 2004. The campaign holds weekly noise demonstrations outside the factory. Over the years campaigners have organised countless lock-ons, roof-top occupations, acts of sabotage, mass mobilisations against the factory, and protest camps.

Activists face the police at a mass demonstration outside EDO MBM/ITT, Brighton (UK Indymedia 2009)

In January 2009, as Gaza was being bombarded by Israel, a group of activists broke into the EDO MBM factory with the aim of 'decommissioning' the production of weapons. The damage caused is estimated to have cost the company £189,000[49] and succeeded in closing the factory for several days,[50] until the assault on Gaza had come to an end. In court in 2010, the defendants argued their actions had been to prevent the greater war crimes being perpetrated by Israel in Gaza. All were found innocent. During the trial, Judge George

---

[49]http://www.brightonandhovenews.org/2010/09/brighton-factory-targeted-in-fresh-protest/, [accessed September 2011] and http://www.youtube.com/watch?gl=GB&hl=en-GB&v=iQhzTn3H4sE, [accessed September 2011].
[50]Evidence of Paul Hills, Hove Crown Court, July 2010. Authors personal notes.

Bathurst-Norman offered the opinion that End User Certificates required for arms export licences were "not worth the paper they are written on".[51]

The biannual arms trade fair, **Defence and Security Equipment International (DSEi)**, held in London's Docklands in September, has also been a long-term target of anti-militarists. The fair allows buyers and sellers to come together, network and make deals. UK arms companies exhibit at the fair, along with hundreds of others from across the globe – and they don't appear too concerned with the end use of their products. Along with Israel, delegates from Iraq, Angola and Colombia shop side-by-side.[52]

Creative and varied actions have taken place against DSEi for over 10 years. These have included mass blockades of train lines, the dock and the exhibition centre itself, stunts such as die-ins, spoof newspapers, pouring red dye into central London fountains, and demonstrations against the financial institutions which invest in the exhibiting companies.[53]

Prior to the 2003 fair, Palestine solidarity activists staged a rooftop protest at the **Caterpillar** HQ in Desford, near Leicester. The action was to highlight the use of Caterpillar bulldozers in demolishing Palestinian homes in the run up to the company appearing in DSEi.[54]

Caterpillar has also been subject to sustained opposition from the 'Caterkiller' campaign which began in 2004. Actions ranged from occupations and blockades, to high street 'street theatre' actions, resulting in some churches divesting from the company *(see our earlier chapter on Israel's walls for a full run-down)*.

A variety of actions have also been taken against BAE Systems over the last few years. CAAT launched a Ban BAE counter-recruitment campaign in autumn 2010 calling on students to oppose BAE's presence at careers fairs for students and graduates. Protests took place at the Guardian's London Graduate Fair and at Bristol University, where a group of students staged a 'die-in' in front of BAE's stand. Other protests have taken place at Warwick, Southampton, Edinburgh, London and Exeter.[55]

In late 2009, the Target Brimar campaign was launched against Brimar. A march on the company's headquarters took place after the group produced a dossier titled 'The case against Brimar' which outlined the company's complicity in Israel's atrocities in the occupied territories.[56]

---

[51]Marsh C (7 July 2010), Activists found not guilty of decommissioning weapons factory, *Electronic Intifada*. Available: http://electronicintifada.net/content/activists-found-not-guilty-decommissioning-weapons-factory/8904, [accessed June 2011].
[52]http://www.sibat.mod.gov.il/sibatmain/exhibitions/DSEI, [accessed June 2011].
[53]http://www.dsei.org/wp-content/uploads/2011/06/disarmdsei-2011-pamphlet.pdf, [accessed September 2011].
[54]http://www.ism-london.org.uk/253, [accessed September 2011].
[55]http://www.indymedia.org.uk/en/regions/manchester/2010/11/467268.html, [accessed September 2011]
[56]See, for example, http://www.indymedia.org.uk/en/2009/08/436518.html, [accessed September

Raytheon is no stranger to protest, and has been a long-term target of anti-war campaigners due to its role in various conflicts, notably the US/UK invasion of Iraq. Some actions against the company have been in specific response to its relationship with the IDF.

9 anti-war activists, who became known as 'the Raytheon 9', forced entry into the plant at Derry, Northern Ireland, in August 2006 and destroyed the main server. This was based on the information that Raytheon missiles were being used by Israel in the invasion of Lebanon. All were acquitted in the trial two years later, after the defendants argued that they were acting to prevent war crimes.[57]

The Raytheon 9 were acquitted by a jury in Belfast after breaking into Raytheon's offices in Derry and disabling the server during the bombing of Lebanon in 2006 (Raytheon 9 2006)

The company once again became a target in January 2009, but this time it was Raytheon's involvement in the Gaza massacre that prompted direct action. 9 women chained themselves together to obstruct the doors of the Derry plant. The women were hoping to bring down the computer system and thereby prevent or delay Israeli war crimes in Gaza but were unable to gain entry. The women demanded that the local police investigate the links before they removed themselves, which the police agreed to.[58] All defendants were acquitted in 2010.

The company closed its Derry plant in February 2010. A document obtained at the time noted: "Raytheon's US senior management continue to be dismayed and disappointed by this outcome. Unfortunately, it would appear that the view of senior US management is that the

---

2011].
[57]See http://raytheon9.org/home.html, [accessed September 2011].
[58]http://www.raytheon9.org/9womenhome.htm, [accessed September 2011].

legal system in Northern Ireland does not offer the degree of protection to their business that could be expected in other parts of the world."[59]

Where next?

As previous direct action campaigns against arms companies show the anti-militarist movement and the BDS movement have a shared aim as Israel continues to commit war crimes in the West Bank and Gaza Strip. Campaign group Smash EDO is planning a Summer of Resistance in 2012 against EDO MBM/ITT.[60] Local groups around the UK could emulate the Smash EDO and Target Brimar campaigns, aimed at closing down local weapons producers. Continuing actions at the DSEi arms fairs are an effective way to highlight the issue of arms trading with Israel generally, as well as drawing attention to specific companies. Actions at universities' recruitment fairs raise awareness of the deadly truth behind these companies' ethical propaganda.

Pressure also needs to be applied to the investors in the arms trade. British pension funds and banks invest in the arms industry. *For more information on how these investments should be targeted by divestment campaigns see the following sections on British pension funds and banks.*

---

[59] Author not stated (January 12 2010), Raytheon to pull out of Londonderry, *Londonderry Sentinel*. Available: http://www.londonderrysentinel.co.uk/news/local/raytheon_to_pull_out_of_londonderry_1_2099755, [accessed September 2011].

[60] For more information see www.smashedo.org.uk, [accessed September 2011].

27
Israeli Companies with British Shareholders

According to Bureau Van Dijk[1] there are 103 Israeli companies which have British shareholders:

Israeli Company	British Investor
Teva	Baillie Gifford and Co
	Old Mutual plc
B Communications	Black Rock (US company with offices at London Bridge)
Checkpoint Software	Schroders plc
	Old Mutual plc
	Egerton Capital
	Investec plc
Hot Telecommunication Systems	Cool Holdings ltd
Nice Systems	Egerton Capital
	Polar Capital
Orbotech Ltd	Old Mutual plc
	Oxford Asset Management
Internet Gold	Eurocom
Leadcom Integrated Solutions	Goldman Sachs International
	Rathbone plc
Ceragon	Barclays
	Polar Capital
	Aberdeen Asset Management
	Oxford Asset management
	Old Mutual plc
Taldor Computer Systems	DBS Investments ltd
Syneron Medical	BT plc
	Polar Capital
	Marshall Wace
	Aberdeen Asset Management
Ituran Location and Control	Barclays
	Aviva
Radware	Barclays

---

[1] Orbis database, Bureau Van Dijk, [accessed August 2011].

Israeli Company	British Investor
BATM Advanced Communications	Henderson Group Gartmore Investment ltd Standard Life Hambro Walkers Crisps Herald Investment Management Close Brothers Group River and Mercantile Legal&General HSBC Dalton Strategic Partnership Jupiter Fund Management Aberdeen Asset Management
Nova Measuring Instruments	Old Mutual plc Aberdeen Asset Management
Visonic	Forest Investment
Clicksoftware Technologies	Polar Capital
Allot Communications	Polar Capital
Oridion Systems	Chase Nominees Schroders Cazenove Capital Old Mutual plc
SHL Telemedicine	Schroders
Dori Media Group	AXA Framligton
Silicom ltd	Polar Capital Oxford Asset Management
MTI Wireless Edge Ltd	Polar Capital CFI Independent ltd
Bio View	MRC Investments ltd
Procognia (Israel)	Procognia ltd
Start Net	Smile Media
Nirshamim Lalimudim	Smile Media
Morgan Stanley Israel	Morgan Stanley International
Deutsche Securities Israel	DB Overseas Holdings
Overseas Tobacco	British-American Tobacco
Tate&Lyle Gadot	Tate&Lyle plc
Escrow Europe (Israel)	NCC Group
Cemex Holdings Israel ltd	Cemex Investments Cemex UK
MS Global	Bunzl
Axismobil	Synchronica
Servision ltd	Servision plc
Holiday Travel	Tui Travel

Israeli Company	British Investor
Mondi Paper Hadera	Mondi Plc
Taldor Communications ltd	Taldor Computer Systems ltd
Grafinir Paper Marketing	Mondi Plc
Yavnir	Mondi Plc
Stepac LA	DS Smith plc
CBD Technologies	Futuragene
Reuvent-Pridan IPG	Lowe&Partners Worldwide
Koffolk Animal Health	Phibro Animal Health
Hashmira	G4S
Kata Vitec	The Vitec Group
Shalmor Avmon Amichay Advertising	WPP plc
Y&R Interactive	WPP plc
Itis Traffic Services	Itis Holdings
Semitool Israel	Semitool Europe
012 Telecom	B Communications
Hype Active Media	Smile
Seret	Smile
Smile Lerimudin	Smile
Ester Neurosciences	Amarin Corporation
Apax Holdings Israel	Apax Partners
Apax Leumi	Apax Partners
Singlesource Research	WPP plc
Telegal	WPP plc
Telemessage ltd	WPP plc
Taylor Nelson Sofres	Messaging International plc WPP plc
Pilat Media Israel.	Pilat Media Global
Timestrip Technical Services	Timestrip
MT Labs	Mobile Tornado Group
Davidoff Howden Insurance	Hyperion Insurance Group
Repair and Overhaul Techjet Aerofoils	Rolls Royce
Media Edge	WPP plc
Meishav Hfakot	WPP plc
Reckitt Benckiser (Near East)	Reckitt Benckiser
BAE Systems Rokar International	BAE Systems
Zoko ltd	CP Holdings
Bateman Engineering	Bateman BV
Industries Development Corporation	Bateman BV
Psagot Investment House	Apax Partners
Mellamox Technologies ltd	Herald Investment Management Barclays plc Aberdeen Asset Management

28
Banks

British bank holdings in Israel are small but significant. One British bank, HSBC, has branches operating in Israel (all HSBC companies are now subsidiaries of HSBC UK). Another, Barclays, has an office in Israel and, in August 2011, was granted permission to operate Israeli branches.[1] Barclays also has the most significant investments in Israeli companies and companies complicit in Israeli militarism, colonisation and apartheid of any British bank.

Company profiles

Barclays is the only major British high street bank with significant investments in Israel, holding shares in 8 Israeli companies: **Tower Semiconductor**, **Gilat Satellite Networks, Ceregon Networks Ltd, Ituran Location and Control Limited, Radware Ltd, Ezchip Semiconductor Ltd, Mellanox Technologies Ltd** and **Teva.** All eight companies are registered on the NYSE.

Tower Semiconductor (Tower Jazz) is a developer and manufacturer of semiconductors and integrated circuits for the electronics industry. The company, operating in Israel, the US and Japan, specialises in inbuilt flash memory.[2] Gilat Satellite Networks is a satellite communications company which provides antennae for Israeli military checkpoints in the West Bank.[3] Ceregon Networks Ltd is a wireless communications company based in Norway and Tel Aviv. Ituran Location and Control Limited is a manufacturer of GPS systems based in Israel, Argentina and Brazil.[4] Radware Ltd provides software to banks, insurance companies, manufacturing and retail, government agencies, media companies, and service providers.[5] Ezchip Semiconductor is involved in the development of ethernet networking. Mellanox Technologies Ltd is an ethernet connectivity company based in Israel and the US.[6]

Barclays also holds shares in **Teva**, an Israeli pharmaceutical company with a large share of the generic drug market *(See our previous chapter on pharmaceuticals).*

Barclays is clearly attempting to expand into the Israeli High St. The bank has recently successfully applied for a license to operate bank services in Israel. The bank invests in a number of companies linked to Israel's settlements: **Unilever**, which owns **Beigel&Beigel,** a

---

[1] http://www.ynetnews.com/articles/0,7340,L-4109211,00.html, [accessed September 2011].
[2] http://www.hoovers.com/company/Tower_Semiconductor_Ltd/cyxyhi-1.html, [accessed September 2011].
[3] http://www.whoprofits.org/Company%20Info.php?id=670, [accessed September 2011].
[4] http://www.zacks.com/commentary/16491/Ituran+Location+%26+Control+Ltd., [accessed September 2011].
[5] http://investing.businessweek.com/research/stocks/snapshot/snapshot.asp?ticker=RDWR:US, [accessed September 2011].
[6] http://www.mellanox.com/content/pages.php?pg=company_overview, [accessed September 2011].

company based in Barkan settlement industrial zone;[7] **France Telecom,** which owns the **Orange** brandname (Orange's franchisee, **Partner Communications,** owns mobile phone antenna in the settlements);[8] **G4S**, which provides services to Israeli and West Bank prisons and police stations;[9] **Motorola** which supplies security equipment and communications equipment to the Israeli army, settlements and for use in the apartheid wall[10] and **F&C Reit**, owner of settlement real estate through **British Israel Investments**.[11] The bank also owns shares in **Tesco** and **Sainsbury**, High Street stores that sell settlement produce in the UK.

Barclays is the largest global investor in the arms trade[12] and holds shares in several companies supplying arms to Israel: **Smiths, Rolls Royce, Meggit, Raytheon, BAE, Chemring** and **Ultra Electronics**. Barclays provides market maker services to **ITT** on the NYSE.[13]

Protest against Barclays Bank's investments in the arms trade and services to EDO MBM/ITT (Smash EDO 2010)

HSBC are currently the only British High Street bank to operate branches in Israel.[14] The bank holds shares in **BATM Advanced Communications**, an Israeli data and telecommunications company listed on the London Stock Exchange; **Veolia** and **F&C Reit.**

---

[7]http://www.whoprofits.org/Company%20Info.php?id=579, [accessed September 2011].
[8]http://www.whoprofits.org/Company%20Info.php?id=713, [accessed September 2011].
[9]http://www.whoprofits.org/Company%20Info.php?id=596, [accessed September 2011].
[10]http://www.whoprofits.org/Company%20Info.php?id=544, [accessed September 2011].
[11]http://www.whoprofits.org/Company%20Info.php?id=834, [accessed September 2011].
[12]See War on Want (2009), *Banking on bloodshed*, Available: http://www.waronwant.org/campaigns/corporations-and-conflict/banking-a-the-arms-trade/inform/16327-banking-on-bloodshed, [accessed September 2011].
[13]http://www.nyse.com/about/listed/lcddata.html?ticker=itt, [accessed September 2011].
[14]Bank of Israel, *Israel's banking system, Idem.*

The bank also has significant arms trade holdings including in several companies that supply arms to Israel: **General Dynamics, Raytheon, Boeing, BAE** and **ITT**.

Lloyds holds shares in **F&C Reit** and **BAE Systems** and is a customer of Israeli company **NICE Systems**. Santander, a Spanish bank with branches in the UK, has investments in BAE.

Anti arms trade campaigner outside AXA's offices in the City of London. During the DSEi arms fair in 2009 activists targeted investors in the arms trade (SchNEWS 2009)

29
Retail

All major UK supermarkets sell Israeli goods, and most of them sell produce from illegal Israeli settlements in the West Bank. Some have made statements in support of Zionism and some have contracts with Israeli companies.

Tesco

Tesco stock fresh food and clothing from Israel and Israeli settlements, including **Montagne Jeunesse** Dead Sea products and a large amount of produce grown in the occupied territories, including fruit and vegetables supplied by **Carmel Agrexco**.[1] Israeli products stocked by Tesco include fruit juice, mangoes, avocados, grapes, stonefruit, dates, herbs, pickled cucumbers, Exquisa potatoes, mixed peppers (from Israel and a second country of origin), **Barkan** wine, **Yarden** wine, biscuits, cold meat, dips, **Osem** soups and cakes, snacks by **Beigel&Beigel, Telma** (soup mixes and cubes, noodles etc) and socks (Tesco's own brand).

The company admitted sourcing 'a number of products' illegal settlements, including avocados, herbs, grapes and stonefruit, such as peaches, from farms in the West Bank and occupied Syrian Golan.[2] In 2006 War on Want reported that Tesco was selling Beigel & Beigel products sourced from settlements.[3] Beigel&Beigel Ltd is located in the Barkan industrial zone in the occupied West Bank and produces pretzels, savoury biscuits and crackers *(see our previous chapter on industrial zones for more information on Beigel&Beigel)*

Mehadrin-Tnuport Export Company (MTex) supplies Tesco with settlement fresh fruit[4] and the store also stocks fresh produce from the **Arava** settlement company.

Tesco also sells gas cylinders for products made by **Soda Club**, which has a factory in the settlement industrial zone of Mishor Edumim, and repackages settlement dates from Hadiklaim as Tesco own brand dates.

Other links to Israel: John Porter, one of the principal shareholders in Tesco, also has substantial investments in Israeli companies. The multi-millionaire is the son of Tesco heiress Shirley Porter, daughter of Tesco's late founder, Sir Jack Cohen. The family own property in the wealthy Herzliya Pituach district just outside Tel Aviv, where Shirley Porter

---

[1] See www.corporatewatch.org/?lid=3192. [accessed September 2011].
[2] http://www.guardian.co.uk/world/2008/jul/06/israelandthepalestinians.supermarkets, [accessed September 2011].
[3] War on Want (2009), *Banking on bloodshed, Idem.*
[4] http://www.corporatewatch.org.uk/?lid=3625, [accessed September 2011].

now resides.[5] Shirley Porter took her name from late husband Leslie Porter, Tesco chairman between 1973 and 1985. After retiring Leslie Porter spent much of his time in Israel and became chancellor of Tel Aviv University (TAU). Shirley Porter is still a member of the TAU Board of Governors.[6] Through the Porter Foundation the couple are major donors to projects at the university, including the Porter Institute for Poetics and Semiotics.[7]

Tesco has also signed a number of contracts with Israeli high-tech firms for in-store and back-room software. The retailer awarded a $1 million IT contract to Israel's **Tescom** to provide solutions for the company's Year 2000 conversion requirements. Another deal saw Ra'anana-based **Retalix** sign a $10 million contract to upgrade store management systems in Tesco branches[8] and in 2004 the shopping chain adopted Retalix's 'BackOffice' solutions in all its stores across Europe and Asia.[9] Retalix produce point of sale and inventory management software and have been working with Tesco since 1995.[10]

Corporate response to BDS campaigners: In October 2007, a group of campaigners from the Brighton Tubas Friendship and Solidarity Group entered Tomer settlement in the occupied Jordan Valley and photographed medjoul dates, packaged by Carmel Agrexco, labelled 'Made in Israel' and marked as bound for Tesco stores. Products exported as 'Made in Israel' benefit from the preferential trade terms of the EU-Israel Association Agreement, which came into effect in 2000. Settlement products, however, are excluded from the beneficial terms of the EU-IAA. When ITN screened an expose in 2007 accusing supermarkets of misleading British consumers, Tesco admitted it had acted "in error" and stated that Israeli dates "originating solely in the West Bank will [in the future] be labelled as such."

Tesco says that 'freedom of choice' is one of the company's priorities and consumers can choose not to buy Israeli products. However, in correspondence with campaigners in 2006, Tesco representatives said they were phasing out Tesco's line of Israeli peppers due to consumer pressure.[11]

Resistance: Tesco has repeatedly been targeted by BDS campaigners because of its continued sale of Israeli and settlement goods. In 2009 campaigners in Swansea damaged settlement products in a Tesco store on the grounds that they came from stolen land.[12] The

---

[5] http://www.independent.co.uk/news/obituaries/sir-leslie-porter-529813.html, [accessed September 2011].
[6] http://www1.tau.ac.il/bog/members.php, [accessed September 2011].
[7] http://www.guardian.co.uk/travel/1999/feb/28/foodanddrink.jayrayneronrestaurants.restaurants, [accessed September 2011].
[8] http://www.haaretz.com/print-edition/business/retalix-signs-contract-to-upgrade-tesco-stores-1.165094 [accessed September 2011].
[9] http://www.haaretz.com/print-edition/business/retalix-s-backoffice-wins-tesco-contract-1.128287 [accessed September 2011].
[10] *Ibid.*
[11] Correspondence between Tesco and consumers, forwarded to authors, 2004-2011.
[12] http://www.quaker.org.uk/friends-action-much-ado-about-dates, [accessed September 2011].

Tesco AGM has repeatedly been a focus for BDS campaigners and in Summer 2011 a group in Cambridge occupied their local store and blocked the checkouts with trolleys filled with Israeli goods.[13] Tesco's store in Covent Garden has been the scene of repeated theatrical actions by BDS campaigners.[14]

(Above) BDS campaigners picket a Tesco store in Covent Garden and *(Below)* occupy the store (London BDS 2010)

---

[13]Examples of BDS actions sent to Corporate Watch during Summer 2011.
[14]http://londonbds.org/2011/08/18/ahava-and-tesco-bds-protests-sat-august-13, [accessed September 2011].

Marks & Spencer

M&S stocks Israeli grapes, lychees, figs, plums, dates, fresh herbs, sweet potatoes, potatoes (Maris Piper, Desiree, Jacket, Marfona, and King Edward). Many of these products are imported through **Carmel Agrexco**.

M&S also stocks large quantities of **Delta Galil** clothing, largely underwear. Delta Galil is Israel's largest manufacturer and marketer of textiles *(for more on Delta Galil see our previos chapter on textiles)*. Marks and Spencer also sells textiles produced by Israeli firms, **Solog** and **Polgat**.

Until 2008 M&S openly sold products from illegal Israeli settlements. *The Guardian* reported in 2004 that the company stocked an extensive range of settlement products. Since 2007, however, M&S has made repeated statements claiming that it does not stock goods from the occupied territories.[15] In 2008, the store wrote: "We do not buy products from the West Bank, Golan Heights or Gaza as we cannot safely visit the suppliers in these areas because of the current security situation." It seems probable that the move to cease selling settlement products was, in fact, due to effective campaigning, protests and fear of adverse press coverage.

Despite the above assurance, there is evidence that M&S continues to stock **Hadiklaim** dates packaged as an M&S own brand product. In correspondence with the School of Oriental and African Studies in 2008,[16] David Gregory, Technical Food Director for M&S, stated the following: "In the past, we have sold dates from this region. However, we made a policy decision sometime ago to cease all purchases from this area. However, our UK suppliers do buy raw material (dates) from the organisation Hadiklaim on our behalf. The contract explicitly prohibits purchase from Palestinian Territories and Hadiklaim source the dates from elsewhere within Israel to satisfy our requirements. Traceability systems are in place to confirm the source of the dates." *(to read more about Hadiklaim see our earlier chapter on agriculture)*.

Other links to Israel: Historically, Marks & Spencer has made statements in support of Zionism. Lord Sieff, chairman and founder of M&S who died in 2001, made several statements in support of Israel's military policies. In 1941, Sieff said that "large sections of the Arab population of Palestine should be transplanted to Iraq and other Middle-Eastern Arab States".[17] In 1990, Sieff, in a book entitled 'On Management: The Marks and Spencer Way', wrote that one of the fundamental objectives of M&S was to "aid the economic development of Israel." There have, however, been no reports of M&S openly showing ideological support for Israel since 2004.

---

[15]For example, see http://link.brightcove.com/services/player/bcpid1184614595?bctid=16537, [accessed September 2011].
[16]Private correspondence made available to the authors by SOAS, 2009.
[17]*Jewish Chronicle*, 21/09/1941.

The retail company has repeatedly asserted that "[it has] no 'special' relationship with any government, political party or religious group" but accepts that M&S does "make representations to governments in support of [its] commercial aims." M&S management has not, to our knowledge, commented on Lord Sieff's remarks in support of Zionism and has not made a statement as to whether the current management stands by them.

In 1998, Sir Richard Greenbury, then CEO of Marks & Spencer, received the Jubilee Award from Israeli Prime Minister Binyamin Netanyahu. In 2000, the Jerusalem Report stated that "M&S supports Israel with $233 million in trade each year."

In October 2000, the Jewish Chronicle reported that the **British-Israel Chamber of Commerce (B-ICC)** had held meetings at Marks & Spencer's offices in Baker Street. However, in 2008 the store claimed that M&S "do not host meetings on our premises for the B-ICC."[18] Nevertheless, in December 2004, Stuart Rose, CEO of Marks and Spencer at the time, was a listed speaker at the annual dinner of the B-ICC.

Corporate Response to BDS Campaigners: When questioned in correspondence about the sale of Israeli goods in M&S stores in 2008, an M&S spokesperson said that the company buys "from Israel as… from 70 other countries…" and went on to state that the company would continue to do so. The letter continued to say that, "[w]e always put the country of origin on the products we sell. Where we buy Israeli products we label them as products of Israel."[19]

Resistance: M&S has faced sustained protests due to their historic ideological support for the Israeli state and because of their policy of stocking Israeli goods. Pickets have been held and store signs and billboards subvertised.[20] M&S has repeatedly ignored campaigners' representations against the continued sale of Israeli goods.

ASDA

ASDA sells Israeli basil, tarragon, rosemary, sage, chives, dill, mint, thyme, passion fruit, mangoes, Blackfine plums, autumn red plums, medjoul dates, dragon fruit, pomegranates, avocados, organic sweet potatoes, sweet pointed peppers (red), sweet potatoes ("Georgia Jet"), frozen meat, biscuits, table wine (red, white, rose & sparkling), **Keter Plastic** garden storage units and tinned grapefruit. ASDA also sells **Carmel Agrexco** products, potatoes from **Mehadrin-Tnuport Export Company (MTex)** and Dead Sea mud, packaged by **Montagne Jeunesse**.[21]

Corporate response to BDS Campaigners: Since ITN's 2007 report, ASDA has made several statements denying that it stocks goods in its stores from the 'West Bank' (i.e.

---

[18]Private correspondence made available to the authors, 2009.
[19]*Ibid.*
[20]For example http://northern-indymedia.org/articles/645, [accessed September 2011].
[21]Observed in an ASDA store by Corporate Watch researchers in June 2011

settlement goods). However, in 2009 ASDA made several ambiguous statements contradicting its earlier stance. A spokesperson from the company recently wrote "I am sure you can imagine it is very difficult for ASDA to take a position on behalf of all our customers over politically controversial issues such as the current conflict you refer to (the occupation of Palestine). On the sourcing of products from overseas we are always guided by the position of the UK Government and by the European Union on trade policy."[22]

Resistance: Campaigners held many pickets of ASDA stores in Brighton and London in 2009 protesting against their sale of Israeli goods. Regular pickets of ASDA have continued in Brighton.

A picket during a coordinated BDS day of action (UK Indymedia 2006)

The Co-operative Group

Despite the Co-operative family of businesses' ethical image, the shelves of its supermarkets and high street stores have been found to carry Israeli products, including **Carmel** mangoes, sweet potatoes, peppers, sweet peppers (grown by Sulat), cherry tomatoes, herbs, passion fruit, **Jaffa** oranges and own brand tinned grapefruit. Goods supplied by settlement companies **Carmel Agrexco** and **Arava**.[23]

Other links to Israel: In November 2008, YNet claimed that the Co-op had met with the Co-op Israel (a separate organisation) and agreed to open a chain of kosher supermarkets which would be equally owned by Co-op Israel and the UK Co-op. The UK Co-op has refuted this claim but admitted that a meeting took place with Co-op Israel.

---

[22]Private Correspondence forwarded to the authors, 2009.
[23]Correspondence between the Co-Op and campaigners, 2010

Corporate response to BDS campaigners: In 2008 the Co-op board undertook to look into conditions on settlement farms. Throughout the year, the issue was raised with Co-op management by members of the Co-op and its customers.

On the 5th January 2009 Len Wardle, Co-operative Group chair, wrote "The Co-operative Group board has decided to suspend sourcing products from illegal West Bank settlements. However, we will continue to trade with Israel and will seek to develop trading links with Palestinian farmers. The Co-operative Group only rarely curtails trade with particular countries or regions. However, in the case of the illegal settlement in the Israeli controlled occupied territories, it has proven to be all but impossible to ensure that supplies derived from the region are not perpetuating injustice and unfair terms of trade. We will no longer source dates, grapes and a number of herbs from the illegal West Bank settlements and will be phasing out the use of similar items from our own brand products."[24]

In making this statement, the Co-op was the first store to base its reasons for ceasing the sale of settlement goods on ethical concerns. The statement is weaker in some ways than that of M&S, but only in that it precludes the sale of West Bank goods and not produce from the occupied Syrian Golan. It is also unclear whether the Co-op's definition of the West Bank includes East Jerusalem.

The Co-operative Group has failed to offer assurance that it will not sell 1948 Israeli products supplied by companies which source products from both the settlements and 1948 Israel, such as **Hadiklaim, M-Tex** and **Carmel Agrexco**.

Campaigners have put a lot of effort into trying to persuade the Co-Op not to source goods from Agrexco. In 2010 the Cooperative Group wrote to campaigners saying that it would continue to stock Agrexco products but that it had met with Agrexco representatives and was planning 'third party audits' to ensure that the goods they bought from them were not from settlements. They also confirmed that they sourced goods from **Arava**.[25]

In December 2010 Len Wardle assured campaigners that his colleagues were 'comfortable that the relationship with Agrexco does not breach our recently agreed Human Rights and Trade policy' and that '..it may well be that you are looking to move the Group into an anti-Israeli goods policy. That would be a new area for us, and one which would take some achieving.'[26]

The Co-operative Group now also owns the **Somerfield** chain, and whilst many of the latter's stores are being changed into Co-Op outlets it is unclear whether those stores still trading as Somerfield have adopted the Co-Op's stance on settlement goods.

---

[24] Correspondence between the Co-Op and Brighton and Hove Palestine Solidarity Campaign, April 2010
[25] *Ibid.*
[26] Correspondence between the Co-Op and Brighton and Hove Palestine Solidarity Campaign, December 2010.

Resistance: The Co-Op has faced pickets and repeated representations from consumers and campaigners over its sale of Israeli produce. In 2011 campaigners attended dozens of the Co Ops regional AGMs in England, Scotland and Ireland calling on the Cooperative Group to 'completely suspend trade with Carmel Agrexco, Arava and with any other businesses that are actively involved in the agricultural colonization of the West Bank.'[27]

Waitrose/John Lewis

Waitrose stocks Israeli basil, tarragon, thyme, lemon thyme, rosemary, chives, sage, oregano, mint, curly leaf parsley, 'Red Rosa' pears, sharon fruit, passion fruit, figs, lychees, oranges, lemons, grapefruit, grapes, strawberries, pomelos, pomegranates, galia melons, dragonfruit, organic medjoul dates, hadrawi dates, "Deglet Nour" dates, cherry tomatoes, sweet potatoes, 'Pamino' peppers, 'Red Romano' peppers, mixed peppers, goods from the **Tivall** vegetarian food range, 'Food for Thought' snacks supplied by **Beigel&Beigel**, cold meat, biscuits and dips.

Campaigners report that Waitrose also stock fresh produce sourced from **Valley Grown Salads**, which owns a stake in **EDOM**, a company which sources produce from the Arava region and which has exported from growers in Tomer settlement *(for more on EDOM see our earlier chapter on agriculture)*.

According to a 2008 *Observer* article the settlement farms Waitrose source from are near the illegal settlements of Mehola, Argaman and Roi in the Jordan Valley.[28]

Corporate response to BDS campaigners: Waitrose has refused to enter into any debate about the sale of Israeli goods and its management has repeatedly refused to meet with campaigners. In February 2009, a spokesperson for the store reiterated that Waitrose was "unable to arrange a meeting". In a letter to one customer, a representative of Waitrose wrote "Whatever our own views may be about Israeli products, we do not think it is right to ask our buyers to base their choice of products on any other criteria than the commercial ones of quality and value for money."[29]

Waitrose stocks goods from illegal Israeli settlements and has been unresponsive to the ITN and More 4 reports which have led other stores to label their goods more clearly. The supermarket chain stocks a large range of products sourced from **Carmel Agrexco**, including a wide variety of organic herbs and vegetables grown on Israeli settlements, mainly in the Jordan Valley, and certified as organic by the **Soil Association**.

---

[27] Correspondence between the authors and BDS activists in Brighton and Sheffield.
[28] http://www.guardian.co.uk/world/2008/jul/06/israelandthepalestinians.supermarkets, [accessed September 2011].
[29] Correspondence between a Palestine Solidarity Campaign activist and Waitrose, forwarded to the authors in 2010.

Waitrose claims that, if it ceased to deal with Israeli settlements, it would impact on Palestinian farmers. In correspondence with consumers, the retailer has described the settlement farms it works with are "joint Israeli and Palestinian" enterprises. In February 2009, a spokesperson wrote: "We currently take organic cut herbs from two farms in the West Bank on which a mixed Palestinian-Israeli workforce have worked side by side for many years."[30]

Waitrose has responded to some concerns about the conditions of labourers on settlement farms. However, the response has been to assure customers that each 'supplier' audits the relevant settlement farms using a "tight criteria" that relates to "worker hours, salaries and employment contracts."[31] This effectively means that Waitrose entrusts the auditing of settlement farms to the settlement company supplying the produce.

Waitrose claims that its technical directors have inspected its supplier farms in the West Bank. Overall, Waitrose has been one of the most intransigent British supermarkets when faced with concern over sale of Israeli produce and Israeli settler produce.

The **John Lewis Partnership**, of which Waitrose is a part, has announced that it will discontinue the sale of Ahava Dead Sea beauty products, most likely as a response to concerted BDS campaigning.[32]

Resistance: The chain has been the subject of protests and pickets across the UK, including in Brighton and London where, in 2009, protesters dressed as burglars and displayed banners claiming "Waitrose sells stolen goods". In 2011 Waitrose in Brighton was occupied in protest at the death of Palestinian activist Jawaher Abu Rahma.[33]

Sainsburys

Sainsbury's sells Israeli oranges, grapefruit, avocados, strawberries, thyme, tarragon, parsley, coriander, rosemary, passion fruit, sharon fruit, 'Shelly' mangoes, mejdoul dates, lychees, fresh figs, plums, fruit juice, minneola (tangerines), potatoes ('Desiree', 'Vivaldi', 'Rooster', white, baking, baby, salad), sweet potatoes, peppers ('Ramiro'), pickled cucumbers, pickled olives, radishes, 'Splendid' flowers, 'Basics' flowers, 'Saveur Mediterranean' hummous, turkey, smoked chicken breast, Rumples party pretzels, **Osem** croutons, **Telma** chicken soup mix and soups, feta cheese, **Tivall** vegetarian food range, 'Food for Thought' dips, table wine (red, white, rose & sparkling), **Kiddush** and **Yarden** wine, **Osem** foods and products from **Soda Club**.

---

[30] *Ibid.*
[31] *Ibid.*
[32] http://www.palestinecampaign.org/Index7b.asp?m_id=1&l1_id=4&l2_id=25&Content_ID=1693, [accessed September 2011].
[33] See, for example, http://www.indymedia.org.uk/en/2010/03/448411.html, [accessed September 2011].

Corporate response to BDS campaigners: Sainsburys has said, in correspondence with Boycott Israeli Goods Campaign supporters, that the store is 'not a political organisation and it does not boycott products from any country'.[34] In the same letter Sainsburys acknowledges that "ethical trading is a growing area of concern for our company and consumers."

Sainsburys says it is committed to 'informative labelling', despite describing one piece of produce as being from 'Gaza Strip, Israel'. After the 2007 ITN report about mislabelling of settlement Medjoul dates as 'Produce of Israel', Sainsburys admitted that it had mislabelled and has since promised to label goods from settlements as 'West Bank' produce.[35]

In 2010 Sainsburys claimed that it no longer stocked goods from Israeli settlements but that this decision was purely based on the restrictive price. The store continues to refuse to take an ethical stance on settlement produce.

Resistance: Palestine solidarity campaigners have attended Sainsburys PLC shareholders meetings several years running, in an attempt to persuade the company to stop selling Israeli goods and to label its produce more accurately. Sainsburys have been picketed across the UK by campaigners calling for a boycott of Israeli goods.[36]

Company Profiles

Debenhams sells **Dead Sea Magik** beauty products, supplied by **Kent Cosmetics**. These products contain minerals extracted from the Dead Sea and, as such, contribute to the environmental exploitation of the Dead Sea region by Israeli industry *(for more on the Dead Sea minerals industry see our earlier chapters on the Dead sea and on extractive industries)*.

Holland and Barrett sell **Dead Sea Magik** products, supplied by Kent Cosmetics, and vegetarian products made by Israeli company, **Tivall**. The store have ignored repeated approaches by Corporate Watch and others over their sale of Israeli produce. Two pickets of Holland and Barrett have been held in Brighton over the stores sale of Dead Sea beauty products.

The Soil Association is a UK organisation registered as a charity and a not-for-profit limited company. They are the largest organic certification body in the UK. In 2007 it became apparent that the Soil Association was certifying produce as organic from Israel and Israeli settlements including the Tomer settlement, in the Jordan Valley.

In 2008 Corporate Watch wrote to the Soil Association (SA) pointing out that some of the fresh goods that it certified were produced on illegal Israeli settlements in the West Bank and

---

[34] Correspondence between Sainsburys and the Palestine Solidarity Campaign, forwarded to the authors in 2009.
[35] Personal meetings between the authors and Sainsburys management, 2008-2010.
[36] See, for example, http://www.palestinecampaign.org/index7b-2.asp?m_id=1&l1_id=3&l2_id=19&content_ID=1617, [accessed September 2011].

that Palestinian workers involved in their production were underpaid, not allowed to unionise and often under 18. These were issues which had been brought to the Soil Association's attention by consumers and campaigners over a number of years. However, the association's initial reaction had been to ignore and deflect the criticisms. When Corporate Watch wrote to the SA, it clearly took the approach more seriously, presumably because of the implicit threat of publication, and agreed to meet with us.

A Corporate Watch researcher visited the SA in 2009 and met with an operations manager and a director of the organisation. The atmosphere was informal and the researcher was told that the SA was sympathetic to the concerns we had raised.

At first the SA attempted to deny the claims, stating it could not be sure where the goods it certified came from, as it took the word of the Israeli certifier, **Agrior**, that the goods were organic. In the course of Corporate Watch's discussions with the SA, which carried on for several months in the form of emails and phone calls, it became clear that the SA did certify Israeli settlement products as organic.

The SA ignored the concerns raised relating to worker's rights and repeatedly attempted to frame our concerns as being purely about the legality of the settlements. This tactic of honing in on one issue appeared to be an attempt to obfuscate wider concerns.

During our talks with the SA, our researcher mentioned that there was a possibility that a legal opinion would be produced on the legality of selling settlement goods. In the event, such a legal opinion never appeared. The SA used the absence of this legal opinion as an excuse to carry on business as normal, despite the concerns we had raised about child labour and non-payment of the minimum wage, contravening IFOAM's organic standards, which should have given the SA reason enough to reassess its supply chains.

Corporate Watch's engagement with the SA carried on until the Summer of 2009, during which time we sent the organisation videos showing that child labour was used at an Israeli settlement, Tomer. The SA admitted that it had certified food grown in the settlement. In Summer 2009, despite the severity of the issues Corporate Watch was raising, calls and emails stopped being answered.

The SA has since written to the growers it provides certification for in Israel/Palestine asking them to ensure that Israeli settlement produce is labelled as such. No move, however, has been made to exclude Israeli, or Israeli settlement goods, from organic certification.

Howard Shultz, the chairman of **Starbucks**, is thought to be an active Zionist. This is based on the fact that he was given the 'Israel 50th Anniversary Friend of Zion Tribute Award' by the staunchly Zionist **Fund of Aish HaTorah** for his services to the Zionist state by "playing a key role in promoting close alliance between the United States and Israel."

Shultz received this award in 1998 and, by 2001, Starbucks made attempts to aid Israel's failing economy by opening coffee shops in Israel through a joint venture company, **Shalom

Coffee Co, which was owned by publicly traded Israeli conglomerate **Delek Group** and **Starbucks Coffee International**. The plan was to open 15 coffee shops by the end of 2002, but Starbucks only opened 6 shops, which had to be closed down in April 2003, due to financial losses caused by Israel's recession.

Interestingly, after the shops closed, Zionists such as the **Anti-Defamation League (ADL)** criticised Starbucks for pulling out of Israel. Others, such as the **Jewish Council for Public Affairs**, defended Starbucks, reassuring us that Shultz was indeed an 'avid Zionist' and 'doing his best' for Israel.

According to **isrelate.com**, a Zionist website, Starbucks sponsored a 'Bowl 4 Israel' fundraiser for a paratrooper unit in the Israel Defense Forces in 2003.

Even though Starbucks has recently made a statement saying it is a non-political organisation there are references to its Zionist connections on a number of pro-Israel websites as well as calls to boycott the company coming from a wide variety of groups.

When sports fans from across the globe descend on East London for the Olympic games in 2012 more than half of them will have to pass through the giant **Westfield** shopping complex at Stratford City. The Westfield Group is owned by Czech-born Australian-Israeli mogul Frank Lowy, an ex-IDF commando and one of the richest men in Australia.[37] His malls can also be found in Broadmarsh, Belfast, Derby, the West Midlands, Tunbridge Wells, Guildford and Shepherds Bush.[38]

Lowy went to British-mandate Palestine at the end World War 2 and fought alongside Ariel Sharon in the Haganah during 1948.[39] His ties to the highest echelons of Israeli politics meant that he forged close relationships with former Israeli prime minister Ehud Olmert and Dan Meridor, who served as both justice minister and finance minister with Likud during the 1990s.[40] Meridor is currently vice-chair of the Institute for National Security Studies, a hawkish think tank attached to Tel Aviv University and chaired by Lowy.[41] Lowy is a major funder of the Institute for National Security Studies and a funder of *Keren Hayesod*, a partner of the Jewish Agency for Israel which works "to further the national priorities of the State of Israel".[42]

---

[37] http://www.forbes.com/lists/2011/78/australia-billionaires-11_Frank-Lowy_CXFY.html [accessed September 2011].
[38] http://uk.westfield.com/uk/ [accessed September 2011].
[39] http://www.smh.com.au/business/the-quiet-benefactor-lowys-close-ties-with-israel-20080928-4ppd.html and http://fr.jpost.com/servlet/Satellite?cid=1148482069344&pagename=JPost/JPArticle/ShowFull [accessed September 2011].
[40] *Ibid.*
[41] *Ibid.*
[42] http://www.kh-uia.org.il/EN/AboutUs/our-mission/Pages/OurMission.aspx [accessed September 2011].

Robert Dyas, a well known DIY store, sells **Sodastream** products,[43] made by **Soda Club**, at several of its stores. Soda Club have a factory in the West Bank settlement industrial zone of Ma'ale Adumim[44] *(for details see our earlier chapter on industrial zones)*.

---

[43] Direct observation by the authors, 2010.
[44] http://www.scribd.com/doc/49588306/Januar-2011-WhoProfits-Production-in-Settlements-SodaStream, [accessed September 2011].

30
Universities

Corporate Watch carried out research, using the Freedom of Information act, into several universities' investments, procurement of service providers and joint projects. The aim was to examine whether the BDS movement should target British university links with Israeli universities, investment in companies complicit in Israeli apartheid, militarism and occupation and procurement of services from complicit firms.

The following is a list of:

- university collaborations with Israeli companies and universities
- investment in, donations from or procurement from Israeli settler companies, Israeli companies, companies selling arms to Israel, companies selling Israeli goods, companies with assets or investments in Israel, companies with significant investments in any of the above.

This is not a 'boycott list', simply a guide for campaigners considering launching divestment campaigns against universities. Campaigners may wish to cherry-pick companies for divestment who, for example, are directly involved in business in Israeli settlements or aiding Israeli militarism.

The list has been compiled with the boycott call from the Palestinian Academic Boycott Initiative (PACBI) in mind:

"We, Palestinian academics and intellectuals, call upon our colleagues in the international community to comprehensively and consistently boycott all Israeli academic and cultural institutions as a contribution to the struggle to end Israel's occupation, colonization and system of apartheid, by applying the following:

1. *Refrain from participation in any form of academic and cultural cooperation, collaboration or joint projects with Israeli institutions;*
2. *Advocate a comprehensive boycott of Israeli institutions at the national and international levels, including suspension of all forms of funding and subsidies to these institutions;*
2. *Promote divestment and disinvestment from Israel by international academic institution[1]'s."*

---

[1] Read the full PACBI call at http://www.pacbi.org/etemplate.php?id=869

University links with companies complicit in Israeli apartheid, militarism and colonisation:

Company	Details	University			
		SOAS	Sussex	Edinburgh	Reading
Aviva	Aviva is an investor in several companies selling arms to Israel including **Raytheon**.[2]		Investor		
Barclays	Barclays holds shares in **Raytheon**[3] and provide market maker services to **ITT**.[4] The bank holds shares in eight Israeli companies and in **G4S, France Telecom** and **Unilever**, companies that do business in the settlements *(see our earlier section on banks)*.[5]	Service Provider	Investor / Service Provider		
BNP Paribas	BNP Paribas operates bank branches in Israel.[6]	Service Provider			
BT	BT is part of a partnership with Israeli telecommunications firm **Bezeq**.[7]	Investor / Service Provider	Service Provider		Investor
Cisco	Cisco has R&D investments in Israel.[8] The company is a customer of **Marvell Systems Solutions Israel**.[9]	Investor			

---

[2] Orbis database, Bureau Van Dijk, [accessed August 2011] and http://www.waronwant.org/campaigns/corporations-and-conflict/banking-a-the-arms-trade/inform/16327-banking-on-bloodshed, [accessed August 2011].
[3] http://www.waronwant.org/campaigns/corporations-and-conflict/banking-a-the-arms-trade/inform/16327-banking-on-bloodshed, [accessed August 2011].
[4] http://www.nyse.com/about/listed/lcddata.html?ticker=itt, [accessed August 2011].
[5] Orbis database, Bureau Van Dijk, [accessed August 2011].
[6] http://www.bnpparibas.co.il/en/locations/agencies.asp, [accessed August 2011].
[7] http://www.btplc.com/news/articles/showarticle.cfm?articleid={a21ff7f3-0965-4753-9174-6489ec5c1a83}, [accessed August 2011].
[8] http://www.slideshare.net/IsraelExport/new-mediaisrael-export-institute, [accessed August 2011].
[9] http://www.ivc-online.com/G_info.asp?objectType=1&fObjectID=9irgcbaw2en&CameFrom=GoogleSearch&utm_so

Company	Details	University			
		SOAS	Sussex	Edinburgh	Reading
Coca Cola	Coca-Cola's Israeli franchise owns **Tara** whose subsidiary has a dairy farm in the occupied Jordan Valley.[10] **Coca Cola Israel** is supplied by **Adir Plastic Packaging**, a company based in the settlement industrial zone of Mishor Adumim.[11]		Service Provider		Investor
Dell	Dell is a customer of Marvell Systems Solutions Israel.[12]	Service Provider	Service Provider		
Eden Springs	Eden Springs is an Israeli company based in the occupied Syrian Golan which extracts and bottles local water resources.[13]				Service Provider
EADS	EADS currently manufactures Eagle 1 drones together with **Israeli Aircraft Industries**.[14]			Donor	
General Electric	GE are a partner of **IC Technologies**, manufacturer of surveillance equipment used on the apartheid wall.[15]		Investor		
G4S	G4S delivers services to Israeli prisons and illegal settlements.[16]		Investor		Service Provider

urce=google&utm_medium=google_pages&utm_campaign=google_pages, [accessed August 2011].
[10] http://www.whoprofits.org/Company%20Info.php?id=783, [accessed August 2011].
[11] http://www.whoprofits.org/Company%20Info.php?id=806, [accessed August 2011].
[12] http://www.ivc-online.com/G_info.asp?objectType=1&fObjectID=9irgcbaw2en&CameFrom=GoogleSearch&utm_source=google&utm_medium=google_pages&utm_campaign=google_pages, [accessed August 2011].
[13] http://www.whoprofits.org/Company%20Info.php?id=503, [accessed August 2011].
[14] http://www.corporatewatch.org.uk/?lid=3455, [accessed August 2011].
[15] http://www.whoprofits.org/Company%20Info.php?id=917, [accessed August 2011].
[16] http://corporateoccupation.wordpress.com/2011/03/27/g4s-delivers-services-to-israeli-prisons-and-

Company	Details	University			
		SOAS	Sussex	Edinburgh	Reading
Hebrew University	Israeli University with part of its campus on stolen Palestinian land in East Jerusalem.	Service Provider			
Heineken	Heineken own 40% of the Israeli company **Tempo Beverages**, which has 44.7% share capital and voting rights in **Barkan Wineries**, producer of wine from the occupied Syrian Golan.[17]			Investor	
Hewlett Packard	HP operates in Ra'anana high-tech park and has a laboratory in Haifa's Technion.[18] The company is also a provider of the Basel system, an automated biometric access control system for Palestinian workers through subsidiary **EDS Israel**.[19]	Service Provider			
Honeywell	Honeywell is a partner of **ICx Technologies**.[20]	Service Provider			Service Provider
HSBC	HSBC has branches in Israel and is an investor in **General Dynamics, Raytheon, Boeing, BAE Systems** and **ITT**, suppliers of arms to Israel.[21] The bank has shares in **F&C Reit** and **Veolia**.	Investor	Investor	Investor	Investor

---

illegal-settlements/, [accessed August 2011].
[17] http://www.whoprofits.org/Company%20Info.php?id=466, [accessed August 2011].
[18] http://www.hpl.hp.com/israel/, [accessed August 2011].
[19] http://www.whoprofits.org/Company%20Info.php?id=624, [accessed August 2011].
[20] http://www.whoprofits.org/Company%20Info.php?id=917, [accessed August 2011].
[21] Orbis database, Bureau Van Dijk, [accessed September 2011].

Company	Details	University			
		SOAS	Sussex	Edinburgh	Reading
IBM	IBM has been working in Israel since the 1970s and has facilities in Tel Aviv, Herzliya, Rehovot, Jerusalem and Haifa. The company also run an R&D lab on **Haifa University** campus, employing over 500 hundred staff and students.[22] The lab collaborates with other multinational companies, including **Samsung**.[23]			Service Provider	Investor
ISS	ISS provides 'manpower' services in Israeli settlements.[24]	Service Provider			
John Lewis	**Waitrose**, a part of **John Lewis**, sells goods from Israel and Israeli settlements.[25]	Investor			
Johnson& Johnson	Johnson&Johnson opened an office in Israel near Shfayim. Took-over **Biosense**, a Haifa-based producer of medical equipment.[26]	Investor		Investor	
Lloyds TSB	Lloyds hold shares in BAE, supplier of arms to Israel.[27]	Investor	Investor / Service Provider	Investor	

---

[22]http://www.israel21c.org/technology/ibm-israel-and-samsung-develop-software-reuse-technology, [accessed August 2011].
[23]*Ibid.*
[24]http://www.whoprofits.org/Company%20Info.php?id=855, [accessed August 2011].
[25]http://www.easi-piesi.org/Waitrose.html, [accessed August 2011].
[26]http://www.israelemb.org/economic/uscompanies.htm, [accessed August 2011].
[27]Orbis database, Burea Van Dijk, [accessed August 2011].

Company	Details	University			
		SOAS	Sussex	Edinburgh	Reading
L'Oreal	L'Oreal operates in Israel. Its Israeli subsidiary's HQ is in Migdal Ha'emek, on land expropriated from the Palestinian community of Mujaydil.[28] L'Oreal owns **Vichy**, whose products are sold/promoted in several pharmacies in settlements in the West Bank.[29]	Investor		Investor	
Meggitt	Meggitt are a supplier of arms to Israel. Specifically avionics for Apache Helicopters.[30]			Investor	
Mitsubishi	Mistsubishi's products are distributed in Israel by Israeli company **Mayer Cars and Trucks**, which owns a depot in the Mishor Adumim industrial zone.[31] Mitsubishi generators are distributed by **Orcal Industries and Mechanisation**, whose generators are used in Atarot military checkpoint in the West Bank.[32]	Investor			

---

[28] http://electronicintifada.net/content/boycott-loreal-makeup-israeli-apartheid/887, [accessed August 2011].
[29] http://corporateoccupation.wordpress.com/2010/12/22/open-letter-to-vichy/, [accessed August 2011].
[30] http://www.stoparmingisrael.org/info/companies.php, [accessed August 2011].
[31] http://www.whoprofits.org/Company%20Info.php?id=798, [accessed August 2011].
[32] http://www.whoprofits.org/Company%20Info.php?id=678, [accessed August 2011].

Company	Details	University			
		SOAS	Sussex	Edinburgh	Reading
Nestle	Nestle owns 50.1% of the Israeli **Osem** corporation. Osem plans to build a factory for Nestle in Israel,[33] and is a customer of 2 companies based in settlements.[34]	Investor			
Prudential	Prudential has investments in several companies supplying arms to Israel including **Boeing** and **Raytheon**.[35]	Investor	Investor / Service Provider	Investor	Investor
Selex	Selex are a military communications company working on a joint communications project with Israeli company **Maxtech**. The project has military applications.[36]			Donor	
Sainsburys	Sainsburys sell Israeli and Israeli settlement produce.[37]		Investor		
Siemens	Siemen's traffic control systems are installed by its Israeli representative, **Orad Group**, on apartheid roads (roads on which only Israelis are allowed to travel).[38]		Service Provider		
Tesco	Tesco sells Israeli and Israeli settlement products.[39]	Investor	Investor	Investor	

[33] http://www.globes.co.il/serveen/globes/docview.asp?did=1000645119&fid=1725, [accessed August 2011].
[34] http://www.whoprofits.org/Company%20Info.php?id=524 and http://www.whoprofits.org/Company%20Info.php?id=518, [accessed August 2011].
[35] Orbis database, Bureau Van Dijk, [accessed August 2011].
[36] http://www.maxtechnetworks.com/press/pr_130410.aspx, [accessed August 2011].
[37] http://corporateoccupation.wordpress.com/2009/02/23/profiting-from-the-occupation-agrexco/, [accessed August 2011].
[38] http://www.whoprofits.org/Search%20Results.php?sStr=siemens, [accessed August 2011].
[39] http://corporateoccupation.wordpress.com/2009/02/23/profiting-from-the-occupation-supermarkets-tesco, [accessed August 2011].

Company	Details	University			
		SOAS	Sussex	Edinburgh	Reading
Thermo Fischer	Thermo Fischer is a partner of **ICx Technlogies**, supplier of security systems for the settlements, apartheid wall and checkpoints.[40]	Investor	Service Provider		
3M	3M is a customer of **Ofertex**, an Israeli company based in Barkan settlement Industrial Zone in the occupied West Bank.[41]	Service Provider			
Unilever	Unilever fully owns **Beigel&Beigel**, a baked goods factory in Barkan settlement industrial zone, in the occupied West Bank.[42]	Investor	Investor		
Veolia	Veolia is part of the Citypass consortium building a tramway through occupied East Jerusalem. The company also operates buses between Israel's West Bank settlements and maintains a waste dump and settler waste collection services in the occupied Jordan Valley.[43]		Service Provider		
Wal Mart	Wal Mart owns **Asda** which sells Israeli and Israeli settlement produce.[44]			Investor	

---

[40] http://www.whoprofits.org/Company%20Info.php?id=917, [accessed August 2011].
[41] http://www.whoprofits.org/Company%20Info.php?id=813, [accessed August 2011].
[42] http://www.whoprofits.org/Company%20Info.php?id=579, [accessed August 2011].
[43] http://www.bigcampaign.org/veolia/, [accessed August 2011].
[44] http://www.easi-piesi.org/asda.html, [accessed August 2011].

Relationships with Israeli Universities

SOAS Faculty of Arts and Humanities is funding several academics who are participating in a joint programme with the **Hebrew University** (Israel) and **Al Quds University** (Palestine) called 'Sensory City'.[45] The project explores how "sensory landscapes, performed behaviours and the built environment shape narratives of place, space and community in the Old City of Jerusalem."

Academics in the Department of the Study of Religions are currently preparing a conference on "Jewish Art in its Roman-Byzantine Context" in conjunction with the Hebrew University Jerusalem. This conference is scheduled to take place in Jerusalem in May 2012.

Both projects break the boycott of Israeli academic institutions called for by the Palestinian Boycott National Committee (BNC) and the Palestine Academic Boycott Initiative (PACBI).

One course at **Oxford University** has an Israeli sponsor organisation: 'Tradition and its Discontents; Ruptures in the Abrahamic Religions'. The sponsor is **Yad Hanadiv**, which acts in Israel on behalf of a number of Rothschild family philanthropic trusts. Projects undertaken by Yad Hanadiv have included the building of the Israeli Knesset and the Israeli Supreme Court.[46]

Lancaster University is part of an EU funded project working jointly on communications with the Israeli company **Yitran Communications** and the **Israel Electric Company**.[47]

Reading University signed a memorandum of understanding with the University of Haifa in 2010 to promote "academic, scientific and cultural collaborations between the institutions". The memo goes on to set out several areas of collaboration aiming to:

8. "Foster opportunities for collaborative research, publications and collouqia, particularly in the field of drama education and initial teacher training;
9. Promote staff and postgraduate research student exchanges for the purpose of personal and professional development in the field of arts education;
10. Extend collaboration and develop taught student exchange links, especially in relation to the teaching of theatre, music, art and English language and literature;
11. Develop taught programmes, particularly in the field of drama education and initial teacher training;
12. Exchange academic materials and publications;
13. Provide cultural and intellectual enrichment opportunities for staff and students."

---

[45] http://www.soasalumni.org/Page.aspx?pid=598, [accessed August 2011].
[46] http://www.yadhanadiv.org.il/general-page/about-yad-hanadiv, [accessed August 2011].
[47] http://cordis.europa.eu/fetch?CALLER=PROJ_ICT&ACTION=D&CAT=PROJ&RCN=93781, [accessed August 2011].

The memorandum is not financially or legally binding and can be terminated with three months notice by either university.

The signatory of the memo for Haifa was Yossi Ben-Artzi, the university's rector. Ben Artzi had previously made the following statement: "Haifa University is proud to continue being the academic home for the security forces and to teach the IDF leadership a large number of different and diverse perspectives. This is the sole way to be better people and better commanders."[48] Ben-Artzi is also implicated in the harassment of Israeli historian Ilan Pappe because of his outspoken criticism of Israel's ethnic cleansing while Pappe was in post at Haifa.[49]

---

[48] http://cosmos.ucc.ie/cs1064/jabowen/IPSC/php/authors.php?auid=3698, [accessed August 2011].
[49] http://ceasefiremagazine.co.uk/new-in-ceasefire/book-review-pappe/, [accessed August 2011].

31
Pension Funds

British pension funds have a range of investments in companies complicit in Israeli colonisation, militarism, occupation. The table below lists investments in:

- Israeli companies
- Companies working in settlements
- Companies selling military equipment to the state of Israel
- Companies operating in Israel
- Investors in any of the above
- Companies in business relationships with any of the above

KEY

1. North Yorkshire pension Fund
2. Universities Superannuation Scheme
3. Lothian pension fund
4. Camden pension fund
5. East Sussex pension fund
6. Surrey pension fund

Company	Details	1	2	3	4	5	6
3m	3M is a customer of Ofertex, an Israeli company based in Barkan settlement Industrial Zone in the occupied West Bank.[1]	X					
Alstom	Alstom is a French company involved in the construction of a light railway in occupied East Jerusalem[2]		X	X	X	X	X
American Express	Bank Hapoalim, through its subsidiary, **Isracard**, is the franchisee for **AMEX** in Israel.[3] Hapoalim operates bank branches on Israeli settlements.[4]	X					
Apple	Apple is a customer of **Marvell Systems Solutions Israel**.[5]	X	X		X		

---

[1] http://www.whoprofits.org/Company%20Info.php?id=813, [accessed August 2011].
[2] http://www.whoprofits.org/Company%20Info.php?id=580, [accessed August 2011].
[3] http://www.globes.co.il/serveen/globes/docview.asp?did=769384, [accessed August 2011].
[4] http://www.whoprofits.org/Company%20Info.php?id=570, [accessed August 2011].
[5] http://www.ivc-online.com/G_info.asp?objectType=1&fObjectID=9irgcbaw2en&CameFrom=GoogleSearch&utm_source=google&utm_medium=google_pages&utm_campaign=google_pages, [accessed August 2011].

Company	Details	Pension Fund					
		1	2	3	4	5	6
AS&E American Science and Engineering	Supplier of cargo inspection scanner systems to the Israeli army.[6]	X					
Assa Abloy[7]	Assa Abloy manufactures and distributes locks worldwide. The group owns **Mul-T-Lock**, which has a factory at the Barkan Industrial Zone.[8]		X				X
Aviva	Aviva is an investor in several companies selling arms to Israel including **Raytheon**.[9]	X	X	X		X	X
AXA	AXA owns shares in **BAE Systems, Boeing** and **Raytheon**, suppliers of arms to Israel.[10]	X	X	X	X	X	X
BAE Systems	BAE is a supplier of arms to Israel.[11]	X	X	X			
Barclays	Barclays holds shares in **Raytheon**[12] and provide market maker services to **ITT**,[13] The bank holds shares in 8 Israeli companies and in **G4S, France Telecom** and **Unilever**, companies that do business in the settlements *(see our earlier section on banks)*.[14]	X	X	X	X	X	X
Bezeq	Bezeq is an Israeli state owned telecommunications firm. It refuses to provide services to unrecognised villages in Naqab *(see our earlier chapter on telecommunications)*.		X				
Blackrock	Blackrock is an investor in **CRH**, which has a controlling stake in Nesher, supplier of cement for the wall.[15]				X		X X

---

[6] http://www.whoprofits.org/Company%20Info.php?id=612, [accessed August 2011].
[7] http://www.whoprofits.org/Company%20Info.php?id=481, [accessed August 2011] and observation by Corporate Watch researchers, April 2010.
[8] *Ibid.*
[9] Orbis database, Bureau Van Dijk, [accessed August 2011].
http://www.waronwant.org/campaigns/corporations-and-conflict/banking-a-the-arms-trade/inform/16327-banking-on-bloodshed, [accessed August 2011].
[10] Orbis Database, Bureau Van Dijk, [accessed August 2011].
[11] http://www.baesystems.com/WorldwideLocations/Regions/MiddleEast/Israel/, [accessed August 2011].
[12] http://www.waronwant.org/campaigns/corporations-and-conflict/banking-a-the-arms-trade/inform/16327-banking-on-bloodshed, [accessed August 2011].
[13] http://www.nyse.com/about/listed/lcddata.html?ticker=itt, [accessed August 2011].
[14] Orbis database, Bureau Van Dijk, [accessed August 2011].
[15] http://www.whoprofits.org/Company%20Info.php?id=614, [accessed August 2011].

Company	Details	Pension Fund					
		1	2	3	4	5	6
Blockbuster	Blockbuster stores and vending machines can be found across Israel. Blockbuster vending machines can be seen in the settlements of Modi'in Illit, Pisgat Ze'ev, Ariel,[16] and Givat Ze'ev. [17]						X
Blue Nile	Blue Nile sells diamonds hand-crafted in Israel.[18]						X
BNP Paribas	BNP Paribas operates branches in Israel.[19]	X	X	X	X	X	X
Boeing	Boeing supplies arms to Israel.[20]	X			X	X	
BT	BT is part of a partnership with Israeli telecommunications firm **Bezeq**.[21]		X	X			X
Carlsberg	Carlsberg's Israeli distributor is the **Central Bottling Company** which owns **Tara**, whose subsidiary, **Meshek Zuriel Dairy**, has a dairy farm in the Jordan Valley.[22]				X	X	X
Caterpillar	Caterpillar is a supplier of military bulldozers to Israel.[23]	X			X	X	
Chemring	Chemring is a supplier of arms to Israel.[24]		X				X

KEY

1. North Yorkshire pension Fund
2. Universities Superannuation Scheme
3. Lothian pension fund
4. Camden pension fund
5. East Sussex pension fund
6. Surrey pension fund

---

[16]Corporate Watch personal observation, March 2010
[17]http://www.whoprofits.org/Company%20Info.php?id=500, [accessed August 2011].
[18]http://www.countercurrents.org/clinton250611.htm, [accessed August 2011].
[19]http://www.bnpparibas.co.il/en/locations/agencies.asp, [accessed August 2011].
[20]Data from Import Genius database, [accessed March 2010].
[21]http://www.btplc.com/news/articles/showarticle.cfm?articleid={a21ff7f3-0965-4753-9174-6489ec5c1a83}, [accessed August 2011].
[22]http://www.whoprofits.org/Company%20Info.php?id=783, [accessed August 2011].
[23]http://www.waronwant.org/campaigns/justice-for-palestine/hide/inform/17109-caterpillar-the-alternative-report, [accessed August 2011].
[24]http://business.timesonline.co.uk/tol/business/movers_and_shakers/article7066375.ece, [accessed August 2011].

Company	Details	Pension Fund					
		1	2	3	4	5	6
Chevron	Chevron's Israeli representative is **Dor Alon**, the Israel company with a monopoly on the sale of fuel to the Gaza Strip.[25]	X	X	X		X	
Cisco	Cisco has R&D investments in Israel. The company is a customer of **Marvell Systems Solutions Israel**.[26]	X	X	X	X	X	X
Cobham	Cobham is a supplier of arms to Israel. The company manufactures parts for the F-35 fighter plane,[27] which Israel has acquired to replace their F16s as the IAF's main attack weapon. Cobham's Israeli representative is **Bartek Aviation**.[28]			X			
Coca Cola	Coca-Cola's Israeli franchise owns **Tara**. Tara's subsidiary has a dairy farm in the occupied Jordan Valley.[29] **Coca Cola Israel** is supplied by **Adir Plastic Packaging**, a company based in the settlement industrial zone of Mishor Adumim.[30]	X	X	X	X	X	
Covidien	Covidien are a customer of **Avgol**, which have a factory in Barkan settlement industrial zone.[31]	X			X		
CRH	CRH has a controlling stake in **Nesher**, supplier of cement for the apartheid wall.[32]			X			
Danone	Danone operates a research institute in Israel.[33]	X	X	X	X	X	
Dell	Dell is a customer of **Marvell Systems Solutions Israel**.[34]			X			X

---

[25]http://www.whoprofits.org/Company%20Info.php?id=469, [accessed August 2011].
[26]http://www.ivc-online.com/G_info.asp?objectType=1&fObjectID=9irgcbaw2en&CameFrom=GoogleSearch&utm_source=google&utm_medium=google_pages&utm_campaign=google_pages, [accessed August 2011].
[27]http://www.dailytech.com/Israel+to+Buy+20+F35+Fighters/article19837.htm, [accessed August 2011].
[28]http://www.cobham.com/about-cobham/mission-systems/about-us/life-support/davenport/global-support/bartek-aviation.aspx, [accessed August 2011].
[29]http://www.whoprofits.org/Company%20Info.php?id=783, [accessed August 2011].
[30]http://www.whoprofits.org/Company%20Info.php?id=806, [accessed August 2011].
[31]http://www.whoprofits.org/Company%20Info.php?id=456, [accessed August 2011].
[32]http://www.whoprofits.org/Company%20Info.php?id=614, [accessed August 2011].
[33]http://www.danoneinstitute.org/our_network/fiche_institut.php?other_org_id=9, [accessed August 2011].
[34]http://www.ivc-online.com/G_info.asp?objectType=1&fObjectID=9irgcbaw2en&CameFrom=GoogleSearch&utm_so

Company	Details	Pension Fund					
		1	2	3	4	5	6
Estee Lauder	Ron Lauder is a JNF board member.[35]						X
Finmeccanica	Finmeccanica has a contract with **Israel Post**.[36]			X			X
France Telecom	France Telecom control **Orange** whose franchisee, **Partner Communications**, own communications infrastructure in Israeli settlements.[37]	X	X				
G4S	G4S delivers services to Israeli prisons and illegal settlements.[38]				X		X
Glaxosmithkline	GSK distributes within Israel.[39]	X					
Google	Google operates an R&D centre in Israel.	X	X	X	X	X	
Heidelberg Cement	Heidelberg Cement bought Hanson (UK) and thus became the owner of three plants in West Bank settlements and one Israeli aggregates quarry in the occupied West Bank through **Hanson Israel**.[40]	X	X	X	X	X	
Heineken	Heineken own 40% of the Israeli company, **Tempo Beverages**, which has 44.7% share capital and voting rights in **Barkan Wineries**, producer of wine from the occupied Syrian Golan.[41]				X		X

KEY

1. North Yorkshire pension Fund
2. Universities Superannuation Scheme
3. Lothian pension fund
4. Camden pension fund
5. East Sussex pension fund
6. Surrey pension fund

---

urce=google&utm_medium=google_pages&utm_campaign=google_pages, [accessed August 2011].
[35] http://www.jnf.org/about-jnf/our-leadership/board-members/ronald-s-lauder.html, [accessed August 2011].
[36] http://www.euroisrael.com/2010/10/thanks-to-euroisrael-elsagdatamat-finmeccanica-group-wins-a-10m-euro-contract-with-the-israel-post/?lang=en, [accessed August 2011].
[37] http://www.whoprofits.org/Company%20Info.php?id=713, [accessed August 2011].
[38] http://corporateoccupation.wordpress.com/2011/03/27/g4s-delivers-services-to-israeli-prisons-and-illegal-settlements/, [accessed August 2011].
[39] http://www.gsk.com/worldwide/il.htm, [accessed August 2011].
[40] http://www.whoprofits.org/Company%20Info.php?id=597, [accessed August 2011].
[41] http://www.whoprofits.org/Company%20Info.php?id=466, [accessed August 2011].

The UK - Bringing the Fight Home: Pension Funds

Company	Details	Pension Fund 1	2	3	4	5	6
Hewlett Packard	HP operates in Ra'anana high-tech park and has a laboratory in Haifa's Technion.[42] The company is also a provider of the Basel system, an automated biometric access control system for Palestinian workers through subsidiary **EDS Israel**.[43]	X	X		X	X	X
Honda	**Honda's** Israeli distributor, **Mayer's Cars and Trucks**, own a controlling share in **Merkavim**, which manufactures armoured buses used in the settlements.[44]				X		
HSBC	HSBC has branches in Israel and is an investor in **General Dynamics, Raytheon, Boeing, BAE Systems** and **ITT**. suppliers of arms to Israel.[45] The bank has shares in **F&C Reit** and **Veolia**.	X	X	X	X	X	X
Ingersoll Rand	Ingersoll Rand owns **Recognition Systems (RSI)**, supplier of biometric systems for Israeli checkpoints.[46]	X			X	X	
Intel	Intel operates in Israel.	X					
Investec	Investec Sponsored the **Jewish National Fund's** 2011 Gala Dinner in London.[47]		X	X			
Israel Chemicals Ltd	ICL owns the **Dead Sea Works** on the South Coast of the Dead Sea. The company supply chemicals to **Ahava**, whose factory is in Mitzpe Shalem. The exploitation of the Dead Sea by Israeli companies, of which ICL is the protagonist, is causing shrinkage of the Dead Sea.[48]				X		
ITT	ITT is a supplier of arms to Israel.[49]						X
John Lewis	**Waitrose**, a part of **John Lewis**, sells goods from Israel and Israeli settlements.[50]			X			

---

[42] http://www.hpl.hp.com/israel/, [accessed August 2011].
[43] http://www.whoprofits.org/Company%20Info.php?id=624, [accessed August 2011].
[44] *Ibid.* Also see www.mct.co.il, [accessed August 2011].
[45] Orbis database, Bureau Van Dijk, [accessed September 2011].
[46] http://www.whoprofits.org/Company%20Info.php?id=646, [accessed August 2011].
[47] http://www.jnf.co.uk/events.html, [accessed August 2011].
[48] http://www.washingtonpost.com/wp-dyn/content/article/2005/05/18/AR2005051802400_pf.html, [accessed August 2011].
[49] http://defense.itt.com/ausa2010/assets/ES/DataSheets/ITT_ES_RRAS_Bro_R3.pdf, [accessed August 2011], p.10.
[50] http://www.easi-piesi.org/Waitrose.html, [accessed August 2011].

Company	Details	Pension Fund					
		1	2	3	4	5	6
Johnson & Johnson	Johnson&Johnson opened an office in Israel near Shfayim. Took-over **Biosense**, a Haifa-based producer of medical equipment[51]	X		X	X	X	
L'Oreal	L'Oreal operates in Israel. Its Israeli subsidiary's HQ is in Migdal Ha'emek, on land expropriated from the Palestinian community of Mujaydil.[52] L'Oreal own **Vichy**, whose products are sold/promoted in several pharmacies in settlements in the West Bank.[53]		X	X	X	X	
L3 Communications	L3 Communications supply security systems to the Israeli Airports Authority.[54]						X
Legal&General	Legal&General are an investor in **Boeing** and **Raytheon**, suppliers of arms to Israel.[55]	X	X	X		X	X
Lloyds	Lloyds is the principal banker for **BAE**.[56]	X	X	X	X	X	X
Maersk	Maersk make numerous voyages from Israeli ports to Europe and the US. Companies which have shipped goods on Maersk's vessels include **Carmel Agrexco**, arms company **Elbit** and settlement company **Avgol** (based in Barkan settlement industrial zone).[57]				X		

KEY

1. North Yorkshire pension Fund
2. Universities Superannuation Scheme
3. Lothian pension fund
4. Camden pension fund
5. East Sussex pension fund
6. Surrey pension fund

---

[51] http://www.israelemb.org/economic/uscompanies.htm, [accessed August 2011].
[52] http://electronicintifada.net/content/boycott-loreal-makeup-israeli-apartheid/887, [accessed August 2011].
[53] http://corporateoccupation.wordpress.com/2010/12/22/open-letter-to-vichy/, [accessed August 2011].
[54] http://www.airport-int.com/article/l3-communications-selected-israel-airport-authority-supply-examiner-explosive-detection-system-ben-gurion-airport.html, [accessed August 2011].
[55] Orbis database, Bureau Van Dijk, [accessed August 2011].
[56] *Ibid.*
[57] Import Genius database, [accessed March 2010].

Company	Details	Pension Fund					
		1	2	3	4	5	6
Marks and Spencer	M&S are a customer of **Delta Galil**, Israeli textile company manufacturing goods in Barkan settlement industrial zone.[58]		X	X			
McDonalds	McDonalds operate a franchise in Israel.		X		X	X	
Meggitt	Meggitt is a supplier of arms to Israel. Specifically avionics for Apache helicopters.[59]	X	X				
Microsoft	Microsoft have a development Centre' in Ra'anana, north of Tel Aviv.[60]	X	X	X		X	X
Mitsubishi	Mitsubishi's products are distributed in Israel by Israeli company **Mayer Cars and Trucks**, which owns a depot in the Mishor Adumim settlement industrial zone.[61] Mitsubishi generators are distributed by **Orcal Industries and Mechanisation**, whose generators are used in Atarot military checkpoint in the West Bank.[62]	X		X	X	X	X
Mizrahi Tefahot Bank	Mizrahi Tefahot is an Israeli bank providing financing for the construction of housing projects in Israeli settlements, loans and financial services to local authorities of settlements and loans for Israeli businesses operating in the occupied territory. The bank also provides mortgages for home-buyers in settlements and has branches in the West Bank settlements of Alon Shvut, Karnei Shomron, Kedumim and Ramat Eshkol.[63]					X	

---

[58] http://www.textilesintelligence.com/tistoi/index.cfm?pageid=3&repid=TISTOI&issueid=141&artid=1503, [accessed August 2011].
[59] http://www.stoparmingisrael.org/info/companies.php, [accessed August 2011].
[60] http://www.microsoft.com/Israel/rnd/, [accessed August 2011].
[61] http://www.whoprofits.org/Company%20Info.php?id=798, [accessed August 2011].
[62] http://www.whoprofits.org/Company%20Info.php?id=678, [accessed August 2011].
[63] http://www.whoprofits.org/Company%20Info.php?id=468, [accessed August 2011].

Company	Details	Pension Fund					
		1	2	3	4	5	6
Nestle	Nestle owns 50.1% of the Israeli **Osem** corporation. Osem plans to build a factory for Nestle in Israel.[64] Osem is a customer of two companies based in the settlements.[65]	X	X	X	X	X	X
Occidental	Occidental is a shareholder in **Dolphin Energy**, which is a shareholder in **Paz**.[66] Paz has a monopoly on the sale of fuel to the PA in the West Bank and, as such, is taking advantage of the captive Palestinian market created by Israel's occupation.[67]		X		X	X	X
Pepsico	Pepsico's Israeli distributor is **Tempo Beverages**, which has 44.7% share capital and voting rights in **Barkan Wineries**, producer of wine from the occupied Syrian Golan.[68]				X		
Procter and Gamble	Customer of **Avgol.** Avgol have a factory in Barkan settlement industrial zone.[69]	X	X	X	X	X	
Prudential	Prudential has investments in several companies supplying arms to Israel including **Boeing** and **Raytheon**.[70]		X	X	X	X	X
Raytheon	Raytheon is a supplier of arms to Israel.[71]						X

KEY

1. North Yorkshire pension Fund
2. Universities Superannuation Scheme
3. Lothian pension fund
4. Camden pension fund
5. East Sussex pension fund
6. Surrey pension fund

---

[64] http://www.globes.co.il/serveen/globes/docview.asp?did=1000645119&fid=1725, [accessed August 2011].
[65] http://www.whoprofits.org/Company%20Info.php?id=524 and http://www.whoprofits.org/Company%20Info.php?id=518, [accessed August 2011].
[66] http://www.dolphinenergy.com/Public/our-company/aboutus-shareholders.htm, [accessed August 2011].
[67] http://www.whoprofits.org/Company%20Info.php?id=470, [accessed August 2011].
[68] http://www.whoprofits.org/Company%20Info.php?id=466, [accessed August 2011].
[69] http://www.whoprofits.org/Company%20Info.php?id=456, [accessed August 2011].
[70] Orbis database, Bureau Van Dijk, [accessed August 2011].
[71] http://www.bigcampaign.org/israel-and-the-arms-trade/, [accessed August 2011].

Company	Details	Pension Fund					
		1	2	3	4	5	6
Rolls Royce	Rolls Royce is an arms manufacturer working on joint projects with Israeli companies.[72] The company manufactures components for the F-35, which Israel is currently purchasing to replace their F16s.[73]		X	X			X
Sainsbury	Sainsbury sells Israeli and Israeli settlement produce.[74]	X	X	X			
Santander	Santander is an investor in **BAE Systems**[75]	X	X	X	X	X	X
Siemens	Siemen's traffic control systems are installed by its Israeli representative, **Orad Group**, on apartheid roads (roads on which only Israelis are allowed to travel).[76]		X	X	X	X	X
Smiths Group	Smiths Group is a supplier of arms to Israel. Specifically components for F-16 aircraft and for Apache helicopters to the Israeli air force.[77]		X	X			X
Tesco	Tesco sells Israeli and Israeli settlement products.	X	X	X	X	X	X
Teva	Teva is an Israeli pharmaceutical company.				X	X	
Terex	Distributes **American Truck Company** trucks (used to build the apartheid wall and the A1 trainline) through **COMASCO**.[78]	X					
Thales	Thales is an arms company working jointly with **Israeli Aerospace Industries** and **Elbit**.[79]				X		X

---

[72] http://www.prnewswire.co.uk/cgi/news/release?id=15074, [accessed August 2011].
[73] http://www.prnewswire.co.uk/cgi/news/release?id=15074, [accessed August 2011].
[74] http://corporateoccupation.wordpress.com/2009/02/23/profiting-from-the-occupation-agrexco/, [accessed August 2011].
[75] Orbis database, Bureau Van Dijk, [accessed August 2011].
[76] http://www.whoprofits.org/Search%20Results.php?sStr=siemens, [accessed August 2011].
[77] www.caat.org.uk/publications/countries/israel-0605.pdf, [accessed August 2011] and http://www.stoparmingisrael.org/info/companies.php, [accessed August 2011] and http://corporateoccupation.wordpress.com/2009/02/23/profiting-from-the-occupation-supermarkets-tesco, [accessed August 2011].
[78] http://www.whoprofits.org/Company%20Info.php?id=916, [accessed August 2011].
[79] http://www.satnews.com/cgi-bin/story.cgi?number=1434977902, [accessed August 2011] and http://corporateoccupation.wordpress.com/2010/11/08/israeli-company-to-supply-british-forces-in-afghanistan/, [accessed August 2011].

Company	Details	Pension Fund					
		1	2	3	4	5	6
Thermo Fischer	Thermo Fischer is a partner of **ICx Technlogies**, supplier of security systems for the settlements, apartheid wall and checkpoints.[80]	X					
Total	Total own part of **Dolphin Energy**, a shareholder in **Paz**.[81] Paz has a monopoly on the sale of fuel to the PA in the West Bank and, as such, is taking advantage of the captive Palestinian market created by Israel's occupation.[82]		X	X			X
Toyota	Toyota is a shareholder in **Manitou**, whose cranes have been used in construction and maintenance of the apartheid wall.[83]						X
Tyco Electronics	Tyco Electronics is a global provider of electronic parts based in Switzerland. In 1999 Tyco merged with **Raychem**. Raychem components were found on pieces of the apartheid wall close to the West Bank village of Jayyous.	X			X	X	
UBS	UBS is a shareholder in **CRH**[84], which owns a controlling share in **Mashav** which owns **Nesher**, supplier of cement for the apartheid wall[85]				X	X	X

KEY

1. North Yorkshire pension Fund
2. Universities Superannuation Scheme
3. Lothian pension fund
4. Camden pension fund
5. East Sussex pension fund
6. Surrey pension fund

---

[80] http://www.whoprofits.org/Company%20Info.php?id=917, [accessed August 2011].
[81] http://www.dolphinenergy.com/Public/our-company/aboutus-shareholders.htm, [accessed August 2011].
[82] http://www.whoprofits.org/Company%20Info.php?id=470, [accessed August 2011].
[83] http://www.whoprofits.org/Company%20Info.php?id=561, [accessed August 2011].
[84] http://crh-annual-report-2010.production.investis.com/, [accessed August 2011].
[85] http://www.whoprofits.org/Company%20Info.php?id=614, [accessed August 2011].

Company	Details	Pension Fund					
		1	2	3	4	5	6
Ultra Electronics	Ultra Electronics is an arms company working jointly with Israeli state owned company **Rafael**.[86]		X				X
Unilever	Unilever fully owns **Beigel&Beigel**, a baked goods factory in Barkan industrial zone, in the occupied West Bank.[87]	X	X	X		X	X
Veolia	Veolia is part of the Citypass consortium building a tramway through occupied East Jerusalem. The company also operate buses between Israel's West Bank settlements and maintains a waste dump and settler waste collection services in the occupied Jordan Valley.[88]		X	X			
Vodafone	**Vodafone Ventures** is a shareholder in mobile company **Perfecto Mobile**, which trades in Israel.[89]	X			X	X	X
Volvo	Volvo is a supplier of construction equipment used in building the wall and settlements.[90]			X			
Wal Mart	Wal Mart owns **Asda** which sells Israeli and Israeli settlement produce.[91]	X	X	X	X	X	X

---

[86] http://www.ultra-os.com/acoustic.php, [accessed August 2011].
[87] http://www.whoprofits.org/Company%20Info.php?id=579, [accessed August 2011].
[88] http://www.bigcampaign.org/veolia/, [accessed August 2011].
[89] http://uk.reuters.com/article/2010/06/22/perfecto-vodafone-idUKLDE65L1W620100622, [accessed August 2011].
[90] http://corporateoccupation.wordpress.com/2010/06/16/volvo-equipment-effective-tool-in-the-israeli-occupation-of-palestine/, [accessed August 2011].
[91] http://www.easi-piesi.org/asda.html, [accessed August 2011].

32
Charities

A number of organisations that raise funds for the Israeli army and illegal settlements currently enjoy charity status in the UK. This grants them a wide range of tax benefits.[1]

British charities have sent over £1 million to Israeli West Bank settlements in the last five years. In recent years Israeli *yeshivas*, Jewish religious education institutions, have received over half a million pounds. Beitar Iillit received £70,000 over three years, Ramot Polin received £200,000 in five years, Kfar Etzion received £70,000 in four years and Alon Shvut received £120,000 in 2009.[2]

The table below reveals details of 15 UK charities whose recent accounts show that they have funded settlements, IDF projects or *Hesder Yeshivas* (colleges in Israel that combine religious study with IDF training).

There are a further 24 charities in the UK that have funded settlements or the IDF in the past but that no longer give a breakdown in their accounts of who they donate money to.[3]

Campaigners have sought to draw attention to, and challenge, the charity status of some of these organisations, arguing that support for illegal settlements and for an occupying army that is regularly accused of committing human rights abuses runs contrary to the principles of charity work and may arguably be illegal under domestic and international law.[4]

---

[1] These benefits include exemption from capital gains tax, income tax and corporation tax on income; the ability to recover income tax deducted from deeds of covenant and receipts under gift aid; exemption from inheritance tax for donors to institutions; and substantial relief on business rates. See http://www.lfhe.ac.uk/governance/legal/charitablebenefits.html, [accessed September 2011].
[2] All information taken from charity accounts.
[3] The information in the table was uncovered by searching the charity commission website and charity annual accounts.
[4] For the relevant domestic legislation see
http://www.legislation.gov.uk/ukpga/2001/17/notes/division/4/5?view=plain, [accessed September 2011].

Charities donating to illegal settlements include:

Charity	Charity No.	Settlement donated to	Activities	Sums donated	Address
British Friends of *Yeshiva* Bircas Mordechai	1119274	Beitar Illit	Funds *Yeshiva* Bircas Mordechai in Beitar Illit settlement.	£73,500 since 2008	19 Brantwood Road, Salford, Lancashire, M7 4EN
Gainsborough Trust	1008543	Modi'in Illit	Stated aim is "to benefit inhabitants of Modi'in Iillit, Israel and the surrounding areas with facilities for health and recreation and relief of financial distress."[5] Funded a swimming pool in Modi'in Illit, which borders Bil'in village.	£119,500 since 2006	7 Garrick Avenue, London, NW11 9AR
Friends of Nahalat Moshe (Nahalat Moshe)	327229	Ramot Polin/Ramot Alon	Supports a *Talmudic* college in Ramot Polin/Ramot Alon settlement in Jerusalem.	£210,000 since 2005	64 Princes Park Avenue, London, NW11 0JT Tel: 020 8731 9553
UK Friends of *Yeshiva* Mekor Chaim	1111779	Kfar Etzion	*Yeshiva* in Kfar Etzion settlement.	£73,500 since 2007	11 Leabourne Road, London Tel: 0208 800 6313

---

[5]See description of the charity's activities at http://www.charity-commission.gov.uk/Showcharity/RegisterOfCharities/CharityWithoutPartB.aspxRegisteredCharityNumber=1008543&SubsidiaryNumber=0, [accessed September 2011].

Charity	Charity No.	Settlement donated to	Activities	Sums donated	Address
The Friends of the *Yeshivat* Har Etzion Trust	298814	Alon Shvut	*Yeshiva* in Alon Shvut settlement	£191,000 since 2006	33 Felbridge Avenue, Stanmore, Middlesex, HA7 2BZ Tel: 0208 427 0793
Supporters of Israel's Dependants	1112009	Sde Bar Farm/ Outpost	Sde Bar Farm is an outpost in the West Bank. The charity also builds "educational clubhouses for young Israeli conscripts."[6]	£376,000 since 2007	Tel: 020 7724 7434
The British Friends of *Yeshivat* Birkat Moshe	1009686	Ma'ale Adumim	*Yeshivat* Birkat Moshe is a *Hesder Yeshiva* located in the Mitzpeh Nevo neighbourhood of Ma'ale Adumim settlement.	£14,300 since 2006	West Heath Drive, London, NW11 7QG Tel: 0208 458 5771
Friends of Nefesh B'Nefesh	1136918	Various, including Ma'ale Adumim	A newly registered *Aliyah* charity that funds Jewish immigration to Israel and advertises settlements on its website.	N/A – newly registered	65 Watford Way, Hendon, London NW4 3AQ

---

[6] http://www.charity-commission.gov.uk/Accounts/Ends09/0001112009_AC_20080331_E_C.PDF, [accessed September 2011], p.1 of 2008 accounts.

Charity	Charity No.	Settlement donated to	Activities	Sums donated	Address
World Action Ministries/ Christians 4Israel	295793	Unspecified	World Action Ministries sends money to Christian Friends of Israeli Communities (CFOIC). This is a Dutch Charity that funds settlements in the West Bank. According to its 2010 accounts, "this organisation supports projects in Judea and Samaria."[7]	£35,397 since 2009	PO Box 789, Sutton Coldfield, West Midlands, B73 5FX Tel: 0121 355 8333

Charities making military-related donations include:

Charity	Charity No.	Details of donations and activities	Sums donated	Contact
Jewish National Fund UK	225910	The JNF-UK's links to JNF-Israel are obscured but the latter contributes to refurbishing military bases; building security patrol roads in Gaza and Lebanon borders for IDF use; building a park for soldiers at the IDF's Negev Ramon Airforce Base complete with military parade ground, picnic tables and waste water recycling. JNF-UK takes donations from the Benji Hillman Foundation.	?	JNF House, Spring Villa Park, Edgware, Middlesex, HA8 7ED Tel: 020 8732 6100
Licia Crystal Charitable Trust	1010585	In 2008 it donated, via the JNF, to the park at the IDF's Ramon Airforce Base.	£31,500 since 2010.	7 Sedley, Southfleet, Gravesend, DA13 9PE Tel: 01474 834069

---

[7] http://www.charity-commission.gov.uk/Accounts/Ends93/0000295793_AC_20100331_E_C.PDF, [accessed September 2011], see p.8 of 2010 accounts.

Charity	Charity No.	Details of donations and activities	Sums donated	Contact
UK Friends of the Association for the Wellbeing of Israel's Soldiers	1084272	Supports the IDF. Abbreviated to UKAWIS or Friends of AWIS. Receives donations from many other UK charities.	£800,741 since 2010.	235 Old Marylebone Road, London, NW1 5QT Tel: 020 3210 3060
UK Friends of Nahar Deiah	1096177	Supports an IDF *Yeshiva* in Naharia, Israel. "*Yeshivat Hesder* Nahar Deiah, Nahariya combines intensive study of Torah with active service in the Israel Defence Forces in a warm family-like atmosphere."[8]	£430,000 since 2010.	Simon A Lopian, Lopian Gross Barnett & Co, Harvester House, 37 Peter Street, Manchester, M2 5QD Tel:0161 832 8721
Yeshivat Kerem B'Yavneh Foundation	313687	Supports the IDF *Yeshivat* Kerem B'Yavneh. Its website states that "Almost all *Hesder Yeshiva* students serve in the army as combat soldiers."[9]	£967,594 since 2006.	Unit 5, Etrona Buildings, 172-174 Granville Road, Cricklewood, London, NW2 2LD Tel: 020 8202 8470

---

[8] http://www.nahariya.co.il/Eng/Index.asp?CategoryID=86, [accessed September 2011].
[9] http://www.kby.org/english, [accessed September 2011].

Charity	Charity No.	Details of donations and activities	Sums donated	Contact
Samuel Sebba Charitable Trust	253351	Supports the IDF *Yeshivat* Kerem B'Yavneh.	£45,000 since 2008.	25-26 Enford Street, London, W1H 1DW Tel: 020 7388 3577

Aside from *yeshivas*, the charity **Supporters of Israel's Dependents** (SID), funds a youth project called Sde Bar farm. Its accounts say Sde Bar Farm provides "social and welfare support where needed to young adults who have no parents living with them in Israel."

But Sde Bar Farm is actually a settler outpost next to Nokdim settlement. Since 2007, SID has donated over £300,000 to the farm. Recently, SID stopped naming Sde Bar farm in its accounts but referred to donations for "youth projects". The charity also builds "educational clubhouses for young Israeli conscripts."

Dutch charity **Christian Friends of Israeli Communities (CFOIC)** receives donations via **World Action Ministries UK**. On its website, CFOIC solicits donations to pay for settler libraries, community centres and even walkie-talkies for settlement security. Their web pages show pictures of settlers armed with M-16's. In two years, World Action Ministries sent £35,000 to CFOIC.[10]

World Action Ministries is one of a number of UK registered Christian Zionist charities that ideologically support West Bank settlement. Another is **John Hagee Ministries** which hosts a satellite TV station called **Global Evangelism Television** and runs **Christians United for Israel** which has over half a million US members. John Hagee, who raised £300,000 in the UK last year. preaches Christian Zionism at large public rallies and recently told Prime minister Netanyahu that it was "Israel's sovereign right to grow and develop the settlements of Israel as you see fit."[11]

Nefesh B Nefesh, a charity promoting *aliyah* (Jewish migration) to Israel, is also now registered in the UK after many years receiving donations via the **Jewish National Fund**. Its purpose is to provide funds for Jewish people from around the world to move to Israel by covering their flights and moving costs. Nefesh B Nefesh openly advertise Israeli settlements as places for new Jewish migrants to live.[12] Their website, which reads like an estate agents guide, describes Efrat settlement as being "a popular destination for English-speaking *Olim*. The community offers excellent schools, a close proximity to Jerusalem, a

---

[10] http://www.cfoic.com/emergencyprojects.jsp, [accessed September 2011].
[11] http://peacenow.org/entries/christians_united_for_israels_cufi, [accessed September 2011].
[12] http://www.nbn.org.il/aliyahpedia/community-a-housing/community-guide-beta-listings.html, [accessed September 2011].

supportive community and a wide range of services."

The **Gainsborough Trust** describes its activities as " to benefit inhabitants of Modiin Illit, Israel and the surrounding areas, with facilities for health and recreation and financial distress." Modiin Illit, which received a swimming pool from the Gainsbourough Trust, is located in the West Bank, not Israel, and is built on land belonging to the Palestinian village of Bil'in.

The **Lewis Group Trust**, in its accounts, lists donations to Keshet Yehuda, a pre-military training college that prepares teenagers for the army, particularly for entry into combat units. It is based in the Occupied Syrian Golan.[13]

However, some charities no longer give a breakdown of donations. For example, between 2003 and 2004, **Alliance Family Foundation** donated £9,000 to **El Ad**, a settler organisation taking over Palestinian houses and land in East Jerusalem *(see our previous chapter on East Jerusalem)*. Nowadays, this particular charity simply lists that it gives £110,000 to "individuals and organisations". There is no further explanation of who those individuals and organisations are.[14]

There are at least 1,150 British charities donating to Israel. It is essential that the BDS movement monitors their activities and pressures the Charity Commission to provide a check and balance.

Sign on the gate to an olive grove donated to the settlers of Maskiot by a registered charity (Corporate Watch 2010)

---

[13] See http://www.aliyah18.org, [accessed September 2011].
[14] Alliance Family Foundation accounts. (Charity Number: 258721).

The criteria for charity status

Campaigners in the UK have begun to question the legitimacy of these organisations' charity status. Not only does this status bring with it the tax benefits outlined above, but the title 'charity' also bestows upon these projects a benevolent, humanitarian image.

In the UK, the Charity Commission is the body that grants charity status and is, therefore, the body to which appeals questioning the charity status of such organisations must be submitted. These challenges must be made on the grounds that an organisation and/or its activities do not conform to the UK Charity Commission's list of charitable purposes. The regulatory body uses this list as a test of whether or not an organisation's projects are in the public benefit when making a decision on granting it charity status. The Commission has "the same powers as the court when determining whether an organisation has charitable status."[15] Its website states that it will "interpret and apply the law as to charitable status in accordance with the principles laid down by the courts.. The Register of Charities is therefore a reflection of the decisions made by the courts and our decisions following the example of the courts."[16]

The Charities Act 2006 provides 13 purposes or activities that would qualify as 'charitable'. An organisation seeking charity status must, therefore, show that its activities fall under one of the following categories:

- The prevention or relief of poverty
- The advancement of education
- The advancement of religion
- The advancement of health or the saving of lives
- The advancement of citizenship or community development
- The advancement of the arts, culture, heritage or science
- The advancement of amateur sport
- The advancement of human rights, conflict resolution or reconciliation or the promotion of religious or racial harmony or equality and diversity
- The advancement of environmental protection or improvement
- The relief of those in need, by reason of youth, age, ill-health, disability, financial hardship or other disadvantage
- The advancement of animal welfare
- The promotion of the efficiency of the armed forces of the Crown, or of the efficiency of the police, fire and rescue services or ambulance services
- Any other purposes currently recognised as charitable and any new charitable purposes which are similar to another charitable purpose.[17]

---

[15] http://www.charity-commission.gov.uk/Publications/RR1a.aspx, [accessed September 2011]
[16] http://www.charitycommission.gov.uk/publications/rr1a.aspx#4, [accessed September 2011].
[17] http://www.charitycommission.gov.uk/Charity_requirements_guidance/Charity_essentials/Public_benefit/charitable_purposes.aspx, [accessed September 2011].

The charities in question here will tend to fall under the 'advancement of religion' and 'advancement of education' categories. Challenges to this can be made, as will be shown below. While there is clear scope for charities to support "the armed forces of the Crown", it is far from certain whether support for a foreign army is acceptable, especially when that army is an occupying force.

More important than simply fitting one of these categories, perhaps, is that the organisation must also demonstrate that its aims are "for the public benefit". The Charity Commission publishes extensive guidance on what is meant by its criteria for charitable status, most of which is wordy and vague. However, in the section on public benefit its website states that the benefits of a charity's aims to some of the public must be weighed against the possible harmful effects of those aims to other members of the public: "In assessing the public benefit of individual organisations, we will consider any evidence of significant detrimental or harmful effects of that organisation carrying out its aims in its particular circumstances. There would need to be some real evidence of detriment or harm; it cannot just be supposed.. If the detrimental or harmful consequences are greater than the benefits, the overall result is that the organisation would not be charitable."[18] This would seem to offer hope for challenges to the charity status of organisations that support Israel's illegal settlements and the IDF.

Challenges to charity status

The Charity Commission was asked by campaigners whether an organisation could gain or retain charitable status while raising and donating funds in support of settlements that are illegal under international law. The Commission replied that "the legal status of an area does not prevent charities from operating there. If the inhabitants meet the criteria of a particular charity, they may receive charitable relief for any of the [thirteen charitable] purposes.. Charities must only raise funds and undertake activities within the charitable purposes for which they are established."[19] This means that challenges to charity status would have to be made on the basis of their stated purpose and whether those purposes, and only those purposes, are being fulfilled. Challenges based on the legal status of the settlements are likely to be ignored for the time being.

In the US, however, campaigners, particularly the American Arab Anti-Discrimination Committee (ADC), have challenged the tax-exempt status of charities funding settlement construction. This created a good deal of publicity around the issue: the *New York Times* published a lengthy report naming US tax-exempt charities that support illegal Israeli settlements and drawing attention to how this arrangement implicates US tax payers in settlement expansion projects.[20] The contradiction between the US government's stated, though rarely evident, opposition to settlement expansion and the US Treasury's support for

---

[18] http://www.charitycommission.gov.uk/Charity_requirements_guidance/Charity_essentials/Public_be nefit/public_benefit.aspx#e, [accessed September 2011].
[19] Correspondence forwarded to Corporate Watch, September 2011.
[20] http://www.nytimes.com/2010/07/06/world/middleeast/06settle.html?_r=1&pagewanted=1

those settlements through tax breaks for these organisations has embarrassed the US administration. The ADC filed a number of administrative complaints to the US Treasury, demanding investigations into those tax-exempt organisations donating money to settlement projects. In early 2010, it was reported that Commissioner Doug Schulman of the IRS had agreed to "go after" any charity supporting West Bank settlement expansion.[21]

Corporate Watch asked UK tax experts whether a similar challenge could be mounted in the UK via HMRC. Unfortunately it seems that HMRC essentially outsources the tax-based vetting of current and potential charities to the Charity Commission. The Commission is the final arbiter in these matters and, as has been shown, challenges based on the legal status of the settlements will likely be ignored.

The case of 'Good News for Israel'

The case of Good News for Israel (GNFI) is illuminating, as the UK Charity Commission rejected this organisation's application for charity status because one of its purposes was deemed controversial. The Charity Commission's report on this decision states that one of the GNFI's objectives is to "advance the Jewish religion by (amongst other means) promoting the doctrine of Aliyah, being the promotion of the return of Jewish people to the land promised to them by God. " GNFI could not adequately prove that this was for the public benefit, so the Commission concluded that "promotion of a particular religious doctrine is not necessarily advancement of religion in the charitable sense."[22]

Crucially, the Commission followed the decision made in the case of *Keren Kayemeth Le Jisroel v IRC [1931]*, where it was accepted that "settling people in the Holy Land was not an exclusively charitable purpose as advancing the Jewish religion as it involved considerations which went beyond the religious and spiritual".[23] This implies an understanding of the political and social implications of GNFI's objectives.

The Keren Kayemeth case dealt with an organisation (the JNF – *see below for further details on this organisation*) seeking to establish the state of Israel as a theocratic state. However, the fact that Israel now exists does not, according to the Commission, make any difference with regard to the charitable status of a mission to settle Jewish people in the Holy Land:

> "[T]he Commission did not accept that the establishment of the state of Israel meant that the settlement of Jewish people in the Holy Land can now be accepted as furthering a religious purpose when previously it could not. There continue to be implications which go beyond the spiritual and religious, and which raise political,

---

[21]http://www.adc.org/media/press-releases/2010/january-2010/adc-commends-irs-decision-to-investigate-settlement-funding/, [accessed September 2011].
[22]http://www.charitycommission.gov.uk/Charity_requirements_guidance/Charity_essentials/Public_benefit/public_benefit.aspx#e, [accessed September 2011], p.1.
[23]http://www.charitycommission.gov.uk/Charity_requirements_guidance/Charity_essentials/Public_benefit/public_benefit.aspx#e, [accessed September 2011], p.3.

economical, social and civil order issues. The Commission understood the state of Israel to have a policy of encouraging and assisting Jewish people to settle there. However, whether or not practical assistance to Jewish people to travel to Israel is facilitating a particular policy of the state of Israel, such assistance cannot be considered to be exclusively concerned with the advancement of religion.[24]"

In light of these decisions, it would appear that there is plenty of scope to challenge the charity status of organisations funding settlements, the IDF and military training on the grounds that public benefit cannot be ascertained given the negative political, social and civil order repercussions of these activities in the context of the on-going occupation of Palestine and oppression of Palestinians. The failure of GNFI to secure charity status on the basis of its commitment to promote Aliyah could provide a framework for a challenge to Nefesh B'Nefesh, a newly registered charity that encourages and supports Aliyah and helps establish new homes and families in illegal settlements.[25]

The JNF

The JNF, or *Keren Kayemet LeYisrael* (KKL), is currently the main target for campaigners in the UK seeking to revoke the charity status of organisations supporting Israel's occupation of Palestine. The Stop the JNF Campaign aims to challenge the organisation's charity status not only by questioning the extent to which its ambitions are charitable, but also by exposing its past and present activities as illegal under domestic and international law.[26]

The JNF is as old as Zionism itself; it emerged from the debates during the First Zionist Conference at the end of the 19th century. In discussing how to establish a Jewish state, it was posited that a fund should be established to secure land for the creation of this state (at the time Jews in Palestine owned just 7% of the land), and that this fund should be inalienable: once land became Jewish, it must be kept in trust for all Jews and never again be made available to non-Jews.

Thus, the aim of the JNF was "to purchase, take on lease or in exchange, or otherwise acquire any lands, forests, rights of possession and other rights... in [Palestine, Syria, Sinai, Turkey]... for the purpose of settling Jews on such lands".[27] The fund went about acquiring these lands in a variety of ways. One was to accept donations of land, dunum by dunum (1 dunum is around a quarter of an acre), from the Jewish diaspora. Contrary to the JNF's own

---

[24] http://www.charitycommission.gov.uk/Charity_requirements_guidance/Charity_essentials/Public_benefit/public_benefit.aspx#e, [accessed September 2011], p.5.
[25] http://www.nbn.org.il/about/about-nbn-services.html and http://www.nbn.org.il/aliyahpedia/community-a-housing/community-guide-beta-listings.html, [accessed September 2011].
[26] http://www.stopthejnf.org/index.html, [accessed September 2011].
[27] JNF/KKL memorandum of association, (1907).

self-sponsored mythology, this did not contribute a huge amount of land. Before May 1948, just 936,000 dunums had been acquired.[28]

The JNF also 'redeemed' land more aggressively, often at the expense of the Arab *fellahin* (peasants). This process was to escalate dramatically in the wake of the establishment of the State of Israel in 1948. As Palestinians were forced off their land or fled in fear of Jewish troops, the JNF plundered the rewards. Most of the land now owned by the JNF was conquered during the *Nakba*. This land was the holdings of Palestinian refugees or of 'present absentees' and acquiring it through other parties is illegal under international law, as land acquisition and settlement by an occupying power contravene The Hague Regulations of 1907 and the 1949 Geneva Convention.

One would think that the JNF would have withered away after 1948; it had served its purpose when the state of Israel was born. But rather than taking over the JNF's land following the victory in 1948, the state perpetuated the organisation's existence due to the UN resolution on Palestinian refugees at the time. The United Nations had resolved in December 1948 (Resolution 194) that 'those refugees wishing to return to their homes and live in peace with their neighbours,' should be given that option.[29] If the nascent state were to take over Palestinian land directly it could face severe consequences under international law. Instead, the JNF continued to exist and act as a holder of that land in order to circumvent this legal issue. Palestinian lands were formally taken over by the 'Custodian of Absentee Property' and sold to a fictitious 'Development Authority' that had the option of selling the land to the state, to the JNF, to municipalities, or to 'an institution for settling landless Arabs'. The latter option was not used, of course; most of the land was sold to the JNF. Today, around half of the JNF's land belonged, or should belong, to Palestinian refugees.

Thus, the JNF sits at the heart of the complications surrounding Palestinian refugees' right to return and, though it was created as a spur for the establishment of a Jewish state, it has now morphed into a prop of Israel's ongoing apartheid policies. Its mandate to lease only to Jews has seen the JNF criticised by even the Israeli high-court on the grounds of discrimination against Palestinians. Each time, though, loopholes are found to allow the JNF to continue its work. The JNF forms a majority on the board of the **Israel Land Administration (ILA)**, the Israeli government's organ for orchestrating land distribution in Israel. In an Israeli High Court petition begun in 2004, the attorney general's office stated that the ILA could not discriminate against Arab citizens of the state in the marketing and allocation of lands it manages, even those belonging to the JNF. The JNF's response to accusations of discrimination was forthright: "The JNF is not the trustee of the general public in Israel. Its loyalty is given to the Jewish people in the Diaspora and in the state of Israel... The JNF, in relation to being an owner of land, is not a public body that works for the benefit of all citizens of the state. The loyalty of the JNF is given to the Jewish people and only to them is

---

[28] Lehn, W and Davis, U (1988), *The Jewish National Fund*, London and New York: Kegan Paul International, p.70.
[29] http://domino.un.org/unispal.nsf/0/c758572b78d1cd0085256bcf0077e51a?OpenDocument, [accessed September 2011].

the JNF obligated. The JNF, as the owner of the JNF land, does not have a duty to practice equality towards all citizens of the state."[30] Such views have been supported in law thanks to bills passed in the Knesset, notably Uri Ariel's bill submitted in 2007.[31]

The JNF has provided land for over 1,000 settlements. It has built national parks on the still-visible ruins of Arab villages. It is a central administrative prop of Israel's discriminatory land administration and supports the ongoing expansion of Israel's settlements. The Stop the JNF Campaign, launched in 2011 on March 25th, Palestinian Land Day, seeks to use these facts and arguments to tear apart the tightly maintained veil of legitimacy that disguises the JNF's activities.

See our earlier section on the Naqab for more on the Stop the JNF campaign

Where next?

Because the Charity Commission uses the principles of case law to decide whether to grant an organisation charitable status, energy should be channelled into one campaign that might set a precedent that can be used to challenge the status of other organisations raising charity funds to support Israel's occupation.

Given the Charity Commission's reliance on precedent in its decision-making, if campaigners were able to have the charity status of one of these organisations revoked on the grounds that it does not work for the public benefit (or at least that the harm they cause outweighs the benefits they bring), there is no reason why each of the others should not lose their charity status as a result. As yet, there has been no clear and coherent challenge to any of these organisations on the basis of public benefit. This must be rectified. It will also be necessary to demand that charities not publishing a breakdown of their donations are forced to release details of the beneficiaries of their funds so that the commission can make an informed decision on their suitability for charity status.

Requests for a review of the decisions of the Charity Commission must be made by submitting an application online or by downloading, printing, completing and posting an application. The Commission's decisions can also be appealed to and reviewed by a tribunal. The Commission's website states that "[t]he First-tier Tribunal (Charity) is an independent legal body which has the power to look again at some of the decisions made by the Commission and to quash, change or add to them."[32]

While the loss of income to the Zionist enterprise would not be huge were the UK to revoke the charity status enjoyed by these organisations, there is a tendency for countries to fall into

---

[30] http://www.badil.org/en/article74/item/429-the-jewish-national-fund-jnf, [accessed September 2011].
[31] http://www.haaretz.com/print-edition/opinion/a-mazuz-bypass-law-1.226259, [accessed September 2011].
[32] http://www.charitycommission.gov.uk/About_us/Complaining/Complaining_about_our_decision_index.aspx, [accessed September 2011].

line with these kinds of regulations. Changes in the UK would give succour to campaigns in Europe and elsewhere in the world. It has been shown that European-wide tax breaks for charities supporting settlements amount to very significant amounts of money.[33] A successful campaign to end this European tax-payer sponsorship of the Israeli occupation would deal a significant blow to the viability of a number of new and existing settlements in the West Bank.

---

[33] http://ipsnews.net/news.asp?idnews=52983, [accessed September 2011].

A BDS Handbook

IN 2002 ISRAEL BEGAN BUILDING THE 700 KILOMETRE LONG WALL. THE WALL IS INTENDED TO STEAL MORE PALESTINIAN LAND, GHETTOIZE PALESTINIANS AND ANNEX MANY ISRAELI SETTLEMENTS TO THE WESTERN SIDE OF THE WALL.

PALESTINIANS IN THE WEST BANK AND GAZA NOW EXIST ON 26% OF HISTORICAL PALESTINE. ISRAEL HAD KILLED 6500 PALESTINIANS IN ITS CRUSHING OF THE PALESTINIAN UPRISING, WHICH HAD BEGUN IN LATE 2000.

ISRAELI TANKS ROLLED INTO ALL MAJOR PALESTINIAN CITIES IN THE WEST BANK AND GAZA, DESTROYED GOVERNMENT BUILDINGS AND POLICE STATIONS USING F16s OR BULLDOZERS AND KILLED OR IMPRISONED THOUSANDS.

Boycott Divestment and Sanctions by Sean Michael Wilson and Rejena Smiley

IN 2004, A CASE WAS BROUGHT IN THE INTERNATIONAL COURT OF JUSTICE IN THE HAGUE. THOUSANDS OF PEOPLE TRAVELLED TO THE HAGUE TO DEMONSTRATE OUTSIDE THE COURT AGAINST ISRAEL'S WALL, KNOWN AS THE APARTHEID WALL.

THE COURT'S ADVISORY RULING WAS THAT THE WALL WAS ILLEGAL -- AND THAT 'ALL' STATES ARE UNDER AN OBLIGATION NOT TO RECOGNIZE THE ILLEGAL SITUATION RESULTING FROM THE CONSTRUCTION OF THE WALL AND NOT TO RENDER AID OR ASSISTANCE IN MAINTAINING THE SITUATION CREATED BY SUCH CONSTRUCTION'.

THE RULING ADDED WEIGHT TO THE PALESTINIANS STRUGGLE AGAINST APARTHEID AND OCCUPATION. A CALL FOR SOLIDARITY WAS MADE SO THAT EVERYONE COULD PLAY A PART IN THE FIGHT AGAINST ISRAELI OCCUPATION.

A BDS Handbook

BUT A POPULAR MOVEMENT AGAINST THE WALL HAS GROWN ACROSS PALESTINE, WITH WEEKLY DEMONSTRATIONS BEING HELD IN VILLAGES LIKE BUDRUS, BIDDU, MAS'HA, JAYYOUS, BIL'IN, NIL'IN AND NABI SALEH. IN 2005, PALESTINIANS UNITED BEHIND A CALL FOR A BOYCOTT OF ISRAEL UNTIL IT COMPLIED WITH INTERNATIONAL LAW. THE CALL FOR BDS ENCOMPASSED EVERYTHING FROM BOYCOTTING ISRAELI GOODS TO PUSHING STATES TO IMPOSE MILITARY SANCTIONS.

RECENTLY THE BOYCOTT OF ISRAELI GOODS HAS BEGUN TO BITE. ISRAELI COMPANIES ARE BEGINNING TO WORRY ABOUT A DROP IN EXPORTS. TOURING ISRAELI SPORTS TEAMS HAVE HAD THEIR PITCHES INVADED AND STATE-SPONSORED MUSICIANS HAVE HAD THEIR CONCERTS DISRUPTED. PEOPLE HAVE OCCUPIED SUPERMARKETS SELLING ISRAELI GOODS, BLOCKADED THE DEPOTS TRANSPORTING THE GOODS AND PREVENTED ISRAELI GOODS BEING UNLOADED.

ACTIVISTS HAVE BROKEN INTO FACTORIES MANUFACTURING WEAPONS FOR ISRAEL AND DISABLED THE PRODUCTION LINE—JURIES HAVE REFUSED TO CONVICT THEM. IT IS CLEAR THAT THE LIGHT AT THE END OF THE TUNNEL IN THE PALESTINIAN STRUGGLE FOR LIBERATION IS NOT IN GOVERNMENTS AND POLITICIANS, BUT IN THE SOLIDARITY AND RESISTANCE OF ORDINARY PEOPLE!

Select Bibliography

Adalah (2011), *New Discriminatory Laws and Bills in Israel*. Available: http://www.adalah.org/upfiles/2011/New_Discriminatory_Laws.pdf

Alenat, S (2010), *Working for Survival: Labor Conditions of Palestinians Working in Settlements*, Kav LaOved.

Amnesty International (2009), *Fuelling Conflict: Foreign Arms Supplies to Israel/Gaza*. Available: http://www.amnesty.org/en/library/info/MDE15/012/2009

Applied Research Institute Jerusalem (2005), *Report on the Israeli Colonization activities in the West Bank and the Gaza Strip*. Available: http://www.arij.org/publications(8)/Monitoring%20Report/81.pdf

B'Tselem and BIMKOM (2005), *Under the Guise of Security*. Available: http://www.btselem.org/download/200512_under_the_guise_of_security_eng.pdf

BRICUP (2007), *Why Boycott Israeli Universities?*, British Committee for the Universities of Palestine. Available from Bricup, www.bricup.org.uk

Corporate Watch (2009), *Profiting from Occupation..* Available: http://www.corporatewatch.org/?lid=3395.

Hanieh, A (2003), *From State-led Growth to Globalisation: The Evolution of Israeli Capitalism*, Journal of Palestine Studies, Vol 32:4.

Hever, S (2010), *The Political Economy of Israel's Occupation: Repression Beyond Exploitation*, Pluto Press.

Human Rights Watch (2010), *Separate and Unequal: Israel's Discriminatory Treatment of Palestinians in the Occupied Palestinian Territories*. Available: http://www.hrw.org/sites/default/files/reports/iopt1210webwcover_0.pdf

Hunaiti, H (2008), *The Arab Jahalin: From the Nakba to the Wall*, Stop the Wall. Available: *www.stopthewall.org/.../pdf/Jahalin-EN1.pdf*

Lehn, W and Davis, U (1988), *The Jewish National Fund*, Kegan Paul International.

Locke, S (2010), *Gaza Beneath the Bombs*, Pluto Press.

Ma'an Development Center (2008), *Salfit: From Agricultural Heaven to Industrial Ghetto*. Available: *http://www.maan-ctr.org/pdfs/Salfeeteb.pdf*

Machover, M and Orr A (2002), *The Class Character of Israel,* International Socialist Review, *Issue 23, May-June 2002.*

Niewhof, A (2011), *Multinational Companies Mining Occupied Palestinian Land,* Electronic Intifada. Available: http://electronicintifada.net/content/multinational-companies-mining-occupied-palestinian-land/9974

Nitzan, J and Bichler, S (2002), *The Global Political Economy of Israel*. Pluto Press.

OECD (2009), Economic Survey of Israel 2009. Available: http://www.oecd.org/document/53/0,3746,en_2649_33733_44384757_1_1_1_1,00.html

OECD (2010), *OECD Review of Agricultural Policies: Israel*. Available: http://www.oecd.org/dataoecd/53/0/45189389.pdf

Paltrade (2010), *Movement of Goods from the West Bank to East Jerusalem and Israel*. Available: http://www.lacs.ps/documentsShow.aspx?ATT_ID=2486

Pappe, I (2006), *The Ethnic Cleansing of Palestine*, One World Publications.

Rosenthal, N (2010), 2010 Activity Summary Report – Migrant Workers in Agricultural Settlements, *Kav LaOved*. Available: http://www.kavlaoved.org.il/UserFiles/File/Thaieng.pdf

Stop the Wall (2007), Exporting Occupation: the Israeli Arms Trade. Available: http://www.stopthewall.org/downloads/pdf/Exportoccupation.pdf

Stop the Wall (2008), *Development or Normalisation: A Critique of West Bank Development Approaches and Projects*. Available: http://www.stopthewall.org/briefing-development-or-normalisation-critique-west-bank-development-approaches-and-projects

Swirski, S (2008), The Burden of Occupation, Adva Center. Available: http://www.israeli-occupation.org/2010-04-16/shlomo-swirski-the-burden-of-occupation/

War on Want (2005), *Caterpillar: the Alternative Report*. Available: http://www.waronwant.org/attachments/Caterpillar-%20The%20Alternative%20Report.pdf

White, B (2009), *Israeli Apartheid: a Beginner's Guide,* Pluto Press

Who Profits (2010), *Financing the Israeli Occupation*. Available: http://www.whoprofits.org/articlefiles/WhoProfits-IsraeliBanks2010.pdf

Who Profits (2010), *Crossing the Line: The Tel Aviv-Jerusalem Fast Train, a New Israeli Train Line Through West Bank Areas*. Available: http://www.whoprofits.org/articlefiles/WP-A1-Train.pdf

Who Profits (2011), *Soda Stream: A Case Study for Corporate Activity in Illegal Israeli Settlements*. Available: http://www.whoprofits.org/Article%20Data.php?doc_id=990

Yacobi Keller, U (2009), *The Economy of the Occupation: Academic Boycott of Israel*, Alternative Information Center: A Socioeconomic Bulletin, No. 23-24. Available: http://electronicintifada.net/v2/article10945.shtml

Glossary

Places

1948 Israel: the areas of historic Palestine which fell within the state of Israel in 1948 including Palestinian areas which were colonised after the Israeli ethnic cleansing of Palestine. Israel's population currently stands at almost 7.3 million[1] (excluding Israeli settlers living in the West Bank). This figure includes over 1.5 million Palestinian citizens of Israel.

West Bank: The West Bank is part of historic Palestine. From the end of the 1948 war through to the 1967 war the West Bank was occupied and controlled by Jordan and Palestinians living there became Jordanian citizens. It was the Jordanian authorities who coined the term 'West Bank'. The Israeli state refers to the West Bank as 'Judea and Samaria', names for areas of the kingdom of Israel referred to in the Bible. The West Bank has a population of 2.6 million, including over 500,000 settlers[2] and is controlled by Mahmoud Abbas' Palestinian Authority (PA).

East Jerusalem: Jerusalem was partitioned in the 1948 war and East Jerusalem was controlled by Jordan until its conquest and occupation by Israel in 1967.

Gaza: the Gaza Strip is a small area of land – around 25 miles long and 6 miles wide – located to the south-west of Israel bordering Egypt and the Mediterranean Sea. It is home to more than 1.5 million Palestinians. Gaza was created in 1948 after the *Nakba*. It was controlled by Egypt until 1967 when it was occupied by Israel. Today it is politically controlled by Hamas, while its borders with Israel are strictly controlled by the Israeli military which restrict Palestinian freedom of movement and the flow of goods entering, thus suffocating the Gazan economy.

Occupied Syrian Golan: an area in the south-west of Syria which was occupied by Israel during the 1967 War driving more than 100,000 Syrians from their homes. It is commonly referred to as the 'Golan Heights', a term which ignores the illegality of Israel's occupation of a neighbouring state and people. There are 18,000 indigenous Syrians and 17-20,000 Israeli settlers.[3] In 1981 the Golan Heights Law extended Israeli law to the occupied Syrian Golan, a *de facto* annexation which is not accepted by the majority of Syrian residents of the Golan or by international law.[4]

---

[1] http://www1.cbs.gov.il/reader/cw_usr_view_Folder?ID=141, [accessed October 2011].
[2] http://www.indexmundi.com/west_bank/demographics_profile.html, [accessed September 2011].
[3] http://www.golan-marsad.org/Images/022011/Study%20Changing%20the%20landscape.pdf, [accessed October 2011].
[4] http://www.mfa.gov.il/MFA/Peace+Process/Guide+to+the+Peace+Process/Golan+Heights+Law.htm, [accessed October 2011].

Occupied Palestinian Territories/Occupied Palestine: The Palestinian areas under Israeli military occupation: the West Bank (including East Jerusalem) and Gaza.

Occupied Territories: All areas under Israeli military occupation. We have used the term occupied territories throughout this book to refer to the occupied Palestinian territories and the occupied Syrian Golan.

Al-Khalil: the Palestinian name for Hebron. Al-Khalil means 'friend' or 'the friend of God', referring to Abraham who is thought to be buried there. Similarly, the Israeli term Hebron (or *Hevron* as it is also known) derives from the Hebrew word for friend.

Al Quds: the Islamic name for Jerusalem, meaning 'The Holy'.
Naqab: the Palestinian name for the desert situated in what is now southern Israel (known as the *Negev* in Hebrew), covering around 60 per cent of the country's land mass.

People

Palestinian-Israeli: Palestinian citizens of Israel. We have chosen to use this term rather than Arab-Israeli as the term 'Arab' is used in Zionist colonial discourse to negate the Palestinian right to the land.

Bedouin: primarily nomadic or semi-nomadic pastoralists who live in the deserts of North Africa and the Middle East. Prior to Israel's creation the majority of Palestinian Bedouin esided in the south of Palestine, in BirSaba, the Naqab and south of Al-Khalil. Whilst most of the Palestinian Bedouin were forcefully expelled from these areas by Jewish forces during the *Nakba*, around 130,000 remain in the Naqab.

Jahalin: the *Jahalin* (or Arab *Jahalin*) are the largest group of Bedouin living in the West Bank, and originate from the Naqab desert. They were expelled from the Naqab to Hebron and eastern Bethlehem by Jewish forces in the lead up to the creation of Israel in 1948. Today Jahalin Bedouin live predominantly in the outer Jerusalem area of the West Bank.
Ashkenazi: Israeli-Jews who are of northern and central European descent, particularly those from Germany. In Israel the political, military and business elites are disproportionately *Ashkenazim*.

Sephardi: Jews descended from the Jews of the Iberian Peninsula who were expelled from there in the 15th Century.

Mizrahi: Israeli-Jews who are descended from Jewish communities living in the Asia, the Middle-East and the Caucasus. Mizrahi Jews have historically been the target of discrimination from Ashkenazi Jews in Israel and no Mizrahi Jew has yet held the position of Prime Minister.

Events

Ottoman rule: Palestine was captured by the Ottoman empire in 1516 and remained, save for a brief period of Egyptian rule, part of that empire until 1917.

British mandate: the British captured Jerusalem in 1917 and assumed control over Palestine formally in 1922. The mandate was officially terminated in 1948.

Nakba: the term *al Nakba* (the catastrophe) is used by Palestinians to describe the ethnic cleansing which led to the establishment of the State of Israel in 1948. However, in many textbooks and historiographies of the West it is described as the Israeli 'War of Independence'. The term *al Nakba* is used throughout this book.

The 1967 War: an attack by Israel against its Arab neighbours Egypt, Syria and Jordan that resulted in the Jewish state occupying the West Bank and Gaza Strip, as well as Egypt's Sinai Peninsula and the Syrian Golan. The popular term for this event is the Six Day War. This term celebrates Israel's supposed military superiority and we prefer to refer to the war as simply 'the 1967 war'.

The 1973 War: a coordinated but unsuccessful attempt by Egypt and Syria to win back from Israel the territories taken in the 1967 War. It is popularly known as the Yom Kippur War, but as with the 1967 War this terminology creates a false narrative portraying Israel as the benign defender against Arab aggression. The hostilities paved the way for the 1979 Camp David Accords which resulted in the Sinai Peninsula being handed back to Egypt.

Intifada: the two Palestinian popular uprisings against the Israeli occupation between 1987-1993 and 2000–2004. Literally translated, *Intifada* means 'shaking off'.

Oslo Accords: a set of agreements signed in 1993 between the late PLO leader Yasser Arafat and then Israeli Prime Minister Yitzhak Rabin. The Accords, brokered by the Clinton Administration, were announced with much fanfare to the international community as the first step towards a Palestinian state and peace in the Middle East. In reality, they merely cemented Israel's occupation of the West Bank and Gaza Strip, and legitimised the system of apartheid Palestinians are forced to endure daily.

Under the accords the West Bank was carved up into three areas: A, B and C. Area A, which was predominantly Palestinian urban centres, was to be controlled by the soon to be created Palestinian Authority (PA) and Israeli troops were to withdraw as Palestinian security forces took control. In Area B, administration was to be carried out by the PA whilst security fell under the remit of the Israeli Defence Force. Lastly, all land designated Area C (around 60 per cent of the occupied Palestinian territories) was to be fully controlled and administered by the Israeli military.

The Accords were merely a statement of principles before planned 'final status talks', which never reached any agreement. Thus the Oslo process did nothing to address the problem of Israel's illegal settlements and effectively de-railed any attempt to solve the problem of Palestinian refugees scattered across the Middle East.

Terms

Apartheid: term meaning a legal system of racial segregation originally used to describe the policies of the White National Party governments ruling South Africa between 1948 and 1994. The definition of the crime of apartheid, as defined by the 2002 Rome Statute of the International Criminal Court, is inhumane acts "committed in the context of an institutionalized regime of systematic oppression and domination by one racial group over any other racial group or groups and committed with the intention of maintaining that regime."[5] We believe the term apartheid accurately reflects Israel's policies against Palestinians in the West Bank and Gaza, as well as within Israel itself.[6]

Ethnic Cleansing: a term which was first used to refer to the atrocities committed during the break-up of the former Yugoslavia. It has been defined as a "policy of a particular group of persons to systematically eliminate another group from a given territory on the basis of religious, ethnic or national origin. Such a policy involves violence and is very often connected to military operations. It is to be achieved by all possible means, from discrimination to extermination"[7] In *The ethnic cleansing of Palestine*, Israeli historian Ilan Pappe argues that this term can be used to describe the destruction of villages, expulsions, murder and massacres which occurred during the colonisation of Palestine from 1947-9.

There are problems with this term as the word 'cleansing' implies the presence of impurity. However, 'ethnic cleansing' has become a popular term to describe a particular type of crime against humanity and we have used it throughout this book to describe the actions of armed Jewish groups before, during and after the 1948 war. The term can also be applied to the expulsions of Palestinians from the West Bank during the 1967 war. Smaller scale acts of ethnic cleansing are perpetrated regularly by the Israeli state, most recently communities in the Jordan Valley and the Naqab have been destroyed, accompanied by the threat of or the use of violence, and attempts have been made to bar the previous residents from returning to the area.[8]

---

[5]http://untreaty.un.org/cod/icc/statute/99_corr/2.htm [accessed October 2011].
[6]For more information see White, B (2009), *Israeli apartheid: a beginners guide*, Pluto Press and Davis, U (1989), *Israel: an apartheid state*, Zed Books.
[7]Petrovic, D (1994), *Ethnic cleansing – an attempt at methodology*, quoted in Pappe, I (2006) *The ethnic cleansing of Palestine*, Oneworld Publications, p.1.
[8]For example the village of Al Araqib has been destroyed 21 times since 2010 to make way for a Jewish National Fund forest. See http://www.alternativenews.org/english/index.php/topics/news/3384-el-araqib-destroyed-for-21st-time-jnf-changing-facts-on-ground.

Judaization: the systematic attempts by the Israeli government and settler organisations to move Jewish people into areas populated by Palestinians in order to alter the demographic balance in favour of Jews. Judaization is often coupled by the systematic denial of services to Palestinian areas in 1948 Israel and East Jerusalem.

Normalisation: a term used to describe the promotion of economic, cultural and political ties with Israel with the aim of consolidating Israeli occupation and apartheid.

Settlement: this refers to the transfer and settlement of an Israeli-Jewish population into the occupied territories of the West Bank, East Jerusalem and Syrian Golan. It covers not only the act of settling in these territories, but is also used to describe the communities which Israeli-Jewish settlers establish. Some, including many Palestinians, rightly refer to settlements as colonies but we have decided to use the word 'settlement' as it is both the legal and popular term.

The Rome Statute of the International Criminal Court defines the "transfer, directly or indirectly, by the Occupying Power of parts of its own civilian population into the territory it occupies" as a war crime.[9] More than 500,000 Jewish settlers currently live in the West Bank, whilst an estimated 20,000 live in the occupied Syrian Golan. These settlements are not only built on land stolen from Palestinians and Syrians, but they also continually rob the local populations of other resources such as water.

However, the Israeli state and Israeli Zionist organisations also pursue a process of land grabs and colonisation within Palestinian areas inside 1948 Israel. This occurs in the Naqab where state policy and parastatal organisations are being used to evict Bedouin and plant a **Jewish National Fund** forest. We see little difference between Israeli policies of colonisation within 1948 Israel and its settlement policy in the West Bank.

Siege of Gaza: the economic blockade and military strikes carried out by Israeli on the Gaza Strip since the 2005 disengagement, effectively rendering it an open prison. Both Human Rights Watch and Amnesty International have denounced the siege as illegal, with Gaza's Palestinian inhabitants living in poverty and shut off from the outside world.
With Israel controlling all but one of Gaza's four borders, and Egypt operating similar policies on the fourth, limited amounts of goods are allowed to pass in and out of the strip and 90 per cent of industry has shut down. This has been coupled with targeted Israeli air strikes against factories, universities and schools which are aimed at destroying the infrastructure and institutions needed to build Palestinian livlihoods.

---

[9]http://untreaty.un.org/cod/icc/statute/romefra.htm [accessed October 2011].

War crime/crime against humanity: Where we have used these terms they are as defined in the Rome statute of the International Criminal Court.[10]

Zionism: an ideology and political movement whose origins date from the 19th Century, which asserts that all Jews constitute one nation and advocated the creation of a Jewish homeland.

Yeshiva: a Jewish school or institute of learning where students undertake the study of sacred Jewish texts.

Hesder Yeshiva: a type of Yeshiva which combines religious study with service in the Israeli army.

Kibbutz/Moshav: types of Israeli-Jewish collective community traditionally based on agriculture. Today there are more than 250 *kibbutzim* and 450 *moshavim* in 1948 Israel.

---

[10]http://untreaty.un.org/cod/icc/statute/99_corr/2.htm.

INDEX

A

Aberdeen Asset Management 206, 279, 281, 283, 288-90
Absentee Property Act 244-5, 248
Abu Dis 97-8
Academia 77-8, 80, 82, 84, 86
academic boycott 77-82, 85-6, 156
ACRI (Association for Civil Rights in Israel) 251
actions, legal 24, 30, 119, 204, 208
ADC (Anti-Discrimination Committee) 337-8
ADL (Anti-Defamation League) 305
Advanced Technology Park *see* ATP
AFI 183
Africa Israel 6, 166, 183-4, 187-8, 192
Africa-Israel 164, 183
Africa Israel Investments 184
Africa-Israel Investments 164
Africa Israel Real Estate 184
agreements, accompaniment 11-12
Agrexco 3-4, 23-4, 27, 30-1, 68-70, 234, 239, 300
Agrexco distribution centre in Hayes 31
Agrexco's UK logistics centre 71
agricultural policies 16-18, 22-3
agricultural production 16-17, 22, 107, 233
agricultural settlements 21, 222, 234, 237, 259
agricultural workers 19, 21, 92, 235
agriculture 3, 8, 16, 18-20, 22, 24, 26-8, 30, 71, 92, 95, 112, 114, 223-4, 260-2
agriculture industries 100, 231
Ahava 39-40, 44-6, 90, 167, 257-8, 322
AHMSA (Altos Hornos de Mexico SA) 38
AIC (Alternative Information Center) 77, 117, 156, 266
Airgate Israel 71
al-Araqib 261-2, 266-7
al-Bustan 243-4, 254
al-Faluja 154-5

Al-Khalil 95, 260
Al-Kurds 249-50
Al-Marsad 221-2
Aliyah 338-9
Allianz SE 197, 279, 281-2
Alon Shvut 324, 329, 331
Alstom 189, 194, 252, 317
Alternative Information Center (AIC) 77, 117, 156, 266
Alternative Tourism Group 66-7
Altos Hornos de Mexico SA (AHMSA) 38
Aluminum Construction CL Israel 102
American Century Companies 197
American Express 14-15, 152, 317
ammunition 124-5, 127, 144
Anglo Palestine Bank *see* APB
Anglo Palestine Company (APC) 8
Angola 131, 161, 163-4
Anti-Defamation League (ADL) 305
Anti-Discrimination Committee (ADC) 337-8
Antiquities Authorities 244, 248
Apache Helicopters 283, 312, 324, 326
apartheid 32, 34, 57, 63-4, 67, 81-2, 85-7, 159-60, 189, 291
apartheid wall 41, 58-9, 62, 94, 97, 103, 106, 118, 125, 134, 143, 185, 204, 209-12, 326-7
Apax Holdings Israel 290
Apax Partners 59-60, 207, 290
APB (Anglo Palestine Bank) 8
APC (Anglo Palestine Company) 8
apples 25, 223-4
Arab Association for Development 222-3, 228
Arab Jahalin 38, 97, 255
Arava region 20, 26, 234, 301
Ariel 78, 91-2, 106-8, 164, 185, 210, 217, 319
Ariel settlement block 106
Ariel University Centre 78
Arison Group 6, 185, 189

arms 1, 79, 115, 125, 129, 143-4, 163, 172, 176, 207, 277-8
　supplier of 311-12, 318-20, 322, 324-6
arms companies 129, 277-8, 280, 282, 284, 286-7, 326, 328
arms trade 278-9, 287, 292-3
ASA (Advertising Standards Authority) 66
Asda 257, 298-9, 314, 328
Ashdod 68-70, 90, 190
Ashtrom 190, 212
Ashtrom Group 44, 190
Assa Abloy 318
Association for Civil Rights in Israel (ACRI) 251
Association of University Teachers (AUT) 85
Atarot 44, 91, 103-5, 114, 210
Atarot settlement 90, 103, 105, 171, 212
ATP (Advanced Technology Park) 263
AUT (Association of University Teachers) 85
authorities, local 10, 136-8, 159, 324
Auto Chen 104
Avgol 51, 90, 320, 325
　settlement company 70, 323
Avi Cranes 198
Aviva 206, 279, 283, 308, 318
AXA 197, 206, 279, 281-3, 318

B

B-ICC 298
BAE 279, 285, 292-3, 311, 318, 323
BAE Systems 278-9, 285, 290, 318, 326
Bank Hapoalim 7-8, 10, 12, 317
Bank Leumi 7-8, 14, 183
Bank of Jerusalem 9-10
Banking and Financial Services 7-8, 10, 12, 14
banks 7-9, 11-15, 281, 287, 291-3, 308, 310, 318, 322, 324
Bar Man Food Industries 105
Barad Company for Landworks Developments and Roads 187, 196, 198

Barclays 9, 15, 206, 279, 283, 288, 291-2, 308, 318
Barkan 38, 91, 106-10, 112, 118, 225, 294, 328
Barkan settlement 70, 89-90, 106, 109, 111, 292, 314, 320, 323-5
Barkan settlement Industrial Zone 314, 317
Bateman BV 290
Bayti Real Estate Investment Company 185
Bedouin 120, 122, 256, 260-1, 263, 265, 267-8
beer 115, 161, 164
Beigel&Beigel 108-9, 291, 294, 301, 314, 328
Benz, Mercedes 104
Beqa'ot 28
Beresheet 25, 224
Bethlehem 63, 117-18, 134
Bezeq 55-6, 59-60, 252, 308, 318-19
BG Group 53
BII (British Israel Investments) 205-8, 292
Bil'in 139-40, 143, 146, 148, 188
　village of 165, 167, 186, 188
Bino Holdings 50
Bio-Negev 264
Black Rock 206, 281, 283, 288
Blackrock 129, 279, 282, 318
Blockbuster 217, 319
Blue Nile 167, 319
Blueprint Negev 23, 265
BNC (Boycott National Committee) 24, 63, 65, 130, 144, 166, 315
Bnei Yehuda 10, 115, 129, 223, 225, 228
BNP Paribas 9, 197, 279, 281, 308, 319
Boeing 126-7, 282, 293, 310, 318-19, 322-3
Boeing Israel 80
bomb racks 280
Boycott Israeli Goods Campaign 303
Boycott National Committee *see* BNC
BRICUP 82, 85, 243
Brighton 280-1, 284, 299-300, 302-3
Brighton Jordan Valley Solidarity 29, 231, 233, 239
Brimar 283, 285

British-Israel Chamber of Commerce 298
British-Israel Communications and Research centre 206
British Israel Investments *see* BII
British Medical Journal 176
British pension funds 44, 287, 317
BT 60, 308, 319
B'Tselem 23, 41-2, 48, 140, 164
bulldozers 127, 200, 202, 209, 237

C

CAA (Coalition Against Agrexco) 30
CAEC (Committees on Arms Export Controls) 278
Camden pension fund 317, 319, 321, 323, 325, 327
Canada 90, 100, 110, 131, 188
Capital Group 204, 279, 281-2
Carmel Agrexco 23, 30, 294-5, 297, 301, 323
Carmel-Agrexco 3, 23, 69-70
Carmel Agrexco, settlement companies 299
Caterpillar 198, 200, 202-3, 209, 211, 214, 237, 269, 285, 319
Caterpillar D9 200, 202-3
Cellcom 56, 58
cement 1, 10, 64, 98, 104-5, 196, 198-9, 203, 212
Cement Roadstone Holdings *see* CRH
Cemex 42-3, 114, 199
Cemex Holdings Israel 289
Cemex Israel 43
Central Bottling Company 319
Ceregon Networks Ltd 291
CFOIC (Christian Friends of Israeli Communities) 332, 334
charity status 329, 336-9, 341
checkpoints 16, 20, 44, 55, 103, 125, 132-4, 138, 182, 185, 195, 209, 211-13, 222, 235
chemicals 1, 36, 94-5, 105, 112
Chemring 319
Christian Friends of Israeli Communities *see* CFOIC

CIA 47-8
Cisco 154, 158, 308, 320
Citypass 189, 194
Citypass consortium 189-90
Citypass tramline 193
Clima Israel Aluminum 105
Clinton 161-2
Co-op 299-301
Co-op Israel 299
Co-operative Group 299-300
Coalition Against Agrexco (CAA) 30
Cobham 320
Coca Cola Israel 265, 320
Coca-Cola's Israeli 309, 320
Combined Systems (CSI) 140, 142-3
Commission, Charity 335-8, 341
Committees on Arms Export Controls (CAEC) 278
companies
  agricultural 23, 224, 234
  chemical 104
  construction equipment 212
  credit card 7
  ethernet connectivity 291
  foreign 141, 233
  freight 71
  military 144
  recycled wood 96
  retail 298
  satellite communications 291
  scrap metal 96
  state-owned 47, 49, 51, 55, 75, 127
  telecommunications 292
  traded 217
conflict diamonds 165, 167
construction 10-11, 76-7, 92, 97-8, 113-14, 164, 178, 180-8, 190-2, 195-6, 198-9, 201-2, 204, 206-7, 211-13
Construction and Real Estate 178, 180, 182, 184, 186, 188, 190, 192, 194, 196, 198, 200, 202, 204, 206
construction companies 180, 183, 188
  largest 183
  largest private 190

construction companies building 11
construction equipment 100, 178, 198-9, 209-10, 212-14, 328
construction industry 43, 113-14, 182, 211, 237
construction materials 36, 40, 42, 105, 178
Cooper, Lee 215-16
Cooperative Group 300-1
Corrie family 203
Cosiarma 69, 72
Cosmetics, Kent 257, 303
Covidien 90, 320
CRH (Cement Roadstone Holdings) 196-8, 203-4, 212, 318, 320, 327
Cross Israel Highway 192
Cross-Israel Highway 185, 191-3
CSI (Combined Systems) 140, 142-3

D

Dan 73
Dan Gertler Israel *see* DGI
Danya Cebus 166, 183, 187-8, 192
David Visitors Center 246
Dead Sea 36-40, 46, 61, 65, 90, 230-1, 255-9, 298, 303, 322
Dead Sea Magik products 257, 303
Dead Sea Products 90, 257
Dead Sea Works 37-9, 255, 257, 322
decisions 63, 80, 82, 175, 242, 245, 268, 303, 336, 338-9, 341
DEFRA (Department for Environment, Food and Rural Affairs) 29
Delek 48, 51
Dell 154, 309, 320
Delta Galil *see* DG
Democratic Republic of Congo 141, 161, 163
Democratic Republic of the Congo *see* DRC
demolitions 106, 200, 202, 210-11, 237, 240, 243, 266-7
Department for Environment, Food and Rural Affairs (DEFRA) 29
Deutsche Bank 197, 206, 279, 281-2
Deutsche Securities Israel 289

Dexia 9, 15
Dexia Israel 9, 12, 15
DG (Delta Galil) 89, 111, 297, 324
DGI (Dan Gertler Israel) 164-5, 167
diamonds 1, 88, 141, 161-7, 319
Digal 11
Dimona 130, 259
Diners Club Israel 49
divestment campaigns 188, 203-4, 214, 287
Dolphin Energy 50-1, 54, 325, 327
Dor Alon 47, 49, 54, 218, 320
DRC (Democratic Republic of the Congo) 141, 161, 163, 165
drones 131-2, 141, 279-80, 309
DSEi 285

E

EADS 309
East Jerusalem 12-13, 49, 66, 96, 174, 189-90, 192-3, 213, 216, 218, 237, 240-6, 248, 250-4, 335
  occupied 11, 61, 64, 103, 314, 317, 328
East Jerusalem and Israeli settlements 16
Eden Springs 227-8, 309
Edinburgh 84, 87, 285, 308-14
EDO MBM/ITT 280, 284, 287, 292
Edom 26, 301
Edom Israel 26
Edom UK 25-6, 234
Efrat settlement 334
Egged 73, 76, 194
Egypt 48, 53, 68, 88-9, 155, 201-2, 259
Ein Gedi 256
Ejector Release Unit (ERU) 280
El Ad 244-8, 253-4, 335
Elbit 116, 129, 131-2, 138, 142, 198, 204, 279
electricity 47-8, 56, 251-2
Elqana settlement 43
energy 16, 31, 47-8, 50, 52, 54, 84, 251, 341
energy companies 51, 68, 218
  largest Israeli 49, 51
ERU (Ejector Release Unit) 280

ethnic cleansing   127, 178-80, 231, 233, 237, 245, 265-6, 268, 316
EU funding grants to Israeli   85
EU-Israel Association Agreement   29, 152, 295
EU Israeli Association agreement   119
exports   1, 3-4, 16, 18-19, 25-7, 29, 40, 88, 100, 105-6, 110-11, 113, 167-8, 174, 277-8
Extal   100
extractive industries   36, 38, 40, 42, 44, 46, 256-7, 303

F

F-35s   280, 283, 326
Farisiya   237
F&C Reit   205-6, 208, 292
Fermentek's website   104
FIBI (First International Bank of Israel)   6-7, 13
FIBI Holdings   6-7
Field Replaceable Connector System (FRCS)   280
Finder's Health   257
Finmeccanica   321
First International Bank   6-7, 13
First International Bank of Israel (FIBI)   6-7, 13
flowers   17-18, 23, 302
France   3, 15, 23, 30, 46, 51, 63, 110, 117, 131, 175, 177, 194, 199, 263
France Telecom   58-9, 218, 292, 321
France Télécom   56-7
franchisees   49, 215, 217-18, 317, 321
franchises   15, 56, 58, 215-18, 324
FRCS (Field Replaceable Connector System)   280
Freight Transport   24, 68, 70, 72
French companies   54, 189, 317
French Hill   192-3
fruit   17, 20, 23, 27-8, 263
   passion   298-9, 301-2
fuel   47, 83

G

Galilee   23, 25, 80, 102, 224, 226, 264-5
gas   47-8, 53, 102, 139-40, 142
Gaza   3, 53-4, 59, 74, 76, 80, 84, 86-7, 101, 118, 133-5, 200-1, 241, 259-60, 284
Gaza Freedom Flotilla   71-2
Gaza Marine Field   48, 52-4
Gaza Power Plant   47
Gaza Walls   200, 202
GDUK (General Dynamics UK)   281
General Dynamics   140, 280-1, 293, 310, 322
General Dynamics UK (GDUK)   281
General Mills   104
Germany   23, 89-90, 96, 109, 117, 131, 199, 212, 263
Gertler   161, 163
Gertler, Dan   161, 163-5, 167
GF Group   69-70, 72
Gilat Satellite Networks   291
GNFI (Good News for Israel)   338-9
Golan   58, 114, 221-8
Golan Heights   16, 42, 221, 297
Golan Heights Winery   226
Golan settlements   229
Good News for Israel (GNFI)   338-9
goods
   high-tech   1
   organic   19, 26
grapes   27-8, 223, 225-6, 294, 300-1
Green Patrol   261

H

Haaretz   76, 80, 110, 156, 159, 163, 165, 246-7
Hadidya   237
Hadiklaim   26-7, 31, 234, 294, 297, 300
Haifa   70, 77, 80-3, 105, 129, 151, 154, 156-7, 190, 206, 215, 265, 311, 315-16
Haifa refinery   48
Haifa University   80-1, 83, 244, 315-16
Hanson Israel   43, 106, 321

Hapoalim 7, 9, 13-14, 165, 317
Hashmira 133, 290
Heftsiba 12, 165
Heidelberg Cement 43-4, 321
Heineken 310, 321
helicopters 282-3
Herzliya Interdisciplinary Center 77
High-Tech 149-50, 152, 154, 156, 158, 160
high-tech companies 138, 152, 156, 158, 160, 195
  international 138-9, 157-8, 264
high-tech sector 77, 149, 151-3, 156, 159-60, 168
H&M 216-18
Hofrey Hasharon 44, 191, 193
Holding Companies 6
Holland 46, 76, 96, 110, 199, 234-5, 257, 303
Honeywell 281, 310
HSBC 9, 14-15, 206, 279, 281, 289, 291-2, 310, 322
Hutchison Whampoa 57

I

IAA (Israeli Antiquities Authority) 64, 244, 248
IAI (Israeli Aerospace Industries) 6, 124, 127-8, 131, 157, 228
IBM 151, 153, 311
ICL (Israel Chemicals Limited) 38-9, 322
IDF (Israel Defense Forces) 83, 102, 104, 113, 115, 125, 129, 133, 137-8, 176, 185, 203, 259, 266, 280-1
IDI (Israeli Diamonds International) 163, 165
IEC (Israeli Electric Company) 6, 48-9, 252
IFOAM (International Federation of Organic Agriculture Movements) 19
Ikea 215
ILA (Israel Land Administration) 22-3, 179, 261, 340
IMA (Israeli Medical Association) 175-6
IMI (Israel Military Industries) 124, 127

Industrial Buildings Corporation 187
industrial parks 91-2, 97, 103, 106, 153, 264
industrial zones 19, 38, 42-4, 48, 70, 88-96, 98, 100-3, 105-12, 114-19, 211-13, 223, 294, 306, 323-5
infrastructure construction 189-90, 192, 194, 198, 207
infrastructure projects 178, 189-90, 193, 195
Ingersoll Rand 139, 322
Insightec 171
Intel 149, 151, 154, 156-60, 322
Intel Israel 154
IPSC (Irish Palestine Solidarity Campaign) 142, 167
Ireland 40, 66, 131, 196, 203, 216, 301
Irish Palestine Solidarity Campaign (IPSC) 142, 167
Iscar 153
Israel Aerospace Industries 157, 199, 228
Israel Aerospace Industries/Golan Industries 228
Israel Chemicals Industries 39
Israel Chemicals Ltd 6, 37, 46, 68, 255, 258, 322
Israel-controlled Jerusalem Municipality 240
Israel Corporation 6, 38-9, 51, 68
Israel Discount Bank 7, 51, 207
Israel Electric Company 315
Israel Export Institute 3
Israel Infrastructure Fund 189
Israel Land Administration *see* ILA
Israel Manufacturers Association 3
Israel Military Industries (IMI) 124, 127
Israel Missile Defence Association 80
Israel Natural Gas Lines Ltd 48
Israel Petrochemical Enterprises 51
Israel Railway case 76
Israel Salt Company 37, 39-40
Israel Science Foundation 152
Israeli academia 77, 79
Israeli Airports Authority 104, 323

Index

Israeli Antiquities Authority (IAA) 64, 244, 248
Israeli arms trade 124, 144
Israeli Atomic Energy Commission 130
Israeli banks 7, 13-15, 324
Israeli Bio-Organic Agriculture Association 27
Israeli bombing of Islamic University of Gaza 79
Israeli Central Bank 149
Israeli Council of Higher Education 77
Israeli diamond industry 161-2, 167, 208
Israeli diamond sector 188
Israeli Diamonds International (IDI) 163, 165
Israeli Electric Company *see* IEC
Israeli Electric Corporation 252
Israeli exporters, largest 164
Israeli exports to Europe 31
Israeli F-16 280
Israeli fruit export 17, 25
Israeli Government Tourism Office 64
Israeli Lands Council 179
Israeli Medical Association (IMA) 175-6
Israeli mercenaries 141
Israeli Military Industries 6, 127, 140, 142
Israeli Ministry of Finance 125, 178
Israeli Ministry of Health 174
Israeli Ministry of Tourism 61-2, 65-7
Israeli National Tourism Office 63
Israeli oil sector 48
Israeli Osem corporation 313, 325
Israeli products 294-5, 298-301
Israeli quarrying 41-2
Israeli textile sector 88
Israeli UAV companies 131
Israeli universities 77-9, 86-7, 129, 138, 307, 310, 315
Israeli wine companies 225
Israel's Walls 195-6, 198, 200, 202, 204, 285
ISS 137-8, 311
ISS Israel 137

ISTAR (Intelligence, Surveillance, Target Acquisition and Reconnaissance) 131
Italy 23, 30, 69, 190
ITT 281, 292-3, 308, 318, 322
Ituran Location and Control Limited 291

J

Jahalin 97-8
Japan International Cooperation Agency (JICA) 238
JCB 209, 211, 214, 237
JDEC (Jerusalem District Electric Company) 49, 251-2
Jenin 117-18, 233
Jerusalem 9-10, 12, 62-4, 67, 73, 75, 84, 96-8, 103, 152, 154, 241-2, 247, 250-4, 315
Jerusalem District Electric Company *see* JDEC
Jerusalem Light Rail (JLR) 13, 189
Jerusalem settlement of Homat Shmuel 207
Jerusalem settlement of Nof Zion 190
Jerusalem settlement of Pisgat Ze'ev 218
Jewish National Fund *see* JNF
JICA (Japan International Cooperation Agency) 238
JLR (Jerusalem Light Rail) 13, 189
JNF (Jewish National Fund) 22-3, 179, 186, 222, 235-6, 245, 263, 265-9, 272, 274, 322, 332, 334, 338-41
JNF Campaign 268-9, 339, 341
joint PA-Israel initiatives 67
Jordan River 27, 222-3, 230-1
Jordan Valley 16-18, 20, 22-3, 25, 27-9, 64, 116-18, 128, 158, 209-10, 230-9, 255, 301, 303, 319
Jordan Valley Solidarity 210-11, 239

K

Kalia Israel Ammunition Co 102
Kalia settlement 26
Karnei Shomron 116, 324
Katz controversy 81

Katzrin   48, 51, 114-15, 213, 223, 226-7
Katzrin settlement   42, 114-15
Kav LaOved   19-21, 92-3, 99, 102, 235
Keren Kayemet LeYisrael (KKL)   339
Keter   109
Kfar Etzion   329-30
KFC and Pizza Hut   218
Khalil   61-2, 64-5, 116, 139
Kibbutz Kalya   40, 256
Kiryat Arba   64, 116
KKL (Keren Kayemet LeYisrael)   339

L

labelling   28-30
labour, child   20, 304
Lee Cooper Group   215-16
Legal&General   206, 279, 281-3, 323
lestinians-vacate-Israeli-hospitals   173
Leumi   7-9, 11-13, 15
Leumi Le'Israel   8
Lev Leviev   6, 161-2, 164, 166-7, 183-4, 188
Leviev   161, 164-6
Lewis, John   99, 311, 322
Lichtenstein   206-7
Lipski Plastic Industries   109, 112
LLD Diamonds Ltd   164-5
Lloyds   206, 279, 293, 311, 323
Lockheed Martin   126-7, 279-80
London   3, 8-9, 14, 37, 44-6, 59-60, 66, 68, 79, 90, 109, 166-7, 206, 330-1, 333-4
Lord Sieff   297-8
Lothian pension fund   44, 317, 319, 321, 323, 325, 327
Lowy   305
lychees   25, 297, 301-2

M

Ma'ale Adumim   12, 96-7, 205, 215-16, 306, 331
Ma'an Development Center   106-8
Maersk   68, 70, 72, 323
Manitou   198-9, 327

manufactures   95-6, 104, 109, 128, 131, 144, 157, 169, 172, 280, 322
manufacturing   88, 90, 100, 102, 168, 170, 291
Marathon Asset Management   279
Marks & Spencer   27, 89, 297-8
Marvell Semiconductor Israel Ltd   154
Marvell Software Solutions Israel (MSSI)   154
Marvell Systems Solutions Israel   308-9, 317, 320
Mashav   196, 327
Masri   186
Mavi Marmara   74, 76, 138
Maxima Air Separation Center   102
McDonalds   324
Meggitt   283, 312, 324
Mehadrin   27-8, 31, 225, 234
Mehadrin settlement growers   28
Mei Golan   48, 224
Merkavim   210, 322
Merom Golan   24-5, 50, 65
Meshulam Levinstein   207
Mezan Center for Human Rights   135
Microsoft   153, 158-9, 324
migrant workers   20-1, 181
Mineral extraction   36-8
Ministry of Construction and Housing (MOCH)   182
Minrav Group   187, 191-2
MIRS   56, 58-9, 139
Mishor Adumim   91-2, 96-102, 114, 312, 324
  industrial zone of   309, 320
Mishor Edomim   44
Mitsubishi   212, 214, 282, 312, 324
Mitzpe Shalem   39-40, 322
  illegal West Bank settlement of   39, 90
MOCH (Ministry of Construction and Housing)   182
Modiin Ezrachi   245-6
Modiin Illit   335
Modi'in Illit   167, 193, 217, 319, 330
Mod'In Illit   179, 182, 184
Mondi Plc   290

Index **364**

Mordechai Aviv Construction Industries 187
Morgan Stanley Israel 289
Motorola 59-60, 151, 153, 158-9, 292
Motorola handsets 59-60
Motorola Israel 58-9, 129, 153, 202
Mount Hermon 221, 226-7
Mount Scopus 192-3
M&S 89, 297-8, 300, 324
MSSI (Marvell Software Solutions Israel) 154
MTex 27, 234, 294, 298
Mul-T-Lock 108, 318

N

Nahalat Moshe 330
nanotechnology 46, 174, 264
nappies 90, 111
Naqab 23, 39, 55-6, 97, 102, 130, 157, 209-10, 222, 259-70, 318, 341
National Health Service *see* NHS
National Priority Areas 157-8
National Union of Journalists' (NUJ) 175
National Union of Students (NUS) 86-7
Nazareth 80, 180
Nazareth Illit 180, 183
Neged Neshek 125
Negev 97, 259, 264-5
Negev Advanced Technology Park 263
Nesher 193, 196, 198, 207, 212, 318, 320, 327
Nesher Israel Cement Enterprises 10
Nesher Israel Cement Enterprises Ltd 212
Nestle 313, 325
Netherlands 17, 31, 69, 72, 99, 110, 131, 194
Neuman Steel Industries for Construction 213
Neumann Steel Industries for Construction 113, 187
Neve Ativ 226-7
New York Stock Exchange *see* NYSE
NGO Pax Christi International 261

NHS (National Health Service) 170, 177, 228
Nice Systems 152, 288, 293
Nitzanei Shalom 91, 93-6
Noe, Leo 205, 208
North Yorkshire 317, 319, 321, 323, 325, 327
Northern Ireland 286-7
Norway 28, 31, 71, 197, 204, 206, 281, 291
NUJ (National Union of Journalists') 175
NUS (National Union of Students) 86-7
NYSE (New York Stock Exchange) 49, 54, 109, 212, 291-2

O

Oakland 72, 165
Occidental 325
occupied Syrian Golan 10, 12, 24-5, 36, 41, 43, 48, 50-1, 56, 59, 64-5, 114-15, 212-13, 224-5, 309-10
OCS (Office of the Chief Scientist) 151
OECD (Organisation for Economic Cooperation and Development) 16-18, 22-3, 47-9, 61-3, 74, 88, 126, 161, 179-82, 253
Ofakim 264-5
Office of the Chief Scientist (OCS) 151
Oil Refineries Ltd (ORL) 48, 51
Old Mutual 281, 288-9
Om Brothers Construction Works Investment and Development Company 187
Orange Israel 56
Orcal Industries and Mechanisation 312, 324
Oreal 312, 323
Oslo Accords 13, 22, 55, 91, 97, 150, 191, 200, 233
Oxford Asset Management 288-9

P

PA-initiated industrial zones 117-18

PACBI (Palestinian Academic Boycott Initiative) 85, 307, 315
Palestine Solidarity Campaign 59, 202, 301, 303
Palestinian Academic Boycott Initiative *see* PACBI
Palestinian banks 13
Partner Communications 56-9, 218, 292, 321
Pelephone 55-6, 59
Pension Funds 194, 317-28
peppers 26, 299, 301-2
Pepsico's Israeli 325
Peres Centre for Peace 103
petrol stations 49-51
PGFTU 93-4
pharmaceutical companies 168-9, 173-4, 176, 291, 326
pharmaceuticals 168, 170, 172-4, 176, 291
Philadelphi Corridor 200, 202
Physicians for Human Rights 173
Pisgat Ze'ev 217-18, 319
Pizzarotti 190-1
Polar Capital 288-9
Political Economy of Israel's Occupation 31
Post, Israel 321
products
  cleaning 102, 111, 113, 115
  plastic 113-14
Prudential 206, 279, 281-3, 313, 325
Public Transport 73-4, 76

Q

QIP (Quick Impact Project) 63
Qiryat Gat 154, 158
QIZ (Qualified Industrial Zone) 88

R

Ra'anana 153, 310, 322, 324
Radware Ltd 291
Rafael 6, 128, 130-1, 171, 174

Rafael Arms Development Authority 124, 128
Railways, Israel 75-6
Ramat Gan Diamond Centre 163
Ramat Hovav 267-8
Ramet 187, 192-3
Ramot bridge 192-3
Rawabi 185-6
Raychem 196, 199, 327
Raytheon 126, 283, 286-7, 292-3, 308, 310, 313, 318, 322-3, 325
Readymix 42-3, 114, 199, 213
Reckitt Benckiser 40, 290
Recognition Systems (RSI) 322
Regional Council of Unrecognised Villages (RCUV) 55
REIT 205-6
REIT/British Israel Investments 208
Retail 294, 296, 298, 300, 302, 304, 306
Riwal 199, 204, 212
Rolbit 110
Rolls Royce 290, 292, 326
Rolls-Royce 283
RSI (Recognition Systems) 322
Rubin Landsman Building Engineering 187

S

SA (Soil Association) 301, 303-4
Sainsbury 100, 292, 302, 326
Sainsburys 257, 302-3, 313
Sakawe Mining Corporation 165
Salfit 106-8
Samicor 165
Santander 279, 293, 326
Saudi Arabia 278-9
Scanning Radar (SPIDER) 198
School of Oriental and African Studies *see* SOAS
Schroders 197, 281, 283, 289
Scotland 227, 283, 301
Sde Bar Farm 331, 334
Sderot 264-5
Selex 313
Semitool Israel 290

Sete 70-1
settlement construction 12, 183, 212
  charities funding 337
settlement wineries 225
Shamir Salads 110-11
Shapir 191
Shapir Pizzarotti Railways (SPR) 191
Sheikh Jarrah 248-50
Shepherd Hotel 250
shipping 9, 68
ships 68-9, 125
Shir Hever 7, 31, 117-18, 169, 173, 247
SIBAT 129
SID (Supporters of Israel's Dependents) 125, 334
siemens 158, 191, 313, 326
Silwan 64, 210, 242-4, 246-8, 253
  neighbourhood of 243-4
Sinokrot/Palestine Gardens 28
Siyag 260
SJP (Students for Justice in Palestine) 159
Smile 290
Smile Media 289
Smiths Group 326
SOAS (School of Oriental and African Studies) 84-6, 297, 308-14
Soda Club 99-101, 294, 302, 306
Soda Stream 91, 93, 99-102
Soda Stream products 99, 101
Soil Association *see* SA
Solel Boneh 185, 187, 189, 192-3, 198
Solmoran 95
Solor Gas Industries 95
SPIDER (Scanning Radar) 198
SPR (Shapir Pizzarotti Railways) 191
Stanley, Morgan 197, 279, 281-2
Starbucks 304-5
State Street Corporation 197, 279, 281-2
stonefruit 294
Stop Arming Israel 279, 283
Students for Justice in Palestine (SJP) 159
Sun Capital Partners 215-16
supermarkets 29-31, 102, 143, 237, 299
Supporters of Israel's Dependants 331

Supporters of Israel's Dependents (SID) 125, 334
Surrey pension fund 317, 319, 321, 323, 325, 327
sweet potatoes 297-9, 301-2
Swirski 49, 55-6, 78, 88, 91-3, 96, 132, 150, 180, 182-3, 191, 195
Switzerland 100, 114, 131, 194, 196, 199, 327
Syria 222-3, 228, 339
Syrian Golan 115, 221-4, 226-9
Syrian villages 223-4

T

Taldor Computer Systems 288, 290
Tara 309, 319-20
Taro 168, 172
TASE *see* Tel Aviv Stock Exchange
TAU (Tel Aviv University) 84, 295, 305
Technion 77, 79-80, 138, 157-8
Technion Israeli Institute of Technology in Haifa 153
Tel-Aviv 77
Tel Aviv Stock Exchange (TASE) 5, 39, 73, 169, 172, 185, 190, 207
telecommunications 55-6, 58, 60, 218, 251, 318
Temsa Global 104
Terex 199, 212, 326
Tesco 27-9, 102, 109, 257, 292, 294-6, 313, 326
Teva 168-70, 175-7, 288, 291, 326
Teva Naot 89
Teva UK 170, 177
textiles 1, 88, 98, 111, 113, 297
Thailand 21, 131
Thales 132, 326
Thermo Fischer 314, 327
toiletries 90
tomatoes 26
Tomer 26-7, 237, 304
Tomer settlement 25, 29, 301, 303
Toronto Dominion Bank 279

Total Produce 24
tourism 1, 18, 37, 61-7, 226, 235-6, 253, 256
Tovlan landfill 238
Tower Semiconductor 291
Toyota 327
Tribunal, Russell 133-4, 189, 196, 199, 203-4
Tulkarem 91, 93-5, 107, 117-18
Tyco Electronics 196, 327
Tzifha International 188

U

UAV Engines Ltd (UEL) 279
UAVs (unmanned aerial vehicles) 112, 130-2, 228, 283
UBS 129, 279, 281-2, 327
UEL (UAV Engines Ltd) 279
UK arms companies 283, 285
UN Global Compact 43-4
UN Human Rights Council 261
UNICEF 166
Unilever 108-9, 291, 314, 328
Unishipping Israel 71
United Nations Relief and Works Agency (UNRWA) 248
universities 46, 77-8, 80-7, 138, 151, 157, 171, 264, 287, 295, 307-14, 316
Universities Superannuation Scheme (USS) 39, 44, 206, 279, 317, 319, 321, 323, 325, 327
University of London Union (ULU) 86
unrecognised villages 55-6, 261, 268, 318
UNRWA (United Nations Relief and Works Agency) 248
US 1, 15, 23, 48-51, 70-1, 88-90, 110, 126-7, 130-1, 133, 198-9, 202-3, 277-81, 283, 291
US arms transfers 282-3
USS see Universities Superannuation Scheme
UTI 68

V

Valley Grown Salads (VGS) 25-6, 301
Vanunu 130
Veolia 73, 76, 189, 194, 237, 314, 328
Veolia/Connex Israel 74
VER-2 280
VGS (Valley Grown Salads) 25-6, 301
vineyards 225-6
Volvo 100, 198, 209-11, 214, 237, 266, 269, 328
Volvo Buses 209-10
Volvo Construction Equipment 209
Volvo Group 100, 209-10

W

Wadi Hilweh 243-4, 246-7, 254
Wadi Hilweh Information Center 253-4
Wagner, Roy 19-21
Waitrose 27, 301-2, 311, 322
Wal Mart 314, 328
Wal-Mart 89
Wall Street Journal 149-50, 152
Wardle, Len 300
WDC (World Diamond Council) 162, 166
Wikforss 209
William Goldberg Centre 165
WMA (World Medical Association) 176-7
workers 20-1, 23, 28, 37, 72, 76, 92-3, 99, 106, 110, 118-19, 137, 167, 180-2, 235
World Action Ministries 332, 334
World Bank 172-3
World Diamond Council see WDC
WPP plc 290
WTO (World Trade Organisation) 174

Y

Yad Hanadiv 315
Yatir quarry 42, 213
Yesh Din 42
Yeshivat Birkat Moshe 331

Z

Zabludowicz 206
Zabludowicz Trust 206-7
Zim 6, 68-9, 71-2
zones, joint industrial 117-18